AMERICAN HORTICULTURAL SOCIETY

Southwest

SMART GARDEN™ REGIONAL GUIDE

AMERICAN
HORTICULTURAL
SOCIETY

AMERICAN HORTICULTURAL SOCIETY

Southwest

SMARTGARDEN™ REGIONAL GUIDE

RITA PELCZAR
AND PAT WELSH

DK Publishing, Inc.

LONDON, NEW YORK, MUNICH,
MELBOURNE, AND DELHI

Senior Editors Jill Hamilton, Anja Schmidt
Senior Art Editor Susan St. Louis
Designers Melissa Chung, Miesha Tate
Creative Director Tina Vaughan
Project Director Sharon Lucas
Production Manager Chris Avgherinos
DTP Co-ordinator Milos Orlovic
Picture Research Chrissy McIntyre
Horticultural editor Trevor Cole
Editorial assistance Rip Noyes, John Searcy
DK Photo Access Library Neale Chamberlain, Richard Dabb

First American Edition, 2004
00 01 02 03 04 05 10 9 8 7 6 5 4 3 2 1

Published in the United States by
DK Publishing, Inc.
375 Hudson Street
New York, New York 10014

DK Publishing, Inc. offers special discounts for bulk purchases for sales
promotions or premiums. Specific, large-quantity needs can be met with
special editions, including personalized covers, excerpts of existing guides,
and corporate imprints. For more information, contact Special Markets
Department, DK Publishing, Inc., 375 Hudson Street, New York, NY 10014
Fax: 800-600-9098.

Library of Congress Cataloging-in-Publication Data available

Reproduced by Colourscan, Singapore
Printed and bound in Spain by Artes Graficas, S.A.

See our complete product line at

www.dk.com

CONTENTS

Foreword 6

PART I

THE TEN
SmartGarden™ TENETS

Know yourself 10

Assess your site 16

Adapt when necessary 26

Pick the best plants 32

Take good care of the earth 40

Work with nature 52

Manage pests for a healthy garden 60

Keep a garden journal 70

Consult the pros 74

Have fun 78

PART II

PLANT CATALOG

Catalog Contents 82

Woody Plants 84

including trees, conifers, palms,
shrubs, and climbers

Herbaceous Plants 256

including perennials, wildflowers,
groundcovers, ornamental grasses, bulbs,
aquatic plants, annuals, and biennials

PART III

GARDENING TECHNIQUES

Selecting Plants 362

Planting 366

Pruning 374

Propagation 380

APPENDICES

Government resources 386

Horticultural organizations and gardening
websites 386

Seed and plant catalogs 387

Botanical gardens, arboreta, and parks 387

Index 390

Acknowledgments 399

Photo credits 400

FOREWORD

For a horticulturist, flying from the East Coast to cities such as San Francisco, Los Angeles, and Albuquerque, is always a bit like visiting another planet. In contrast to temperate East Coast vegetation, southwestern landscapes seem so exotic and diverse. Fragrant Mediterranean-style plantings in one region merge with lush tropical vegetation or striking desert landscapes in other areas. In the Southwest, the availability of water, elevation, and proximity to the Pacific Ocean or other water bodies play a critical role in the type of plantings that succeed.

No matter where you live, successful gardening is based on coordinating factors such as light, temperature, water, and nutrients, and coping with the elements, critters, and the gardener's age. Advances in technology, such as the development of the AHS Plant Heat Zone Map in 1997, are making plant selection easier, too. Gardeners can now use the Heat Zone Map in conjunction with the USDA Plant Hardiness Zone Map to easily determine the full range of temperature tolerance for any cultivated plant.

The passage of time has also brought many innovations to gardening in the Southwest, yet in my travels, I still see the mistakes that people live with in their gardens day after day that reduce the pleasures of gardening. Too many gardeners put up with plants that have outgrown their space, or are barely surviving.

This leaves the gardener with crucial questions to answer. How can I replace and replant with the most desired effects and create a SMARTGARDEN™? What tasks can I attempt and what should I have a professional do? And how do I do this while being a good steward of the earth? The SMARTGARDEN™ program described in this book answers these questions and many more. Using these ideas and techniques, you can create a garden that is beautiful, successful, environmentally responsible, easy to maintain, and – most important – fun!

This Southwest SMARTGARDEN™ Regional Guide will be something you can turn to again and again for down-to-earth advice and suggestions for plants suited to any garden situation. I know you will enjoy the process of re-evaluating your garden and your gardening practices from this new perspective!

H. MARC CATHEY, PHD
PRESIDENT EMERITUS,
AMERICAN HORTICULTURAL SOCIETY

PART I

THE TEN SmartGarden™ TENETS

These tenets offer the key to a scientifically sound, environmentally responsible approach to gardening. An assessment of your site and lifestyle directs your gardening choices with maximum efficiency. Integration of new technologies with proven practices and the effective use of available resources provide guidance for selection and maintenance of your garden plants. Most importantly, each practice is considered with respect to its environmental impact, to help you make the most responsible gardening choices.

KNOW YOURSELF

A lot of thought should go into gardening before you even pick up a trowel. Since you are going to determine the garden's dimensions, style, and makeup – and you will be primarily responsible for its maintenance – the best place to begin is to take a reading of your personal likes and dislikes and your abilities and limitations. In subsequent tenets we will consider the characteristics of the site, appropriate criteria for selecting plants, and ways to ensure that your gardening efforts reap successful results by using an environmentally responsible approach. But before you can begin to put that important information to good use, it is critical to examine your preferences, priorities, and point of view.

Be realistic

As much as you would enjoy spending many hours in your garden, you have other commitments that limit your availability, and you may be sharing your outdoor space with others who prefer nongardening activities. Physical constraints might also inhibit your gardening pursuits, and your budget may not accommodate your elaborate gardening visions. However, with some thoughtful planning and a bit of compromise, your SMARTGARDEN™ can oblige your varied outdoor requirements, limitations in time and physical ability, and, yes, even a budget that lacks a certain desired heft.

In a nutshell: think about your time, your physical condition, and your budget, and take on a garden only of the size and complexity you can handle.

The space-time continuum

Once you know where a garden best fits within the overall landscape, the next step is to determine its size and shape. While the shape is largely a design consideration, the size depends a great deal on the plants you want and the time you have to tend them.

Some gardens will require little of your time once they are established. A bed of flowering shrubs underplanted with a groundcover needs only occasional attention. An extensive flower bed or large vegetable patch, on the other hand, needs regular tending throughout the growing season. Of course, the bigger the garden, the more time it requires to plant, weed, harvest, deadhead, edge, and prune. The best plan is to start small, then expand if you find you have the space, time, resources, and energy.

Dramatic impact
Few plants can lend such drama to a garden as cacti and euphorbias while asking for so little in return, as proved here at Lotus Land in Santa Barbara by the late innovative plants-woman Ganna Walska.

Planning the site

When you are deciding where you should place your garden and what size to make it, you need to consider not only the conditions that make it suitable for growing plants, but also how the garden will be integrated into the landscape as a whole. For example, if you have children who need space for a swingset or to play basketball or frisbee, siting your garden at the other end of the yard might be wise – at least until they outgrow these activities. Obviously, you need a plan.

What you want
The owner of this property made careful decisions about how she wanted to use this area (each year wildflowers are planted from seeds in fall). Another owner might have covered the space in lawn, or built a pool or koi pond surrounded by decks. A third might have created a playground.

Garden plans

Whether your garden aspirations are complex and ornate or you are planning on a somewhat more modest scale, you should map out your garden on paper before you pick up your trowel or buy your first plant. Although these garden plans may vary in complexity from a rough sketch to an exquisitely executed artwork, there are just a couple of basic types of sketches that you need to use at this stage. The first one is used to map out existing features and microclimates, information that you need to determine which plants will thrive and where. A more detailed garden sketch, which should be done on graph paper to scale, shows your entire property – both physical features and garden areas.

Unless you are starting with an empty lot, you will need to sketch the existing features of your landscape, such as the house, walkways, and driveway. The more accurate your sketch, the more useful it will be for planning. Don't forget to note sunny and shady areas, hedges and fences that block the wind, unusually wet or dry spots, neighboring buildings, attractive or unattractive views, and other positive and negative features.

You may find that you want to make adjustments: remove a tree, repair or improve a walkway, relocate the doghouse. Some of these changes will be easy; those that are more complex can be completed over time. Make corresponding notes on your plan to track the direction in which you are heading.

Next make a list of the activities that you enjoy doing in the yard. Of course, you also need to consider anyone who may spend a significant amount of time in the yard, whether it be your spouse or partner, children, or anyone else. The landscape use checklist (opposite) will help you identify the various uses and activities and that fit your space and budget.

Once you have a prioritized list of gardening and nongardening activities for your yard, you can begin designating areas for each. Some areas will overlap, so make sure that the activities are compatible for use of the same space – playing football in the herb garden just won't work. On the other hand, patios and decks are perfect locations for container gardens and adjacent raised beds. Keep in mind that different kinds of plants (for example, perennials, vegetables, and shrubs) can often be combined in the same garden area as long as they have similar cultural requirements.

Making a Plan

This exercise is useful for those who have just acquired a new property as well as for those who are considering a major (or even minor) relandscaping project. Documenting existing conditions will point you in the right direction when the time comes to choose specific elements.

FEATURES TO CONSIDER FOR THE SKETCH

When drawing a sketch of your property, include all features that are permanent or at least long-term. Once your sketch is completed, you may want to make several copies. That way you can try out different designs for arranging beds and hardscaping features on paper before you actually get to work.

Don't forget to include any of the following features that are applicable. There may well be more features in your yard that you should include.

- Perimeter of the yard
- House
- Driveway
- Walkways and paths
- Garage, shed, or other service outbuildings
- Gazebo, patio, deck
- Hammock
- Swingset/sandbox
- Pool

- Doghouse, kennel, run
- Existing trees
- Existing beds or gardens
- Hedges, fences, walls
- Water faucets
- Areas of sun and shade
- Wet or dry areas
- Views to highlight
- Views to hide

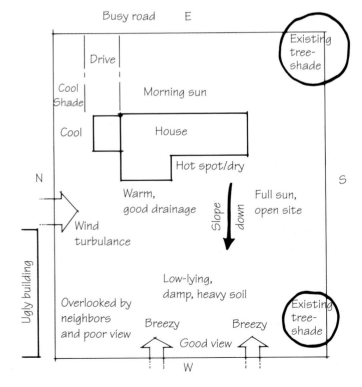

Putting it down on paper
All of the important cultural and design elements of the property have been included in this sketch. Note that there are no specific plant features indicated except for the trees, which are being considered more as producers of shade than as living plants. Consideration of individual plants comes later.

KEEP YOUR PLANS FLEXIBLE

Don't fret if there isn't room in your landscape to accommodate all of the activities you have in mind. Long-range planning can extend your choices, and spreading the implementation of your plan over the course of several years also reduces the shock to your bank account.

As you and the others who use your yard mature, priorities for landscape use will change. The area designated for a sandbox for youngsters might be transformed into a patio after a few years. Once the old swing set in the back yard has lost its appeal, it can be replaced with a mixed border or small vegetable garden.

Like children, plants grow up, and their increasing size alters the landscape. Perennials that once filled in between young evergreen shrubs may need to be moved as the shrubs reach their mature size. Aggressive perennials may be overrunning your borders. Choices must be made; something will need to go. As your trees expand in height and spread over the years, the area beneath them becomes shadier. If the grass growing in the trees' shadow becomes thin and weak, it may be time to replace it with a shade-loving groundcover or a simple mulch, or perhaps you will choose to thin or raise the crown of the tree (*see p. 29*) to allow more light to reach the grass.

Remember: plants don't live forever. The demise of a plant often opens up opportunities for including new and perhaps more interesting plants in its place.

Adapting to physical challenges

If you or members of your household have physical limitations, these need to be considered in your planning. Raised beds and containers can be built and placed with accessibility in mind. Paved walkways can put outlying beds within easy reach of those who might otherwise be able to enjoy them only from a distance, and stepping-stones or paths within planting areas afford easier and safer movement through the garden for maintenance.

Careful selection and placement of plants within the landscape is important for physically challenged gardeners. Once established, many trees, shrubs, and groundcovers will require a minimum of care. These can be placed at the periphery of the yard. More labor-intensive gardens should be placed where they are most easily accessed and where tools and water

LANDSCAPE USE CHECKLIST

Planning space to accommodate your outdoor pastimes will help you determine the best placement and size of your plantings, and prioritizing these areas will help you develop a working plan.

Nongarden areas/activities:
- Relaxing (including deck and/or patio)
- Outdoor cooking/eating
- Swimming
- Sports and active play
- Sandbox, tree house, playhouse, swing set
- Utility areas: trash cans, air conditioning/heating units, compost pile

- Work and storage spaces: garden shed, cold frame, firewood storage
- Pet areas
- Paths and walkways
- Driveway/parking
- Lawn
- Other, including walls and fences and overhead structures

Garden areas:
- Vegetable/fruit
- Herbs
- Flowerbeds
- Woodland garden
- Shade trees
- Wildflower meadow or naturalized area
- Foundation planting

- Pond
- Containers
- Raised beds
- Cut flowers
- Hedges
- Specimen trees and shrubs

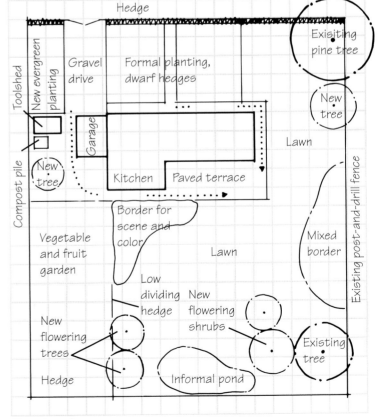

One step closer
The first sketch shown to the left is now fleshed out with desired planted areas (beds, borders, hedges, and the like) and hardscape features (driveway, terrace, and pond). The template is now ready to be made into a reality.

mobility or strength. Your SMARTGARDEN™ should become easier to maintain as plants mature, but no garden is maintenance-free. Fortunately, physical limitations needn't eliminate gardening activities, especially if they are considered in your garden plan.

Lawns and turf alternatives

The majority of homeowners consider a lawn an essential part of the garden, although it is the most labor-intensive and the most demanding in terms of resources and money. A well-maintained lawn, fertilized in spring, mown regularly, and watered during periods of drought, forms a solid green sward that stands up to traffic. Given little maintenance and no supplemental water, however, lawns go brown and dormant during drought, and they quickly become infested with perennial weeds that smother the grass.

One repetitive chore that consumes a great deal of gardening time is mowing the lawn, and maintaining a healthy lawn can be a genuine challenge in many parts of the country. Irrigation systems may be necessary in areas that experience extended periods of dry weather during the growing season. Weeds, insect pests, and diseases may necessitate the use of pesticides or biological controls that can be costly and time-consuming to apply. This doesn't mean that

A creative approach
Raised bed with mixed-media murals made of brick, Mexican river rock, tile, memorabilia, and "found" objects, including old garden tools.

are located nearby. Also remember the potential danger posed by thorny trees and shrubs, low branches, and surface roots. Of course, these points apply to any sensibly designed garden, but they are of more obvious and immediate importance to the physically challenged.

A number of ergonomically designed gardening tools make gardening easier if physical ability is limited. Despite our best efforts to remain fit, chances are that eventually we will all lose some

LAWNS AND ALTERNATIVES

A healthy lawn ties the garden together and creates space.

Many people feel that lawns don't belong in the dry Southwest. Alternative groundcovers, such as lippia or achillea can provide the feeling of greensward while conserving water. However, if you have children and dogs you may want a lawn for now to replace later with a patio. First decide whether to install from seeds, sod, or stolons.

Planting from seeds or stolons is less expensive, but sod provides an instant and weed-free lawn. Zoysia and Bermuda can be planted from sod or stolons, but stolons need late-spring or early-summer planting for the best start.

All grasses fall into two main categories: cool-season grasses, such as Fescue, perennial rye grass, bent grass, and Kentucky bluegrass, which grow more rapidly in cool weather and thrive along the coast, and warm-season grasses, such as Bermuda, zoysia, buffalograss, blue gramma grass, and St. Augustine, which grow more in summer and do better inland. Buffalo grass and blue gramma are often mixed for a drought-resistant meadow. Bermuda and zoysia are also drought-resistant. St. Augustine needs a lot of water but can take some shade. If there's a Bermuda-grass golf course in your neighborhood, the grass will invade your lawn, so choose Bermuda in the first place. Start with a hybrid variety, plant from sod, and the more weedy Bermuda won't invade it.

Consult your Cooperative Extension Office for a list of grasses best adapted to your region. The best

grass choices make chemicals unnecessary and conserve water. Bluegrass and bent grass, for example, fall prey to diseases in the Southwest. The best choices are selections and hybrids, such as zoysias 'De Anza' and 'Victoria' that stay green year round, and 'Santa Ana' Bermuda grass, which is the most drought-resistant lawn. Some grasses have special characteristics, such as the ability to cover bare spots. For example, older types of tall fescue mend well after dog damage and can take some shade. Newer dwarf types don't mend well and can't take shade.

One alternative to grass is a paved patio, here ornamented with a raised bed and a mural.

you should exclude all turf from your landscape, but be aware that it is an area that requires a significant investment in time and money. To reduce the expense, reduce the size of the lawn. A small area of grass is much easier to maintain than a large expanse.

If you decide to reduce the lawn area of your yard, you have a number of options. Consider a wildflower meadow or a large bed of groundcovers, which will require some seasonal care – perhaps two or three times a year – but not nearly the time and effort involved in trying to maintain a perfect lawn.

Another alternative to lawns are the various soil coverings, such as paving, gravel, or mulch. These can serve as walkways or seating areas. Individual planting beds and trees can be extended by removing the turf between them and connecting the areas with mulch. Use broad curves for the outline of the mulched area to facilitate mowing, because mowing around a large area that contains several trees takes much less time than mowing around individual trees. Although the initial cost and labor output of creating these areas may be greater, the reduction in maintenance time and expense over the long run may be significant.

Low-maintenance plantings

Every garden – even the simplest container garden – requires some maintenance, but there are definitely some plants that require less attention than others. Consult your nursery, extension service, and other local experts (*see* Appendix, *pp.386–389*) to identify such plants for your immediate area. Also, there are certain strategies that minimize the effort you must put into a planting for it to look good.

Many of these strategies are simply a matter of working with nature rather than against it: select plants that are adapted to the specific conditions present in your yard; water plants deeply rather than frequently so that roots grow downward and are capable of retrieving water over a greater area; remove weeds before they set seed and spread; and use mulch to conserve water and suppress weeds. Building raised beds and containers and filling them with soil may seem like a lot of work initially, but once constructed, they can provide a planting area that is within easy reach for maintenance.

A SMARTGARDEN™, when carefully analyzed, designed, implemented, and maintained, can reward any gardener for years.

Stay off the grass
The brick area in this picture was once a lawn. When the children grew up and the owners' lifestyles changed, they replaced the lawn with a patio and grew plants in containers watered by a drip system.

ASSESS YOUR SITE

The best place to begin your journey toward a SMARTGARDEN™, as with any project that involves major change, is first to determine where you stand. Take a look around your property. Observe the existing vegetation, the lay of the land, the soil, the degree of light and shade, and determine both your average temperature range and your first and last expected frost dates.

Evaluating strengths & limitations

If your yard is shady, plants that thrive in low light levels will be the most successful. If part of your yard is shaded and another area receives full sun, your options increase; however, siting a plant in the area that satisfies its particular light requirement is essential. If your region receives limited precipitation during the growing season, consider xeriphytic plants (those with low water requirements); if you have wet areas, a bog garden might be your best choice. Although these factors limit gardening options, each can be viewed as a strength if the appropriate plants and garden style are chosen.

Examine the existing plants carefully. Are there trees or shrubs that are struggling to survive or that require excessive maintenance? Plants that outgrow their space or suffer from chronic disease or pest problems may be the wrong ones for your site, and it may be best to remove them entirely.

Evaluating the existing nonplant features in your landscape is an important part of your site analysis. Are there problem areas – a steep slope or an awkward swale? Are your walkways functional? Have you set aside areas for relaxation? Does everyone have space to pursue outdoor interests?

Your observations will point you toward those improvements that need to be made to maximize your gardening success and satisfaction with the least amount of strain on you, your resources, and the environment. Your site analysis will also provide clues for selecting plants (or other nonplant features) that will fit in with your conditions.

It helps to know something about basic plant requirements with respect to the environment, including aspects of soil; how temperature, shade, and exposure define your selection of garden plants; and how microclimates present options for savvy gardeners. After you examine your existing growing conditions, you may decide to make some changes or improvements. In Tenet 3, methods for modifying your site will be outlined. But first let's take a look at what you have to work with.

Get to know your soil

Becoming familiar with the character of your soil is key to your gardening success. Important aspects include texture, structure, drainage and water-holding capacity, pH (acidity or alkalinity), and fertility.

One way to get to know your soil is to have it professionally analyzed. A soil test reveals details about your soil's chemistry that cannot be observed with the naked eye. Soil test kits for home use are available in a wide range of prices and sophistication. You can also send a soil sample to a local soil-testing lab. Public soil-testing labs are relatively inexpensive, but they may be slow during peak seasons. Private soil-testing labs may be a bit more costly, but they are often faster and some offer more extensive tests than those available through the extension labs.

An outdoor kitchen
Facing south, between the house and the swimming pool, is a space for outdoor living under a grape arbor ornamented with lavender and disease-resistant rose, 'Iceberg'. The ground is covered with decomposed granite. Built-in cabinets contain an oven, cooking range, and tile-covered storage for plates, napkins, and silverware.

Metamorphosis
By layering hay with horse manure to make compost, a gardener has transformed an old lemon orchard on poor clay soil and a steep slope into a thriving garden of wildflowers and deeply rooted climbing roses. The formerly hard, alkaline, non-draining soil is now friable with excellent drainage.

SOIL TEST REPORT

A soil test report provides basic information about the fertility of your soil. It is very useful when you are determining the amounts of fertilizer to add (or not to add) to your soil.

Minerally rich soils, such as decomposed granite, contain potassium.

Magnesium is essential for plant activites, most notably for photosynthesis, and its chemistry is closely linked to pH and calcium levels

Adequate levels of calcium exist in most Southwestern soils since irrigation water is akaline and contains calcium.

Phosphorus moves through soil fairly quickly but is easily replaced

NOTE *Optimum levels are based on general garden conditions for a wide range of plants. Some vegetable crops and ornamentals require different levels.*

Macronutrients (pounds/acre)

Phosphorus: 67 (Below Optimum)
Potassium: 360 (Above Optimum)
Magnesium: 202 (Optimum)
Calcium: 1917 (Above Optimum)

by Mehlich 3 extraction

	Below Optimum	Optimum	Above Opt.
P			
Mg			
Ca			

Very Low | Low | Medium | High | Very High

Soil texture

All soils are made up of solid material and spaces between the solids – in roughly equal proportions by volume. About 90 percent of the solid portion of most soil is weathered rocks and minerals. These particles are classified according to size, and are, from smallest to largest, clay, silt, and sand. Most soils are a combination of particle sizes, often with one or another predominating. The relative amounts of each type of particle determines the soil texture. Loam is a soil that contains roughly equal amounts of all three soil particle types and is usually well suited for growing a very wide range of garden plants.

A soil's texture has a major influence on such soil characteristics as water retention and nutrient movement. For example, a sandy soil drains faster than a clay soil, and a clay soil retains nutrients better than a sandy one; therefore, watering and fertilizing schedules should be adjusted accordingly.

Soil texture will also influence your selection of plants. Some plants – those that generally have low water requirements – thrive in a sharply drained, sandy soil. Others benefit from a more constant supply of moisture and nutrients; these usually grow better in a loam or clay loam, which hold on to water longer and release it more slowly than sandy soil. You can get an idea of the texture by rubbing some dry soil between your fingers. Sandy soil has a gritty feel to it; silt is much smoother; and clay, when dry, forms dense, hard clumps that are not easily broken apart. When wet, clay can be formed into balls or ropes.

50% pore spaces (air and water)

45% weathered rock and mineral particles

About 5% organic matter

Ideal growing conditions Adding plenty of organic matter will help plants to grow in a more arid and compacted soil than the optimum conditions shown in this chart.

Soil structure

The structure of a soil is determined by how the various solid portions of the soil are arranged – particles can be separate, as in the case of pure sand, or bind together to form clusters, or aggregates (tiny clusters of particles). The arrangement has significant impact on the movement and retention of water, nutrients, and air in the soil.

The remaining solid part of the soil is organic matter, which makes soil more conducive to plant growth by enabling the formation of soil aggregates. Aggregates form when soil organisms break down organic matter into humus, an amorphous, gummy material that binds particles together (*see* The nature of humus, *p.31*). Pore spaces between the aggregates are relatively large, and yet smaller spaces between soil particles occur within the aggregates. This combination provides a balance between the movement of water and air and the retention of moisture and nutrients, and makes it easier for plant roots to grow down through the soil.

To improve soil structure, spread organic matter on the soil surface and incorporate it into the upper six to eight inches (15–20cm) of soil every year in areas that are cultivated on an annual basis. For more permanent areas, work organic matter into the soil at planting time. After that, organic mulches can be applied around plants each year; the activities of soil organisms and other natural processes will incorporate much of the organic matter into the soil.

Drainage/water-holding capacity

Plant roots require both air and water for healthy growth. The pore spaces in soil accommodate both, but during rain or irrigation, water forces air out of the pores. Drainage refers to the movement of water through the soil; water-holding capacity is the ability of a soil to retain water after rainfall or irrigation. During dry periods, air-filled pores predominate. Coarse-textured (sandy) soils tend to drain quickly, retaining little water. They also warm up faster in the spring and are generally easy to work. Fine-textured (clay) soils retain both water and nutrients longer than a sandy soil and may become waterlogged. The same material – organic matter – that improves the drainage of a heavy clay soil can increase the capacity of a light sandy soil to retain water.

Different areas of your property may drain very differently. After a heavy rain, one area may stay wet much longer than others. If you plan to garden in a wet spot, you should choose plants that are well adapted to such conditions.

SOIL DRAINAGE TEST

To assess your soil's drainage, perform the following test. Wait at least a few days after the last rain until your soil has dried a bit, then dig a hole 4 inches (10cm) deep, large enough to accommodate a 46-ounce (1.4kg) can. Remove the top and bottom of the can and place it in the hole, firming the soil around the outside. Fill the can to the top with water, then observe how long it takes to drain. Ideally, the water level will drop about 2 inches (5cm) in an hour. This indicates that your soil drains well but also will retain the moisture necessary for the healthy growth of a wide variety of garden plants.

If the water level drops less than an inch (2.5cm) after an hour, your soil does not display sufficient drainage to accommodate many plants. Either limit your choice of plants to those that like constant moisture, or take measures to improve the drainage. If the water level drops 4 inches (10cm) in an hour, your soil drains too fast, and unless you plan to grow only plants that tolerate very dry soils, you will need to add organic matter to help retain soil moisture (and will also need to water as necessary).

Remember that different areas of your landscape

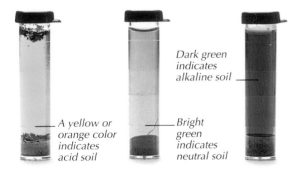

Dark green indicates alkaline soil

A yellow or orange color indicates acid soil

Bright green indicates neutral soil

Determining pH
Kits are available for testing the acidity, neutrality, or alkalinity of your soil at home. They give a good general indication of pH.

may display marked differences in drainage and this test should be done in each one.

Soil pH

The acidity or alkalinity of your soil is critical to plant health. The measurement of the degree of acidity or

alkalinity, the pH scale, rates solutions from most acidic (0) to most alkaline (14), with 7 being neutral. The pH of your soil is determined by many factors, such as the type of rock from which the soil originated, the amount of precipitation, and the type of vegetation growing on it.

The optimal soil pH for most plants is between 6.0 and 7.0. Deficiencies of essential nutrients often occur outside of this range, damaging plants and sometimes making them more susceptible to diseases and pests. Furthermore, alkaline soils inhibit the survival of certain beneficial organisms, including earthworms, mycorrhizal fungi, and many bacteria. These organisms are responsible for the decay of organic matter and thereby help plants obtain nutrients.

Soil pH can be modified (to change soil pH, _see p.30_), but to determine which materials and how much you will need to add to your soil, you will first need to perform a soil test (see the opposite page).

Soil fertility

There are 16 essential nutrients necessary for plant growth. Carbon, hydrogen, and oxygen are derived from air and water, and the remaining nutrients are supplied from the soil. The macronutrients – nitrogen (N), phosphorus (P), and potassium (K) – are needed by plants in large quantities; the secondary nutrients – calcium (Ca), magnesium (Mg), and sulfur (S) – are needed in moderate quantities; and the trace elements – boron (B), chlorine (Cl), copper (Cu), iron (Fe), manganese (Mn), molybdenum (Mo), and zinc (Zn) – are essential but needed only in very minute quantities. Determining the existing nutrient levels in your soil can help identify the kind and amount of fertilizers needed.

Right at home
Azaleas growing in acid soil under pine trees, watered by a circle of laser-cut drip line around each plant, mulched with pine needles on a north-facing bank, the perfect exposure for camellias and azaleas. Standard types of azaleas keep blossoms above the ground, away from snails, and get less blossom blight.

pH
| 4 | 5 | 6 | 7 | 8 | 9 |
Acidic | | | Neutral | | Alkaline

nitrogen
calcium and magnesium
phosphorus
potassium
sulfur
iron, magnesium, zinc, copper, cobalt
molybdenum
boron

Not all are alike
The availability of nutrients in the soil depends on the pH level. Note how many of them are less available in alkaline soils.

Avoiding chlorosis
Yellow leaves with dark green veins on citrus, azalea, and some other plants is a sign of chlorosis, a mineral deficiency often caused by soggy or alkaline soils. To control, improve drainage, add organic matter, and/or treat the ground with chelated iron.

Types of fertilizers

There are many different kinds of fertilizers available that can supply essential nutrients to your plants. Derived from a variety of sources, both natural and synthetic, they are available in a range of formulations that have been developed for different uses, from fast-acting foliar sprays to timed-release pellets. Some contain a single nutrient, and others multiple nutrients.

The three mineral nutrients used in the greatest quantity by plants are nitrogen (N), phosphorus (P), and potassium (K). A fertilizer that contains all three macronutrients is called a complete fertilizer. The three numbers on a bag of a complete fertilizer – the analysis – refer to the percentages by weight of nitrogen (N), phosphorus (phosphate, expressed as P_2O_5), and potassium (potash, expressed as K_2O), in that order.

Many complete fertilizers contain other nutrients that are also essential for healthy plants but are used in smaller quantities (secondary and micronutrients). These are usually listed on the label.

Organic fertilizer is derived from an organic – or once-living – source. Cow, horse, poultry, and sheep manures, fish emulsion, alfalfa and soybean meals, wood ashes, and compost are examples of organic fertilizers. Since most are somewhat lower and more

Apply it correctly
Spread the appropriate amount of fertilizer in a ring around a plant at and beyond its dripline – the outermost reach of its branches – then work it into the soil or cover it with mulch.

variable in nutrient content than chemical fertilizers, you will need to use more of the material to obtain the nutrition your plants require. Because organic fertilizers are typically slow to break down in the soil, they have several advantages over chemical fertilizers: they remain available to plants over a longer period of time, they don't leach out of the soil as quickly, and they don't usually "burn" (dehydrate) roots. One of the most significant qualities of organic fertilizers is that they improve the structure and ecological balance of soil, which promotes healthy plant growth.

FERTILIZER FORMULATIONS

Fertilizer comes in many forms. Many synthetic fertilizers are available in a dry, granulated form, which is easy to spread, and the nutrients are usually readily available. Some granulated fertilizers are coated with sulfur or plastic so that their nutrients are slowly released over time.

Some synthetic fertilizers are sold as concentrated liquids or powders that require diluting. These are applied as liquids to the soil around plants or as a foliar spray. Foliar fertilizing using a water soluble solution can provide quick relief for plants that are suffering from a nutrient deficiency.

Fertilizer spikes are compressed, dry fertilizer that has been formed into a stakelike solid. Commonly used for trees and shrubs, they are inserted into holes drilled into the soil around the root zone.

Manure can be fresh or dried, resulting in a considerable difference in weight and nutrient content, not to mention smell.

NUTRIENT CONTENT OF FERTILIZERS
(ALL VALUES ARE APPROXIMATE)

	% Nitrogen (N)	% Phosphorus (P_2O_5)	% Potassium (K_2O)
Organic			
Animal manure	0.6	0.1	0.5
Compost	0.5	0.3	0.8
Bone meal	2	14	-
Sewage	7	10	-
Seaweed meal	2.8	0.2	2.5
Blood meal	12	-	-
Mushroom compost	0.7	0.3	0.3
Rock phosphate	-	26	12
Wood ash	0.1	0.3	1
Cocoa shells	3	1	3.2
Inorganic			
Balanced fertilizers	available in various proportions		
Ammonium nitrate	35	-	-
Superphosphate	-	20	-
Muriate of potash	-	-	60
Potassium sulfate	-	-	49

Urban soils

Soils in urban environments often suffer from detrimental affects of construction and high-density populations. Compaction, contamination, poor drainage, nutrient imbalances, and excess temperatures are common. When the force of foot and vehicular traffic is exerted on the soil, it compresses and compacts the soil and breaks up soil aggregates. Compacted soil is a major cause of tree decline in urban environments.

Soil contamination occurs when building materials are spilled or dumped. Some contaminants are toxic to plants, while others cause more indirect damage, such as altering the soil pH. Gardening on badly contaminated sites may be limited to growing in raised beds and containers filled with imported soil.

In addition to suffering nutrient imbalances, many urban soils are infertile simply because topsoil and organic matter are often removed during construction, leaving an infertile subsoil that drains poorly and has very poor aeration. Taking the time to improve your soil is usually the best solution (*see* Building soil with organic matter, *p. 30*).

Heat absorbed by buildings, roads, sidewalks, and vehicles adds considerably to the air temperature of the urban environment, which in turn raises the soil temperature. This "heat-island effect" can significantly alter the chemical and biological characteristics of soil. One of the easiest and safest ways to counteract this effect is to apply an organic mulch to the soil surface (*see* The mulch advantage, *p. 47*).

Temperature ranges

All plants have an optimal temperature range for growth. They also have temperature limits (both high and low), beyond which injury or death is likely to occur. These temperatures vary from one plant to another – some plants have a wide temperature range, others are far more limited – a major reason that locations with widely different climates support distinct plant species. Gardeners deal with this preference for temperatures on a daily basis.

Seeking a difference
In order to bloom, large-flowered cymbidiums need a 20°F (11°C) difference between day and night at the warmest time of the year. This could be provided by subtropical zones of coastal California, some mountainsides in Hawaii, or a cool greenhouse.

Sky lovers
Planted out in October to bloom in February, cinerarias (right) need a special microclimate – cold weather but frost-free, in "sky shine," under the open sky, to the north of a house or tree.

Chilling out
Tulips (left) and hyacinths must have winter chill in order to bloom. In frost-free climates, gardeners fool tulips into thinking they've gone through a cold winter by placing bulbs in a paper sack in the refrigerator (not freezer) for six weeks prior to planting.

USDA Hardiness Zones

Winter hardiness is the ability of a plant to survive the winter conditions in a given location. Cold is an important feature of the winter environment, but several other factors influence hardiness, including soil moisture, relative humidity, and buffeting winds. For example, while a dianthus may tolerate frigid temperatures in a garden, it often fails to survive winters where soils stay wet, and although a number of broad-leaf evergreens thrive in cold temperatures, these evergreens may suffer severe desiccation if they are exposed to winter winds.

To assist gardeners with identifying plants that will survive the winter temperatures in their gardens, a system of mapping and coding was developed. The USDA Plant Hardiness Zone Map, which was revised and updated in 2003, identifies 15 hardiness zones in the United States according to the average minimum temperatures experienced.

Thousands of plants have been coded to the USDA Plant Hardiness Zone Map according to the low temperatures they will survive. Also considered in the rating is the plant's cold requirement: many plants require a certain amount of cold in order for their buds to break dormancy in the spring. Therefore, the hardiness rating is actually a range from the coldest zone in which the plant will survive to the warmest zone that satisfies its cold requirements.

The influence of cold temperatures on plant survival is more complicated than simply the lowest temperature experienced by the plant. Other factors such as the rate of temperature drop, the duration of the cold, the amount of temperature fluctuation, and the snow or mulch cover on the soil surrounding the plant affect its ability to survive winter conditions.

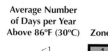

F°	Zones	C°
below -50°	1	below -46°
-50° to -40°	2	-46° to -40°
-40° to -30°	3	-40° to -34°
-30° to -20°	4	-34° to -29°
-20° to -10°	5	-29° to -23°
-10° to 0°	6	-23° to -18°
0° to 10°	7	-18° to -12°
10° to 20°	8	-12° to -7°
20° to 30°	9	-7° to -1°
30° to 40°	10	-1° to 4°
above 40°	11	above 4°
	12	

AHS Heat Zones

On the opposite end of the thermometer, the amount of heat that plants are exposed to in summer is equally critical. For this reason, the American Horticultural Society Plant Heat Zone Map was developed in 1997. AHS President Emeritus Dr. H. Marc Cathey supervised the development of the map, using data collected from the National Climatic Data Center and the National Weather Service. The map divides the US into 12 heat zones according to their average annual number of "heat days." A heat day is defined as a day in which temperatures reach or exceed 86° F (30° C). AHS Heat Zone 1 averages less than one heat day per year, while Zone 12 averages more than 210 heat days.

Like hardiness zones, the heat zones for a particular plant are given as a range. The first number indicates the hottest zone in which it will grow successfully; the second represents the zone with the minimum amount of summer heat necessary for it to complete its annual growth cycle.

As for cold hardiness, heat tolerance in plants involves more than just temperature. Summer rainfall – and the lack of it – limits the successful cultivation of many plants. High humidity rings the death knell for many plants that thrive in drier conditions with similar heat. Some plants are able to thrive in warmer zones if nights are cool. Qualities of the soil – its fertility, acidity or alkalinity, and drainage – also influence the summer survival equation. These factors should also be taken into account when selecting plants.

Although temperature is not the only determinant involved in a plant's ability to thrive in summer conditions, it is an important factor, and one that has been extensively assessed for the use of gardeners. For specific zones for many plants that grow in the Southwest, see the Plant Catalog.

Average Number of Days per Year Above 86°F (30°C)	Zone
<1	1
1 to 7	2
>7 to 14	3
>14 to 30	4
>30 to 45	5
>45 to 60	6
>60 to 90	7
>90 to 120	8
>120 to 150	9
>150 to 180	10
>180 to 210	11
>210	12

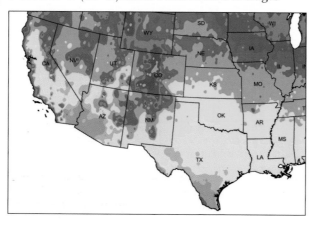

Identify light and shade levels

As you stroll around your yard, observe which areas receive full sun and which areas are shaded by trees or surrounding structures. Because light levels change with the time of day, the season, and from one year to the next, this is an ongoing project. As the sun travels across the sky, a shady morning garden may be basking in full sun by early afternoon. In summer, when deciduous trees are in full leaf, a bed that received spring sun may be densely shaded. The angle of the sun as seasons change also alters the level of light in a garden. Furthermore, as trees mature, they cast increasingly broader shadows – beds that were planted in full sun several years ago may become cloaked in the shade of trees that grow nearby.

As your garden matures, stay abreast of changing light levels and the impact on your plants.

To assess your garden's current level of light, examine the shade patterns several times during the course of a sunny day. Note areas that receive shade in the morning, midday, and early and late afternoon. By noting the position of surrounding trees (taking into consideration whether they are deciduous or evergreen) and estimating the changing angle of the sun, you should be able to approximate the light levels in your garden for the entire year with reasonable accuracy.

Identifying your garden areas according to the light categories on this page will help you select plants with corresponding light requirements.

Full sun
All vegetable crops and most flowering plants require full sun. As gardens mature and trees grow, gardeners must either change their palette to shade loving plants or thin trees to maintain an area of full sun.

Full shade
In deep shade under *Leptospermum laevigatum*, where almost nothing will grow because of dense roots, plectranthus, ferns, and other all-green plants in hanging baskets and containers are the best choices.

Partial shade
One way of providing partial shade is by installing lath panels for the summer. Make sure the lath goes north and south, so shadows will move across the plants as the sun makes its way across the sky.

Identify your microclimates

Areas within the same yard can present quite a variety of growing conditions, and it is important to recognize the garden limitations and possibilities of each. A microclimate – a portion of your yard where growing conditions differ from surrounding areas – can be a dry, shady spot or one that is constantly wet. It may be a narrow strip that is protected by a hedge, or an area warmed by its proximity to a building or stone wall.

To identify microclimates in your yard, note areas that seem slightly out of sync with the rest of the yard or other yards in the neighborhood – spots where spring flowers open earlier or later than others of the same kind, locations where blooms last longer, or areas that require more or less frequent watering than surrounding areas. These observations will suggest the need for plants that accommodate the nuances of your microclimate. They may also offer the opportunity to grow plants beyond the prevailing cultural limitations (particularly the overall hardiness and heat zone ratings) of your landscape.

EXISTING VEGETATION
Trees provide shade, and shady areas are typically several degrees cooler than adjacent areas in the sun. Shady spots also tend to stay wetter longer. Some plants that thrive in the sun where summers are cool can be grown in warmer climates if they are provided some shade. Dense vegetation can also block or reduce winds that cause a rapid loss of moisture by

plants and soil. Planting a windbreak to provide protection from prevailing winds is one way you can help create a microclimate in your yard.

Microclimates are not static, however, especially those influenced by vegetation. As plants grow or are pruned or removed, conditions can be dramatically altered: a sunny garden may become shaded as the tree canopy expands; a wet area may become drier as groundcover plants grow and absorb more water; and a shade garden may be exposed to full sun if an old tree becomes damaged and needs to be removed. gardener, as always, must be adaptable.

STRUCTURES AND HARDSCAPING
A house, garage, fence, or wall can also serve as a windbreak. These structures cast shade as well – the north side of a wall running east to west tends to be cooler and damper; the sunny south side will be notably warmer and drier. Such a wall creates two distinct microclimates that are separated by mere inches. Each side will support a culturally distinct set of plants. Although the difference in climate on either side of a wall that runs north to south is more subtle, the west side will tend to be warmer than the east side.

In temperate zones, a south-facing wall, particularly if it receives full sun, is a great place to grow sun-loving tropical or subtropical vines – such as *Bougainvillea* and black-eyed Susan vine (*Thunbergia alata*) – as annuals. The soil warms earlier in the spring, boosting early growth, and because the wall collects and holds heat,

Water world
Ponds provide habitat for a wide range of beneficial creatures, including frogs and dragonflies, and need to be sited in full sun. Most pond plants, such as water lilies, are sun lovers.

Moisture lovers
Plants such as acorus, mondo grass, *Sisyrinchium bermudiae,* and exotic ferns are best grown close to the house, where you can provide the moist conditions they desire.

moderating cooler night temperatures, growth will continue later into the autumn.

Because the area is cooler, plants growing on the north side of a building emerge from dormancy later than those on the south side. Air temperatures are influenced by the material and color of nearby structures: White or light colors reflect daytime light and heat back onto the plants; dark colors absorb heat.

SOIL SURFACES
The color of paved surfaces and mulch has a similar effect on nearby plants. Dark mulches absorb heat and can be used to warm the soil. Light-colored paving reflects light and heat back to surrounding areas. Heat-tolerant plants that thrive in sunny locations are usually the best choices near unshaded driveways and sidewalks.

WATER
Large bodies of water have a moderating effect on temperature, but even a backyard pond or pool can contribute a similar influence. Plants located at the edge of a pond not only have more water available in the soil, but they also benefit from a more humid environment created by evaporation from the pond.

COASTAL GARDENS
Gardens located near the seashore have special requirements. Plants must be able to tolerate salt spray, strong winds, and sandy soil. However, the moderate temperatures and higher humidity allow

for growing a broader palette of plants, including marginally hardy ones. Soil can be improved by adding organic matter, and windbreaks can provide protection. Surprisingly, solid walls do not afford as much protection as salt-tolerant trees and shrubs, which act as filters to the salt spray as well as a buffer to the wind. Once a living barrier is established, less tolerant plants can be grown and benefit from the nurturing aspect of the ocean.

TOPOGRAPHY
Unless your yard is flat, its topography will influence your growing conditions. Marginally hardy plants and those that produce cold-sensitive, early spring flowers are more likely to be damaged by frosts if they are located in a frost pocket. Slopes also affect runoff: water can collect in a low area, making an ideal location for a bog garden. Steep slopes can be tamed and runoff reduced by using retaining walls to create level planting areas. Now let's explore ways to modify your existing garden conditions.

Dry garden in full sun
Run-off from heavy winter rains on this steep slope of hard clay soil is prevented by a dry stream bed edged with groundcovers of weeping lantana and green apple ice plant.

Protection from wind
If your summer patio is comfortably cool in summer but cold and windy in winter, look for a warmer microclimate in the garden where you can make a winter patio like this one. In a hollow and protected by a wall and hedges, it's too hot in summer but warm and comfortable in winter.

ADAPT WHEN NECESSARY

So you've assessed yourself and your lifestyle and have critically analyzed your site. Now it's time to make some decisions about your gardening conditions. Reconciling your personal interests, style, and budget with the physical limitations of your yard may require some compromises. But if any reasonable improvements to your site will enhance the long-term success of your garden, they should be considered. Drastic changes are not recommended for a SMARTGARDEN™, particularly those that will be difficult or time-consuming to maintain.

Fixed and variable factors

Certain aspects of a gardening site – temperature extremes, rainfall, elevation, proximity to city or the ocean – cannot be altered, and the plants you grow should be inherently compatible with those existing conditions. Radical attempts to change your microclimate are generally unfruitful and a frustrating waste of your time.

On the other hand, some modifications can alter the growing conditions significantly to the advantage of your gardens. Adding soil amendments such as organic matter (*see p. 30*) or limestone or iron sulfate to decrease or increase the acidity (*see* Adjusting soil pH, *p. 30*) is often necessary, particularly in areas where builders have removed topsoil. Regrading a

Plants aren't always the answer
Sometimes the land itself speaks. Here's a place where nothing would grow. Everything planted promptly died, but by adding an arbor, the gardener made it into a special haven.

backyard to improve drainage, or removing trees to allow more light into an area, may dramatically expand your gardening opportunities. The cost of such major modifications should be evaluated against the potential results. Sometimes compromises in garden size, placement, plant selection, and hardscaping options (nonplant features, such as patios) offer satisfying and less costly solutions.

Conditions vary, depending on the location of your garden within the landscape. Parts of your yard may be in full sun while others are shaded; some areas may be exposed to persistent winds from which other areas are protected; drainage patterns may result in a wet zone in one part of the yard and dry conditions in another. Identifying the distinct characteristics of each area provides the gardener with an opportunity to grow plants with varied requirements within a single landscape. Matching the requirements of the plants you want to grow as closely as possible to the conditions of a particular site will minimize adaptations that are necessary for healthy growth.

Eastern glow
East-facing shade in a hot interior climate zone, under an overhang next to a large gravel expanse, provides the perfect microclimate and moist soil for a few colorful semi-shade lovers such as impatiens, hippeastrum, and primrose.

Terracing sloping ground
The historic answer to sloping ground is a terrace, creating a raised bed. Full sun, well-amended soil, and a modern drip system on a timer result in a bountiful garden and abundant crops in a small space.

The benefits of time

Keep in mind that time is an important dimension in gardening. An instant SMARTGARDEN™ is an oxymoron. Good things take time. Building a healthy soil doesn't happen overnight; it is an ongoing process. Likewise plants, particularly trees and shrubs, increase in size over the years, and they should be spaced with an eye toward their mature size. Although you may be tempted to purchase large plants in order to give your garden an established feeling from the start, this strategy has its drawbacks: larger plants are more expensive, and they often have more difficulty becoming established than smaller stock. By the time a large plant has settled in and has begun to produce significant growth, a specimen that was smaller at planting time might even have caught up with the larger one.

Time can be viewed as a wonderful dynamic – you can witness your garden's change with the passage of the seasons and the years as the design you envisioned becomes a reality. As plants and beds mature, they often require less maintenance because after their roots become well established, appropriately selected trees and shrubs will not require much attention, and, as groundcovers fill in, the need for weeding is reduced.

Three stages of landscape renewal
Top: The existing overgrown plants were removed, the soil amended, and a retaining wall built. Right: Urns were added and ready-mix concrete bags were arranged as steps, well watered, and given time to harden before the paper was torn off. Bottom: Drought-resistant species were planted and well mulched.

Raised beds for variety

Sometimes the plants you want to grow are at odds with your soil. Plants that require excellent drainage are poor choices for heavy, clay soils. On the other hand, a light, sandy soil will not sustain plants that require abundant moisture without reliable, abundant irrigation. If you want to include plants in your landscape with requirements that vary significantly from your native soil, consider growing them in raised beds or containers. Given the finite quantity of soil involved, its characteristics can be easily manipulated to suit the needs of desired plants.

Although limited in space, these gardens can be constructed or placed in sun or shade, protected or exposed locations, and watered frequently or minimally. They can also be built to accommodate easy access for gardeners who have difficulty bending or working in ground beds. The flexibility of raised beds gives the gardener an enormous selection of plants that might otherwise be ill suited for the conditions of the site (*see also p.13*).

Culling the existing landscape

Before you begin adding plants to your landscape, it is important to review those that are already there. Some may have suffered damage or neglect and are now simply eyesores. Others may require a bit (or more) of maintenance. Certain plants in your yard may require significant time and energy to keep them healthy and attractive. This is particularly common with plants that were sited in inappropriate conditions in the first place. Transplanting to a different spot in the landscape or removing them altogether may be necessary.

Small trees and shrubs are often planted too close together. Although the short-term effect may be pleasing, after a number of years plants eventually become too crowded for their space. If such plants exist in your yard, determine if their value is worth the effort of constant pruning. Is transplanting them to another location a possibility, or should you simply remove them?

Most suburban lots can accommodate very few large trees. If the trees that were planted decades ago have overtaken the lot, you may want to consider removing one or two, or at least thinning their branches to allow more light to penetrate. Limbing up the tree – that is, removing the lower branches – can increase light penetration as well, and it opens the area beneath the tree for use.

Severe damage from disease, insects, winds, lightning, or other environmental stresses may have affected some trees and shrubs in your yard. Ask yourself if they are worth saving – it may be time to consider a replacement. Pruning or removing large trees may require a professional arborist.

WHEN TO CALL THE ARBORIST

Trees are a common and essential element of the southwestern landscape, providing shade to your home, garden, and leisure areas while lending a graceful aesthetic presence to your surroundings with views of foliage, fruit, bark and habit throughout the year. To protect these valuable horticultural commodities, there are times when a certified arborist must be brought in to evaluate or treat declining, sick, or damaged trees.

Arborists, popularly known as tree surgeons, are professionals trained in tree care. They can diagnose problems, recommend treatments, fertilize, prune, spray, and remove trees safely.

Contact an arborist if large or out-of-reach limbs have broken, often a result of storm damage, or when large-scale pruning must be done. A proper cut, made either from the ground or in the tree's canopy through the use of ropes and harnesses, will enable

the tree to heal quickly and eliminate entry points for insects or disease. Pine trees, cypress, and citrus trees can be especially vulnerable to wounds that are not properly treated.

When insects or diseases become a problem for your trees, arborists can recommend and provide a number of helpful remedies. In cases where specific pests besiege a species or an entire genera, such as long-horn borers and the lerp psyllid on eucalyptus trees, an arborist can prescribe a number of remedies to control the problem and, in some cases, encourage regenerative growth. Arborists can also recommend and perform removal of dead or declining trees. Consult your state association of arborists for a list of certified professionals.

A job for the professional
Removing large limbs and felling trees are both best left to trained professional arborists.

Thinning and limbing up

When large trees limit the opportunities for growing other plants in a yard, either because they take up a great deal of space, or they cast dense shade, removal is not your only option.

Thinning a tree involves removing a percentage of its branches so that more air and light can penetrate through the remaining canopy without stimulating a great deal of vigorous, new growth. This is accomplished by cutting specific branches back to where they connect to a larger limb. This type of pruning is often beneficial to the tree: weak, unhealthy, and crowded branches can be removed, and air circulates better through the canopy. Plants that are growing beneath the tree will receive more light. If you want grass to grow under a tree with a dense canopy, thinning is critical.

Limbing up involves removing low limbs back to the main trunk in order to allow access to the area beneath the canopy; it effectively raises the crown. Ideally this process should begin early in the tree's training, but it can be done to large trees as well. When you are removing lower limbs from a young tree, do it gradually – this will cause less shock and promote a stronger trunk. As the tree gains height and girth, continue to remove the lowest branches. Generally, the best time to prune trees is when they are dormant, during the fall and winter.

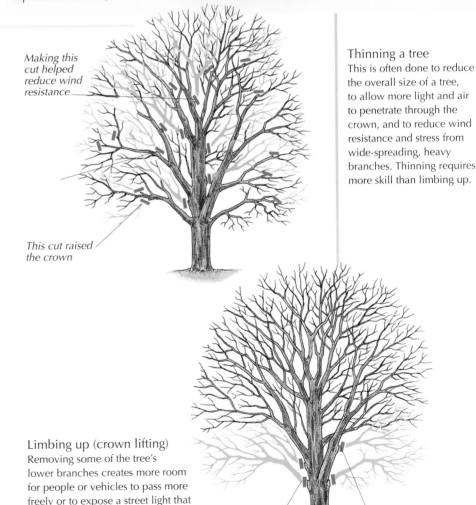

Making this cut helped reduce wind resistance

This cut raised the crown

Thinning a tree
This is often done to reduce the overall size of a tree, to allow more light and air to penetrate through the crown, and to reduce wind resistance and stress from wide-spreading, heavy branches. Thinning requires more skill than limbing up.

Limbing up (crown lifting)
Removing some of the tree's lower branches creates more room for people or vehicles to pass more freely or to expose a street light that has become hidden in the branches. This is generally the easier of the two options presented here.

Entire branch was removed

Part of this large branch was removed

USING GYPSUM TO IMPROVE DRAINAGE

When poor drainage of clay soils is caused by alkalinity (sodium), adding gypsum can improve drainage and help plants to grow. Alkalinity pulls clay particles closer together, making soil denser and impervious to water. The calcium in gypsum combines with exchangeable sodium in the clay, releasing soluble calcium and replacing some of the sodium. This creates a more open soil structure, allowing clay to drain better.

Gypsum is inexpensive and readily available at garden centers. Choose a soluble type and apply 2 to 5 pounds per 100 square feet. If possible, work gypsum into the ground before planting. As much as 10 pounds per 100 square feet can be used prior to installing lawns from seed or sod. It may take up to 2 years for gypsum to take full effect. Reapply it from time to time (annually for roses), spreading it on top of the ground and watering it in. To improve drainage in planting holes, mix 2 or 3 cups of gypsum into the soil in the bottom of each hole under the roots of plants.

Gypsum will not correct poor drainage when it's caused by fine texture or by compaction. These can be overcome by adding organic matter.

Adapting soil conditions

Whether refining an existing garden or working an area that is new to cultivation, a number of conditions can be fairly easily modified, such as adjusting pH and modifying drainange and structure.

Many of these changes – particularly those involving the soil – are most easily addressed prior to planting. Once a garden has been planted, your ability to incorporate soil amendments is restricted. Whenever you dig soil, take the opportunity to incorporate amendments. It takes much longer for fertilizer and limestone to reach plant roots when placed on the surface of the soil than it does when those materials are mixed throughout the root zone.

ADJUSTING SOIL PH

As mentioned in Tenet 2, a soil test provides important information about your soil. If your existing soil pH restricts your selection of plants, you can adjust it by mixing certain minerals into the soil. Limestone – usually ground or dolomitic – is applied to raise the pH (decrease the acidity). Wood ashes also tend to raise the pH of soil. Elemental sulfur or iron sulfate are the most commonly recommended supplements for lowering pH. Aluminum sulfate can also be used to decrease acidity, but it may cause aluminum toxicity in some plants.

Many sources of organic matter, including pine needles, oak leaves, unlimed compost, and green manure (cover crops that are plowed into the soil), will increase the soil acidity as they are broken down by microorganisms. Peat moss is also an acidifier, but its use should be avoided because it takes so long – centuries, in fact – for it to regenerate in its native bogs. The amounts of various materials needed to produce the desired pH level will vary depending on your soil texture and the amount of change needed. Modifying the soil pH takes time; it may require repeated applications.

DEALING WITH DRAINAGE

If your soil drains too slowly, you have several options. You can limit your selection to plants that like wet soils, add material to the soil to improve drainage, or build raised beds and fill them with good, loamy soil before planting. To improve drainage of a compacted soil, add organic matter. If the subsoil is compacted, you may need to break up the hardpan or add subsurface drainage tiles to carry excess water away from planting areas.

For vegetable gardens with poor drainage, a hill-and-furrow planting method can be used: broad rows can be built up above the soil surface, with furrows running between the rows to divert excess water. Conversely, if your soil drains too quickly, use the furrows for planting. Rain or irrigation water will be channeled into the furrows where plants are growing.

For gardens where the soil drains too quickly, the addition of organic matter will improve water holding capacity, and mulching will reduce evaporation loss. But supplemental irrigation may be necessary unless you choose plants that thrive in dry soils.

Building soil with organic matter

Organic matter – compost, leaf mold, grass clippings, rotted manure, or any material that was once alive – has a nearly miraculous power to improve almost any soil. Added to a clay soil, it facilitates drainage by creating soil aggregates with pore spaces between them; in a sandy soil, it bolsters water retention. The best way to provide continuous, well-balanced nutrition for plants is to build up the soil with organic matter.

As both microscopic (for example, bacteria) and macroscopic (such as earthworms and fungi) soil organisms digest organic matter, they release

Using a cover crop One of the best ways to improve your soil, including drainage, is to plant a cover crop, such as scarlet clover (shown here) or crown vetch, from seeds in fall and dig it into the ground in spring.

nutrients in a usable form for plants to absorb through their roots. Unlike quick-release chemical fertilizers that offer a glut of nutrients that may wash away with the next rain, decomposition of organic matter is a continuous process; nutrients are released slowly over a long period of time.

There are many good sources of organic matter, and many of them are free and readily available. Kitchen and yard wastes can be composted and within a few months yield a rich soil supplement (*see* Composting wastes, *p. 58*). Leaves raked during the fall become crumbly leaf mold, especially if they are chopped and mixed with a bit of soil to encourage their decomposition. Manure is often free for the hauling from a nearby farm or stable, or it can be

Mushroom compost   *Peat*   *Manure*

Brown gold
Here are just three of the many different kinds of organic matter that can be added to the soil in order to improve the structure and water retention.

purchased in bags from a home-supply or hardware store. Green manure is a cover crop that is sown, grown, and then turned back into the soil. A winter cover crop is an efficient method of adding nutrients and organic matter to a vegetable garden.

A distinction is often made between leguminous and nonleguminous cover crops. Both add organic matter to the soil, but legumes, such as clover and vetch, contribute additional nitrogen as a result of their symbiotic relationship with nitrogen-fixing *Rhizobium* bacteria in the roots. As the legume roots decompose, nitrogen is released back into the soil. Of course, the amount of specific nutrients any given organic matter contains depends on the source and condition of the organic matter. For example, most compost contains 1.5 to 3.5 percent nitrogen, 0.5 to 1 percent phosphorus, and 1 to 2 percent potassium. Wood ashes – which tend to raise pH – contain little nitrogen, 1 to 2 percent phosphorus, and 3 to 7 percent potassium.

A soil that is well furnished with organic matter will sustain a healthy population of organisms, resulting in both improved soil structure and a good source of the raw materials needed by your garden plants. This is recycling at its best.

DO'S AND DON'TS FOR GARDEN SOILS

Most soils in the Southwest are alkaline, and notoriously poor; they drain badly and contain little natural humus or nitrogen. Regular applications of organic matter and wise use of organic fertilizers, can gradually build the worst garden soil into a dark, productive, and loam-like material in which most plants thrive. But the road to good soil also has pitfalls. Two of the most common are adding raw sawdust to garden soil and adding sand to clay soil.

Raw sawdust is a cheap soil amendment, but it subtracts nitrogen from soil in order to rot. Never add sawdust to garden soil unless you add enough nitrogen (ammonium sulfate) to enable it to rot. Add 1–1½ pounds of nitrogen for every 100 pounds of raw shavings. After tilling the sawdust and nitrogen into the soil, continue feeding plants regularly.

Tests performed by the Extension Service and the USDA prove that adding sand to clay soil can ruin clay's ability to drain. You end up with something akin to concrete. Healthy soil has plenty of air holes surrounding soil particles. Never try to change a soil's structure, don't take out all the rocks or mix in another type of soil, such as sand into silt, or clay into sand. Work with what you've got by mixing in organic matter every time you plant. Add gypsum to clay soil. Mulch the ground once or twice a year with organic mulch such as homemade compost, composted manure, or composted wood products. Even planting trees, shrubs, and vines benefits the soil. Their roots penetrate the soil, breaking up the ground and improving drainage.

The nature of humus

After organic matter is thoroughly decomposed by soil microorganisms, it produces a material called humus, which exists as a very thin layer around soil particles. There is some misunderstanding about this term. The material commonly sold in bags that bear the label "humus" – usually compost or peat – would be more accurately labeled "humus-producing material," because microorganisms use it to make true humus, which is the end product of organic matter decomposition.

Humus contributes significantly to the soil environment by facilitating the aggregation of soil particles (which improves soil structure), holding nutrients against the force of leaching, increasing aeration, retaining water, and acting as a buffer to moderate a soil's acidity or alkalinity.

The carbon:nitrogen ratio

One of the most critical characteristics of organic matter in terms of plant nutrition is the carbon to nitrogen ratio (C:N ratio). Fresh organic matter has a high carbon content compared to its nitrogen content. As the organic matter breaks down, the ratio changes as the relative amount of nitrogen increases. In most fully matured compost, the C:N ratio is between 30:1 and 10:1. When organic matter with a high C:N ratio (above 30:1), such as sawdust or grass clippings, is added to soil, microorganisms use nitrogen from the soil, and a temporary nitrogen deficiency can occur in plants. To avoid this deficiency, use composted organic matter. If mulching with a noncomposted organic material, apply a top-dressing of a nitrogen fertilizer prior to spreading the material.

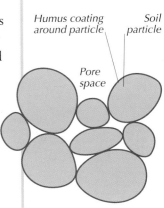

Humus coating around particle   *Soil particle*

Pore space

Up close
This diagram shows a much enlarged view of a few particles of soil. Each particle is coated with humus, the end product of microbial breakdown of organic matter. Humus aids in the retention of moisture and nutrients and promotes the formation of aggregates, which in turn leads to increased pore space and improved percolation.

PICK THE BEST PLANTS

One of the most important steps in establishing and maintaining a SMARTGARDEN™ is selecting the right plants. Matching the cultural requirements of plants with your specific garden environment significantly increases the likelihood of successful cultivation and minimizes the maintenance effort. Preferences for water, light, soil type and acidity, tolerance of wind, humidity, salt spray, and air pollution, and resistance to diseases and pests are important factors in plant selection. Some conditions, such as soil pH, can be adjusted to accommodate the needs of desired plants. Others, such as salt spray near coastal regions or air pollution near industrial areas, are essentially fixed and limiting factors in the selection process.

Practical considerations

Identifying the USDA Plant Hardiness and AHS Heat Zones of your site is a logical first step in choosing plants you would like to grow. If a plant does not have the hardiness or heat tolerance for the zone in which you garden, you should choose another plant, unless you are willing to take extra measures to protect it. For example, tropical and subtropical plants can be grown in a container outdoors in temperate zones and brought indoors for winter, but it's best to choose plants appropriate for your zone. Consult the Zone maps on p. 22 to determine your USDA Hardiness Zone and your AHS Heat Zone. Use those numbers as a starting point to select plants that will thrive in your garden's temperatures.

There may be areas of your yard that are unsuitable or impractical for growing plants of any kind. Consider a nonplant alternative such as a fence (in place of a hedge), a walkway, patio, or deck (in place of a lawn, bed, or similar planting), or a gazebo (in place of a large shade tree). These spaces are important elements of a landscape because they provide you with a minimum-maintenance area for moving through your gardens comfortably, or room for relaxing and enjoying your planted areas.

So you have an area in your yard and you want it to do something, but you need to consider the options: Provide shade? Simply look nice? Attract birds? Smell good? Block a view? Separate one area from another? Cover the ground? Provide a space for active play?

What are the site's physical factors, including sun, water, soil, wind, and microclimate? Will it support plants? If no, use the site for some other purpose, or think hard about what you would need to do to modify it. If yes, consider the specific plant features you'd like and require: leaves, flowers, fruit, form, bark, fragrance, size, shape, longevity, adaptabilty, productivity, hardiness, specific needs such as pruning, support, or deadheading to look its best, and susceptibility to pests and diseases.

Choose plants that meet the desired criteria and will grow well in the available microclimate, and determine how many will be needed.

The next consideration is your budget. If you can wait for a small plant to grow to its mature size, or let groundcovers and other similar plants multiply, you will spend less. You should also determine the most appropriate time for the plant to be purchased and planted.

Borrowed scenery
A savvy gardener created this satisfying garden with a minimum of work and no water; a few inches of gravel, a table and chairs, and – *voila!* – an instant comfortable patio.

Difficult plant area
One of the most difficult areas for planting – a small, west-facing patio, surrounded by a house – is perfect for a secluded hot tub. Potted plants can be changed with the seasons.

Compromise
In a site facing north, problems included invasive tree roots and dry sandy soil – not good for shrubs or flowers but perfect for a brick-floored pergola covered with Chinese wisteria, which needs well-drained soil.

Plant categories

Plants are grouped according to their lifespan. The major categories are annuals, biennials, herbaceous perennials, and woody plants.

ANNUAL

An annual completes its life cycle in a single season. It grows from seed, develops vegetatively, bears flowers, and produces seed for the next generation and then dies, all in less than a year.

Hot-weather lover
Sunflowers thrive in warm weather and can be planted from seeds in late spring or early summer for summer and fall bloom.

Heat-loving perennial
Valerian (*Centranthus ruber*) will survive for many years with little care or water in sun or part-shade, seeding itself around the garden, even thriving in vacant lots.

PERENNIAL

A perennial is a plant that lives for more than two years, and a herbaceous perennial is a nonwoody plant that survives from one growing season to the next because its roots or underground storage organs (such as a bulb, corm, or tuber) persist.

BIENNIAL

A biennial requires two growing seasons to complete its life cycle. Most biennials produce vegetative growth their first season; they flower, produce seed, and die their second season.

It takes two
Tall Shirley foxgloves are true biennials that take two years to complete their life cycle. If planted from seeds in June or from plants in fall (any time before December 20th), they will bloom the following spring, after which they will die, leaving plenty of seeds for another year.

Cool-weather lover
Fairy primrose is a true winter annual that will bloom all winter if planted from transplants in October. Hanging baskets keep plants above slugs and snails.

WOODY PLANT

A woody plant is also a type of perennial, but it possesses a more permanent structure that persists above ground from season to season. Woody plants may be deciduous (shedding their leaves each year) or evergreen. Examples include shrubs, trees, and some climbers and groundcovers.

Storing water in leaves
As has often been said, all cacti are succulents but not all succulents are cacti. Here (near left), non-spiny varieties provide year-round color and drought resistance on a steep site.

Continental color
Provence lavender (far left) is a flowering shrub often combined with perennials in flower gardens or grown here as a groundcover, lending the atmosphere of southern France or Italy.

Perennials grown as annuals

Some plants are referred to as annuals, when they are actually perennial in their native habitat or in another Hardiness Zone. This has led to some confusion among gardeners. True annuals – plants that grow, flower, produce seed, and die in a single growing season – have a Hardiness Zone of zero because they cannot tolerate cold winter temperatures, and so hardiness is not an issue.

Many plants that are grown as annuals in temperate climates, such as sweet basil, snapdragon, coleus, and moonflower, are perennial in warm climates; such plants are sometimes referred to as horticultural annuals, meaning that they can be grown as annuals in regions where they will not survive as perennials. They may also be referred to as tender perennials.

California poppy is an example of a perennial plant usually grown as a winter or cool-season annual, planted from seeds in fall for spring bloom.

Impatiens is an example of a perennial plant that is grown as a warm-season annual in cold-winter climates, but stays alive year-round in frost-free climates.

Monkey flower is a native perennial well-adapted to gardens. Though short-lived, it is highly desirable for its drought resistance and long-lasting color.

Plant adaptations

Why do some plants flourish in full sun, while others languish or outright die unless they are provided with at least some shade during the hottest part of the day? Why do some plants thrive in bogs and open water, and others are perfectly at home in deserts or on cliffsides? Although most garden plants have roughly the same structure – roots, stems, leaves, flowers – nuances in their morphology equip them for a wide variety of conditions. This is fortunate, because this means there are plenty of plants, both naturally occcurring and selected, whose requirements and preferences match your conditions. Understanding the characteristics that make a plant suited to particular conditions will help you recognize those that are likely to do well in your garden environment.

SHADE

Plants that grow best in the shade tend to have large, flat leaves with a fairly thin outer layer of cells. This allows maximum area and minimum resistance for absorbing light needed for photosynthesis and growth. In general, plants that grow in shady conditions produce fewer flowers and seeds than those grown in sun – this limited reproductive activity conserves a great deal of energy that can be directed toward vegetative growth. Thus, the ornamental display of many shade gardens relies more heavily on foliage color and texture than on flowers.

HEAT AND DROUGHT

Xeriphytic plants have developed several strategies for reducing water loss and dealing with high temperatures. Many have smaller leaves with a thick, waxy layer, called the cuticle, on the leaf surface that protects it from drying out as well as providing some protection against insects. The reduction in both surface area and protective coating minimize moisture loss. Alpine plants that survive in areas where soil water is frozen for much of the year, and unavailable for absorption by plants, often exhibit similar traits.

Shady situation
Hanging baskets on a drip system plus containers on stepping stones light up an entranceway where invasive tree roots would have made it impossible to grow plants in the ground.

Good companions in full sun
Native plants in the background are combined with colorful plants such as bougainvillea, succulents, and watsonia from other dry climates around the world. Roses are planted at the bottom of the slope, where they get more irrigation.

Another adaptation that enables many plants to tolerate dry climates is pubescence – the presence of fine hairs – on leaves. These hairs help shade the leaf surface from the hot sun and trap moisture lost by the leaf through transpiration, thus maintaining a higher humidity level immediately around the leaf surface. The higher humidity reduces the transpiration pressure in the leaf, slowing the rate of moisture loss. Leaf arrangement and color also affect the absorption of heat. Leaves that point upward, arranged vertically toward the sun – such as *Yucca* and *Phormium* – absorb less heat than those with leaves oriented at right angles to the stem. Light-colored plants (typical of many heat-tolerant plants, including several species of *Euphorbia, Sedum,* and *Verbascum*) absorb less heat than dark plants.

Tough tomatoes
Tomato Better Boy VFN is a main crop or standard tomato that is resistant to *Verticillium* and *Fusarium* wilts and nematodes, thus providing abundant crops in many Southwestern soils and climate zones.

COLD AND WIND

Some plants that grow well in cold, windy sites (such as along the coast, on open plains and priairies, or at the tops of mountains) have a prostrate growth habit, minimizing their exposure to drying winds. Trees and shrubs that survive in regions with cold winters are sensitive to environmental signals such as dropping temperatures and decreasing day length, initiating changes that induce dormancy to prepare them for winter, often indicated by leaf drop or a change in evergreen foliage color. As temperatures decrease, certain solutes – dissolved substances – accumulate in cells, reducing the likelihood of their freezing and rupturing. This is essentially making use of plant "antifreeze."

Site-specific challenges

Identifying the varied growing conditions of your site will help you select plants that will thrive with the least amount of assistance on your part. For example, an area of your yard that drains poorly and remains wet for long periods of the season is a likely site for a bog garden. The sunny strip alongside the street or driveway, subject to reflected heat and baking sun and far from the water faucet, lends itself to a xeriphytic planting of drought- tolerant plants. The shady north side of your house is a likely spot for shade-loving shrubs and groundcovers.

The conditions of some gardening sites are more challenging than others, and they may significantly restrict plant selection. If you live by the seashore,

Four solutions to challenging sites
On the north side of a house (upper left), where there is a difficult shadow and alkaline soil, a gardener opts to solve the problem with a fountain arising from a small pond. In the open, dappled shade of a redbud (*Cercis canadensis* 'Forest Pansy', upper right), South African bulbs, including babiana, flourish. A bank adjacent to a swimming pool in full sun (bottom left) is covered with drought-resistant plants that prevent erosion, including blue pride of Madeira (*Echium candicans*), yellow gazanias, and pink rock rose (*Cistus* 'Doris Hibberson'). A pool in a hot interior climate (bottom right) is tucked into a narrow side yard where half-shade and an all-green landscape keep the water pleasantly cool in summer.

you should select plants that tolerate salt spray and wind. If your soil is rich in limestone, plants that thrive in alkaline soil are a logical choice. Trees that have proven to adapt to the stresses of air pollution and compacted soil are the best options for planting alongside busy streets and in high-traffic urban areas. The lists in the Plant Catalog offer you a guide to regionally adapted plants to use in the variety of specific conditions that may be present in your garden.

Some areas may represent exceptions to the general conditions that are present in your yard and may offer possibilities for growing plants beyond those typically suited for your region or location (see Identify your microclimates, p. 24).

Plants for local conditions

For centuries, plant breeders have selected and developed varieties of plants with qualities that make them particularly well adapted to certain conditions, often extending the area in which that plant has traditionally been grown. New heat-tolerant perennials, such as dianthus, are an example.

Many, if not most, of the cultivated plants that we grow have been selected because someone thought they were (for example) showier, bigger, smaller, healthier, or more fruitful than other plants like it. It may have been a planned cross that was part of a breeding program at a major seed company, or it may have been a serendipitous event – a gardener noticing a plant that was somehow different in some significant way than others. Sometimes seed of the selection observed and saved by a gardener is passed around to friends and handed down to children.

New varieties are continually being developed, grown, and compared at commercial seed companies and public institutions. Many regional plant breeding programs are associated with land grant colleges (see Appendix p. 386) or botanic gardens and arboreta (see p. 388).

Research has led to the breeding and selection of plants that better withstand environmental adversity. This means that certain varieties may extend the growing range or conditions where the plant can be successfully grown.

Discriminating variety selection can also reduce the impact of pests and diseases that frequently infest gardens in your locale. There may be varieties of the plants you want to grow that display an inherited resistance or tolerance to the problem. This preventive approach to pest and disease control is a simple way to reduce the need for applying pesticides. Local garden centers and Extension Services are often able to provide the names of disease- and pest-resistant varieties of fruits, vegetables, and ornamental plants for your area.

UNDERSTANDING MEDITERRANEAN AND SOUTHWEST CLIMATES

Mediterranean climates occur on Southwestern corners of large continental land masses and are characterized by dry sunny summers, with almost all rainfall concentrated during the mild winter months. Worldwide, there are five main areas: southern California, central Chile, the western cape of South Africa, western and southwest-central Australia, and northern and western parts of the Mediterranean basin. In all these regions, the modulating affect of the ocean brings about a temperate climate with mild winters, while prevailing westerly winds and the proximity of a large land mass results in warm dry summers and wet winters. Many plants native to Mediterranean climates have drought-resistant characteristics: roots that store water, seeds germinated by fire, rapidly growing tap roots, fine surface roots, and leaves that resist dehydration through their leathery, succulent, gray, hairy, or summer-deciduous natures. Typical plants, such as olive and carob trees, Mediterranean fan palms, bougainvillea, oleander, rosemary, rock rose, yucca, and aloe can survive summer drought with little if any irrigation.

This Southwest book covers Texas, Oklahoma, New Mexico, Arizona, Nevada, Hawaii, and California—a vast region—but only southern parts of California west of the mountains have a Mediterranean climate. The interior Southwest has a largely dry and, in many cases, desert climate with temperatures that are more extreme. The weather of most of the Southwest is determined by the pattern of the continental air mass as it moves over mountains and other topographical features from west to east.

However, large areas of the Southwest are influenced by seasonal moisture circulating up from the Gulf of Mexico bringing summer rains, called monsoons, to New Mexico, Arizona, and other hot, dry interior regions. Also, while Western Texas has a typically dry Southwest climate, Eastern and coastal Texas are more subtropical with a damp hot climate. No part of Hawaii has a Mediterranean climate; rainfall can happen at any time of the year. Some mountainside Hawaiian communities are

Glorious Californian
Matilija poppy (*Romneya coulteri*) will thrive on steep slopes in full sun and dry rocky soil.

cool enough to allow growth of short-day onions, camellias, azaleas, and cymbidium orchids, also widely grown in coastal California.

Mature size and growth habit

Trying to achieve a mature appearance in your new garden is tempting, but it can lead to problems. If you space your plants too closely together, the result is almost always unsatisfactory. Plants soon become crowded, they may become more susceptible to disease, and they compete for water and light. Flower and fruit production may be reduced. Often, their growth habit is altered – instead of full, wide-spreading branches, plants may appear sparse and gangly as they stretch in search of light.

When deciding which plants to include in your yard and where you want to place them, be sure you have room to accommodate the mature size of each selection, no matter what its eventual size will be. Repeated pruning of a shrub during the growing season will be made unnecessary if your initial selection is based on the desired mature size. Many nurseries supply the mature dimensions on the plant tag or label. Consult the Plant Catalog to avoid making a major mistake.

If the growth habit of a plant is something worth featuring, be sure to provide adequate room. For example, a Harry Lauder's walking stick (*Corylus avellana* 'Contorta') is best placed in an open area where its unusual form can be appreciated. A low, spreading plant such as creeping juniper needs plenty of lateral room to develop; otherwise, it may overtake nearby plants or walkways.

Training plants from an early age to enhance their natural habit or to direct growth in a certain manner can be an effective way to manage plant size. Carefully pruned specimen plants can serve as focal

points and accents, esepecially in a small garden. Some plants can be trained to grow against a wall, a technique known as espalier; this requires a minimum of garden space and is an effective use of a blank wall.

Another choice you will be confronted with when selecting your plants is which size to purchase. Although a larger plant may give you a fuller look than a smaller version of the same plant, you will need to weigh the additional expense against the immediate effect. In a few seasons, small plants often catch up to plants that were larger at the time of purchase (*see* The benefits of time, p. 28).

If you do start with young plants, it is still possible to achieve a mature look while waiting for them to grow. Maintain temporary herbaceous plantings in the space between young woody plants. Annuals survive for only a single season, and as your trees and shrubs spread in the coming years, perennials can be dug and transplanted to other areas.

Espaliered apple tree
Some deciduous fruit trees adapt well to training and growing as an espalier against a fence or wall, including this low-chill apple, 'Anna', which needs a pollinator but can bear fruit in a frost-free climate.

Tree forms

Trees may be the biggest of all the voices in your garden choir, but they do show a remarkable range of differences. Use these differences to create a varied backdrop for the rest of your garden plants and structures. Remember, it may take several to many years for the tree to develop its fully mature form.

Half-standard   *Fastigiate*   *Multistemmed*   *Weeping standard*

Growth habits

There are many shapes a plant can take, whether naturally or by manipulation though horticultural practices. It is often best to consider a plant's shape before thinking about its flowers – the shape will remain long after the flowers are gone. The Plant Catalog presents some options for selecting plants based on their habit.

Cushion- or mound-forming   *Clump-forming*   *Climbing and Scandet*

TAKE GOOD CARE OF THE EARTH

Every garden activity we undertake has a ripple effect on our plants, soil, water, and wildlife. We apply fertilizer to our lawns and, depending on the type and quantity, it can either bolster a healthy soil environment or leach through the soil and pollute local streams. By encouraging certain plants to grow and removing others, we influence whether and what wildlife inhabits our gardens. The material that we select to surface our paths and driveways also has an impact – positive or negative – on water runoff and soil erosion.

Choices and compromises

In our efforts to develop and maintain satisfying landscapes, we must try to achieve our goals without putting a strain on our environment. Simply by adjusting watering schedules, selecting the most effective mulch material, or timing the application of a pest control measure with precision, we can increase the efficiency of our gardening efforts and minimize the effect on the environment.

Some of the modifications we make in our gardens may require a balanced counteraction. For example, removing debris from a bed to keep it neat deprives soil of organic matter. Replacing the leaves with an organic mulch such as compost or shredded bark, however, supplies the organic matter while achieving the desired tidy appearance. Recognizing the impact of our activities, using resources efficiently and avoiding waste, must become second nature in the SMARTGARDEN™.

Whether you are planning a new bed, maintaining a lawn, or pruning a tree, your gardening activities require choices. Careful consideration of environmental consequences should be an important part of the criteria you use for selecting one technique over another.

Basic decisions such as whether an area should be maintained as lawn or developed into a bed, whether to encourage wildlife (and if so, which kind), and whether a tree that casts dense shade should be removed all need to be weighed against their impact on the overall landscape. Sometimes a compromise in expectations, technique, or timing can be effective in achieving the desired change without affecting significant environmental consequences.

Another good example of compromise is reducing the amount of nitrogen fertilizer applied to those plants that are subject to water stress – vegetative growth may be reduced, but so will the water needs of the plant.

Providing pollen
A raised bed, filled with pollen-bearing wildflowers planted in fall, blooms from winter through spring and attracts many beneficials.

Attracting butterflies
Viceroy and other species of butterflies are attracted to many native plants including the elegant evergreen shrub or tree, Mescal bean (*Sophora secundiflora*).

Serious disease or pest problems can be reduced by adjusting your planting schedule for several vegetable crops. Thinning a tree canopy that casts dense shade, rather than removing the tree, can accomplish the desired outcome of increasing light penetration without destroying a habitat and food source that supports a variety of wildlife.

Conserving water

Given the droughts and high average temperatures many parts of the country have been experiencing in recent years, not to mention the increase in population density, water consumption for

Bird feeder
Giving supplemental food to seed-loving birds may keep them in your garden year-round.

gardening is a growing concern. There are a variety of conservation strategies you can use in your garden to reduce water consumption

While all plants need water to thrive, some need less than others, and some plants are better equipped than others to obtain and retain water. For instance, succulent plants store water in their fleshy leaves or their stems and underground srtuctures for use when needed. Leaves of lamb's-ears (*Stachys* spp.) and wormwood (*Artemisia* spp.) are covered with fine white hairs that shade the leaf surface and prevent moisture loss. Many ornamental grasses and prairie natives have deep roots that range far to seek water. Some leaves are oriented so that the minimum amount of sunlight falls on their surfaces, reducing leaf temperature. These and other characteristics of drought-tolerant plants minimize the need for supplemental watering (*see* Plant adaptations, *p. 36*).

You do not need to limit your plant selection to drought-tolerant species. Plants that require more frequent watering, however, should be grouped together, ideally close to a water source. By designing your garden according to the plants' water requirements, it is easier to develop efficient watering systems tailored to the needs of different sections of the garden.

REDUCING RUNOFF

A great deal of potentially beneficial garden moisture is lost to runoff. Grading your beds can help direct the flow of water to where it will be most useful. Studies suggest that significantly more water penetrates into the soil through a diverse planting of groundcovers than through turf, and reducing lawn area will increase water absorption.

A rain barrel that collects water from the roof saves water that would otherwise be lost as runoff. Several manufacturers produce plastic rain barrels with hardware to connect the downspout with the barrel, and a faucet so you can access the water. Rain barrels can be attached to drip irrigation systems or simply used to fill your watering can. An added benefit of collecting rainwater in areas with wells that supply hard water – water that contains a high level of soluble salts – is that since rainwater is soft, it will not cause mineral deposits that can clog up drip irrigation nozzles, and you can use the water on plants that need acidic soil conditions. Don't forget to cover barrels and other containers to control mosquitoes.

Solid-surface walkways and driveways prevent water from penetrating into the soil, and the water

Not thirsty
Flowers on drought-resistant lavender cotton (*Santolina*) can be enjoyed in spring, then sheared off after bloom to maintain the compact shape of the plant.

REDUCING RUNOFF AND RECYCLING NATURE

The Southwest region has little water and few rivers. Natural freshwater lakes are almost non-existent. To provide for the demands of an increasing population, engineers in the early twentieth century designed huge dams and aqueducts to collect and carry water hundreds of miles from its sources to population centers. At the time, little thought was given to the long-term impact of man-made changes in river valleys, but today new dams and pipelines are often challenged by environmentalists. Water disputes have proliferated. People have come to realize that water is a precious commodity and the supply is limited.

Increased population has also led to contamination of ground water and runoff into coastal waters. Contaminants on roads, parking lots, and driveways are washed into storm drains during heavy rains and end up in watersheds, eventually reaching underground aquifers, rivers, lakes, and the ocean.

Contamination also comes from excess fertilizers and chemicals that leach into the soil from farming and gardening. These increase the alkalinity of soil and water, upsetting the balance of nature and threatening the health of wildlife. For example, many fertilizers contain nitrogen in the form of nitrates or ammoniums. Nitrates are fast-acting but also water-soluble and can leach into ground water. Ammonium and organic nitrogen fertilizers are better choices because they are released more slowly

and last longer in the soil. Some synthetic organic fertilizers also last longer because they must be converted into nitrates by microbes before they can be absorbed by plant roots.

There is no immediate or quick answer to the water problems facing the Southwest, but gardeners alert to the needs of our environment can take steps not to further deplete our natural resources. Water conservation is the first concern. By growing plants consistent with our dry climate, gardeners can save much-needed water. Using organic fertilizers and refraining

from the use of chemical sprays will help protect aquifers, watercourses, and the ocean from the accumulation of damaging salts, heavy metals, and poisons. Established gardens, in which the plants are well-adapted, the surface of the ground frequently mulched, and leaves allowed to remain where they fall, can survive on their own refuse, as they would in nature, with little added fertilizer.

Most drought-resistant native plants need no chemical fertilizers whatsoever and little or no organic fertilizer.

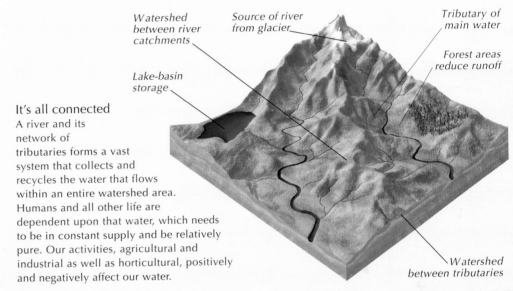

It's all connected
A river and its network of tributaries forms a vast system that collects and recycles the water that flows within an entire watershed area. Humans and all other life are dependent upon that water, which needs to be in constant supply and be relatively pure. Our activities, agricultural and industrial as well as horticultural, positively and negatively affect our water.

Watershed between river catchments

Source of river from glacier

Tributary of main water

Forest areas reduce runoff

Lake-basin storage

Watershed between tributaries

that runs off of these surfaces often leads to erosion or drainage problems. When installing a driveway or walkway, consider using a permeable surface through which rainwater can be absorbed. Driveways can be constructed of gravel, and beautiful walks and patios can be fashioned from unmortared stone set in sand.

Supplementing nature
Water requirements are affected not only by the type of plant and the density of the planting, but also by a number of environmental variables, such as temperature, wind, sunlight, and season.

Dry quarters
A dry streambed and a raised bed can reduce your garden's water needs.

Soils also vary in their capacity to retain water. Thus there is no fixed rule for how often you will need to water: observing your plants and checking your soil offer the best clues.

Plants provide several clues when they are suffering from a lack of water. The observant gardener looks for these signs and waters thoroughly before the plant suffers long term or irreversible damage. The following are common symptoms or clues to water stress. The symptoms you first notice will vary somewhat from one kind of plant to another:

• dullness or a subtle change in foliage color
• reduced growth
• reduction in flowers or fruit
• wilting or curling of leaves
• footprints remain when grass is walked upon
• lawn turns dull, then bluish, and eventually straw-colored or brown

All plants should be watered when they are first set out, and regular watering should continue until their roots are well established. It is important to water thoroughly (and at the base of the plants; you don't need to give plants a shower when you water them) to encourage deep root development. Plants with an extensive and deep root system can obtain more water from the soil and are less subject to injury from temperature fluctuations.

Early morning or evening (in other words, before or after the heat of the day), are the best times to water – less will be lost to evaporation. Avoid wetting plant foliage, because wet leaves are more prone to disease.

WHEN TO WATER

Hard and fast guidelines about how often to water simply don't exist. You need to take into account the individual microclimate of your garden, the nature of your soil, and the quantity and size of the plants you are growing. Then you need to factor in the weather. Temperature, humidity, and wind velocity all contribute to the loss of moisture from the soil, especially when coupled with plants that have a relatively large leaf surface to transpire water. This loss of water from the soil is known as the evapotranspiration rate, and, coupled with the water-holding capacity of your soil, determines how frequently supplemental water will be required.

As you can see from the map below, the Southwest is a largely dry region, except for Hawaii and parts of Texas. You will need to grow plants adapted to these conditions, watching them for signs of stress during the warmest periods of the year, and adjusting your sprinkler systems to water less frequently during seasonal rains. Remember, too, that new plants do not have an extensive root system and are more likely to suffer from dryness than well-established plants. Also plants with large soft leaves are more prone to dryness than those with stiff leaves. It is often possible to conserve water by watering individual plants showing signs of stress to save them, rather than by applying water to an entire bed.

Your soil type also governs the frequency of watering. Light sandy soils need more frequent watering while clay soils retain water longer. Adding organic matter to the ground can help sandy soils retain water and will assist clay soils to drain (*see p.31*). Where soils are poor and water is at a premium, consider planting xerophytic plants (those requiring little water) in preference to more commonly grown woody plants and perennials.

HAND WATERING
Using a watering can or hose with a water breaker to deliver a drink to your gardens allows you to get "up close and personal" with your plants on a regular basis. You are likely to detect disease and insect problems soon after they appear. However,

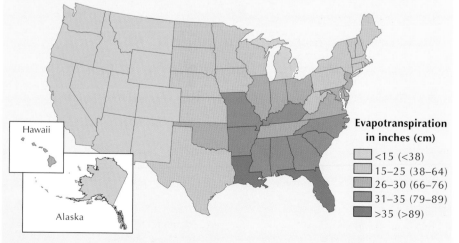

Evapotranspiration in inches (cm)
- <15 (<38)
- 15–25 (38–64)
- 26–30 (66–76)
- 31–35 (79–89)
- >35 (>89)

Hawaii

Alaska

Between-meal snacks
Keeping a filled watering can next to thirsty plants, such as snowbush (*Breynia*) or coleus (*Solenostemon*), makes it easy to give them a quick drink between watering days.

this system requires a great deal of time and may be impractical for large gardens. It is, however, perfectly suited for special, individual plants, small beds, and for those plants growing in containers.

TRICKLE IRRIGATION

One of the most efficient watering systems is drip or trickle irrigation. Although it takes some effort to set up initially, in the long run it saves time. Trickle systems can be designed to accommodate any garden size or style. Water is delivered directly to the root zone of desired plants or areas through emitters at the end of water tubes. Little water is lost to evaporation or wasted on areas between plants. The spacing of emitters and rate of flow can be adjusted as necessary. This system can also be used for container plants.

If your water is hard, however, you may find that the narrow tubes of a trickle irrigation system become clogged with minerals. If a tube is clogged or becomes displaced, plants can suffer before the problem is noticed and rectified.

SOAKER HOSE

Also called a seep hose, a soaker hose allows water to drip out slowly into the soil along the length of the hose. Soakers are similar to drip systems but are easier to move from place to place. They are particularly useful in vegetable gardens, where they can be stretched along the rows, and in densely planted flower beds where they can wind through the entire planting area.

SPRINKLERS

For permanent plantings, an underground, automated sprinkler system can be installed, preferably before the garden is planted. The hardware of these systems must be checked and maintained for efficiency, and plants near nozzles must be monitored; if they grow over the nozzles, they may block or divert the spray. These systems can be programmed to run on a timer.

Portable sprinkler systems are relatively inexpensive and versatile, but they rarely deliver

Efficient irrigation
Low-volume sprinklers water a front lawn of drought-resistant tall fescue, while losing less water to evaporation than high-volume sprinklers. Shrubbery of Indian hawthorn (*Rhaphiolepis*, right foreground) edges the drive so all irrigation water is used and none hits the pavement.

Soaking a raised bed
Raised beds sometimes dry out quicker than the surrounding soil. A soaker hose or drip system can keep the ground moist for vegetables.

Mulching strawberries
Clear plastic mulch is often used over drip lines installed down the center of a mound. Thus, fruit is kept clean and freer of pests than strawberries grown over straw mulch, which attracts sowbugs in the Southwest.

a uniform spray. Hoses connect the water source with a variety of sprinkler attachments – fans, oscillators, pulsating heads. A significant amount of water from sprinklers is lost to evaporation, and use of overhead sprinklers may lead to an increase in foliar disease problems.

Mulching for moisture

Mulching around plants conserves moisture in a number of ways. By physically covering the soil, less daytime moisture is lost to surface evaporation, and the temperature in the root zone in mulched soil is less than for bare soil, especially in hot sun. Mulches inhibit the growth of weeds that compete with your plants for water, and mulches help prevent soil crusting, the dry surface layer that impedes water penetration into the soil, leading to runoff and erosion.

Summer mulches are particularly important for soil moisture retention as well as weed control. But wait until the soil has had a chance to warm up in the spring before applying it, or new growth may be delayed. The best time to mulch depends on the plants that you are growing. In the vegetable garden, cool-season vegetables such as peas and spinach can be mulched much earlier than heat-loving tomatoes and melons. Give perennials

enough time to emerge from the soil before mulching your flower beds.

In a climate with cold winters and warm summers, mulching to provide winter protection is most effective when applied after the ground has become cold and plants have entered dormancy. Mulching too early can delay normal hardening of growth for winter. Many perennials will benefit from a winter mulch after their tops have died back. This helps moderate winter moisture and temperature levels in the soil, which are especially critical with new plantings.

There are some disadvantages to mulching that should be recognized; however, when and how much mulch you apply can minimize these. For example, some animals such as mice and rabbits may find an organic mulch to be a suitable spot to build their nests. These garden inhabitants can cause damage to shrubs and young trees in winter if they gnaw at the base of trunks or stems. Do not allow mulch to build up around the base of plants. This problem can be further minimized by waiting until after you have experienced several hard frosts before you apply the winter mulch. Mice and rabbits will likely have already found another location for their winter home by then. In spring, mulch needs to be pulled back from perennials to allow new growth to emerge and to prevent a buildup of excessive moisture around stems, which can lead to disease.

The mulch advantage

Mulching with the right material, applied at a proper depth and at the appropriate time, provides numerous advantages to garden plants in addition to retaining moisture and suppressing weeds. Mulch protects plant roots from extremes of heat and cold and creates a physical barrier between foliage and soil-splashing rain, which helps prevent the spread of disease. In vegetable gardens, mulch keeps fruit —such as tomatoes, squash, cucumbers, and melons—clean, preventing their direct contact with the soil, where fruit-rotting organisms very likely lurk. Also, mulching may reduce the need for fungicides.

Mulching does not warm or cool a soil; rather, it moderates the temperature changes. This influence is accomplished by shading the soil from the hot sun during the day and by the retention of moisture. Water changes temperature more slowly than air. So the more moisture contained in soil,

the slower the rate of temperature change around a plant's roots. Often winter damage occurs to the roots of plants, not because of the low temperature to which they are subjected, but because of rapid changes in temperature of a dry soil. These rapid changes can cause perennials to heave out of the soil, exposing their roots to cold, dry air, killing the plant. Mulching helps minimize such losses.

Protection from birds
This wooden structure with a PVC pipe water system on a timer and a fly-screen cover protects a strawberry crop from birds.

HOW MUCH MULCH

How much mulch should you apply? Too much can impair plant growth by suffocating roots and preventing moisture from reaching the soil, but too thin a layer will not sufficiently suppress weed growth or retain moisture. In general, a 2–3 in (5–8cm) layer of organic mulch is appropriate. Replace the mulch as it breaks down instead of mulching too thickly at the beginning of the season. Always keep mulch away from the crown or stems of plants to avoid the buildup of excessive moisture and increase the likelihood of disease. In vegetable gardens and annual beds, organic mulch can be incorporated into the soil at the end of the season; it will improve soil structure and fertility. Around permanent plantings, mulch breaks down gradually, releasing nutrients that are carried to the roots by rain. In both cases, an organic mulch promotes a healthy soil environment.

Recycling into mulch
All of the mulching materials above (from the top, they are bark, compost, and leaves) could come from the garden to which they are returned. Recycling all heathy plant debris makes good sense.

MULCHING MATERIALS

The material you select for a mulch depends on availability, personal taste, and the type of garden. Both organic and inorganic mulches are available, and each is suited to several different types of garden applications.

Straw works well in the vegetable garden, but can look messy and contribute unwanted weed seeds to a perennial border. More attractive organic mulches, such as shredded bark, pine straw, or cocoa hulls, are a better choice for flowerbeds, trees, and shrubs.

Weed barrier fabrics (landscape fabric or geotextiles) – material made out of polypropylene fibers – allow water and air to penetrate but prevent weed growth. They can enhance the efficiency of an organic mulch. They are usually placed directly on the soil surface and slits are cut through it for planting. An organic mulch, such as shredded bark or cocoa shells, is usually applied on top to hold it in place and provide a more attractive appearance.

Inorganic mulches include plastic, pebbles, and marble and stone chips. Black plastic is often used to mulch melons and cucumbers, since they benefit from the heat captured by the plastic in addition to a virtually total suppression of weeds. Rock gardens and beds of cacti and other succulents generally require drier conditions, and they may resent the moisture retained under a layer of shredded bark. Mulching with gravel or stone is probably the best solution for such gardens.

The color of the mulching material will affect its absorption or reflection of solar heat. Dark-colored mulches absorb more heat, warm the soil earlier in the spring, and maintain the heat later into autumn. Light-colored mulches absorb less heat, and they reflect heat and light upward toward the plants.

Plants themselves can serve as a mulch as they spread to cover the soil surface, crowding out weeds and shading the soil from the heat of the sun. Clematis benefit from such a mulch; many of them requires a cool, shaded location for the roots along with plenty of sun for the above-ground portions of the plant. These requirements are met when the clematis is planted at the base of a coniferous shrub – the shrub provides a living mulch for the roots, as well as support for the clematis vine to grow upon.

Of course, plants require water, so although a mulch of living plants is an effective method of weed control and soil temperature moderation, it may actually increase the water requirement for the area.

In a woodland garden, trees and shrubs annually provide their own mulch of leaves and needles. Be sure that leaves and needles are raked off of desired groundcovers and herbaceous perennials growing beneath trees.

Managing without chemicals

Keeping your garden neat and preventing weeds from taking over doesn't require chemical warfare. Weeds can be pulled, cut, burned (where legal), smothered, and suppressed – the most effective method of control depends upon the types of weeds and the specific garden situation.

Cleaning up the garden
Keep pests and diseases at bay; clean up the vegetable garden and compost the remains at the end of each gardening season – in fall and again in spring.

In a new garden, weeding can require a good bit of effort. But as garden plants become established and spread to cover the open ground, your weeding efforts will lessen, particularly if you practice some routine weed-management tasks. Eliminate your weeds before they become established and reseed themselves. It is more productive to spend a little time weeding on a routine basis than to let the weeds get an upper hand, eventually requiring a major cleanup effort. Mulching after you weed will prevent many weeds from returning (*see* The mulch advantage, *p. 47*).

Solarization provides excellent initial weed control for a new planting. The area to be solarized should be mowed very low and watered well. Cover it with clear plastic, secured at the edges, and leave it for at least six weeks – longer if possible. The temperature in the top several inches of soil rises significantly, baking the surface vegetation as well as most weed seeds, roots, and soil pathogens.

To suppress the germination of weed seeds, corn gluten can be applied to a soil surface. This material, which is a natural byproduct of milling corn, is a good source of nitrogen, and it inhibits seed germination. Applied to established lawns, it prevents the germination of crabgrass and other annual weeds. It can be applied in a vegetable garden after vegetable plants have emerged. It is also useful in establishing a groundcover bed: groundcover plants are set, corn gluten is applied and watered in, the bed is mulched, and weeds are suppressed.

Edging a bed with a solid barrier, such as brick, stone, or wood, helps prevent creeping weeds from gaining entry.

A flame-thrower is an effective tool for weeding nonflammable surfaces such as gravel paths, paved patios, and driveways. But the use of flame-throwers is against the law in most areas of the Southwest

Both useful and beautiful
Handmade structures of wood and bamboo and an edging of flowers transform a garden of warm-season summer vegetables into an ornamental potager.

due to extreme fire danger.

A far safer alternative is boiling water, which has a similar effect on weeds and can be poured onto the ground straight from the kettle off the stove. It is particularly useful for hard-to-weed spaces between pavers or bricks.

Critter-proof crops
This walk-in garden structure, gated, floored, walled, and roofed with a ½in (1cm) hardware cloth, keeps raccoons, ground squirrels, and deer away from vegetable crops. California poppies and other wildflowers provide pollen for beneficial insects.

Encouraging desirable widlife

Every year, more and more land is being cleared for homes and businesses, and wildlife habitats are being reduced or destroyed. Your SMARTGARDEN™ can be a haven for wildlife with a little planning. The three basic needs of wildlife – food, water, and shelter – can easily be met in a garden if you consider the type of wildlife you want to encourage and provide for them by including plants that produce nectar, flowers, seeds, and fruit, a source of water, and suitable habitats for nesting.

Adding feeders to your garden to supplement the plants will carry the banquet through the garden's lean times. Birdbaths or a small pond can provide sufficient water for your visitors, but remember to change the water frequently so it stays clean. If possible, leave some areas of the yard undisturbed for shelter. Dead trees and hollow logs provide homes for many wild creatures, as do unraked leaves (also see the Plant Catalog for plants to attract wildlife).

Maintaining a wildlife-friendly garden contributes to a well-balanced environment. Birds and bats feed on insects; butterflies, bees, and many other insects (and some bats) pollinate flowers; moles feed on grubs of root-eating beetles. Avoid using pesticides that will harm pollinating insects or birds, and be sure to read all pesticide labels carefully for warnings about potential dangers to wildlife.

Of course, not all forms of wildlife contribute to the health of your plants. Some wildlife may not be as welcome to your garden as others. There are some animals you would rather discourage from grazing in your azaleas, nibbling away at your bulbs, or feasting on your sweet corn. Like insect pests, take the approach of determining how much damage the critter is likely to inflict on your plantings, and if the level is unsatisfactory, take precautions to prevent the destruction.

Various techniques can be used to discourage deer, raccoons, voles, squirrels, and other potentially destructive forms of wildlife from damaging your plantings. Selecting plants that are unappetizing to the specific animal is a start – almost nothing eats daffodils! Other methods include fences or barriers, and dogs and cats, who will hunt rodents. Unfortunately, some cats also hunt birds, but the two will often co-exist.

Haven for birds
Many birds, including hummingbirds, are especially attracted to moving water such as in this trickling fountain; its height protects them from cats. Trees and shrubbery provide shelter and forage; a birdfeeder with thistle seeds brings goldfinches.

SOUTHWESTERN WILDLIFE

Anna's hummingbird
Many hummingbirds can be seen feeding on nectar and tree sap, and gorging on insects and spiders.

As ever more land is taken over for business and housing, the areas left for wildlife shrink and many wild species invade urban areas. By creating a wildlife-friendly garden, you can do much to encourage and protect them. A well-planned garden can provide habitat for a wide range of birds, butterflies, small mammals, beneficial insects, and arachnids. By adding a pond you'll attract amphibians, including frogs. All of these creatures can help you keep pests under control. Even snakes, spiders, and toads – fearsome to the unknowing public – are beloved by knowledgeable gardeners for the important role they play in reducing plant problems. By refraining from the use of poisonous sprays and encouraging the balance of nature, you can create a glorious garden while also caring for the wild. The following lists contain a few of the more common wildlife, some of which you may want to attract.

Greater roadrunner
This large cuckoo eats seeds, insects, lizards, rodents, and even snakes.

Birds help the gardener by feeding on caterpillars, weed seeds, and the egg masses of garden pests, but they can also eat seedlings and fruit. You can encourage them to stay around by putting out feeders and providing water, while controlling damage with permanent structures and bird netting. Birds seen in the Southwest are as diverse as the habitats – seacoasts, canyons, coastal ranges, forests, mountains, deserts, and rainforests. The largest number of birds and most diverse species visit gardens in the coastal zones of California or on the migratory pathways. Nonetheless, there are a few birds common to most regions of the Southwest, nesting in some areas, wintering in others, or living year-round. These include:
• greater roadrunner • black-chinned hummingbird • Western scrub jay • Western tanager • hooded oriole • Bell's vireo • canyon wren • Western wood peewee • Western meadowlark • cliff swallow • burrowing owl • red-tailed hawk • dark-eyed junco • spotted towhee.

Gulf fritillary
Plant common passion vine and this lovely butterfly will float around your garden.

Common garden birds include:
Northern mockingbird • house finch • American goldfinch • Bullock's oriole • mourning dove • Bewick's wren • pine siskin • Western bluebird • barn swallow • purple martin • barn owl • white-crowned sparrow (and many other sparrows) • gray catbird • Northern flicker • hairy woodpecker • cedar waxwing • American robin • many species of warblers. Teals, mallards, or pintails have been known to adopt gardens with swimming pools, even to the extent of raising a clutch of ducklings. Even the black-crowned night-heron can be enjoyed if a covering of stout netting is installed to protect precious koi.

Many small mammals will make their home in your garden, feeding on seeds and insects, and sometimes causing damage in the process. Larger animals, such as skunks, raccoons, foxes, badgers, coyotes, and the only marsupial in America, the opossum, may frequent gardens, sometimes causing amusement and at other times trouble.

Striped skunk
Even resident skunks can be the gardener's friends, digging up thousands of destructive grubs in their nightly forays into your yard.

The strangest visitor of all is the armadillo, the only mammal in North America with a hard shell. Larger animals such as deer and black bears are best excluded. You may see some of these:
• raccoon • coyote • kit fox • spotted skunk • striped skunk • bats • blacktail jackrabbit • desert cottontail • Western chipmunk • gray squirrel • deer mouse • desert pocket mouse • brush mouse • pack rat • longtail vole • valley pocket gopher • various ground squirrels.

Most amphibians and reptiles are gardeners' friends. Among those that should be encouraged are: • desert tortoises • gopher snakes • common king snake • coral king snake • common garter snake • rosie boa • rubber boa • Western shovelnose snake • alligator lizard • Swift's lizard (and many other lizards) • water snakes • American toad • tree frog.

Butterflies, moths, and dragonflies add movement to the garden and can be attracted by plants rich in nectar, a patch of wet mud, or a shallow pond. Some of the more common and striking are:
• Gulf fritillary • mourning cloak • monarch • black swallowtail • orange sulphur • viceroy • civil blue • American painted lady • Melissa blue • Western widow • biddie.
Other invertebrates include:
• bees • wasps (many beneficial types) • spiders.

Ladybird beetle
Release at dusk into a moist garden, and they'll stay around and control the pests.

WORK WITH NATURE

Every aspect of gardening, from selecting your site and your plants to accommodating their spread and cleaning up debris, will be easier and more successful if you work with nature to achieve your goals. Although a garden alters a landscape to some extent, it should exist in harmony with its environment. The key is to follow nature's leads and to harness its forces to work on your behalf.

Learning from natural habitats

Plants with similar growth requirements should be grouped together in your garden, growing as they would in their natural habitat. Shrubs and perennials that thrive in low light can be planted beneath trees that furnish the necessary shade; those that require constant moisture can be grouped in a bog garden or at the edge of a pond; and those that thrive in full sun and dry soil can be combined in a sunny rock garden or xeriphytic planting.

In addition to grouping plants that share similar natural habitats, keep in mind any additional cultural requirements or special care that the plants might need when you are planning your garden. For example, vegetables and annual flowers generally require more fertilization and water than established perennials and woody plants. If the vegetable or annual flower beds are positioned within easy reach of a water faucet or rain barrel, their addition needs can be easily accommodated. Natural cycles of growth, reproduction, and decomposition can be put to work to your garden's advantage, and many

problems can be avoided if you mimic natural patterns and solutions for reducing plant stress.

Just as the environment affects the growth of plants in your garden, everything you do in your garden has an impact on the environment. As environmentally responsible gardeners and stewards of the Earth, working in cooperation with nature rather than attempting to control it just makes good sense.

Natives and non-natives

One way to increase the odds that your plants are well adapted to your conditions is to select plants native to your region. By incorporating indigenous species, your garden not only reflects its geography, but it will also help sustain native wildlife.

Be sure that the natural habitats of your plant choices are reflected in the conditions within your yard. If your yard is open and sunny, it may be ideal for meadow wildflowers or rock garden plants. If it is heavily shaded, woodland natives are more appropriate. Regional wildflower and native plant societies can assist you with identifying native species and finding responsible retail sources.
Never collect plants from the wild without permission. Rare plants – those that may be difficult to obtain, but are not necessarily endangered – are put at risk when collectors dig them and remove them from their natural habitat. Many plants can be obtained without exploiting natural populations. Many nurseries, native plant societies, and private growers propagate their own rare plants and offer plants or seed for sale or exchange. Also, permission is sometimes given to individual plant collectors or native plant societies to dig and remove native plants from construction sites before the area is graded or built upon. In this way, many stands of both rare and common natives have been saved from the bulldozer.

Group similar plants
Facing north, under wisteria, water-thrifty drifts of shade-loving clivia and biennial Madeira geranium (*Geranium maderense*) bloom at the same time in spring.

Cooperating with nature
In full sun on a dry bank, lemon eucalyptus (*E. citriodora*) from Australia, and South American bougainvillea, such as the shrubby 'La Jolla', are adapted to a coastal Mediterranean climate, surviving with infrequent irrigation, once established.

REGIONAL HABITATS WORTH EMULATING

Anza Borrego Desert – California
Plants, birds, and animals abound in stunning desert environment to view by car, foot, or horseback. Well-timed rains result in spectacular spring flowers.

The Southwest has a large number of strikingly different habitats, but as population puts pressure on wild lands, plant diversity decreases. Gardeners can help conserve rare plants by recreating elements of their region and growing endemic species.

Chaparral and woodland
The western portion of Southern California was once covered with native chaparral, woodland, and bunchgrasses. Human settlement has since destroyed much of this habitat but pockets of surprisingly diverse chaparral remain.
Garden-friendly plants:
- Torrey pine tree (*Pinus torreyana*)
- Engelmann oak (*Quercus engelmannii*)
- California sycamore (*Platanus racemosa*)
- Matilija poppy (*Romneya coulteri*)
- California lilac (*Ceanothus*)

- Flannel bush (*Fremontodendron*)
- California fuchsia (*Zauschneria californica*)
- Toyon, California holly (*Heteromeles arbutifolia*)
- Laurel sumac (*Malosma laurina*)
- Lemonade berry (*Rhus integrifolia*)
- Scarlet bugler (*Penstemon centranthifolius*)
- Baby blue eyes (*Nemophila menziesii*)
- California wild grape (*Vitis californica*)

Examples of California habitats can be found at:
Point Reyes National Seashore
Santa Monica Mountains National Recreation Area
Torrey Pines State Reserve

High and Low Deserts
As westerly winds carry moist air eastward, rain falls on the mountains creating deserts to the east. Desert plants withstand dry air, hot daytime temperatures, and shallow soils.
Garden-friendly plants:
- Ocotillo (*Fouquieria splendens*)
- Brittlebush (*Encelia farinosa*)
- Bigelow nolina (*Nolina bigelovii*)
- Bush dalea (*Dalea pulchra*)
- Guajillo, Berlandier acacia (*Acacia berlandieri*)
- Saguaro (*Carnegiea gigantea*)
- Baja fairy duster (*Calliandra californica*)
- Teddy bear cholla (*Opuntia bigelovii*)
- Chuparosa (*Justicia californica*)
- Smoke tree (*Psorothamnus spinosus*)
- Globemallow (*Sphaeralcea ambigua*)
- Rabbitbrush (*Chrysothamnus nauseosus*)

Examples of high and low deserts can be found at:
Arizona-Sonora Desert Museum (Arizona)
Joshua Tree National Park (California)
Living Desert State Park (New Mexico)

Akaka Falls State Park – Hawaii
Native and exotic jungle plants ablaze with colorful and fragrant blossoms edge the hiking trail that leads to a stunning, one-hundred-foot-tall waterfall.

Hawaiian forests and coastal habitats
Many Hawaii native plants are nearing extinction. The original Polynesians brought with them approximately twenty-four plants, including coconut, banana, and breadfruit, but these have since been threatened by the more invasive introductions of Europeans.
Rare but garden-worthy species include:
- Loulu leo palm (*Pritchardia hillebrandii*)
- Kopiko'ula tree (*Psychotria hawaiiensis*)
- O'ahu soapberry (*Sapindus oahuensis*)
- Ohe tree (*Tetraplasandra hawaiiensis*)
- Mountain sandalwood (*Santalum paniculatum*)
- Koki'o tree (*Kokia drynarioides*)
- Ohi'a lehua tree (*Metrosideros polymorpha*)
- Koa tree (*Acacia koa*)
- Kulu'i nut (*Nototrichium sandwicense*)
- Beach vitex (*Vitex rotundifolia*)
- Hawaiian tree fern (*Cibotium glaucum*)
- Cabbage lobelia, Olulu (*Brighamia insignis*)
- Yellow hibiscus (*Hibiscus brackenridgei*)
- Hawaiian abutilon (*Abutilon menziesii*)

Examples of Hawaiian habitats can be found at:
Haleakala National Park (Maui)
Hawaii Volcanoes National Park (Hawaii)
Iao Valley State Park (Maui)

Torrey Pines State Reserve – California
Two-thousand acres of wild land preserve the native habitat of the elegant Torrey Pine tree. Hiking paths lead through coastal chaparral to bluffs covered with wildflowers in spring.

Endangered and threatened plant species are those that the federal government has recognized as being in danger of extinction and are protected by law. The most common cause for this status is reduction or loss of the natural habitat of the species, but commercial collection of rare plants has also threatened their survival. Responsible propagation by native plant growers of species that are rare or at risk has increased considerably in recent years; this helps increase the population and the availability of these vanishing plants to consumers. You should always investigate commercial sources of rare plants to be sure they were nursery propagated and were not collected from the wild.

The term "native plant" is the source of some confusion. Plants have been introduced from one area to another throughout the history of mankind, and some plants have adapted so well to their new environments over such a long period of time that it is often hard to distinguish the natives from the introduced species. Some plant traffic between geographic areas predates human history; seeds having been conveyed by glacial movements, floods, prehistoric animals, or other means. The field of botanical archaeology has made interesting discoveries about prehistoric plant movement that continues to shed more light on natural plant history.

For the purpose of this book, a native species is one that, as far as can be determined historically, is indigenous – native – to the *state* or *region*. (More broadly, the issue is defining what is meant by the "region": is it a given continent, country, or state, or is it the area within 25 miles (40km) of your property?) An exotic species is one that has been introduced from outside the region. An invasive exotic is a species that has adapted so well to its new environment that it has escaped cultivation and is capable of overtaking the habitats of native plants, upsetting the balance of nature.

The nativity of species within a genus is often widespread. For example, the genus *Quercus* – the oaks – include species that are indigenous to various regions within North America, as well as Europe, the Middle East, Asia, and Northern Africa. Species of *Iris* hail from countries as widespread as China, Japan, Ukraine, Afghanistan, Turkey, Algeria, and the United States – from Alaska to the Mississippi Delta. Obviously, even though they are closely related, plants with such diverse native habitats have an equally wide range of cultural requirements. So although you can probably grow more than one species of oak or iris in your garden, there will be other members of those genera that require quite a different habitat.

Non-native plants from regions with similar climates and soils can add diversity to your landscape. To get ideas for plants that will grow well in your garden, observe plants that thrive in other nearby gardens, and ask your neighbors and staff at local public gardens as well. But take care to avoid those that are too well adapted. When these plants encroach upon your garden, diligent efforts are often necessary to limit their spread or eliminate them from your yard altogether.

Plants that are recognized as serious pests have been put on federal and state lists of noxious weeds. Legislation and regulation efforts to eradicate stands and control the spread of these pests is ongoing at federal, state, and local levels.

Native treasure
California lilac (*Ceanothus*) comes in white or blue and many sizes and heights from prostrate to a tall, mounded shrub, such as 'Joyce Coulter' pictured here.

Inspiration from nature
Seeing wild ancestors of garden flowers in natural habitats can inspire the creation of gardens in harmony with nature, using plants adapted to your climate zone.

Blooming islander
Tree mallow (*Lavatera assurgentiflora*), an evergreen shrub native to Santa Cruz Island, off the California coast, thrives in gardens with little irrigation.

INVASIVE PLANTS

The majority of the plants we grow are well behaved. Others such as running bamboos, horsetail (*Equisetum hyemale*), and Sprenger asparagus fern (*Asparagus densiflorus* 'Sprengeri') are garden thugs, spreading far beyond where they're wanted but seldom escaping from gardens. More pernicious are the "invasive exotics," which seed themselves into the wild and crowd out native plants; in certain areas it can even be unlawful to plant some species. In the Southwest, Pampas grass (*Cortaderia selloana*) and its weedy cousin (*C. jubata*) have seeds that can travel many miles on the wind. They are a serious problem in many areas and should never be grown or planted near wild lands.

Invasive exotic trees and shrubs include: Spanish broom (*Spartium junceum*), tamarisk (*Tamarix chinensis*), and tree of heaven (*Ailanthus altissima*).
Invasive climbers include: Japanese honeysuckle (*Lonicera japonica*) and blue dawn flower (*Ipomoea indica*).
Some invasive perennials are: Giant reed (*Arundo donax*), pink fountain grass (*Pennisetum setaceum*), maiden grass (*Miscanthus sinensis* 'Gracillimus'), natal grass, (*Tricholaena rosea*), Bermuda grass, Kikuyu grass, and Sea fig (*Carpobrotus*).
Serious plant pests of Hawaii include: Lantana, Kahili ginger (*Hedychium gardnerianum*), Ivy gourd (*Coccinia grandis*), and Miconia (*Miconia calvescens*).

Multiplication and division

Many garden plants reseed themselves. This natural process can work to your benefit – providing new plants for next year's garden and for giving to or exhanging with other gardeners – or it can create unnecessary weeding. Before selecting a plant and placing it in a bed, determine whether and how prolifically it self-sows.

Some biennials – plants that complete their life cycle over the course of two growing seasons – can become permanent features in your garden through the process of self-sowing. The flowers of woodland forget-me-not (*Myosotis sylvatica*), honesty (*Lunaria annua*), and several foxgloves (*Digitalis* spp.) produce seed that germinates and grows vegetatively the first season and develops flowers the next. With such plants, it is important to recognize the nonflowering plant so that it can be left to grow – and not inadvertently weeded – to bloom the following year.

A number of annuals and perennials also self-sow. Some are such prolific seed producers that weeding the seedlings becomes a chore. If this is the case, deadheading the spent blooms before they have a chance to form and disperse their seed will reduce or eliminate the problem. If there is already a problem, diligent weeding should remedy this.

Quite a few of the garden flowers that are sold in nurseries or by seed companies are hybrids – varieties produced by controlled crosses of specific parent lines – so their seedlings often do not resemble the parent plant in some important aspects. Be aware that your seedlings may be shorter, taller, less disease resistant, or a different flower or leaf color (sometimes amazingly unattractively so) than their parent. Open-pollinated varieties, on the other hand, generally produce seed that is "true to type." Seed of such flowers or vegetables can be collected from these plants for growing the following year with some confidence about their inherited characteristics.

Herbaceous perennials that thrive in your garden may require dividing every few years. Take advantage of this natural increase to acquire more plants. For most perennials that bloom in spring, summer or fall division is recommended. Summer or fall bloomers are usually divided in spring.

Although the procedure varies somewhat with specific plants, division generally involves digging the entire clump, cutting it into smaller sections, discarding old, worn-out portions, replanting the vigorous divisions, and watering them thoroughly.

Composting wastes

One way you can work with nature to improve your soil is to build a compost pile or bin. Here, kitchen and garden wastes of many kinds can be converted into a nutrient-rich soil amendment. It takes several weeks to months for raw organic matter to become thoroughly decomposed and garden-ready in an active compost pile. There are a variety of factors that influence the rate of decomposition; the most important being the initial size of the organic matter, moisture in the pile or bin, temperature of both the surrounding air and the compost itself, air circulation

Composting bin
A simple cage constructed from lumber and chicken wire can hold garden refuse and other materials as it breaks down into compost.

within the pile, and the progressive status of the carbon:nitrogen ratio as the materials break down. Organic matter that has been shredded decomposes faster than if it has been left whole, because there is more surface area exposed. Decomposition rates are higher when conditions are warm and damp than when they are cold and dry. Air circulation increases the rate of composting, because the organisms responsible for decomposition need sufficient air to do their job. (For more on the carbon:nitrogen ratio, *see p. 31.*)

However, other than occasional turning, and a bit of added moisture when it's very dry, nature – in the form of industrious micro- and macroorganisms – does most of the work for you.

COMPOST BINS AND TOOLS

A number of useful products are available to help you produce your own compost. Compost bins can be constructed out of wood, heavy-gauge wire fencing, cinder blocks, or other common materials. They can also be purchased ready-made. Designs range from simple bins to more elaborate constructions that feature cone-shaped tubs, interlocking layered shelves, and twist-top ventilation systems. Some designs feature tumblers or drums that rotate to facilitate mixing. Mixing or stirring an open compost pile can be done with a garden fork or a compost aerator, a tool specifically designed for the purpose,

composed of a shaft with handles or a bar at one end for holding, and short paddles on the other end that are inserted into the pile, then turned and lifted.

Vermicomposting is a system using redworms, night crawlers, or earthworms in an enclosed container to break down organic matter such as grass clippings and kitchen wastes. The worm castings that are shed are a rich source of nutrients.

In an undisturbed woodland environment, the seasonal accumulation of leaves on the forest floor is part of a natural recycling process. As the leaves are decomposed by soil organisms, a steady supply of nutrients is released. In an effort to keep a garden neat, this cycle is often interrupted; leaves are raked and removed. The nutrients can be restored, however, and the neatness maintained, if the raked leaves are composted and the finished compost returned to the garden. Once the compost is ready, it can be incorporated into the soil or applied as a topdressing or mulch (*see pp.47–49*). It is also a useful addition to a soil mix for raised beds and containers. In an active compost pile, most weed seeds are killed by the heat generated during the decomposition process, but a few may survive and are usually easily removed.

By composting your kitchen and garden wastes, you are working in tandem with nature to improve the growing conditions for your plants while simultaneously reducing your contribution of solid waste to local landfills.

Prettier and stronger
A more sturdily constructed compost bin (which is easy to build) is more attractive and holds up longer than a simple cage (opposite). It should last for several years.

The view inside
Removing the front panel reveals the correct method of layering different materials, alternating "soft" (grass clippings and weeds) with "hard" (twigs and dead leaves) to speed decomposition.

General household waste
Plant remains are OK, but avoid including meat scraps and bones, which attract vermin.

Old straw
Make sure your compost pile heats up to destroy seeds contained in straw.

Weeds
As with straw above, a properly constructed and managed hot pile kills most weed seeds.

Hedge clippings
The smaller, thinner, and softer the clippings, the faster they will break down.

Bring it on
Good compost is best made from a wide variety of materials. Included on this page are just a few possibilities, including the spent bedding plants at left.

Aiding natural selection

Cleaning up a garden at the end of a growing season will improve its appearance through winter and, more importantly, contribute to its health the next season. This often involves a bit of "editing" – removing plants, plant parts, or pests.

- Branches of trees and shrubs that are damaged beyond repair should be removed with clean cuts. Stems displaying disease symptoms such as cankers or sunken lesions are usually best removed in order to prevent the further spread of disease.
- Minimize next year's insect pests by removing and disposing obvious signs of infestation such as the "bags" of bagworms and the nests of fall webworms.
- Remove weeds before they go to seed.
- Rake leaves to avoid matting that may suffocate lawn or groundcovers; compost both weeds and leaves (but remember: no pest- or disease-infested material onto the pile; this material is best discarded along with your household trash)
- After they have died naturally or succumbed to frost, cut annuals at ground level, leaving the roots to break down in the soil; this is a particularly good practice where erosion is a problem. Or remove the plants, roots and all, then compost everything.
- Clean structures and stakes you plan to reuse. Those that cannot withstand winter weather should be removed, cleaned, and stored until conditions are suitable again in spring.
- Perennial plants that die back in fall can be cut to the ground unless they contribute to your winter landscape or provide food or cover for desirable wildlife.

Eliminating flowered stalks
Removing flowered stalks of herbaceous plants improves their appearance and may also stimulate further flowering.

Reducing stress

Just like humans, garden plants look and perform better if their level of stress is reduced.

Transplanting can be traumatic for plants and may lead to a condition known as "transplant shock." To avoid this, allow seedlings grown indoors to acclimate to their new environment gradually (called "hardening off"). Place them in a protected spot outdoors for a few days before transplanting them. Transplant on a still, overcast day, and drench soil balls with a high-phosphorus liquid fertilizer to stimulate root growth.

During dry weather, wind can cause serious damage by increasing a plant's transpiration (moisture loss) rate. When moisture lost through leaves exceeds the rate at which it is replaced by roots, leaves appear scorched or may drop off. This can happen during cold weather as well, when soil water is frozen and little is available to plants. Siting a garden where plants are sheltered from prevailing winds can prevent such damage, or wind-tolerant plants can be grown as wind breaks to protect nearby plants.

Rapid fluctuations in soil temperature in winter can damage roots. This problem can be avoided by watering and mulching thoroughly in fall. The temperature fluctuates less rapidly in moist soil than in dry soil. In warm climates, mulching and watering provide similar protection, particularly during hot, dry periods when soil absorbs radiant heat during the day. Watering during dry periods and shading the soil with mulch reduce heat and moisture stress that lead to injury.

Safe haven
Hardware cloth under and over vegetables keeps them safe from cabbage butterflies, ground squirrels, raccoons, and gophers. Covering the rounded top with plastic in spring warms early plantings of summer vegetables.

MANAGE PESTS FOR A HEALTHY GARDEN

Integrated pest management (IPM) is a sustainable and environmentally sensitive approach to garden disease and pest problems. IPM was initially developed for commercial growers as a means of merging all available information regarding a crop and its documented or potentially troublesome pests and diseases into a comprehensive plan of action to maximize production and quality and to minimize environmental risks. IPM has been adapted as a useful tool for home gardeners and is a perfect fit with the SMARTGARDEN™ philosophy: to follow nature's leads and to harness her forces to work on your behalf.

Keeping the proper perspective

IPM is a multistep process. It includes taking steps to prevent problems or to reduce their severity, identifying and monitoring problems that do arise (using physical and natural control measures first), and, if necessary, applying the least toxic pesticide at the proper rate and at the proper time. When dealing with garden diseases and pests, it is important to keep in mind that a certain amount of damage is tolerable. Trying to maintain every leaf and flower in perfect condition is impossible. Accepting a level of tolerable imperfection does not mean ignoring damage when it occurs. The SMARTGARDEN™ approach is to assess the damage, identify the cause, estimate the potential for further damage, and, depending on that assessment, continue to monitor the problem and adjust cultural practices to reduce its spread, or proceed with a specific control measure. The key is to strive for balance rather than perfection.

An ounce of prevention

One of the best methods for dealing with plant problems is to prevent them from occurring. Healthy, well-adapted plants are less likely to be seriously damaged by the diseases or pests that invade the garden. They can withstand an infection (from diseases) or infestation (from insects or other animals) better than a plant that is struggling from the stress of neglect or placement in an inappropriate site.

Allies
Ladybird beetles (also widely called ladybugs) and a host of other insect and other creatures can be recruited in the battle against plant pests.

How many should be tolerated?
This colorful caterpillar is the larva of the beautiful black swallowtail butterfly. A few will not cause much damage, but large numbers would pose a threat. It's up to you whether to reduce or eliminate them or leave them alone.

How much is too much?
Gardeners who practice IPM know when the level of damage from a pest's activities has reached an unacceptable level.

will do no damage to your trees or shrubs. An insect that bores into pine trees will probably leave your other trees and shrubs, as well as your herbaceous plants, alone.

Susceptibility to diseases and pests varies from one variety of plant to another. Plant breeders have used this phenomenon to impart disease- and pest-tolerance and resistance to an ever-increasing number of new varieties of the plants we grow in our gardens.

Selecting varieties that are resistant to pests and diseases that are common in your area is an easy way to give your garden plants an advantage. For example, some tomato varieties are resistant to several fungal wilts, viral diseases, and certain nematodes that can devastate a susceptible variety. By selecting varieties of daylily that are resistant to rust (see list in box below), gardeners can combat daylily rust more effectively than by spraying.

SANITATION

Removal and disposal of disease-infected or pest-infested plants and plant remains from the garden is an important cultural tool that should be incorporated into your gardening efforts throughout the growing season. It should also be a designated part of your annual cleanup activities. Remember: although the heat generated by a well-managed compost pile is sufficient to kill pests and most disease-causing organisms, seriously diseased plants are best kept out of the compost pile, just as a precaution.

Many pests and disease-causing organisms overwinter in or on the remains of their former host, and if left in the garden will be ready and waiting to cause problems come spring. When practical, remove the source before the pest or disease has a chance to spread. Also, before you introduce any new plant into your garden, inspect it for pests and the symptoms of disease.

OTHER PREVENTION TECHNIQUES

Other cultural methods for preventing pest and disease problems include mulching to create a physical barrier between soil-borne spores and potential hosts, using physical barriers such as netting or row covers to exclude egg-laying female insects, planting to ensure adequate air circulation between plants, planting early or late to avoid a pest or disease at a predictable time each year, and removal of garden plants or weeds that may serve as alternative hosts to disease organisms or pests.

Natural disease control
Wait three or four years before growing ranunculus (foreground) or stock in the same bed.

RESISTANT VARIETIES

Most plant diseases and many pests are quite specific for the host plants that they will infect or infest. A disease that infects your lawn most likely

PEST-RESISTANT PLANTS

Some plants show a natural resistance to pests or diseases. Remember that resistance does not mean that the plants will not be attacked, just that they are not as susceptible to damage as others.

Daylilies: 'Black-eyed Stella', 'Frankly Scarlet', 'Butterscotch Ruffles', 'Lavender Dew', 'Little Joy', 'Tootsie Rose'.
Fuschias: 'Baby Chang', 'Chance Encounter', 'Dollar Princess', 'Golden West', 'Miniature Jewels', 'Red Spider'.
Plants resistant to *Phytophthera* **root rot:** *Camellia sasanqua, Chamaecyparis*

nootkatensis, Juniperus chinenesis 'Pfitzerana', *Juniperus squamata* 'Meyeri', *Pinus mugo* var. *mugo, Thuja occidentalis*.
Roses: *Rosa banksiae*, 'Dublin Bay', 'Gene Boerner', 'Iceberg', 'Margaret Merril', 'Alba Maxima', 'Pascali', 'Queen Elizabeth', and the 'Carefree', 'Dream', and 'Flower Carpet' Series.
Trees: *Brachychiton, Cedrus, Ceratonia siliqua, Cotinus, Ficus, Franklinia, Grevillea robusta, Koelreuteria paniculata, Podocarpus, Sophora japonica, Ginkgo, Metasequoia, Pistacia chinensis*.
Zinnia: 'Benary's Giant Hybrids'.

CROP ROTATION

Rearranging (rotating) the placement of plants from one season to the next is a valuable means of outwitting pests and diseases in vegetable gardens and annual beds. Most diseases and many insects are rather specific in their selection of host plants, and many survive the winter as eggs or spores in the soil around the plant that was the pest's host during the previous growing season. Replanting the same crop in the same space increases the probability of reinfection. Make it more difficult for the pest or disease: move your beans to the other side of the garden, and plant marigolds where you had China asters last year. This simple avoidance technique can significantly reduce recurring problems.

YEAR 1
LEGUMES AND POD CROPS

Okra
Hyacinth beans
Scarlet runner beans
Lima beans
Snap beans
Peas
Broad beans

YEAR 2
ALLIUMS

Bulb onions
Pickling onions
Scallions
Shallots
Welsh onions
Oriental bunching
Onions
Leeks
Garlic

YEAR 4
BRASSICAS

Kales
Cauliflowers
Cabbages
Brussel sprouts
Sprouting broccoli
Broccoli
Oriental mustards
Chinese broccoli
Bok choi
Mizuna greens
Chinese cabbages
Komatsuna
Kohlrabi
Rutabagas
Turnips
Radishes

YEAR 3
TOMATO AND ROOT CROPS

Sweet peppers
Tomatoes
Loganberries
Eggplants
Celery
Beets
Taro
Carrots
Sweet potatoes
Parsnips
Scorzonera
Salsify
Potatoes

ROTATION OF VEGETABLE CROPS

Vegetables are divided into four groups: legumes and pod crops; alliums; brassicas; and solanaceous, root, and tuberous crops. Sweet corn and summer and winter squash do not fit into the major groups, but they still should be rotated. If you are growing only a small amount of these, it may be possible to include them in one of the groups (such as alliums). Otherwise, treat them as a separate group and rotate everything on a five-year basis.

Diagnosing and assessing damage

If you are unfamiliar with the plant problem confronting you, take a Sherlock Holmes approach: use all available clues and resources to pin down the culprit. Numerous books and publications are available to assist your diagnosis. Furthermore, local Cooperative Extension offices, botanical gardens, nurseries, and plant societies maintain diagnostic clinics and horticultural hotlines. Many of these can be conveniently contacted on the Internet (*see* Appendix, p. 387 for regional resources).

You may have an expert horticulturist to whom you can turn with any plant problems. But no matter whom you ask, the prognosis will be based on the information that you provide. The more detailed observations you make, the more accurate the advice you will receive. Whenever possible, you should provide one or more specimens of the plant that demonstrate progressive symptoms for the expert to examine. Each specimen should be more than just a single leaf; it is helpful and sometimes necessary to see more than one leaf attached to a bit of stem to identify the plant as well as the problem.

Once you identify the specific cause of your problem, the next step is to learn more about the disease or pest and determine how much damage is likely to occur and whether and what type of control measures are warranted.

NOTING DAMAGE

- When did you first notice the damage?
- What are the symptoms? Examine all parts of the plant and be as precise as possible.
- Are the symptoms on more than one plant or kind of plant?
- How rapidly do the symptoms progress?
- How long has the plant been growing in its current location?
- Which kinds of treatment (for example, fertilizer, insecticide, herbicide, mulching) have been applied to the plant or to surrounding areas recently?
- Have you ever noticed this problem before? If so, is it different this time?
- Has there been any change in soil grade in the area surrounding the plants?
- Has there been any other change in the area surrounding the plant?

Know your enemy

Familiarizing yourself with the most common pests and diseases of the plants you grow is a major step to outwitting them. By knowing their appearance, life cycle, feeding and overwintering habits, potential hosts, and natural predators, you can work with nature to tilt the balance in the favor of your garden plants.

For example, fireblight is a bacterial disease that infests apples, pears, pyracantha, hawthorn, quince, and several other ornamental plants, typically causing sudden twig dieback. Serious damage can often be avoided by limiting the use of nitrogen fertilizer on susceptible plants, since succulent new growth, which is stimulated by nitrogen, is most prone to infection. If the disease does cause dieback, pruning out and destroying infected stems will generally stop (or at least slow down) the spread of the disease before it causes serious damage. Left untreated, the infection may move into older wood, where it forms cankers in which the bacteria overwinter. More extensive removal of branches displaying such cankers may be required at this point.

Knowledge of the life cycle of a pest or disease-causing organism enables the gardener to apply countermeasures at the time when they will be most effective. For instance, parasitic nematodes effectively control several

A ROGUE'S GALLERY

Insects:

Aphids: Small and generally on the growing tips or underside of leaves. Attack a wide range of plants, sucking sap and covering foliage with a sticky deposit.

Bugs and beetles: A varied group of hard-bodied insects that feed mostly by chewing holes in leaves and stems.

Caterpillars: The young stage of butterflies and moths (such as gypsy moth) feed on leaves and shoots.

Grubs: The larvae of several beetles (and other insects) that live in soil and eat roots or suck sap.

Miners: Small larvae that tunnel inside a leaf, leaving opaque areas or mines.

Mites: Tiny, red or yellowish, and live mostly on the underside of leaves and spin fine webs between stems. They cause tiny pale spots.

Slugs and snails: Feed on foliage and small plants, mostly at night. Slime trails make their presence easy to detect.

Diseases:

Anthracnose: Fungi that attack a wide range of plants, targeting foliage and fruit.

Blights: Shoots or branches wilt, growth stops, and the affected part dies. In fruit, development ceases and the fruit gradually withers.

Leaf spots: Caused by many different fungi, they occur on a wide range of plants. They start as small pale areas and spread, often coalescing to cover almost the entire leaf.

Mildews: Occur on many plants and are especially destructive during hot, humid weather and on dry soil.

Catch it in time
Diseases such as rusts (above), if caught early in their development, may be controlled by nonchemical means. Severe cases, however, may need chemicals for total control.

lawn pests, including Japanese beetle grubs. But they must be applied when the target pest is active; the nematodes persist for only about two weeks. By knowing that the grubs become active as the soil warms in spring, the nematodes can be applied when the grubs begin to feed.

PHYSICAL CONTROLS

Many pests and diseases can be controlled by physical means. For example, handpicking the pest or pruning diseased stems or branches is sufficient in many cases to prevent further spread. Brute force is sometimes effective: a hard spray of water can knock down a population of aphids or mites to a tolerable level. Colorado potato beetles and tomato hornworms can often be eliminated by hand – the pests are simply picked off the host plant and destroyed. This method is effective, however, only when the gardener is vigilant (and prepared for gore!).

Barriers can also prevent pest damage: a cardboard collar around young vegetable seedlings checks their destruction by cutworms. Tree wraps – sticky bands of material that are placed around the trunk of a tree – prevent the larvae of gypsy moths and similar leaf-eating caterpillars from reaching the tree's susceptible foliage. Tubular plastic cages and wraps placed around young trees protect their bark from the gnawing of mice or rabbits. Floating row covers made of a thin, light, and water-permeable fabric can block many flying pests from infesting vegetable plants. Birds can be thwarted from eating your cherries or blueberries by covering the trees or shrubs with a protective net before the fruit ripens.

When pesticides are necessary

The goal when using a pesticide is to achieve control with the minimum impact on the rest of the environment. Applying the right material at the wrong time, to the wrong plant, or at the wrong dilution can negate its effect or, even worse, cause more damage than the pest itself. Whenever you decide to use a pesticide, it is critical to follow all label instructions for safety.

DIRECTIONS FOR HANDLING
• Eliminate or minimize human, pet, and nontarget plant exposure to the pesticide. This is particularly important when dealing with concentrated formulations.
• Wear protective clothing, and wash it after use, separately from other laundry.
• Wash equipment used for measuring, mixing, and applying the pesticide, and store in a secure, designated location.
• Wash down or flush any hardscaped or soil areas that were exposed to pesticides or where pesticides may have been inadvertently spilled.
• Store pesticides in a safe, secure (preferably locked) location – out of the reach of children and pets – in their original containers and according to the label instructions.
• Thoroughly wash your hands and face – or better, shower – after applying pesticides.
• Dispose of unused pesticides and empty pesticide containers according to the label instructions.
• Keep a record of the application; include date, material applied, and plants treated.

Population explosion
Control greenhouse whiteflies (shown here) and giant whiteflies by growing plants in appropriate light and covering the ground under the plants with a one-inch thick layer of worm castings. A month later, you'll see better, longer-lasting control than with chemicals.

Many synthetic chemical pesticides formerly available have been banned for environmental and safety reasons. A variety of environmentally friendly, nonchemical pest control alternatives have been developed, many derived from plants or minerals. These pesticides generally break down quickly into safe byproducts and thus are good choices for the pests they control. Like any pesticide, they may be toxic to humans or other nontarget animals and should be applied with care according to the manufacturer's instructions.

Types of pesticides

Pesticides work by direct contact, ingestion, or making the plant distasteful to pests. Some pests and diseases are susceptible just during one phase of their life cycle. Therefore, timing may be critical to achieving an acceptable level of control.

Contact pesticides require direct contact with an external part of the pest for effective control. They must be applied where the pest is or will be present. If a pest feeds on the underside of leaves, the pesticide should be applied to the leaf undersides. If only the upper surface of the leaf is sprayed, the pesticide may have little or no effect.

Other pesticides work only after ingestion – they must be consumed by the pest. Leaf-eating caterpillars and beetles are often controlled by an ingested pesticide that is applied to the foliage of the host plant. Many biological controls such as Bt (bacteria that control specific leaf and root eating pests) must also be ingested by the pest to be effective (*see* Beneficial microbes, *p. 69*).

Systemic pesticides are absorbed and carried within a plant. Sprayed on the foliage or applied to the soil, they are taken in by the plant and kill the pest when it feeds on plant tissues.

Repellents do not kill the pest but instead prevent it from harming the host plant by making it less appealing. Hot pepper sprays and predator urine are examples of repellents designed to keep animals from devouring garden plants. These generally require frequent application.

Chemical pesticide formulations

Some pesticides can be applied directly, while others require diluting prior to application. Be sure always to dilute concentrated pesticides to the correct strength for the pest you are trying to control, and the host to which it is applied. Most pesticides are available in one or more of the formulations detailed below:

- Aerosols are ready-to-use sprays – usually contact poisons – that are under pressure. The pesticide is emitted as a fine mist.
- Dusts are finely ground pesticides combined with a fine inert powder that acts as a carrier. These are generally ready to apply from the bag.
- Granular formulations are similar to dusts, but the carrier is a larger particle, usually an inert clay. This formulation is most commonly used for pesticides that are applied to the soil.
- Wettable powders are water-soluble pesticides that are usually combined with a wetting agent to make mixing easier. They are mixed with water prior to application. They are usually applied as a spray but may be watered into soil when appropriate.
- Liquid concentrates are similar to wettable powders except that the concentrated pesticide is in liquid form.

THE WAY CHEMICALS WORK

Different problems require chemicals to be applied in different ways. A combination of application methods may be needed to achieve a satisfactory level of control.

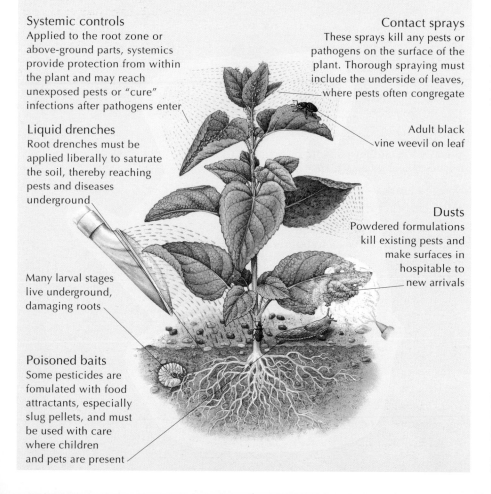

Systemic controls
Applied to the root zone or above-ground parts, systemics provide protection from within the plant and may reach unexposed pests or "cure" infections after pathogens enter

Liquid drenches
Root drenches must be applied liberally to saturate the soil, thereby reaching pests and diseases underground

Many larval stages live underground, damaging roots

Poisoned baits
Some pesticides are fomulated with food attractants, especially slug pellets, and must be used with care where children and pets are present

Contact sprays
These sprays kill any pests or pathogens on the surface of the plant. Thorough spraying must include the underside of leaves, where pests often congregate

Adult black vine weevil on leaf

Dusts
Powdered formulations kill existing pests and make surfaces inhospitable to new arrivals

Chemical pesticide alternatives

There are many alternatives to chemical pesticides that are available for combating garden pests and diseases, and many are just as effective as stronger chemical pesticides if they are used correctly.

BOTANICAL INSECTICIDES

Certain compounds extracted from plants are effective in controlling a variety of pests. Some of the more commonly available are:

• pyrethrum: an effective, broad-spectrum contact poison
• rotenone: commonly applied as a dust for short-term control of many leaf-eating caterpillars and beetles
• sabadilla: both a contact and stomach poison, effective against many true bugs, leaf-eating caterpillars, and thrips
• neem: repels some pests and interrupts the life cycle of many plant-eating caterpillars and beetles after ingestion.
Keep in mind that pesticides classed as botanical may still be very toxic and will still kill beneficials (*see p.68*); rotenone in particular is very toxic to fish. Like any other pesticide, these must be used with extreme care, and always read the label.

INSECTICIDAL SOAPS

Derived from fatty acids and potassium salts, insecticidal soaps are applied as a dilute spray. They damage cell membranes of soft-bodied pests such as aphids, leafhoppers, whitefly, and spider mites, and make them slip off the plant. In order to be effective, insecticidal soaps must come into direct contact with the pest. Some particularly sensitive plants can be damaged by insecticidal soaps; check the manufacturer's instructions and, if you are unsure, test the product on a small part of the plant first.

HORTICULTURAL OILS

These are refined petroleum products that are commonly used on dormant plants to smother overwintering insects and mites. Formulations called summer-weight oils can be applied to many plants during the growing season for controlling scales, whiteflies, and certain diseases. However, some plants are susceptible to damage by oils so, as with all pesticides, you should read all of the instructions carefully.

Vegetable oils, derived from agricultural crops, may also be used to control pests such as aphids, spider mites, whiteflies, thrips, and scales. They should not be used on begonias, fuchsias, or seedlings because they can damage the leaves.

A focused defense
Keep budworms at bay on garden geraniums, like Pelargonium 'Mrs. Henry Cobb', by beginning a monthly spray on the first full moon in April with Bt (*Bacillus thuringiensis*), an environmentally responsible product that kills caterpillars and nothing else.

MINED MATERIALS

Another component of the arsenal of pest control weapons is material that is mined from the earth. Sprinkling diatomaceous earth – fossilized single-celled aquatic organisms – around plants provides a physical barrier against soft-bodied slugs and snails. Copper strips can be used as barriers to prevent damage by slugs and snails. Copper- and sulfur-based sprays and dusts can control fungal diseases such as powdery mildew and botrytis. These products can be detrimental to predatory mites, however, and should not be sprayed on young apples. Furthermore, the buildup of copper in the soil may be harmful to worms and, as it runs off into neighboring waterways, will affect fish.

Nature's pest control

Another method of thwarting garden pests is to enlist their natural enemies to work for you. Insects, nematodes, mites, microbes, and other organisms that feed upon or infect a plant pest are known as biological controls, and they are among the most effective ways of dealing with troublemakers in your garden. Beneficial organisms are fairly specific with respect to creatures they infect or consume, and they pose minimal danger to humans and other nontarget animals.

Some of the organisms that gardeners often lump together under the term "insects" are more correctly known simply as arthropods. Technically, true insects – such as ants, grasshoppers, butterflies, and beetles – are distinguished from other groups of common garden arthropods such as arachnids (spiders and mites) and crustaceans (pillbugs and sowbugs). Most of these creatures are neutral when it comes to their effect on garden plants; that is, they neither harm nor benefit them. They may, however, be a food source for birds, bats, or other wildlife, or they may help decompose organic matter. So in a sense, even though they do not directly help or harm plants,

arthropods help maintain a well-balanced environment. Many arthropods benefit garden plants by hunting and eating other insects and mites that feed on plants. Others parasitize pests, often by laying their eggs inside the body of the pest, where they eventually hatch and consume their host, then the emerging female adults complete the cycle by laying eggs in new hosts. Predatory mites often consume plant-feeding spider mites. Many spiders build webs and feed on whatever prey wanders in and gets stuck. Others, such as wolf, jumping, and crab spiders, actively seek their prey on plants or on the ground. Among the pests they help control are aphids, leafhoppers, and numerous beetles and caterpillars. Avoid spraying pesticides when these garden-friendly creatures are present.

Sowbugs may occasionally be a problem, however, because they are sometimes attracted in large numbers to seedlings, feeding on them at ground level. If necessary, a colony of sowbugs can be destroyed by pouring boiling water on them.

COMMON PARASITES AND PREDATORS

Centipedes: A good scavenger that feeds on a variety of soil-living pests, including millipedes and wireworms.
Ground beetles: These black beetles are often seen running away from an overturned piece of wood. They feed on many pests that live in or near the soil surface, such as cutworms, root maggots, and slugs and snails. Some species climb and help control Colorado beetles and tent caterpillars.

On patrol
A ground beetle actively searches for many kinds of garden pests to eat.

Hover flies: Looking like tiny wasps, these dart about like hummingbirds and feed on aphids.
Lacewings: Seen mostly in early evening, these feed on aphids, small larvae, mites, thrips, and scale insects.
Ladybird beetles (ladybugs): Both the well-known adult and the larvae devour aphids and other plant feeders. They are fairly specific on food choice, so buying them and releasing them in your garden may not work. A recently introduced species from Asia should be viewed with

mixed feelings: while it eats aphids, it also gives people a painful sting.
Parasitic wasps: Varying in size from very small to rather large, these wasps lay their eggs in the bodies of host insects. The larvae then feed on the host and kill it. They may look frightening, but they do not sting people.
Spined soldier bug: One of the stink bugs, with a wide, flat shape, this has pronounced horns on either side of the shell. It feeds on many harmful caterpillars, sawfly larvae, and Colorado beetle larvae.
Tachinid flies: Similar in looks to house flies, these lay their eggs on many pests, including cutworms, army worms, gypsy moth larvae, and tent caterpillars. The resulting larvae feed on the host and pupate on the corpse.

Lone hunter
A solitary wasp has captured an insect to take back to its nest for its young.

Attracting beneficial organisms

You can encourage predators and parasites of plant pests to inhabit your garden. Beneficial organisms can be purchased from distributors of natural pest controls. Make sure that when you release beneficial insects, there are pests for them to feed on; otherwise, they will seek another garden with a more tempting menu. Another potential problem is that some predaceous insects, such as the praying mantis, will feed on beneficial insects as well as your pests.

Either attracting or releasing beneficial insects into your garden will not give you instant results – your pests may be around for several days – but once the predators or parasites arrive, they will

work to control the pest until the pest population is depleted. Do not apply any insecticides to your garden while your beneficials are doing their job or you may eliminate them.

On target
Place containers of beneficial organisms on or near the plants you want to protect.

Beneficial nematodes

Some nematodes – microscopic, eel-like roundworms – are plant pests, but others are beneficial, residing in soils where they attack, and infecting and reproducing in garden pests that spend part of their life cycle in the soil. Beneficial nematodes are effective for managing black vine weevil larvae, white grubs, and Japanese beetle grubs, among others. The nematodes penetrate a host insect through natural body openings, multiply within the host's body, and release bacteria that multiply and kill the pest.

Native populations of beneficial nematodes are generally too low to provide effective pest control. However, beneficial nematodes can be purchased and applied to your lawns and gardens. Timing of the application is critical, and as with all pest-control products, it is important that you follow all of the label directions carefully. When correctly applied, beneficial nematodes not only provide excellent control of the target pest but are extremely safe to humans and other nontarget animals because they can only inhabit particular hosts, for example, the vine weevil.

Beneficial microbes

Some microbial organisms can be recruited to control pests. *Bacillus thuringiensis* (Bt) is a bacterium available in several different varieties, each of which is effective against specific pests. The bacterium produces a protein that is toxic to a variety of insects, causing paralysis of their mouthparts or gut. Bt var. *kurstaki* (Btk) controls several destructive caterpillars, such as cabbage caterpillars, cabbage loopers, gypsy moth, tomato hornworm, and codling moths, as well as corn borers. Other strains, Btt and Bt var. san diego, provide control of leaf-eating beetles such as the Colorado potato beetle. It is important to select the appropriate variety of the bacterium for the pest at hand. Bt degrades in sunlight and, consequently, it must be reapplied in order to remain effective.

A related species, *B. popilliae*, controls Japanese beetles by infecting the grubs – the soil-borne larval stage – with a disease known as milky spore. The bacteria reproduce in the host and remain in the soil when the host dies, providing a long-term source for infection of other grubs.

Attracting predators
Even a small patch of wildflowers planted from seeds in fall will attract large numbers of beneficial predatory and parasitic organisms into your garden.

KEEP A GARDEN JOURNAL

The more you know about your site, your plants, and potential problems you may encounter, the more success you will experience in gardening. Although numerous resources are available to guide your gardening endeavors, the most important is your own experience. Keeping records is among the most valuable gardening activities you can perform. Both your successes and failures provide lessons that will make you a better gardener.

A garden diary

Interrupting your planting or weeding efforts to jot down notes in a diary might seem like a nuisance at the time, but it will help you plan your garden efforts this season and for years to come. Record the names of those plants that have performed famously as well as those you'd rather forget – and be sure to indicate which is which! The moments you take to note your observations will save you time in the long run. When you repeat a mistake because you forgot a previous failure, not only is it a waste of time and effort, but it may result in the loss of an entire growing season or even longer.

A gardening diary is a simple way to keep track of what is happening in your yard. Some allow for multiple years' entries on the same page. Typically, one page is allotted to every week of the year, and it is divided to accommodate four or five years' worth

of records. This allows you to look back to see what was going on in the garden at the same time in previous seasons. However, less elaborate systems can work just as well. A simple notebook or a calendar with enough room for your entries can accommodate any important details. The critical aspect of a garden diary is not what it looks like, but that you write in it. Regularly.

While garden notes needn't be lengthy, a few items are very important to include. Be sure to record the full name, including cultivar or variety, of any plant you acquire. Note the planting date and the plant's location in the yard. Then, when it's time to replant your strawberries and you want the same (or a different) variety than you planted half a dozen years ago (was it 'Camarosa' or 'Chandler'?), it is just a matter of checking your records. When you order vegetable and annual flower seeds, you can sit down with your notes, ordering those varieties you considered tops in the past and avoiding those that were disappointing. Having a record of where you purchased a given plant is sometimes helpful, especially for those hard-to-find varieties.

Diagrams of planting plans are also helpful. A sketch of your vegetable garden will assist planning future crop rotation schedules. A bed layout will remind you of the location of bulbs, ephemeral perennials (plants that complete their annual growth cycle in a very short time), or perennials that emerge late in the season, avoiding accidental damage when you are working in your garden before or after these plants are visible.

Making notes
Recording garden observations as you make them will produce a valuable record for the future. It can be as simple or as literary as you wish.

The four seasons
Many experienced gardeners strive to have something of interest in their gardens throughout the year. Noting when plants bloom or show other interesting features will be useful as you plan color combinations or theme gardens for a particular season. Clockwise from top left: Pink jasmine (*Jasminum polyanthum*) in winter, Pride of Madeira (*Echium fastuosum*) in spring, *Bougainvillea* 'Barbara Karst' in summer, and Mexican flame vine (*Pyrostegia venusta*) in fall.

The march of time
Photographs document a seed bed planted in fall, with pea stakes holding up bird netting, and wildflowers blooming in spring after the netting is removed.

Information to include

Your records should include as much of the following information as possible about your plants and their basic and specialized care:

- Source: where you obtained the plant (nursery, friend, local plant sale)
- Provenance: the plant's place of origin (where it was previously grown)
- Date acquired
- Size and condition
- Special characteristics that set the plant apart
- Exact planting location
- Dates of application of fertilizer and pesticides
- Notes on propagation where applicable
- Pruning schedule
- Additional care required

- Flowering and fruiting times. Observations about plant growth are helpful as you plan additions. Perhaps you want a shrub that blooms at the same time as those in an existing planting, or a raspberry that ripens after your blackberries. Keeping track of planting and harvesting dates in the vegetable garden helps you plan for an extended harvest.
- Diseases, pests, cultural problems. Many pests can be avoided by planting earlier or later than the pest's arrival to the garden (doing this is especially useful in vegetable gardening). This necessitates, however, knowing when to expect the unwanted visitor. Because these dates vary even within a region, the best source of this information is your own garden records. The onset of a disease or pest infestation is equally important to note on ornamental plants so that you can be prepared to minimize damage.

On screen
Suitable computer software can be an invaluable aid in keeping track of the comings and goings (and successes and failures) of your garden plants over the years.

Planting Record.XLS

	PLANT NAME	SOURCE	DATE PLANTED	PLANTING LOCATION(S)	NOTES	F	G	H	I	J
2	Dalea greggii x 12	Desert Gardens	11/12/95	left of drive	little irrigation, good groundcover					
3	Leucophyllum 'Green Cloud' x6	Mesa Nursery	11/14/95	as screen near road	little irrigation, don't prune					
4	Ericameria laricifolia	Oasis Brothers	11/24/94	behind pool	prune dead out in winter					
5	Encelia farinose x 7	Hot Springs Selection	11/3/98	next to rockery	no water once established					
6	Baileya multiradiata x 12	Master Gardener Seminar	10/19/02	in flower border	irrigate every two weeks to keep bloom going					
7	Ceratonia siliqua	Best Desert Trees	10/18/91	behind pool	avoid overwatering					
8	Acacia greggii	Spooks Mountain Nursery	11/20/03	behind cactus mound	native shrub, or tree, if watered					
9	Pinus halpensis	Pines and Palms	9/10/94	near front spruce	a few deep waterings needed in summer					
10	Cupressus sempervirens x 9	Canyon Acres	10/12/90	windbreak on west	water deeply in summer					
11										
12										
13										

Sheet1 Sheet2 Sheet3

Ready — Sum=0 — SCRL — CAPS — NUM

Many gardeners have developed a personal computerized plant record system. Data can be added to files quickly, and multiple years of records can be conveniently stored. You can develop a long-range plan and keep track of your progress. Be sure to keep a backup of all your gardening files just in case something happens to the computer.

Some of the most fascinating garden records are photographs. A spectacular garden is all the more dramatic when you can compare the "before" and "after" shots. Growth of trees, combinations of perennials, and successful container plantings can be documented for future referral. Also, a photograph can be very helpful to someone trying to diagnose a plant problem or identify a plant.

Other items for the record

Always record major modifications you make to your soil, such as double digging and adding replacement soil. Keep your soil tests from year to year, and make note of the kind and quantity of organic and mineral amendments you incorporate. Records of your soil fertility and pH are most useful when changes can be observed over time. Be sure to identify areas that receive different treatments.

Routine maintenance such as mulching, watering, fertilizing, and pruning should be recorded. Knowing the quantities of mulch and fertilizer you use in a season helps estimate future purchases.

By studying the phenology of the plants in your landscape – their cycles of growth and development over the course of the year – you can time gardening activities to your specific conditions. The optimum time to plant particular seeds, to apply insecticides, to release beneficial insects, and other gardening activities can be determined by observing the growth cycle of your plants and relating their various stages to the environment as a whole. Because plants respond to environmental stimuli, such as day length and temperature, their growth cycles can be used to indicate other similarly stimulated events such as the arrival of an insect pest or the emergence of a weed. Applying snail control to clivia spikes to catch snails emerging from winter dormancy is an example of a phenologically based practice. Similarly, when an insect infestation is first observed in your yard, look around and take note of what is blooming. If the insect reappears in following years when the same plant is in bloom, you can reasonably schedule your pest control methods to coincide with that particular plant's blooming time.

Timing is everything
Keep a record of when you cut plants back. For example, when basal foliage sprouting from the ground on plants such as spurge (*Euphorbia characias wulfenii*) is about 4–8in long, you can safely cut back the old foliage.

CONSULT THE PROS

In today's media-rich environment, the challenge is not so much to find information about whatever topic you seek as it is to filter the available resources to make sure you locate those that are most reliable and valuable to you and your gardening efforts. The books, periodicals, websites, television and radio shows, and gardens that are most useful to you are largely determined by two factors: your gardening interests and your location.

Gathering information

If you are investigating the possibility of developing a rock garden, heirloom vegetable plot, or water feature, for example, you can find books, magazines, and websites devoted to the subject. To apply the information you gather to your backyard, you can look to more regional resources, such as a nearby botanical garden, a local chapter of a rock garden society, your state's cooperative extension service, and periodicals with a regional focus. Obtain the best resources available to you, then integrate the information into your garden plan.

The printed word

Certain resources become like trusted friends – you return to them time after time for advice. A stroll down the gardening aisle of a well-stocked bookstore reveals that there are titles for nearly every conceivable aspect of gardening. But all gardening references are not equal. Although some books, like this one, have a regional perspective, many are written from a more general point of view, and some will reflect conditions quite unlike those you confront. Take this into consideration when looking for advice from a nonregional reference.

Magazines and journals can inspire you with examples of what other gardeners are doing as well as keep you up to date on advances in the field. There are many periodicals to choose from, for every level of gardening and for just about any specialty. Some of these are national with a broad scope. Every region and many gardening subjects – from prairie gardens to tomato culture to water gardening – are represented on the periodical shelf at the bookstore. Many plant societies, botanic gardens, and nurseries publish a newsletter, and many of these are packed with useful information. If you are considering subscribing to a gardening magazine or newsletter, ask a gardener who shares your interests for a recommendation.

Local and regional newspapers are another source of timely gardening information. Many run gardening columns each week or biweekly that offer growing tips on a local level. Newspapers may cover gardens worth visiting in your area, as well as local gardening programs and events.

The printed word
Many reference books are available to buy from bookstores or to research at libraries. It's a good idea to consult more than one volume to get multiple (and often different!) insights on a given plant's characteristics and garden potential.

Landscape painters
Employing a professional landscape architect or designer may be more expensive but can lead to lasting rewards. (Pond by Nancy Goslee Power.)

The electronic approach

Websites on virtually every gardening specialty have cropped up over the last few years. A quick search on the Internet can reveal hundreds of articles about any gardening topic. You can spend many hours surfing the Net for specific information, or just enjoy exploring the breadth of subjects covered. Nearly every major garden club, plant society, and botanical garden, as well as many state cooperative extension services and university horticulture departments, have websites that you are welcome to peruse. In many cases, expert advice on almost any gardening subject is often only an e-mail away.

Many organizations may have regional chapters with individual websites. These can be a helpful source of local expert advice and can inform you of meetings, classes, and other events in your area. If you are looking for information on a specific plant, for example daffodils or roses, or a particular gardening topic such as rock gardens or bonsai, start with the appropriate national organization and go from there. Many organizations are listed on more general gardening websites, and the national organizations usually provide links to regional sites (see p. 387).

A gardening list serve – an electronic conversation among a group of gardeners – provides opportunities to ask, receive, and offer advice, and to share gardening experiences. Many organizations sponsor list serves. The accuracy of such advice, of course, depends upon the participants, but conversations are often lively and stimulating. If you are a member of the American Horticultural Society (AHS), you can learn about various list serves by visiting the Society's website (www.ahs.org), then join one of many ongoing conversations on just about any gardening subject that interests you.

Many local radio and cable television stations are getting into the gardening act with shows that highlight local gardens, gardeners, and timely and regionally appropriate gardening information. Tune in and see what's new.

Being there

Although written and electronic references are invaluable aids to gardening, nothing is quite the same as a visit to a real garden for learning what you need to know and for inspiring you with ideas. Regional botanical gardens and arboreta afford visitors a chance to see plants they have read or heard about in a real growing situation, and experts are often available to answer your questions.

Some public gardens offer classes and workshops on a variety of subjects, and some provide training for Master Gardeners (*see* Master Gardeners, *opposite page*). Most offer volunteer opportunities – a great way to work with trained gardening staff, learning garden techniques first hand.

The Huntington Library and Botanical Gardens
A dozen different, appealingly designed, gardens in a parklike, 207-acre landscape, include a Japanese garden, a rose garden, and the largest camellia and outdoor desert collections in the world.

Living Desert Zoological & Botanical State Park, New Mexico
A botanical garden, greenhouse, native-animal zoo, and desert plants available for sale are all at the foot of the arid Ocotillo Hills, covered with cacti, yucca, and other native and exotic desert plants, including flowering shrubs and giant saguaro.

MASTER GARDENERS

The Master Gardeners program began in the early 1970's in Washington State as a way to train volunteers to help gardeners find reliable solutions to their gardening problems. Today there are master gardener programs in every state, coordinated by each state's Cooperative Extension Service.

Programs vary somewhat from one state to another, but in general, volunteers are selected and trained in basic horticultural practices. Training often includes plant identification, diagnosis of plant problems with appropriate recommendations for treatment, soil and fertilizer recommendations, lawn care, pesticide use and safety, organic gardening, ornamental gardening, and a variety of other topics.

In return for their training, Master Gardeners must volunteer a certain number of hours in public service. They may participate in plant clinics, assist with processing soil test reports, answer horticultural hotlines, conduct garden tours, or other activities that are aimed at disseminating reliable gardening information to the public.

Two hundred universities, public gardens, and nurseries throughout the United States and Canada are home to All-America Selection (AAS) display gardens. These gardens provide visitors the opportunity to see how recent award-winning introductions (vegetables, flowers, and herbs) perform in a garden setting (See appendix for a list of AAS display gardens).

Close to home

Don't overlook a garden simply because it doesn't have a name: within your neighborhood there may be landscapes that deserve a closer look. Most gardeners love to show off the fruits of their labor, and some of the best advice available to you may be from the man or woman next door who shares both your growing conditions and your enthusiasm for gardening.

Observing the plants your neighbors grow, how they grow them, and how they tackle problems that arise can provide insight and ideas for your own yard. A gardening acquaintance may alert you to the arrival of a pest or show you a new plant that is just the ticket for your perennial border. Putting your heads together to find a solution for a problem multiplies your available resources.

As your garden comes of age, and neighbors can't help but observe your success, you are likely to be asked for advice from other interested gardeners. Be generous. Share your enthusiasm for gardening and your respect for the environment. You too are a valuable gardening resource.

Cutting edge
Faculty members at local and regional agricultural colleges often spend part of their time researching new techniques and breeding new plants. Their printed and electronic publications are a valuable resource.

EXTENSION SERVICE

During the late 19th and early 20th centuries, Congress dramatically advanced the practice of agriculture by founding land-grant colleges, creating agricultural experiment stations, and founding the Cooperative Extension Service, to deliver the latest agricultural knowledge to farmers. The Cooperative Extension is cooperatively financed and run by the Department of Agriculture and the land-grant university in each state, hence the name. Cooperative funding comes from the federal government, the counties, and farm organizations. Extension officials called Farm Advisors (County Agents) teach farmers and householders the latest scientific methods of farming, gardening, and home economics. Extension offices reflect the needs of each community in which they exist. They offer a wide range of educational materials and advice to residents, including advice in home gardening.

Results of government studies involving such subjects as hybridization, plant selection, soils, fertilizers, irrigation, integrated pest-management, beneficial organisms, pruning, and much more help farmers and gardeners alike. Information is released through bulletins, books, websites, telephone hotlines, and direct consultation. One of the most dramatic discoveries was of plant climates. Maps were created in the 1930s to indicate just where certain plants, such as citrus and avocado, and later all horticultural plants, would survive. Another dramatic discovery was that the flowering of poinsettias was triggered by day length. Chrysanthemums and many other plants were later studied and growing practices rapidly changed. Since the 1970s, the Master Gardener program has allowed horticultural information to be disseminated to the public with increased efficiency (see above).

HAVE FUN

Lots of people have yards; some have gardens. A yard is the area that surrounds your house. A garden, on the other hand, is a creation that enhances that space with sights, fragrances, and sounds that inspire and fulfill. The yard around your house is what you begin with; a garden is what it can become. Whether your garden is a woodland teeming with towering trees and flowering shrubs, a deep border of colorful perennials, a vegetable patch that stocks your table, or a simple windowbox overflowing with annuals, it should be fun for you and for those who visit.

The vision

Visualizing your dream garden can occupy many delightful hours looking through books and magazines for ideas, visiting botanical gardens, and imagining a bed here, a pond there, and over there, perhaps a trellis . . . it's a pleasant thing to daydream about your green activities. Planning for it to become a reality, and taking the measured steps necessary to assure success, is even more exciting. Witnessing the transformation of your yard into a SMARTGARDEN™ through choosing great plants, maximizing efficient practices, and nurturing a friendly, healthy environment, is a thrill that grows over time.

The challenge

Achieving a SMARTGARDEN™ is a challenge beyond simply planting a few perennials and trees around a patch of grass. It requires you to consider the question: how do you develop a garden, making the most of your landscape, while at the same time merging seamlessly into the rhythms and flow of nature? Your answer is both the task and the reward of its creation. Compromises will be necessary, and you may not see instant dividends on your investment, but over time you will enjoy the compounded benefits of a lovely garden and a healthy, balanced environment. Because you planned for it, your investment will continue to grow over time.

The gardening practices described in this book are designed to make the most of your gardening activities, using all available resources to streamline efforts so that you can concentrate on the gardening activities that you find particularly rewarding and have plenty of time to enjoy the fruits of your labor. Of course there will be some surprises. You will make changes as you go along, learning from and adapting to what works best for you. It is dynamic, challenging, and exciting, and, as every gardener comes to know, there is no such thing as a "finished" garden. The ongoing processes of planning, planting, maintaining, experiencing, refining, and sharing is part of the thrill.

The reward

Although many gardens are pleasant to look at, a SMARTGARDEN™ is a delight to experience on many different levels. It harmonizes with its surroundings, and enhances its environment without dominating it. The soil is alive and teeming with beneficial organisms. The plants fit their site and space – and they flourish! Birds and butterflies are welcomed, encouraged by the diversity of vegetation and friendly habitat. It's exciting to know your plants intimately while taking pride in their performances and anticipating their changes through the seasons as well as the years.

People garden for many reasons: to enjoy nature, get some fresh air and spend time outdoors, cultivate particular plants, grow their own food, attract wildlife, and create a pleasing, comfortable environment. For most gardeners, it is a combination of such goals. Some people garden because they enjoy the solitude, while others consider it an opportunity to spend time productively in the company of friends or family. It is a perfect activity for intergenerational bonding: senior gardeners have a wealth of experience they can share with young garden enthusiasts. Whether alone or with company, most of us garden because it's fun.

Some gardeners find satisfaction in neat rows of plump tomatoes, while others take more pleasure in a casual meadow of wildflowers or an elaborate pond for night-blooming waterlilies. No matter which type of garden you choose, it can be grown following these ten tenets. This kind of garden affords you the opportunity to express your taste and style and then to watch it grow, knowing that it is a healthy and safe environment for all who visit. That knowledge will amplify the joy you derive from your garden.

Whether you are beginning from scratch or you are improving an existing garden, smart gardening will help you embrace the vision, meet the challenge, and enjoy the rewards of bringing plants, animals, and structures together into a green and living whole.

Topiary springs to life
Gardening isn't all serious. It's not about overcoming obstacles or striving for perfection – it's about having a good time, throwing your inhibitions aside, and enjoying life.

PART II

PLANT CATALOG

including Woody Plants *and*
Herbaceous Plants

One of the three most critical factors for the
success of any SMARTGARDEN™ is choosing the
right plant for the right spot. In this section, more
than 4,000 plants that grow well in the Southwest
region are grouped by physical characteristics or
horticultural requirements, with information on
light and moisture needs, cold and heat
tolerance, and maximum height and width.
Below is a key of the symbols:

☼	Sun	◗	Some irrigation	Zx–x	USDA hardiness zones
◐	Part shade	◗	Full irrigation	Hx–x	AHS heat zones
☀	Shade	pH	Acidic soil	↕ in/ft (cm/m)	Height of plant
◌	No irrigation	Ⓝ	Native	↔ in/ft (cm/m)	Spread of plant

Plant catalog contents

WOODY

Native trees for desert gardens 86
Shade trees for desert gardens 88
Small trees for desert gardens 90
Treelike succulents for dry gardens 91
Trees that survive without irrigation 92
Drought-resistant deciduous trees 94
Drought-resistant evergreen trees 96
Trees for wet soil 98
Trees for adobe soil 100
Large subtropical flowering trees 102
Trees for tropical gardens 104
Trees for Mediterranean-style gardens 106
Medium flowering trees for mild zones 108
Small flowering trees for mild zones 109
Conifers for mild-winter zones 110
Conifers for interior zones 111
Evergreen conifers for mountain zones 112
Deciduous trees for mountain zones 113
Small trees for patios 114
Small flowering trees for front yards 115
Trees for use near swimming pools 116
Trees for the oceanfront 118

Trees for windbreaks 120
Evergreen trees for screens 122
Trees for informal hedges 123
Trees for espalier 124
Trees with fragrant flowers 126
Trees with colorful fall foliage 128
Trees with ornamental bark 130
Trees for hummingbirds 132
Trees for butterflies 133
Trees for birds 134
Trees with fantastic shapes 136
Trees with a weeping habit 138
Trees resistant to smog 140
Trees resistant to oak-root fungus 142
Citrus trees 144
Deciduous, interior fruit and nut trees 146
Tropical or exotic fruit trees 148
Low-chill fruit trees for mild zones 150
Palms for desert gardens 152
Palms for tropical gardens 153
Drought-resistant palms 154
Palms for damp soil 156
Palms that survive frost 157
Fast-growing broadleaf trees 158

Native shrubs for desert gardens 160
Native shrubs for desert-style gardens 164
Native evergreen shrubs for desert gardens 166
Groundcover shrubs for dry shade 168
Native shrubs for dry shade 170
Non-native shrubs for dry shade 171
Shrubs for moist soil in semishade 172
Shrubs for moist soil in deep shade 173
Shrubs for Zone 3 firebreaks 174
Shrubs with fragrant flowers 176
Shrubs for year-round bloom 178
Shrubs for spring or summer bloom 180
Shrubs for fall and winter bloom 182
Shrubs for tropical gardens 184
Shrubs for subtropical gardens 186
Shrubs with flowers for tropical effects 188
Shrubs for the oceanfront 190
Roses for foggy coastal gardens 192
Shrubs for thorny barriers 194
Shrubs for sandy soil 196
Evergreen shrubs for informal screens 197
Flowering shrubs for informal screens 198
Shrubs for espalier 200
Shrubs with variegated foliage 202
Shrubs with colorful foliage 203
Shrubs for cottage gardens 204
Shrubs for butterflies 206
Shrubs for hummingbirds 208
Hedges for birds 210
Native shrubs for birds 211

Shrubs with fantastic shapes 212
Native shrubs resistant to deer 214
Non-native shrubs resistant to deer 215
Shrubs to plant under windows 216
Small shrubs for herb gardens 218
Shrubs for use near swimming pools 220
Shrubs for containers 222
Shrubby succulents for containers 224
Shrubs for hanging baskets 225
Tall cacti for dramatic effects 226
Small cacti for garden accents 227
Shrubby succulents for
rocky landscapes 228
Climbers for desert gardens 230
Drought-resistant climbers 231
Climbers for subtropical gardens 232
Climbers for tropical gardens 234
Climbers for Mediterranean
-style gardens 236
Climbers for cottage gardens 238
Climbers for groundcover 240
Climbers for groundcover in shade 241
Climbers for butterflies 242
Climbers for hummingbirds 243
Climbers with fragrant flowers 244
Climbers with edible fruit 245
Climbers for chain-link fences 246
Climbing roses for fences and arbors 247
Drought-resistant climbing roses 248
Climbing roses for mild coastal zones 250
Climbing roses for hot interior zones 251
Durable shrub roses 252
Climbing and trailing succulents 254

HERBACEOUS

Perennials for hot interior gardens 258
Perennials for hot dry shade 260
Perennial groundcovers for
Zone 2 firebreaks 262
Mild-zone perennials: spring 264

Mild-zone perennials: summer 266
Mild-zone perennials: fall and winter 268
Perennials for tropical gardens 270
Hardy perennials 272
Perennials for cottage gardens 274
Perennials for full sun 276
Perennials for butterflies 278
Annuals for butterflies 279
Annual wildflowers for desert gardens 280
Wildflowers for mountain zones 282
Wildflowers for Texas 284
Wildflowers for summer and fall 286
Cool-season annual wildflowers 288
Herbaceous plants with fragrant flowers 290
Border perennials: spring 292
Border perennials: summer 294
Border perennials: fall and winter 296
Drought-resistant perennials
for hummingbirds 298
Plants between stepping stones 300
Succulents for dry landscaping
or containers 302
Perennials for hanging baskets 304
Succulent groundcovers for
Zone 1 firebreaks 306
Herbaceous groundcovers for full sun 308
Perennial groundcovers for full shade 310
Native perennial groundcovers: dry shade 312
Native perennial groundcovers:
hot interiors 313
Groundcovers for light foot traffic 314
Ornamental grasses 316
Bamboos 317
Hardy bulbs 318
Bulbs for winter and spring bloom 320
Bulbs for summer and fall bloom 322
Bulbs for naturalizing in
mild-winter zones 324
Orchids for mild zones 326

Daffodils for mild zones 327
Aquatic plants 328
Perennials for shallow water 330
Native perennials for desert gardens 332
Perennials for use near swimming pools 334
Pink drought-resistant perennials 336
Red or purple drought-resistant
perennials 337
Yellow drought-resistant perennials 338
Orange drought-resistant perennials 339
Blue or lavender drought-resistant
perennials 340
White or silver drought-resistant
perennials 341
Perennials for year-round bloom 342
Annuals for cut flowers 344
Perennials for cut flowers 345
Perennials for English-style borders 346
Annuals and perennials for herb gardens 348
Annuals and perennials with
edible flowers 350
Annuals and biennials for semishade 352
Annuals and biennials for
cottage gardens 354
Annuals for summer and fall bloom 356
Cool-season annuals 358

WOODY PLANTS

OFTEN CALLED THE "the bones of the garden," trees and shrubs should be the first plants to go in once the hard landscaping is done. Trees grow slower than perennials or annuals, but eventually make more impact on the landscape. When selecting a tree, consider eventual size, hardiness and heat tolerance, foliage color and density, and flowering time. Trees play a dominant role in the garden and can influence the other plants you grow because of their root systems and the shade they cast. Some shallow-rooted trees can take so much moisture from the soil that it is hard to grow even grass beneath them.

Fremontodendron 'California Glory'
The flannel bush is a colorful California native. This hybrid form blooms prolifically in spring and is good for planting on steep banks.

Maclura pomifera
This intriguing but inedible fruit is borne by the Osage orange, a fast-growing tree, native to Texas and Oklahoma, which endures wind, heat, and poor soil.

Also take into account the winter effect; many trees have brightly colored bark or persistent fruit, which may provide the main winter interest in cold-winter gardens, where there is a lack of year-round bloom.

When it comes to shrubs, there is a selection for every location, soil type, and exposure. Low groundcover species can take the place of grass, tall upright forms make ideal hedges or screens, and spiny ones can make an intruder-proof barrier.

Some shrubs bloom year-round in waves. Others have a specific season of bloom, providing many choices for every time of year. In cold-winter climates, shrubs with colorful stems, fall leaves, or berries can brighten cooler seasons.

The diversity of evergreens is equally broad. Most conifers have needle- or fanlike foliage that may be green, blue, or yellow, while broadleaved evergreens have flowers and fruit. They range from small, columnar plants to large, towering trees. Many make excellent hedges that filter the wind, rather than blocking it, while others are better as specimen plants. They are often used as screens, providing a backdrop to more colorful elements of the garden. Some broadleaved evergreens are grown mainly for their foliage, but in the Southwest, the majority, such as bottlebrushes, camellias, and coral trees, are grown for their flowers.

Plumeria alba
Fragrant flowers are produced summer to fall on white plumeria, which flourishes easily in Hawaii, but on the mainland needs a protected spot.

Tabebuia impetiginosa
In spring, the pink trumpet tree drops its leaves and bursts suddenly into bloom, giving a wonderful show in spots where it is sheltered from wind.

Native trees for desert gardens

Native desert trees can be used in other hot interior climates, saving water. Visit one of the many demonstration gardens exhibiting these trees to observe how attractive they can be when combined with rocks and other desert plants, artistically planted on undulating ground. These landscapes also provide wild desert creatures with food and cover.

Salix gooddingi
SAN JOACHIN WILLOW
Ⓝ ☀ ◊◑ Z7–9 H9–7 ↕↔20ft (6m)
Deciduous, narrow, light green leaves attract good insects like fly catchers. Roots reach deep for water when young. Attractive yellow stems appear in winter.

Washingtonia filifera
CALIFORNIA FAN PALM
Ⓝ ☀ ◊◑◐ Z8–11 H12–8 ↕60ft (18m) ↔20ft (6m)
A native to desert washes and streams, this thick-trunked tree is disease-resistant in interior, not on the coast. Hooded orioles use threads from leaf tips for nests.

Parkinsonia florida
BLUE PALO VERDE
Ⓝ ☀ ◊◑ Z7–12 H12–10 ↕↔30ft (10m)
Small, lightly fragrant flowers appear in March and April. An open structure with blue-green bark that litters from seed capsules. Birds like to nest in this tree.

MORE CHOICES

- *Acacia constricta* H12–10
- *Acacia smallii* Z10–11 H12–10
- *Canotia holacantha* Z8–11 H12–7
- *Cercidium praecox* Z8–11 H12–8
- *Chilopsis linearis* Z8–9 H9–8
- *Cupressus arizonica* Z7–9 H9–7
- *Leucaena retusa* Z8–10 H10–9
- *Lysiloma microphylla* Z9–11 H12–9
- *Olneya tesota* Z8–10 H10–9
- *Prosopis velutina* Z8–11 H12–10
- *Quercus emoryi* Z4–7 H7–1
- *Sophora secundiflora* Z7–11 H12–7

Bursera microphylla
ELEPHANT TREE
Ⓝ ☀ ◊◐ Z13–15 H12–10 ↕15ft (5m) ↔20ft (6m)
Needs a dry winter and some irrigation in summer or foliage drops. Bare trees look upside-down. The massive trunk, like an elephant leg, has peeling bark.

Prosopis pubescens
SCREWBEAN MESQUITE
Ⓝ ☼ ◊◊ z8–11 H12–1 ↕↔15ft (5m)
Flowers in 2in (5cm) spikes appear April to June, and in summer after rain. A shaggy barked, multitrunked tree with deciduous foliage that spines in pairs.

Platanus wrightii
ARIZONA SYCAMORE
Ⓝ ☼ ◊◊◊ z7–9 H8–7 ↕80ft (20m) ↔55ft (17m)
Deciduous, like *P. racemosa*, but with more deeply lobed leaves and stemmed seed capsules in bunches, this is a fine shade tree with summer irrigation.

Prosopis glandulosa
HONEY MESQUITE
Ⓝ ☼ ◊◊ z8–11 H12–7 ↕↔30ft (10m)
Similar to *Schinus molle*, with bright green, feathery foliage that cascades downward on tips, this tree usually has several trunks. 'Maverick' is thornless.

Ebenopsis ebano
TEXAS EBONY
Ⓝ ☼ ◊ z7–9 H9–7
↕30ft (10m) ↔20ft (6m)
Slow-growing thorny tree with fluffy cream-colored spikes of fragrant flowers in summer, Sheds all or most of its leaves in winter.

Acacia farnesiana
SWEET ACACIA
Ⓝ ☼ ◊◊ z9–11 H12–10
↕30ft (10m) ↔25ft (8m)
Fragrant balls of yellow bloom in winter. This thorny tree often freezes to ground. *A. smallii* is spring-blooming and will not freeze.

WOODY PLANTS

Shade trees for desert gardens

Shade trees for hot interior and desert climates need to be able to withstand strong winds and heat that would wilt many of the trees planted in coastal or mountain zones. Choose carefully, taking into account eventual size and possible litter. Site with care so patios and windows remain adequately shaded as shadows elongate in winter and shorten in summer.

Sophora japonica 'Regent'
JAPANESE PAGODA TREE
☼ ◊ Z4–10 H9–1 ↕70ft (20m) ↔60ft (18m)
A uniform and vigorous variety of a spreading deciduous tree that needs good drainage. Attractive, creamy, pea-shaped summer flowers may stain patios.

Gleditsia triacanthos
HONEY LOCUST
Ⓝ ☼ ◊◊ Z3–8 H7–1 ↕70ft (20m) ↔35ft (11m)
A fast-growing, straight-trunked tree with deciduous feathery foliage. Needs a distinct winter. Wild type is thorny and messy; 'Moraine' and others are thornless.

Eriobotrya japonica
LOQUAT
☼ ◊◊ Z8–12 H12–8 ↕↔30ft (10m)
Producing edible fruit, this small ornamental tree is also good for hot interior and coastal gardens. *E. deflexa* is strictly ornamental. 'Champagne' gives better fruit.

Quercus fusiformis
PLATEAU LIVE OAK
Ⓝ ☼ ◊ Z6–9 H9–6 ↕↔40ft (12m)
A briefly deciduous oak, native to Texas, Oklahoma, and New Mexico. Often shrubby, in deep fertile soil it grows faster and becomes a larger tree.

Tilia tomentosa
SILVER LINDEN

☼ ◐ ◗ z6–9 H9–6 ↕50ft (15m) ↔30ft (10m)

Deciduous foliage ripples in the wind, showing silvery backs of leaves. More resistant to heat and drought than most lindens. 'Sterling' has a nice winter shape.

Juglans major
NOGAL, ARIZONA WALNUT

Ⓝ ☼ ◐◗ z6–8 H8–6 ↕↔50ft (15m)

An important shade tree in desert areas that endures wind and heat, this needs moderate water and deep soil. Deciduous divided leaves and small edible nuts.

MORE CHOICES

- *Brachychiton populneus* z9–11 H12–10
- *Ceratonia siliqua* z9–12 H12–10
- *Eucalyptus microtheca* z8–10 H10–8
- *Fraxinus berlandieri* 'Fan-Tex' z7–10 H8–4
- *Olneya tesota* z9–10 H10–9
- *Pinus halepensis* z9–10 H10–9
- *Pistacia chinensis* z6–9 H9–6
- *Populus fremontii* 'Nevada' z3–9 H9–1
- *Populus* x *canescens* 'Macrophylla' z5–9 H9–5
- *Prosopis alba* 'Colorado' z7–11 H12–10
- *Schinus molle* z8–11 H12–8

Celtis laevigata var. reticulata
WESTERN HACKBERRY

Ⓝ ☼ ☼ ◐ z3–9

H9–1 ↕↔30ft (10m)

With pendulous branches and deciduous, oval toothed leaves, its roots go straight down. Good in parking strips, by drives and on patios. A poor choice for the coast, it takes heat, drought, wind, and poor soil inland.

Melia azedarach
CHINABERRY

☼ ◐ z7–12 H12–10

↕↔50ft (15m)

This pictureque decidous tree takes heat, drought, wind, and poor soil. Clusters of fragrant lilac flowers and yellow fruits appear in spring. 'Umbraculiformis' (Texas umbrella tree) is thick and domed, 25ft (8m) tall and wide.

WOODY PLANTS

Small trees for desert gardens

All these trees are native and small enough to fit in a patio or entryway. The best choices are shapely and amenable to pruning. Cleanliness is another good trait, but no tree is perfect. Some of the loveliest drop leaves and seedpods. If the choice is between a flowering tree with some litter and a boring one with none, go for the bloom.

Sophora secundiflora
TEXAS MOUNTAIN LAUREL
Ⓝ ☼ ☼ ◑ Z8–10 H12–7 ↕25ft (8m) ↔15ft(5m)
Slow-growing and shrublike for years, this thrives in alkaline soil and has dense evergreen foliage. Clusters of fragrant flowers appear in late winter and spring. Cut off seedpods to avoid litter; seeds are poisonous.

Leucaena retusa
GOLDEN LEAD BALL TREE
Ⓝ ☼ ◑ Z7–9 H10–9 ↕↔20ft (6m)
Finely divided, fernlike leaves are deciduous in a cold winter, evergreen in mild. One-inch fluffy golden balls fill the tree in spring, followed by flat pods. Good in groves or as a single patio specimen.

Foresteria neomexicana
DESERT OLIVE
Ⓝ ☼ ◑ Z7–10 H12–1
↕18ft (5.5m) ↔12ft (4m)
Seen only in arid regions, use this for a deciduous green screen or prune into a multitrunked small tree. Some plants produce fruit, attracting birds, but others do not.

Parkinsonia florida
BLUE PALO VERDE
Ⓝ ☼ ◑◑ Z8–11 H12–10
↕35ft (11m) ↔30ft (10m)
This fast-growing, tough native to deserts in Arizona, California, and Mexico, has stunning springtime bloom. Disease-free but messy. 'Desert Museum' is litter free.

Chilopsis linearis
DESERT WILLOW
Ⓝ ☼ ◑ Z8–10 H10–8 ↕30ft (10m) ↔20ft (6m)
Its fragrant bloom, spring to fall, brings hummingbirds. This deciduous fast-growing, then slow, tree has shaggy bark and a twisted trunk. Prune in winter.

Olneya tesota
DESERT IRONWOOD
Ⓝ ☼ ◑◑ Z8–10 H10–9 ↕↔30ft (10m)
Slow-growing with thorny hardwood, lavender spring flowers, and evergreen gray foliage, this tree grows tall at first, then spreads in age. Old leaves drop in spring.

MORE CHOICES

- *Parkinsonia aculeata* Z8–12 H12–10
- *Prosopis glandulosa* Z8–11 H12–7
- *Rhus lancea* Z7–10 H8–1

Treelike succulents for dry gardens

Euphorbias and aloes are statuesque succulents that grow well in mild Mediterranean climates. Many euphorbias look like cacti, but there are key differences: euphorbias have white sap, are usually poisonous, have spines arising singly or in pairs, and are mostly from Africa; cacti have clear sap, are non-poisonous, have bunched spines, and originate mostly in the New World.

Euphorbia canariensis
CANARY ISLAND EUPHORBIA
Ⓝ ☼ ☼ ◊ ◐ z10–11 H11–10 ‡40ft (12m) ↔6ft (2m)
Freely branching with caplike cyathea in summer, this spines in pairs on sharp ridges. Often mistaken for a cactus, it needs similar care but is not as cold hardy.

Euphorbia candelabrum
TREE EUPHORBIA
☼ ◊ ◐ z10–11 H11–10 ‡↔30ft (10m)
With a single trunk, cracked bark, and many green curving branches, like giant candelabra, this is long lived given good drainage in frost-free climates.

Aloe thraskii
THRASK'S ALOE
☼ ☼ ◊ ◐ z10–11 H11–10 ‡30ft (10m) ↔10ft (3m)
A trouble-free plant with foot-tall, yellow-orange blooms in panicles above leaves in late winter. Trunk branches in age; old leaves hang down like a thatch.

Aloe dichotoma
QUIVER TREE
☼ ☼ ◊ ◐ z10–11 H12–10 ‡30ft (10m) ↔12ft (4m)
This long-lived plant grows at a moderate rate. It has a single trunk, papery bark, and a branched head. Needs good drainage and summer water for better growth.

MORE CHOICES

- *Aloe bainesii* z10–11 H12–10
- *Cereus uruguayanus* z10–11 H12–10
- *Euphorbia tirucalli* z10–11 H12–10
- *Fouquieria macdougalii* z10–11 H12–1
- *Synadenium compactum* var. *rubrum* z10–11 H12–10

WOODY PLANTS

Trees that survive without irrigation

Throughout the Southwest, cycles of drought alternate with cycles of good rains. In times of drought, water reserves can run out and gardeners must turn off the tap. In some areas there are even fines for watering your garden during a drought. As long as you plant these trees in the correct climate zone, they will still be alive when you turn the faucet back on.

Parkinsonia florida
BLUE PALO VERDE

Ⓝ ☼ ◊◑ Z10–11 H12–10 ‡35ft (11m) ↔30ft (10m)

This fast-growing, tough native has a stunning spring bloom and does not need much care. They are messy but 'Desert Museum' is litter free.

Heteromeles arbutifolia
TOYON, CALIFORNIA HOLLY

Ⓝ ☼ ◊◑ Z8–10 H12–8 ‡↔25ft (8m)

'Macrocarpa' and other cultivars carried by specialty nurseries have better flowers and larger berries. Seeds are spread by birds. Attractive pruned as a small tree.

Prosopis pubescens
SCREW BEAN

Ⓝ ☼ ◊◑ Z7–11 H12–1 ‡↔20–25ft (6–8m)

This multitrunked shrubby barrier or small tree has blue-green, deciduous foliage, green-yellow spring flowers, and spiraled seed pods. Thornless varieties available.

Lagerstroemia indica
CRAPE MYRTLE

Ⓝ ☼ ◑ Z7–10 H10–6 ‡↔25ft (8m)

For a patio or lawn in interior zones only, smothered with bloom in summer. Leaves color before dropping, showing handsome bark.

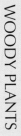

Quercus lobata
VALLEY OAK

Ⓝ ☼ ◊◊ z7–9 H9–7 ↕↔70ft (20m)

Drippy but gorgeous, this is perhaps the largest native oak. It grows straight up, then wide, and has a massive trunk. Limbs shade large patios.

Cercis occidentalis
WESTERN REDBUD

Ⓝ ☼ ◊◊ z8–10 H12–9 ↕35ft (11m) ↔30ft (10m)

Purple, pea-shaped flowers appear in spring. Summer brings heart-shaped, blue-green foliage, while orange pods hang on in winter. Great on dry banks.

MORE CHOICES

- *Acacia smallii* z8–11 H12–10
- *Adenostoma sparsifolium* z8–10 H10–8
- *Ceratonia siliqua* z9–10 H10–9
- *Eucalyptus sideroxylon* z9–11 H12–9
- *Juglans hindsii* z7–9 H9–7
- *Olneya tesota* z9–10 H10–9
- *Prosopis velutina* z9–11 H12–10
- *Prunus ilicifolia* z9–10 H10–9
- *Quercus douglasii* z9–10 H10–9
- *Rhamnus californica* z7–10 H10–7
- *Schinus molle* z8–11 H12–8
- *Schinus terebinthifolius* z9–11 H12–9
- *Umbellularia californica* z7–10 H10–7
- *Yucca brevifolia* z8–10 H10–8

Aesculus californica
CALIFORNIA BUCKEYE

Ⓝ ☼ ◊◊ z7–10 H10–7 ↕25ft (8m) ↔30ft (10m)

A fine native for banks, canyons, and wild gardens, with spring creamy flowers on top of foliage that attracts bees and hummingbirds. Do any pruning in winter.

Fouquiera splendens
OCOTILLO

Ⓝ ☼ ◊◊ z8–10 H10–8 ↕25ft (8m) ↔10ft (3m)

An impressive spring bloom of spires of scarlet flowers that attract hummingbirds. A great plant for hot dry gardens that leafs out several times a year after rain.

WOODY PLANTS

Drought-resistant deciduous trees

Vast areas of the interior Southwest are hot and dry in summer, making cooling shade one of the most important considerations in any landscape. Where winters are cold, deciduous trees give you shade in summer, and sun in winter. They are often cleaner than evergreens, since leaves drop all at once. Trees that cast dappled shade protect garden plants from sunburn.

Acacia willardiana
PALO BLANCO
Ⓝ ☼ ◊◊ Z8–12 H12–8 ‡20ft (6m) ↔10ft (3m)
A small tree for patios, planters, or against walls, its unique bark peels to white in summer. Summer spikes of fuzzy white flowers are shaped like caterpillars.

Acacia schaffneri
SCHAFFNER'S WATTLE, TWISTED ACACIA
☼ ◊◊ Z8–11 H12–10 ‡↔25ft (8m)
This Chihuahuan desert native has thickly spaced, finely divided leaves on short petioles that spring straight from twisted thorny branches. Prune in youth.

Robinia neomexicana
NEW MEXICO LOCUST
Ⓝ ☼ ◊◊ Z5–10 H9–5 ‡25ft (8m) ↔15ft (5m)
Clusters of fragrant flowers appear in June on this often shrubby tree that suckers from roots and creates thorny thickets. It also takes heat and poor soil.

Cercis occidentalis
WESTERN REDBUD
☼ ☼ ◊◊ Z8–10 H12–9 ‡↔20ft (6m)
A large rounded shrub or small tree, often wider than tall. Good on drought-resistant banks. In spring, pea-shaped magenta blooms sprout directly from wood.

Prosopis glandulosa var. glandulosa
HONEY MESQUITE
Ⓝ ☼ ◊◊ Z8–10 H12–10
‡28ft (9m) ↔15ft (5m)
This thorny shrub or small tree is native to desert washes and has fragrant spring flowers and twisted seends.

Celtis reticulata
WESTERN HACKBERRY

Ⓝ ☼ ☀ ◊ Z3–10 H10–3 ↕↔30ft (10m)

A shrub or small tree with rounded uneven growth, pendulous branches, and leaves that are densely netted with veins. Birds love its fruit and deer browse its foliage. A native to moist stream banks.

MORE CHOICES

- Acacia roemeriana Z8–10 H12–10
- Cercidium floridum Z8–11 H12–10
- Cercidium microphyllum Z8–11 H12–8
- Fraxinus cuspidate Z8–11 H12–9
- Prosopis velutina Z8–11 H12–10
- Prunus mume Z6–9 H8–6

Psorothamnus spinosus
SMOKE TREE

☼ ◊◊ Z9–10 H10–9 ↕20ft (6m) ↔15ft (5m)

A large shrub or small tree with a crooked trunk and spiny smokelike branches. In late spring, pea-shaped indigo flowers grow from bare wood. Sparse silver-white foliage appears briefly, then branches stay bare.

Fraxinus angustifolia
MEDITERRANEAN ASH

☼ ◊ Z7–10 H9–6 ↕35ft (11m) ↔25ft (8m)

A small-leaved foliage tree with good branch structure. 'Raywood' (claret ash) needs less irrigation, is available in the West, has purple-red fall color, no seeds, and a compact size.

WOODY PLANTS

Drought-resistant evergreen trees

These stunning beloved trees are heroic in their resistance to drought, but no tree is perfect. Some, including California pepper and silk trees, are best sited at a distance from the house or on banks where their attractive shapes and foliage can be appreciated and bad habits, such as messiness, will not detract. All need regular irrigation to get them started.

Grevillea robusta
SILK OAK
☀ ◊◊◊ Z8–11 H12–8 ↕60ft (18m) ↔35ft (11m)
Orange flowers attract scarlet tanagers and orioles in spring, also when leaves drop messily. This grows in the low desert. Prune to strengthen branches.

Schinus molle
CALIFORNIA PEPPER
☀ ◊◊ Z8–11 H12–8 ↕↔40ft (12m)
Brought by Spanish padres, this is a messy but handsome tree with graceful foliage giving feathery shade. Heat-resistant and fast-growing, it gets Texas root rot and is a magnet for song birds.

Laurus nobilis
SWEET BAY
☀ ☀ ◊ Z8–11 H12–1 ↕↔40ft (12m)
Slow-growing and conelike with edible leaves, this is tub plant in cold zones. 'Saratoga' is resistant to psillid, has broader leaves, and a treelike shape.

Ceratonia siliqua
CAROB, ST. JOHN'S BREAD
☀ ◊◊ Z9–10 H12–10 ↕↔40ft (12m)
A slow-growing, Mediterranean evergreen that grows where citrus grows. Female trees have chocolate-flavored pods, enjoyed by children and animals. Specimens with multiple trunks can be used as a hedge.

Cinnamomum camphora
CAMPHOR TREE
☼ ☼ ◐ ◐ Z8–10 H10–8 ‡50ft (15m) ↔60ft (18m)
This street and shade tree for good drainage has slow growth, a strong trunk, and light green foliage. Keep invasive roots away from pipes and pavement.

Olea europaea
OLIVE TREE
☼ ◐ ◐ Z8–10 H10–8 ‡↔30ft (10m)
Its fast growth slows with age. The smooth gray trunk, finally gnarled, has a wide base. Grow for its olives or choose a fruitless variety. 'Swan Hill' is non-allergenic.

Acacia baileyana
BAILEY'S ACACIA
☼ ◐ ◐ Z9–11 H12–10 ‡30ft (10m) ↔40ft (12m)
Plant multiple trunks on banks or prune as a garden or street tree. Feathery gray foliage bears fragrant blooms in late winter, early spring. Also a purple-leaved type.

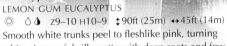

Eucalyptus citriodora
LEMON GUM EUCALYPTUS
☼ ◐ ◐ Z9–10 H10–9 ‡90ft (25m) ↔45ft (14m)
Smooth white trunks peel to fleshlike pink, turning white. A graceful silhouette with deep roots and few fallen leaves. Plant a row to hide a building.

MORE CHOICES

- *Acca sellowiana* Z10–11 H12–9
- *Callistemon viminalis* Z10–15 H12–10
- *Casuarina stricta* Z9–15 H12–10
- *Eriobotrya japonica* Z8–11 H12–8
- *Leptospermum laevigatum* Z9–10 H10–9
- *Lophostemon confertus* Z9–15 H12–10
- *Melaleuca lanariifolia* Z9–12 H12–10
- *Photinia arbutifolia* Z8–10 H10–9
- *Quercus agrifolia* Z9–11 H12–9
- *Schinus terebinthifolius* Z9–11 H12–9

Trees for wet soil

Although all of these trees will tolerate wet soil, their individual ranges of requirements vary widely. Some, such as California sycamore, like wet soil but must have good drainage. Others, such as weeping willow, thrive in a wet spot with or without good drainage. Carrotwood and paperbark can take wet or dry soils. They are drought-resistant yet pests in Florida swamps.

Umbellularia californica
CALIFORNIA LAUREL

Ⓝ ☼ ☼ ☼ ◐ ◐ Z7–10 H9–7 ↕↔75ft (23m)

The size above refers to the wild plant. In gardens, it is slow-growing to 25ft (8m). The bay leaves are edible but strong, so when cooking use a half a leaf.

Magnolia virginiana
SWEET BAY MAGNOLIA

Ⓝ ☼ ☼ ◐ pH Z6–10 H9–6 ↕50ft (15m) ↔20ft (6m)

A swamp plant from the East Coast with fragrant flowers in spring and summer. A deciduous shrub in colder climates; a big evergreen in warm.

Populus fremontii
WESTERN COTTONWOOD

Ⓝ ☼ ◐ Z3–10 H10–1 ↕60ft (18m) ↔30ft (10m)

Grows near streambeds with green summer foliage, bright yellow in fall. 'Nevada' is a fine male variety. A tough tree for hot summers and cold winters.

MORE CHOICES

- *Alnus rhombifolia* Z5–9 H9–5
- *Betula nigra* Z4–9 H9–1
- *Carpinus caroliniana* Z3–9 H9–1
- *Casuarina cunninghamiana* Z8–10 H12–10
- *Celtis laevigata* Z5–9 H9–3
- *Clethra arborea* Z8–9 H9–8
- *Cupaniopsis anacardioides* Z9–13 H12–10
- *Liquidambar styraciflua* Z6–10 H9–6
- *Melaleuca viridiflora* var. *rubriflora* Z9–11 H12–10
- *Platanus wrightii* Z7–9 H9–7
- *Robinia neomexicana* Z5–10 H9–5
- *Salix babylonica* Z6–10 H9–1
- *Sequoia sempervirens* Z8–9 H9–8
- *Thuja occidentalis* Z2–8 H7–1
- *Washingtonia filifera* Z8–11 H11–8

Alnus cordata
ITALIAN ALDER
☼ ◐ ● Z5–9 H7–5 ‡40ft (12m) ↔25ft (8m)
From Corsica, Italy, this fast-growing tree is a vertical spire in youth, then spreads. Popular in low deserts, near creeks, this can be a shade tree or a tall screen.

Platanus racemosa
CALIFORNIA SYCAMORE
Ⓝ ☼ ●● Z8–10 H8–5 ‡80ft (25m) ↔50ft (15m)
Can take much or little water given adequate drainage. Grows in lawns May get Anthracnose fungus if not annually sprayed, but can survive without it.

Acer rubrum
RED MAPLE
Ⓝ ☼◐ ●● Z3–10 H9–1 ‡60ft (18m) ↔40ft (12m)
A fall-color tree that comes from low moist spots in eastern US. Needs non-polluted air. Varieties offer many colors and shapes, from columns to spreading.

Castanospermum australe
MORETON BAY CHESTNUT
☼ ● Z9–12 H12–10 ‡60ft (18m) ↔50ft (15m)
An attractive landscape tree with edible nuts if roasted. Needs much irrigation or a streamside site. Yellow-red, summer flowers appear on stiff stems from main trunk.

Acer macrophyllum
BIGLEAF MAPLE
Ⓝ ☼◐ ●● Z5–10 H9–4 ‡75ft (23m) ↔50ft (15m)
Native to streambeds and moist canyons from Alaska to California, this has winged seeds and a yellow fall color in cold-winter climates. Grow where adapted.

WOODY PLANTS

Trees for adobe soil

Historically, adobe clay was sun-baked into bricks for Southwestern houses and walls, and red or white clay was used for pottery. In gardens, all clays bake hard in the sun and suffer from poor drainage. Fortunately, clay soils are rich in minerals and can be improved by amending (*see p. 30*). Certain plants, including these trees, grow well in heavy clay.

Washingtonia robusta
MEXICAN FAN PALM
Ⓝ ☼ ◊◑ Z9–13 H12–10 ‡100ft (30m) ↔10ft (3m)
More drought-tolerant than the thread-bearing *W. filifera* (California fan palm), this tree has more compact foliage heads and a taller thinner trunk. When mature, no threads are borne on leaves.

Betula nigra 'Heritage'
HERITAGE RIVER BIRCH
Ⓝ ☼ ◑ Z4–9 H9–1 ‡70ft (20m) ↔60ft (18m)
Native from streambeds in eastern North America, this easiest of birches has pink peeling bark when young, then cinnamon peeling bark. Popular in lawns, this is often planted by homesick easterners.

Syzygium paniculatum
EUGENIA
☼ ☀ ◑◑ Z10–11 H12–1 ‡60ft (18m) ↔20ft (6m)
A columnar tree usually used for hedges that can be clipped into arches and bears edible but tasteless fruit. Eugenia psylllid disfigures foliage, but beneficials have been introduced to control it.

Pyrus kawakamii
EVERGREEN PEAR
☼ ◑ Z9–11 H12–9 ‡↔30ft (10m)
A popular small tree. Fireblight, spread by birds, causes dieback of branches. If this occurs, prune out dead wood in winter and destroy. In its best years, foliage is hidden by blossoms in February.

Morus alba
WHITE MULBERRY

☼ ● Z4–10 H8–1
↕↔50ft (15m)
Fast-growing and
deciduous, this is often
smaller than full size. Tolerant
of wind, poor soil, coast, or desert.
Stake when young. 'Fruitless' is best
for shade; 'Pendula' is a weeping form.

Nerium oleander
OLEANDER

☼ ☼ ◊● Z9–13 H12–1 ↕20ft (6m) ↔12ft (4m)
A shrub available as a small staked tree, this is a fine
desert plant, though poisonous and threatened by
glassy-winged sharpshooter. Blooms spring to fall.

Sophora japonica
JAPANESE PAGODA TREE

☼ ● Z5–9 H9–5 ↕↔70ft (20m)
A fine-looking deciduous shade tree where summers
are hot with creamy clusters of bloom. Young gray-
green wood is smooth; bark furrows with age.

MORE CHOICES

- *Cercis occidentalis* z8–10 H12–9
- *Eucalyptus citriodora* z9–10 H10–9
- *Eucalyptus rudis* z9–10 H10–9
- *Eucalyptus sideroxylon* z9–11 H12–9
- *Fraxinus velutina* 'Modesto' z6–9 H8–4
- *Jacaranda mimosifolia* z10–15 H12–10
- *Liriodendron tulipifera* z5–10 H9–1
- *Magnolia grandiflora* 'Magestic Beauty'
  z6–10 H9–7
- *Quercus suber* z7–9 H9–7
- *Rhus lancea* z7–9 H8–1
- *Ulmus parvifolia* 'True Green' z7–10 H9–7

Zelkova serrata 'Japanese Selko'
SAWLEAF ZELKOVA

☼ ◊● Z7–10 H9–7 ↕100ft (30m) ↔10ft (3m)
A spreading variety of an Asian tree grown in place of
an American elm, this can survive Dutch elm disease
and has smooth gray bark and saw-edged leaves.

Large subtropical flowering trees

Imagine an avenue of jacarandas in full bloom, or a single floss silk tree lighting up a neighborhood. This is what planting subtropical trees can achieve. Two or three of these spectacular trees give you color year round. Most are easy to grow and many are drought-resistant, including the silk oak, the gold medallion tree, and coral trees.

Magnolia x *veitchii*
VEITCH MAGNOLIA
☼ ☼ ◐ Z6–10 H9–6 ‡↔30ft (10m)
One of the best deciduous magnolias for southern California, it blooms on bare wood like *M. soulangeana*. Not for hot dry climates; needs some chill.

Brachychiton acerifolius
AUSTRALIAN FLAME TREE
☼ ◐ Z10–15 H12–8 ‡60ft (18m) ↔30ft (10m)
A fun-to-grow tree with a heavy green trunk. Blooms depend on rain, sun, and temperature. Spring brings an all-over bloom; other times only a portion may bloom.

Paulownia tomentosa
EMPRESS TREE
☼ ◐ Z5–9 H8–5 ‡50ft (15m) ↔45ft (14m)
Flower buds form in fall and open in spring with a big show on bare branches, but the climate must be right: if winters are too cold, buds freeze; if too warm, buds fall off. Foliage looks tropical.

Erythrina crista-galli
COCKSPUR CORAL-TREE
☼ ◐ Z9–12 H12–8 ‡↔20ft (6m)
Very attractive with big clusters of red or pink flowers on branch tips several times a year, this tree has handsome rough bark. Hard frosts make it a shrub.

MORE CHOICES

- *Albizia julibrissin* 'Rosea' z6–10 h9–6
- *Bauhinia variegata* z10–15 h12–10
- *Bombax ceiba* z13–15 h12–10
- *Calodendrum capense* z9–15 h12–10
- *Cassia leptophylla* z10–12 h12–10
- *Chorisia speciosa* z9–14 h12–10
- *Dombeya x cayeuxii* z10–15 h12–10
- *Erythrina caffra* z10–11 h12–10
- *Erythrina lysistemon* z10–12 h12–9
- *Eucalyptus erythrocorys* z9–10 h10–9
- *Eucalyptus sideroxylon* z9–11 h12–9
- *Grevillea robusta* z10–11 h12–3
- *Markhamia hildebrandtii* z10–11 h12–10
- *Stenocarpus sinuatus* z10 h12–10
- *Tipuana tipu* z9–15 h12–10

Callistemon viminalis
WEEPING BOTTLEBRUSH

☼ ◐◑ z10–15 h12–10 ↕30ft (10m) ↔15ft (5m)

A weeping tree favored by birds for nesting, the cascade of spring and summer flowers are beloved by hummingbirds. Good in a sheltered spot.

Eucalyptus ficifolia
FLAME EUCALYPTUS

☼ ◐◑ z9–10 h10–9

↕45ft (14m) ↔60ft (18m)

Best on the coast, even on ocean front, the massive bloom appears in summer with benign neglect. Cut off heavy pods every few years. Choose color when the tree is in bloom.

Cassia fistula
GOLDEN SHOWER TREE

☼ ◐ z11–12 h12–10

↕50ft (15m) ↔45ft (14m)

A spectacular flowering tree for Hawaii that blooms better with a little water. *C. leptophylla,* or the gold medallion tree, grows 25ft (8m) tall and 30ft (10m) wide, and is best for planting in southern California.

Jacaranda mimosifolia
BLUE JACARANDA

☼ ◐ z10–15 h12–10 ↕40ft (12m) ↔30ft (10m)

Despite littering and invasive roots, no tree is more desirable in a warm sunny spot. Never plant on the coast or in cold wind, or it will not bloom.

WOODY PLANTS

Trees for tropical gardens

All these trees flourish in Hawaii, and some grow well on the mainland in sheltered coves and coastal banana belts. Favorable microclimates also exist a few miles inland, in steep canyons where cold air slides downhill, or on south-facing, frost-free hillsides. In these special places, tropical and subtropical trees thrive in home-grown jungles among other exotic plants.

Jacaranda mimosifolia
BLUE JACARANDA
☼ ◊ Z10–15 H12–10
↕40ft (12m) ↔30ft (10m)
This blooms at various times in Hawaii, usually June on the mainland, often on bare wood. Give it warmth, facing south or east, out of wind, with reflected heat from a street, patio, or buildings.

Cyathea medullaris
BLACK TREE FERN
☼ ◊◊ Z10–11 H12–10
↕50ft (15m) ↔20ft (6m)
Common in Hawaii, this is a fast-growing, wide-spreading fern with black-stemmed leaves that arch upwards from a black trunk. Plant it in a canyon bottom to see from above.

Spathodea campanulata
AFRICAN TULIP TREE
☼ ◊ Z10–14 H12–10 ↕75ft (23m) ↔50ft (15m)
Orange or red flowers blossom year round in Hawaii, where roots can be invasive. On the mainland, it blooms all summer in a frost-free spot.

Cassia fistula
GOLDEN SHOWER TREE
☼ ◊ Z11–12 H12–10 ↕40ft (12m) ↔35ft (11m)
One of several shower trees for Hawaii. Others include C. javanica (pink and white shower tree) and C. x nealiae 'Wilhemina Telley' (rainbow shower tree).

Tabebuia impetiginosa
PINK TRUMPET TREE
☼ ◊ Z9–11 H12–9 ↕40ft (12m) ↔30ft (10m)
Excellent in Hawaii. Elsewhere, grow it in sheltered spots out of the wind. In youth, prune for strength and shape. Blossoms appear on bare limbs in spring.

MORE CHOICES

- *Albizia lebbeck* Z9–11 H12–10
- *Cassia grandis* Z10–11 H12–10
- *Cassia javanica* Z10–11 H12–10
- *Cassia x nealiae* Z10–12 H12–10
- *Colvillea racemosa* Z10–11 H12–10
- *Cordia sebestena* Z10–11 H12–10
- *Cordia subcordata* Z10–11 H12–10
- *Cybistax donnell-smithii* Z12–13 H12–10
- *Plumeria obtusa* Z10–12 H12–10
- *Plumeria rubra* 'Hawaiian Yellow' Z10–12 H12–10
- *Samanea saman* Z10–11 H11–10

Kigelia pinnata
SAUSAGE TREE

☼ ◑ Z10–11 H12–10 ↕40ft (12m) ↔30ft (10m)

A conversation piece with exotic red hanging flowers that smell unpleasant at night, followed by smooth hanging fruits on a vigorous green tree. In Africa, elephants relish the fruit.

Delonix regia
FLAMBOYANT TREE

☼ ◑ Z11–12 H10 ↕30ft (10m) ↔50ft (15m)

In Hawaii, this has a low-spreading dome that gives open shade; a lawn can survive under its outer edges. Late-winter, early-summer blooms paint the tree orange or scarlet.

Metrosideros excelsa
NEW ZEALAND CHRISTMAS TREE

☼ ◐ ◑ Z10–11 H12–10

↕↔30ft (10m)

Blooms in ocean wind, spring and summer, in coastal California; higher elevations in Hawaii. Prune after bloom but do not overprune. New, light gray foliage turns to dark green.

Thevetia peruviana
YELLOW OLEANDER

☼ ◑◐ Z10–15 H12–10

↕↔30ft (10m)

A small tree in Hawaii, and shrub on the mainland, this is a good front-yard plant that survives with neglect in frost-free gardens and blooms year-round if warm.

Brachychiton acerifolius
AUSTRALIAN FLAME TREE

☼ ◑◐ Z10–12 H12–8

↕40ft (12m) ↔30ft (10m)

Leaves drop on sections of this tree prior to bloom. Its canoe-shaped, woody fruits are loved by flower arrangers. *B. discolor* has pink flowers and a bottle-shaped trunk.

Trees for Mediterranean-style gardens

The Mediterranean style of garden design is based on the stunning landscapes we see in countries surrounding the Mediterranean Sea. All the trees listed here can withstand the long summer drought and strong sunshine of Mediterranean climates (*see p. 38*), and will lend the romantic atmosphere of old Spain or Italy to Southern California and interior gardens.

Populus nigra 'Italica'
LOMBARDY POPLAR
☼ ◊ Z3–9 H9–1
↕100ft (30m) ↔15ft (5m)
Good in dry interior zones, not coastal. White bark, yellow foliage in autumn. Takes wind, cold, and desert heat. Needs irrigation unless roots reach ground water. Suckers profusely.

Arbutus unedo
STRAWBERRY TREE
☼ ☼ ◊◊
Z8–10 H9–6 ↕↔25ft (8m)
Drought- and disease-resistant, easy care. Good for both small or large gardens, slow growth. Flowers, followed by edible but tasteless fruits – loved by birds – provide almost year-round color.

Citrus meyeri 'Improved'
MEYER LEMON
☼ ◊◊ Z9–11 H12–1
↕6–22ft (2–7m) ↔5–10ft (1.5–3m)
Sweet lemons, excellent for cooking. Fragrant flowers, neat shape. Water deeply, rather than often, more frequently in containers. Wash off pests. Fertilize regularly during warm months.

Pinus pinea
STONE PINE, UMBRELLA PINE
☼ ◊ Z9–10 H12–9 ↕50–70ft (15–20m) ↔20–40ft (6–12m)
Often bought as a tiny Christmas tree, becomes a thick-trunked, domed giant, dropping lower branches. Fertilize in spring, water deeply in late summer, early fall to ward off beetles.

Punica granatum 'Wonderful'
WONDERFUL POMEGRANATE

☼ ◊ z8–11 H12–1 ↕↔8–10ft (2.5–3m)

Good for west-facing wall with reflected heat. Prune to show off large globelike hanging fruits that make great jelly. Takes drought, but better fruit with irrigation. Not good along coast. 'Eversweet' has fewer seeds.

Quercus suber
CORK OAK

☼ ◊ z7–10 H9–7 ↕↔70ft (20m)

Massive trunk, textural bark contrasts well with shape of evergreen foliage. Good on dry banks, as shade tree, in groves. Slow growth. Needs drainage, water to establish.

Cedrus atlantica f. glauca
BLUE ATLAS CEDAR

☼ ◊ z6–10 H9–6 ↕to 130ft (40m) ↔30ft (10m)

Lifelong silvery gray foliage, open growth. Grows well near coast. In youth, pinch back long branches to strengthen. Support long heavy branches against breakage in snow. Slow growth.

MORE CHOICES

- *Arbutus andrachne* z7–9 H9–7
- *Ceratonia siliqua* z9–10 H12–10
- *Chamaerops humilis* z9–10 H12–10
- *Cupressus sempervirens* 'Stricta' z8–10 H10–8
- *Ficus carica* 'Mission' z7–10 H9–5
- *Olea europaea* z8–10 H10–8
- *Phoenix canariensis* z9–12 H12–10
- *Pinus canariensis* z9–10 H10–9
- *Pinus halepensis* z9–10 H10–9

Cedrus libani
CEDAR OF LEBANON

☼ ◊ z6–10 H9–3 ↕↔100ft (30m)

Stays small, narrow, pyramidical with bright green foliage for many years. Largely trouble-free, no pruning needed. In Europe some of these trees reach age 500.

Quercus ilex
HOLLY OAK, HOLM OAK

☼ ◊◊ z4–9 H9–2 ↕80ft (25m) ↔70ft (20m)

Smooth gray bark and lance-shaped leaves. Takes salt air or desert winds. Fast-growing, slow along coast. More disease-resistant than native oaks. Can be sheared as hedge.

WOODY PLANTS

Medium flowering trees for mild zones

If you yearn for flowers but lack time for gardening, plant subtropical flowering trees. They put on a great show with little care. Medium-sized trees allow you to extend the bloom season by planting more than one. A stunning way to display these spectacular trees is to place them against a plain background that enhances the color of the blossoms.

Chionanthus retusus
CHINESE FRINGE TREE
☼ ◐◗ Z5–10 H9–3 ↕20ft (6m) ↔15ft (5m)
Breathtaking and white all over when in bloom, fill a parking lot with this tree or, for an element of surprise, hide it around a corner against green trees or a blue sky.

Albizia julibrissin 'Rosea'
SILK TREE, RED MIMOSA
☼ ☼ ◗ Z6–10 H9–6 ↕40ft (12m) ↔80ft (25m)
A fast-growing, low spreading tree with summer flowers that loves heat. For a smaller size, cut back to 10–20ft (3–6m); it is stunning from above.

Koelreuteria bipinnata
CHINESE FLAME TREE
☼ ◐◗ Z6–10 H9–1 ↕↔40ft (12m)
Deep-rooted with no mess, its yellow summer flowers are followed by salmon-colored pods. The attractive foliage drops annually. Blooms poorly in ocean breeze.

MORE CHOICES

- *Erythrina coralloides* Z10–12 H12–10
- *Eucalyptus leucoxylon* subsp. *megalocarpa* Z9–11 H10–9
- *Hymenosporum flavum* Z10–11 H12–9
- *Melaleuca linariifolia* Z10–12 H12–10
- *Stenocarpus sinuatus* Z9–12 H12–10
- *Tabebuia impetiginosa* Z9–11 H12–9

Bauhinia x *blakeana*
HONG KONG ORCHID TREE
☼ ◐◗ Z9–11 H12–10 ↕↔20ft (6m)
Good in a low raised bed, shaded from wind. If cool, its leaves will not drop off. Fall-to-spring blooms appear all over the tree when it is in a warm spot.

Small flowering trees for mild zones

Small flowering trees have a wide variety of uses. They are good choices for patios, planter boxes, parking strips, or as street trees for narrow spaces. In gardens, they can take the place of umbrellas, providing shade for a chair or a bench. They also can be used as sentinels, flanking an entryway, or combined into a miniature avenue, lining straight paths or steps.

Magnolia stellata
STAR MAGNOLIA
☼ ☼ ◐ Z5–10 H9–5 ‡10ft (3m) ↔20ft (6m)
Deciduous white blooms appear in earliest spring. Some varieties are fragrant. Plant early-blooming bulbs beneath. Elegant in front of evergreens.

Rhaphiolepis indica 'Majestic Beauty'
INDIAN HAWTHORN TREE
☼ ☼ ◐◐ Z9–11 H12–7 ‡20ft (6m) ↔10ft (3m)
These clean, healthy, easy-care trees have larger leaves and a thicker trunk than the shrub varieties and light or dark pink spring flowers. Needs little pruning.

Michelia doltsopa
BANANA SHRUB
☼ ☼ ◐ Z9–11 H12–1 ‡25ft (8m) ↔15ft (5m)
A lushly foliaged, fragrant magnolia relative with a profuse winter bloom but slightly messy. Selections may be upright or lower and wider. Prune when young.

Luma apiculata
LEMON-LEAF MYRTLE
☼ ◐◐ Z9–11 H12–10 ‡↔20ft (6m)
A large shrub or small tree from Chile, with lemon-scented foliage, and flaking cinnamon bark. Flowers midsummer to midautumn and gets mites in shade.

MORE CHOICES

- *Acacia baileyana* 'Purpurea' Z10–11 H12–10
- *Brachychiton rupestris* Z10–11 H12–10
- *Cercis occidentalis* Z8–10 H12–9
- *Lagerstroemia indica* 'Tonto' Z7–9 H9–7
- *Leptospermum scoparium* 'Ruby Glow' Z9–10 H10–9
- *Pyrus kawakamii* Z9–11 H12–9

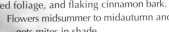

Conifers for mild-winter zones

Some people glance at any tree with needles and cones and instantly suppose it is a pine tree, but although all pines are conifers, not all conifers are pines. "Conifer" is a popular name for a few deciduous and many evergreen trees that have needlelike foliage and conelike fruits, including pines, cypress, sequoias, and more than twenty other groups.

Pinus canariensis
CANARY ISLAND PINE

☼ ◗ ◑ Z9–10 H10–9 ↕80ft (25m) ↔35ft (11m)

With red bark that sunburns and cascading long needles, this upright tree is narrow for many years, then spreads on top. Do not cut off more than 20 percent of its foliage at one time.

Cedrus deodara
DEODAR CEDAR

☼ ◗ Z6–11 H9–6

↕80ft (25m) ↔40ft (12m)

A fast-growing Himalayan tree for a large lawn or wide street. The top of the tree bends and graceful branches weep with upward tips. For a thick, formal Christmas tree, cut back branches in late spring.

Pinus patula
MEXICAN WEEPING PINE

Ⓝ ☼ ◗ ⃝ Z8–11 H9–8 ↕80ft (25m) ↔40ft (12m)

A fast-growing tropical pine from Mexican mountains, this arresting pyramid casts light shade and has draping foliage, red bark, and spaced-out branches.

Araucaria heterophylla
NORFOLK ISLAND PINE

☼ ◗ z9–11 H12–9 ↕100ft (30m) ↔60ft (18m)

An evergreen conifer with large cones, this is a lovely silhouette on Hawaiian coastlines and in Southern California gardens. Leave the lower branches on tree.

MORE CHOICES

- *Juniperus chinensis* 'Torulosa' Z6–10 H9–1
- *Pinus pinea* Z9–11 H12–9
- *Pinus thunbergii* Z5–9 H8–5
- *Podocarpus gracilior* Z7–11 H12–7

WOODY PLANTS

Conifers for interior zones

Some of these trees are appropriate for higher elevations; others survive in desert wind and heat but may need more water in summer. All need good drainage. Some conifers, especially pine trees, need shaping, at least in youth. You can make pine trees denser by cutting back new growth, known as "candles," in spring. To slow growth, cut the candles off.

Pinus densiflora 'Umbraculifera'
JAPANESE RED PINE
☼ ● Z4–9 H7–1 ↕12ft (4m) ↔20ft (6m)
A fast-growing, red-barked tree that dislikes extreme heat or cold and is best inland a few miles from a foggy coast. 'Umbraculifera' is a dwarf shrubby form.

Cryptomeria japonica 'Elegans'
JAPANESE PLUME CEDAR
☼ ● Z6–9 H9–4 ↕60ft (18m) ↔20ft (6m)
Dense and grayish green in summer, purple-bronze in winter, this tree's trunk bends. For a peeling-bark, Oriental look, prune out some branches for layers.

Cupressus arizonica var. glabra
ARIZONA CYPRESS
Ⓝ ☼ ◐● Z6–9 H9–2 ↕40ft (12m) ↔20ft (6m)
In youth, this is squat and spreading with smooth bark. It becomes conical with age, with shredding brown or red bark and thick gray foliage. Use as a screen.

Pinus edulis
PIÑON PINE
Ⓝ ☼ ◐● Z5–9 H8–3 ↕20ft (6m) ↔15ft (5m)
Thick and scrubby in youth, prune to enhance its natural shape that will spread. Good in drought-resistant rock gardens, its edible nuts have wild shapes.

Abies nordmanniana
NORDMANN FIR
☼ ◐ ● Z4–6 H6–4 ↕50ft (15m) ↔20ft (6m)
Slow-growing near the coast and faster inland, this has an upright cone shape, needs little pruning, and can grow in a container for several years. Birds like seeds.

Calocedrus decurrens
INCENSE CEDAR
Ⓝ ☼ ◐ ◐● Z5–9 H8–5 ↕90ft (25m) ↔15ft (5m)
An evergreen from Oregon to Baja, this takes extreme heat and drought in stride. This narrow symmetrical cone needs space for expansion and is fragrant in sun.

MORE CHOICES

- *Juniperus chinensis* 'Torulosa' Z6–10 H9–1
- *Pinus pinea* Z9–11 H12–9
- *Pinus thunbergii* Z5–9 H8–5
- *Podocarpus gracilior* Z7–11 H12–7

WOODY PLANTS

Conifers for mountain zones

Conifers are truly impressive specimens. They include the most massive, oldest, and tallest of all living things. They are resinous, mostly evergreen, with central upright trunks and tiers of branches. Their leaves are usually needlelike, as in pines; flatter as in yews; or scalelike, as in cypresses. Most are hardy forest trees, bearing seeds in cones.

Juniperus scopulorum 'Skyrocket'
SKYROCKET JUNIPER

Ⓝ ☼ ☼ ◊ ◖ ◕ Z3–10 H7–1 ‡20ft (6m) ↔2ft (60cm)

A thin, blue, drought-resistant column, 10ft (3m) high in 10 years, 20ft (6m) in 20, it looks rocketlike when planted alone. In a row, it makes a good screen with no pruning. Endorsed by the US National Arboretum.

Pinus cembra
SWISS STONE PINE

☼ ◕ Z3–9 H7–1

‡70ft (20m) ↔25ft (8m)

A dense, blue-gray pyramid when young, attractive on lawns or in an irrigated garden as it cannot take intense heat. In age, it is picturesque with a wide head. Cones are purple.

Pseudotsuga menziesii
DOUGLAS FIR

Ⓝ ☼ ☼ ◊ ◖ ◕ Z5–8 H7–5 ‡160ft (50m) ↔30ft (10m)

A lumber tree of the Northwest, this is a great garden tree when young, with a pointed shape. Low branches drop off with age; it becomes tall and wide-spreading.

Pinus aristata
BRISTLECONE PINE

Ⓝ ☼ ◊ ◕ Z2–10 H9–1 ‡40ft (12m) ↔15ft (5m)

Small pines, shrublike in youth for a rock garden or pots, form unique sculptures with age. Wild groves in Arizona, Colorado, and New Mexico date to 500 BC.

Sequoiadendron giganteum
GIANT SEQUOIA

Ⓝ ☼ ◕ Z6–9 H9–4

‡100ft (30m) ↔50ft (15m)

Slower-growing, hardier, and more drought-resistant than *Sequoia sempervirens*, this is a dense pyramid in youth. It may get diseases in mild zones; use in cold-winter climates.

MORE CHOICES

- *Abies bracteata* Z7–8 H8–7
- *Abies lasiocarpa* Z5–6 H6–5
- *Abies magnifica* Z6–8 H8–6
- *Pinus coulteri* Z8–9 H9–8
- *Pinus jeffreyi* Z6–8 H8–6

Deciduous trees for mountain zones

When planting trees in mountain gardens, most homeowners think first of evergreen conifers. But deciduous trees provide colorful fall foliage and interesting branch structure when covered with snow in winter. Birds appreciate their foliage and seeds. Prune these trees, if necessary, after they have dropped their leaves in fall.

Acer macrophyllum
OREGON MAPLE
Ⓝ ☼ ◐ ◗◖ Z5–10 H9–4
↕80ft (25m) ↔50ft (15m)
The light green foliage dome gives shade and turns gold in fall. Bare winter branches appear on a red-brown, furrowed trunk. For a large garden.

Acer saccharinum
SUGAR MAPLE
Ⓝ ☼ ☀ ◐◖ Z4–8 H8–1
↕60ft (18m) ↔40ft (12m)
A hardwood garden tree in cold-winter areas of the West that gives sap in climates where frosts and thaws often alternate. Red, orange, and yellow fall color.

Quercus muehlenbergii
CHINQUAPIN OAK
Ⓝ ☼ ◐◖ Z4–9 H8–2 ↕50 ft (15m) ↔60ft (18m)
A long-lived eastern forest oak that was cut for fences, steamboat fuel, or railroad ties, gives summer shade, a reddish gold fall color, and leaf edges like saw blades.

MORE CHOICES

- *Alnus tenuifolia* Z6–8 H8–6
- *Cercocarpus ledifolius* Z6–9 H9–6
- *Populus tremuloides* Z1–8 H8–1
- *Sorbus scopulina* Z6–8 H8–6
- *Ulmus wilsoniana* 'Prospector' Z4–9 H9–1

Populus tremula 'Pendula'
EUROPEAN WEEPING ASPEN
☼ ◖ Z2–8 H8–1 ↕20ft (6m) ↔25ft (8m)
This invasive, European tree has long pendent branches and foliage that moves in slightest breeze. It may get beetles; *Populus tremuloides* is more reliable.

Fraxinus velutina
ARIZONA ASH
Ⓝ ☼ ◖ Z6–10 H9–6 ↕30ft (10m) ↔40ft (12m)
A soft-wooded shade tree, a cone in youth that spreads with age, for cold winters or desert heat. 'Montebello', 'Modesto', and 'Fan Tex' hybrids available.

Small trees for patios

Small trees serve many purposes in patios. They can give you fruit to pick and eat, shade to lounge in, atmosphere to feed your spirit, as well as flowers, fragrance, or a memory of a distant place you love. Before looking for a tree, write down your personal requirements, plus the measurements of the planting area and its degree of sun and shade.

Ficus carica 'Brown Turkey'
EDIBLE FIG
☼ ◐ Z7–11 H12–7 ↕↔30ft (10m)
With large deciduous leaves, this can be espaliered, gives dense shade and a Mediterranean atmosphere, and grows where figs do, including the coast. Smaller in pots, this has big crops of brownish purple fruit.

Plumeria rubra
RED FRANGIPANGI
☼ ◐ Z10–15 H12–10 ↕35ft (11m) ↔20ft (6m)
A fragrant garden tree in Hawaii with many varieties, this gives a tropical atmosphere and is hardier than the white type in frost-free California. Grow from cuttings in spring – can be in a pot.

Phoenix robelinii
PYGMY DATE PALM
☼ ◑ ◐◐ Z9–12 H12–10 ↕10ft (3m) ↔6ft (2m)
This small, long-lived, slow-growing palm gives a tropical atmosphere but is a shade plant for the desert. Its trunk curves to light if not in sun. It browns in frost.

Wisteria floribunda 'Alba'
JAPANESE WISTERIA
☼ ◐ Z5–10 H9–5
↕8ft (2.5m) ↔5ft (1.5m)
This climber makes a fine, spring-flowering tree for containers or the ground. In summer, shear often to maintain desired tree shape and rub off sprouts on trunk. Fertilize lightly when young.

Acer japonicum
JAPANESE MAPLE
☼ ◑ ◐ pH Z5–10 H7–1 ↕↔30ft (10m)
Many varieties in nurseries are tricky as they often die. For reliability and fall color, plant from a backyard seedling and grow in a semishaded patio or a big tub.

MORE CHOICES

- *Acer palmatum* Z5–10 H8–2
- *Anisodontea* x *hypomandarum* Z10–11 H12–10
- *Arbutus unedo* 'Elfin King' Z7–10 H9–6
- *Brugmansia cubensis* 'Charles Grimaldi' Z10–15 H12–1
- *Cassia leptophylla* Z10–12 H12–10
- *Citrus* 'Ponderosa' Z9–10 H10–8
- *Eriobotrya deflexa* Z8–12 H12–8
- *Nerium oleander* Z9–15 H12–1
- *Pinus mugo* Z3–10 H7–1
- *Syringa vulgaris* 'Lavender Lady' Z4–10 H8–1
- *Tibouchina urvilleana* Z10–15 H12–10

Small flowering trees for front yards

When guests arrive, it is nice to have colorful plants saying hello even before they ring the bell. When one of these small trees is in full bloom, you may notice a guest's first remark will be to compliment the display. None of these choices are too large to fit in most front yards, though Bailey's acacia is best for lining drives or leaning over a country fence.

Acacia baileyana
BAILEY'S ACACIA
☼ ◊◗ Z9–11 H12–10
↕30ft (10m) ↔40ft (12m)
Not for manicured gardens, this exudes informal grace, fragrance, and a country atmosphere. Fernlike foliage is weighed down by yellow bloom in February.

Lagerstroemia indica 'Catawba'
CRAPE MYRTLE
☼ ☼ ◗ Z7–13 H12–3
↕10ft (3m) ↔6ft (2m)
This outstanding year-round appearance has spring foliage, summer flowers, fall color, handsome bark, and a shapely trunk after the leaves fall. Mildew-resistant, but do not plant on the coast.

Leptospermum scoparium
NEW ZEALAND TEA TREE
☼ ◊◗ Z9–12 H12–3 ↕10ft (3m) ↔6ft (2m)
Spectacular with long-lasting winter color and cut flowers; a twisted trunk; and masses of tiny pink, red, or white flowers that cover foliage. Prune after bloom.

MORE CHOICES

- *Acacia baileyana* 'Purpurea' Z9–11 H12–10
- *Brachychiton rupestris* Z10–12 H12–10
- *Cercis canadensis* 'Forest Pansy' Z6–10 H9–6
- *Cercis occidentalis* Z8–10 H12–9
- *Leptospermum scoparium* 'Ruby Glow' Z9–12 H10–9
- *Magnolia* x *soulangiana* Z5–10 H9–5
- *Rhaphiolepis indica* 'Magestic Beauty' Z7–11 H12–7

Cotinus coggygria
SMOKE TREE
☼ ☼ ◊◗ Z5–10 H9–3 ↕↔25ft (8m)
A shrub or tree for all zones, good in Texas, place this on the east or west side of a mound, so sunlight shines through. Spent flower stems are lavender-pink.

Trees for use near swimming pools

Trees near swimming pools need to be clean, with large, long-lasting leaves. Some of them will hang onto their leaves forever, or at least long enough for them to be clipped off. Others drop leaves but not often. Large leaves lend a tropical atmosphere and are easy to fish out of the water if one blows in. Make sure to plant trees north of the pool to avoid shade.

Schefflera actinophylla
QUEENSLAND UMBRELLA TREE
☼ ◐ ⬤ Z10–15 H12–10 ↕↔40ft (12m)
A fast-growing, easy tropical tree. Plant 2–3ft (60–90cm) from walls to protect foundations. Unless cut back, all foliage will be atop long leaning trunks.

Rhaphiolepis indica 'Majestic Beauty'
INDIAN HAWTHORN TREE
☼ ◐ ⬤⬤ Z7–11 H12–7 ↕20ft (6m) ↔10ft (3m)
A perfect umbrella that needs good drainage and has few, if any, falling leaves. Prune after bloom if necessary. Pruning in fall or winter prevents bloom. Vigorous ones are darker pink.

Cordyline australis 'Variegata'
VARIEGATED DRACAENA
☼ ◐⬤ Z9–11 H12–1 ↕30ft (10m) ↔12ft (4m)
With many colorful varieties, this tropical tree has thin trunks from a thick base. Cut back a single trunk where you want it to branch. Dead leaves hang on.

Cordyline indivisa
BLUE DRACAENA, MOUNTAIN CABBAGE TREE
☼◐ ⬤ Z9–10 H12–1 ↕25ft (8m) ↔10ft (3m)
Like a stiff, upright, thick-trunked yucca with lacy summer panicles of white flowers, this tolerates oceanfront. A crown of stiff leaves hangs on until cut.

Musa acuminata 'Zebrina'
VARIEGATED ORNAMENTAL BANANA
☼◐ ⬤ Z10–15 H12–7 ↕↔10ft (3m)
A tropical treelike perennial with inedible fruit for a warm garden with no wind. Needs water, humus-rich soil, and frequent feedings. Cut down faded stalks.

MORE CHOICES

- *Cyathea cooperi* Z10–12 H12–10
- *Eriobotrya deflexa* Z8–12 H12–8
- *Ficus auriculata* Z10–11 H12–10
- *Firmiana simplex* Z7–10 H12–8
- *Pittosporum phillyreoides* Z9–10
- *Tabebuia chrysotrycha* Z9–12 H12–10

Strelitzia nicolai
GIANT BIRD OF PARADISE
☀ ◐ ⧫ Z9–15 H12–10 ↕↔30ft (10m)
Plant several around the back of a pool to lend height and a tropical atmosphere, without shading the pool. Faded flowers stay on until cut off.

Magnolia x soulangeana
SAUCER MAGNOLIA
☀ ◐ ⧫ Z5–10 H9–5 ↕↔25ft (8m)
Fragrant blossoms drop after flowering in spring. Big leaves drop off once, in autumn. Non-drippy, green all summer, and sited against a wall with its back from the pool edge, it will take reflected light.

Cupressus sempervirens
ITALIAN CYPRESS
☀ ◐ ⧫ Z7–10 H9–3 ↕60ft (18m) ↔10ft (3m)
A non-drippy tree that will not cast shade on the north side of a pool and adds a Mediterranean atmosphere and height. Feed in spring to hasten growth.

Dracaena draco
DRAGON TREE
☀ ◐ ⧫⧫ Z9–12 H12–1 ↕↔20ft (6m)
This slow-growing tree has leaves that hang on for years before eventually falling off. Flower clusters on branch tips look neater if cut off with a sharp pole pruner.

WOODY PLANTS

Trees for the oceanfront

Many trees are dwarfed by wind on cliffs or the beachfront. Some, including a few listed in the More Choices box on this page, become thick sculptured shrubs under these conditions. Most of these trees, however, are more erect, for streets, parks, and gardens by the ocean. Note the requirements, as they can differ.

Pinus thunbergii
JAPANESE BLACK PINE

☼ ◐ ◑ Z5–10 H8–5 ‡30ft (10m) ↔10ft (3m)
In coastal zones, it is best to control growth by removing or shortening candles in spring. Grown naturally inland, this becomes a tall shapely tree.

Pinus pinaster
MARITIME PINE

☼ ◊ ◐ Z10–11 H12–10 ‡30ft (10m) ↔10ft (3m)
Best when buffeted by ocean wind, this is from the coasts of southern France, and not good inland. Use a humic acid solution after planting to stimulate roots.

MORE CHOICES

- *Casuarina stricta* Z9–15 H12–10
- x *Cupressocyparis leylandii* Z6–10 H9–3
- *Eucalyptus ficifolia* Z9–10 H10–9
- *Leptospermum laevigatum* Z9–10 H10–9
- *Melaleuca nesophila* Z9–15 H12–6
- *Melaleuca viridiflora* var. *rubriflora* Z9–15 H12–10
- *Metrosideros excelsa* Z10–15 H12–10
- *Myoporum laetum* Z10–15 H12–10
- *Paraserianthes lophantha* Z8–10 H10–8
- *Pinus pinea* Z9–11 H12–9
- *Pinus radiata* Z7–10 H9–7
- *Sabal mexicana* Z10–15 H12–10
- *Sabal palmetto* Z10–15 H12–10
- *Sequoia sempervirens* Z8–9 H9–8
- *Vitex lucens* Z6–10 H9–6

Quercus ilex
HOLLY OAK, HOLM OAK
☼ ◊◊ Z4–10 H9–2 ‡↔60ft (18m)
Shrubby and long-lived on a beachfront, it is taller
behind a house, in a garden, or on a street. It has gray
bark and is not as shapely as *Q. agrifolia* (live oak).

Cupressus macrocarpa
MONTEREY CYPRESS
Ⓝ ☼ ◊◊ Z7–11 H12–7 ‡↔40ft (12m)
On an oceanfront, this may live 200 years. Do not
grow even one block inland as it will fall prey to bark
beetles and incurable coryneum canker fungus.

Pinus halepensis
ALEPPO PINE
☼ ◊◊ Z9–10 H10–9 ‡60ft (18m) ↔40ft (12m)
A Mediterranean tree with a twisted shape in strong
ocean wind; crossing branches form natural grafts,
which strengthen the tree and should not be cut out.

Pinus pinea
ITALIAN STONE PINE
☼ ◊◊ Z9–10 H12–1 ‡80ft (25m) ↔60ft (18m)
A great beach tree, this is low and spreading in its first
20 years; a thick-trunked mushroom in the next 30–40;
and a towering, flat-topped umbrella at 75–100.

Pinus muricata
BISHOP PINE
Ⓝ ☼ ◊◊ Z7–10 H9–7 ‡80ft (25m) ↔40ft (12m)
From northern California and the north Baja coasts,
this takes fog, wind, spray, and salty soil. It starts as a
pyramid, then rounds, and finally becomes gnarled.

Trees for windbreaks

Many garden plants cannot take constant wind. On windy hillsides or in valleys with strong afternoon winds, a well-placed row of wind-resistant trees can provide welcome shelter for houses, gardens, and people. Evergreen trees are best, since they provide protection year round, but deciduous trees can be used in deserts, where winds are often less damaging in winter.

x *Cupressocyparis leylandii* 'Haggerston Grey'
HAGGERSTON GREY LEYLAND CYPRESS
☼ ◑ Z6–10 H12–9
‡70ft (20m) ↔15ft (5m)
A gray form of a green, symmetrical spirelike cypress that can be sheared or left natural. Coryneum canker fungus can kill it in the hottest regions.

Markhamia hildebrandtii
GOLD TRUMPET TREE
☼ ◑◕ Z10–11 H12–10
‡40ft (12m) ↔20ft (6m)
A fast-growing tall column that spreads slowly, its pinnate leaves hang on for years. Clusters of large, yellow, trumpet-shaped flowers appear August to December, best after dry winters. Wind strengthens a young trunk.

Picea abies
NORWAY SPRUCE
☼ ☼ ◑◕ Z3–8 H8–1
‡40ft (12m) ↔20ft (6m)
A valuable windbreak in cold zones, this also takes heat and humidity better than most spruces. Dwarf forms are available, but for windbreaks choose a tall type or 'Nidiformis' (bird's next spruce), which grows to 5ft (1.5m).

Lagunaria patersonii
PRIMROSE TREE
☼ ◑ Z9–15 H12–10 ‡50ft (15m) ↔40ft (12m)
A tall tree that is good in groves. Pink to lavender small flowers appear in summer or year round. Tolerates extreme heat, ocean wind and spray, and has brown seed capsules. Handle pods carefully: stiff fibers irritate skin.

WOODY PLANTS

Araucaria heterophylla
NORFOLK ISLAND PINE
☼ ◑ ● z9–11 H12–9 ‡160ft (50m) ↔20ft (6m)
Araucarias are strange-looking conifers from the Southern
Hemisphere that grow slowly. Use as a windbreak in Hawaii or
as an ornament on the mainland. Drought-resistant on coasts.

Eucalyptus globulus
BLUE GUM
☼ ◑◑ z9–10 H10–9
‡160ft (50m) ↔75ft (23m)
The largest messiest eucalyptus can be a big
windscreen for groves and farms, away from
gardens. Trees near the coast or deep-rooted in
groundwater are resistant to psyllids and borers.

MORE CHOICES

- *Acacia saligna* z10–11 H12–10
- *Broussonetia papyrifera* z6–9 H9–6
- *Calocedrus decurrens* z5–8 H8–5
- *Casuarina stricta* z12–15 H12–10
- *Cupressus arizonica* 'Pyrimidalis'
  z7–9 H9–7
- *Cupressus sempervirens* z7–10 H9–3
- *Maclura pomifera* z5–9 H9–5
- *Melaleuca huegelii* z9–15 H12–10
- *Pinus muricata* z7–10 H9–7
- *Populus alba* f. *pyramidalis* z4–9 H9–1
- *Populus nigra* 'Thevestina' z2–9 H9–1
- *Quercus virginiana* z8–10 H10–7
- *Schinus molle* z8–11 H12–8
- *Sequoia sempervirens* z8–9 H9–8
- *Thuja plicata* 'Fastigiata' z6–9 H8–6

Ficus benjamina
WEEPING FIG
☼ ◑◑ z10–12 H12–10 ‡↔60ft (18m)
Often acquired as a houseplant, stuck in the ground, preferably a
good distance from the house as it has invasive surface roots. An
effective screen up to 60 feet in Hawaii; half large on the mainland.

Ficus microcarpa
INDIAN LAUREL FIG
☼ ● z9–12 H12–1
‡60ft (18m) ↔75ft (23m)
A popular screen, clipped or not. Thrips
disfigure foliage in summer. 'Green Gem'
is pest-resistant with dark green foliage.

Evergreen trees for screens

Some evergreen trees are natural columns, with branches to the ground and small leaves. These trees can be used instead of shrubs as screens, needing little or no pruning. If some pruning is necessary, always maintain a shape that is wider below and narrower above, so the sun hits all the foliage. Otherwise, lower branches die off, creating a bare, see-through effect.

Thuja plicata 'Green Giant'
WESTERN RED CEDAR
Ⓝ ☼ ☀ ◗◖ Z6–8 H8–6
↕100ft (30m) ↔60ft (18m)
Its natural shape makes a fine lawn tree with no pruning. Varieties for screens include 'Fastigiata', which is dense and tall, and 'Spring Grove', which can be sheared.

x *Cupressocyparis leylandii*
LEYLAND CYPRESS
☼ ☀ ◗◖ Z6–10 H9–3
↕100ft (30m) ↔60ft (18m)
A popular screen, good as a green background. Gets fungus inland. Can clip or let it grow naturally. More disease-resistant than the Monterey cypress, with a simpler shape.

Ligustrum lucidum
GLOSSY PRIVET
☼ ☀ ◗ Z8–10 H10–8 ↕↔40ft (12m)
If not clipped, many flowers are followed by much fruit. Plant away from sidewalks. For a screen, plant 10ft (3m) apart and never remove the lower branches.

Podocarpus macrophyllus
YEW PINE
☼ ☀ ◗◖ Z7–11 H12–7 ↕50ft (15m) ↔15ft (5m)
Fifty feet tall in Hawaii; 15ft (5m) tall, 4ft (1.2m) wide on the mainland. Good-looking, heat-tolerant, and takes wind. Shear for screen; can also be a street tree.

MORE CHOICES

- *Ficus microcarpa* 'Green Gem' Z9–11 H12–1
- *Leptospermum laevigatum* Z9–10 H10–9
- *Podocarpus macrophyllus* Z7–11 H12–7
- *Syzygium paniculatum* Z10–11 H12–1
- *Taxus baccata* 'Fastigiata' Z7–8 H8–7

WOODY PLANTS

Trees for informal hedges

Many gardens suffer from an ugly view or a lack of privacy. Well-placed trees can be a creative solution to this problem. The best choices can be left to grow naturally with little pruning or special care. Some of these trees should not be grown near houses or sidewalks, because their invasive roots can invade pipes or push up paving.

Acer campestre
HEDGE MAPLE

☼ ☀ ◊ ● Z6–8 H8–4 ‡↔30ft (10m)

Deciduous with yellow fall color, for cooler areas, not deserts. Thinner growth in California than Northwest. A better hedge, 'Queen Elizabeth' has glossy foliage.

Calocedrus decurrens
INCENSE CEDAR

Ⓝ ☼ ☀ ◊ ● Z5–8 H8–5 ‡90ft (27m) ↔15ft (5m)

Slow-growing at first, this takes heat, poor soil, and neglect in the right climate zones. An unpruned screen, windbreak, or street tree that is fragrant in sun.

Prunus lusitanica 'Variegata'
VARIEGATED PORTUGAL LAUREL

☼ ◊◊ Z7–9 H9–4 ‡↔20ft (6m)

As a street tree, it is a formal lollipop. For hedge, choose unpruned plants. Purple fruits, liked by birds, follow flowers. P. l. subsp. azorica is a green column.

MORE CHOICES

- *Cupressus sempervirens* Z7–9 H9–3
- *Ficus microcarpa* var. *crassifolia* Z9–12 H12–9
- *Grevillea robusta* Z10–11 H12–3
- *Juniperus chinensis* 'Robust Green' Z5–10 H9–1

Schinus molle
CALIFORNIA PEPPER

☼ ◊◊ Z8–11 H12–8 ‡↔40ft (12m)

This heritage plant has fast growth, bird attraction, evergreen foliage, and drought resistance. Faults include invasive roots, abundant litter, and pests.

Trees for espalier

Espaliers, plants trained to grow flat against supports, are good choices for narrow beds between walls and walkways. If the wall is tall enough, an espaliered tree is preferable to a shrub. This is also a space-saving way to grow more fruit trees, which tend to bear more abundant blooms and fruit when their branches are arranged horizontally against a wall or on wires.

Pyrus pyrifolia
JAPANESE SAND PEAR
☼ ◐ Z7–9 H9–4 ‡40ft (12m) ↔25ft (8m)
This deciduous ornamental pear does best with winter chill (no coasts or deserts) and has white spring flowers, poor fruit, and orange to purple fall color.

Malus 'Adirondack'
FLOWERING CRABAPPLE
☼ ◐◐ Z4–8 H8–1
‡12ft (4m) ↔18ft (5.5m)
A disease-resistant ornamental tree that flowers usually on bare wood, followed by long-lasting red fruit. Needs winter chill; takes heat, but not low desert.

Laburnum x *watereri* 'Vossii'
VOSS'S GOLDENCHAIN TREE
☼ ◐◐ Z5–8 H8–3 ‡↔30ft (10m) ↔20ft (6m)
Best in cool zones, this needs similar care as lilacs and rhododendrons. Spring flowers are like wisteria. Branches bend onto an arbor or train on a trellis.

Malus 'Anna'
ANNA APPLE
☼ ◐ Z5–10 H8–1 ‡↔20ft (6m)
One of the best low-chill apples, with crisp, juicy red fruit near the ocean. Without a pollinator planted near or grafted on the tree, it bears elongated fruit.

MORE CHOICES

- *Amelanchier alnifolia* 'Regent' Z4–9 H8–3
- *Citrus aurantium* Z11–15 H12–10
- *Diospyros kaki* 'Fuyu' Z7–10 H10–7
- *Eriobotrya deflexa* Z8–11 H12–8
- *Eriobotrya japonica* 'Champagne' Z8–11 H12–8
- *Ficus auriculata* Z10–11 H12–10
- *Ficus carica* 'Genoa' Z7–11 H12–1
- *Ficus elastica* 'Asahi' Z11–11 H12–1
- *Ficus microcarpa* 'Green Gem' Z9–11 H12–1
- *Magnolia* 'Star Wars' Z6–10 H9–6
- *Magnolia grandiflora* 'San Marino' Z6–10 H10–7
- *Malus* 'Pristine' Z5–8 H8–1
- *Podocarpus macrophyllus* Z7–11 H12–7
- *Pyrus communis* 'Hood' Z5–10 H10–1

Magnolia grandiflora 'Little Gem'
LITTLE GEM MAGNOLIA
☼ ☼ ◐ ● Z7–10 H9–3 ‡25ft (8m) ↔15ft (5m)
This small variety bears 5in (1.5cm) fragrant flowers spring to fall, fewer in heat. Good in a container, with branches to the ground. Feed with a balanced slow-release fertilizer. Don't plant too deep.

Citrus reticulata 'Dancy'
DANCY TANGERINE
☼ ● Z9–10 H10–8
‡20ft (6m) ↔15ft (5m)
The standard type bought in markets, the fruit ripens in fall to winter and hangs on until picked. Attractive on espalier, this is easily trained onto a support. Fertilize in February.

Citrus meyeri
MEYER LEMON
☼ ● Z9–11 H12–1
‡12ft (4m) ↔15ft (5m)
A great choice for its fragrant flowers and fine fruit. Only 'Improved Meyer', a disease-resistant variety, is permitted for sale in California. Most lemons make good espaliers, though they are thorny.

Podocarpus gracilior
FERN PINE
☼ ● Z7–11 H12–7 ‡60ft (18m) ↔15ft (5m)
From seed, this grows into a fine shade tree. Grown from cuttings, its willowy branches can be staked as a hedge, screen, or espalier. New foliage is a lovely light green color. This is not a true pine.

Diospyros kaki 'Hachiya'
HACHIYA PERSIMMON
☼ ◐ ● Z7–10 H10–7 ‡↔30ft (10m)
This deciduous tree needs some winter chill. The tree and its fruit are extremely attractive. Large orange fruit may fall off when fully ripe but are still delicious if you get them that day.

Trees with fragrant flowers

Fragrance adds romance and magic to gardens. What traveler home from the tropics can remember plumerias without nostalgia? What displaced Southerner can think of the Deep South without magnolias? Plants originally developed fragrance to attract insect and animal pollinators. Now they also use it to attract human beings, so that we will plant and care for them in our gardens.

WOODY PLANTS

Plumeria alba
WHITE PLUMERIA

☼ ◐ ◊ ◖ Z10–12 H12–10 ‡↔20ft (6m)

A beloved tropical tree, in Hawaii they grow without care. On the mainland, plant in a tub or in the ground in a warm microclimate, on a patio or in a sideyard.

Chionanthus virginicus
WHITE FRINGE TREE

Ⓝ ☼ ◐ ◊ ◖ Z4–10 H9–1 ‡↔20ft (6m)

Narrow greenish white flowers in bigger bunches than the Chinese fringe tree bloom later. This is deciduous, often staying shrubby, with a light fragrance.

Clethra arborea
LILY-OF-THE-VALLEY TREE

☼ ◊ ⌂ Z8–9 H9–8 ‡20ft (6m) ↔10ft (3m)

This small evergreen tree needs no pruning for its naturally upright shape with bronze-green foliage. Spring flowers have fragrance like lilies-of-the-valley.

MORE CHOICES

- *Cinnamomum camphora* Z8–10 H10–8
- *Citrus aurantium* 'Bouquet de Fleurs' Z10–15 H12–10
- *Cladrastis kentukea* Z4–9 H9–1
- *Eriobotrya japonica* Z8–11 H12–8
- *Hymenosporum flavum* Z9–11 H12–9
- *Melia azedarach* Z7–15 H12–10
- *Michelia doltsopa* Z9–11 H12–1
- *Vitex agnus-castus* Z6–12 H9–6
- *Laurus nobilis* Z8–11 H12–1

Franklinia alatamaha
FRANKLIN TREE

(N) ☼ ☼ ● ᴴ Z6–10 H9–6

↕20ft (6m) ↔30ft (10m)

Extinct in the wild, this tree can be shrubby but is usually sold on a single, gray-barked trunk. Flowers appear in late summer and fall, when leaves are green. Grow with camellias and azaleas.

Magnolia grandiflora
SOUTHERN MAGNOLIA

(N) ☼ ● Z7–10 H9–1

↕80ft (24m) ↔60ft (18m)

This lawn or street tree, drippy with leaves and pods, pushes up pavement. Nothing will grow in its shade. Yet it is beloved for its large, leathery evergreen leaves and huge fragrant flowers.

Styrax obassia
FRAGRANT SNOWBELL

☼ ☼ ● ᴴ Z6–9 H8–6 ↕30ft (10m) ↔20ft (6m)

This little-known small tree has 1in (3cm) fragrant spring flowers in bunches and non-invasive roots. Grow with camellias and azaleas. Needs winter chill.

Gymnocladus dioica
KENTUCKY COFFEE TREE

(N) ☼ ● Z5–9 H9–5

↕100ft (30m) ↔50ft (15m)

Fast-growing when young. Female trees bear fragrant spring flowers on branch tips, followed by pods holding seeds that were ground as a coffee substitute by settlers.

Tilia cordata
SMALL-LEAVED LINDEN

☼ ● Z3–8 H8–1

↕50ft (15m) ↔30ft (10m)

Dense deciduous foliage, dark green above, silver beneath, forms a conical shape. Fragrant flowers bring bees. Control aphids with ladybugs. Plant in deep damp soils. Has small nuts in bracts.

Robinia pseudoacacia 'Frisia'
BLACK LOCUST

(N) ☼ ◊●● Z4–10 H9–4 ↕75ft (23m) ↔60ft (18m)

An invasive thorny, but useful, attractive, fast-growing deciduous tree with fragrant bloom for edges of property. Survives drought, wind, and alkaline clay.

WOODY PLANTS

Trees with colorful fall foliage

We do not often associate warm-winter climates with colorful fall foliage. Nonetheless, some deciduous trees have excellent autumn colors in the Southwest. Some can take extreme heat and cold, including staghorn sumac (*Rhus typhina* 'Laciniata'), which turns yellow, orange, and glowing red before dropping its leaves in fall.

Acer palmatum 'Garnet'
JAPANESE MAPLE
☼ ◐ ◦ pH Z5–10 H8–2 ↕9ft (2.5m) ↔12ft (4m)
This mounded plant holds color all summer, turning brighter in the fall before dropping its leaves. Volunteer seedlings more tolerant of wind and drought.

Acer japonicum 'Acontifolium'
FULL MOON MAPLE
☼ ☼ ◦ Z5–9 H7–5 ↕↔15ft (5m)
A shrublike tree with green, deep cut leaves, bright scarlet in the fall where adapted. Needs some shade in warmest regions and little pruning. Good for lawns.

Diospyros kaki
JAPANESE PERSIMMON
☼ ◦ Z7–10 H10–7 ↕9ft (2.5m) ↔12ft (4m)
Fall brings bright yellow foliage and bright orange fruit. Needs chill so keep away from the coast for best color and fruit. Unripe fruit is astringent.

Nyssa sylvatica
SOUR GUM, TUPELO

Ⓝ ☼ ☼ ◊ ◑ ● Z5–9 H9–7 ↕50ft (15m) ↔30ft (8m)

When young, this is wide below with a pointed tip. Red fall foliage, crooked branches, and reddish winter bark are nice. Pollinated females bear fruit.

Pistacia chinensis
CHINESE PISTACHE

☼ ◊ ◑ ● Z6–9 H9–6 ↕60ft (18m) ↔50ft (15m)

A valuable shade tree anywhere away from the coast. Leaves grow 1ft (30cm) long with bright fall color. Needs good drainage; takes heat, wind, and drought.

Lagerstroemia indica 'Tuskegee'
TUSKEGEE CRAPE MYRTLE

☼ ◊ ● Z7–10 H9–7 ↕↔25ft (8m)

A drought-resistant, flowering tree for hot interior zones that gets mildew along the coast. Has bright yellow, fall foliage and an ornamental trunk in winter.

Liquidambar styraciflua 'Festival'
AMERICAN SWEET GUM

Ⓝ ☼ ◊ ● Z6–10 H9–6 ↕60ft (18m) ↔25ft (8m)

Developed in California from an East Coast native, this is an outstanding variety of a widely planted tree for warm-winter zones, with year-round beauty.

MORE CHOICES

- *Cercis canadensis* var. *texensis* 'Oklahoma' Z6–9 H9–6
- *Cornus x rutgersensis* 'Celestial' Z5–8 H8–3
- *Fraxinus angustifolia* 'Raywood' Z6–9 H9–6
- *Gleditsia triacanthos* 'Moraine' Z3–7 H7–1
- *Koelreuteria bipinnata* Z6–10 H9–1
- *Liriodendron tulipifera* 'Majestic Beauty' Z5–9 H9–5
- *Metasequoia glyptostroboides* Z4–11 H12–1
- *Parrotia persica* Z4–7 H7–1
- *Populus fremontii* 'Nevada' Z3–9 H9–1
- *Populus nigra* 'Italica' Z3–9 H9–1
- *Quercus coccinea* Z5–9 H9–4
- *Quercus rubra* Z5–9 H9–5
- *Rhus typhina* 'Laciniata' Z3–9 H8–1
- *Sapium sebiferum* Z8–10 H10–8
- *Styrax japonicus* Z6–8 H8–6
- *Ulmus parvifolia* 'Frontier' Z8–10 H9–5

Ginkgo biloba 'Autumn Gold'
AUTUMN GOLD MAIDENHAIR TREE

☼ ◊ ● Z3–10 H9–1 ↕60 ft (18m) ↔40ft (12m)

A male variety with good shape and choice fall color. Shapely leaves look like gray-green fans. This Chinese conifer relative is a column in youth that spreads later.

Trees with ornamental bark

Tree bark comes in an array of colors and textures. It can be black, gray, brown, white, pink, purple, green, or even multicolored, with textures ranging from smooth to thorny, furrowed, or peeling. If the tree is deciduous, it is nice to have bark that looks attractive when it is bare. If the tree is evergreen, bark should contrast pleasantly with foliage and flowers.

Platanus racemosa
CALIFORNIA SYCAMORE
Ⓝ ☼ ◐ ◑ Z3–10 H8–5 ‡80ft (25m) ↔50ft (15m)
Choose a shapely sapling and plant it to lean in the direction desired. In youth, prune out ungainly growth. White patchy bark contrasts with yellow fall foliage.

Quercus suber
CORK OAK
☼ ◑ Z7–10 H9–7 ‡↔30ft (10m)
Each drought-resistant tree is uniquely shaped and takes desert heat. Evergreen foliage contrasts with thick fissured bark. Plant on banks, groves, and streets.

Lagerstroemia fauriei 'Fantasy'
JAPANESE CRAPE MYRTLE
☼ ◑ Z7–10 H9–7 ‡↔30ft (10m)
This mildew-resistant tree has white summer flowers and light green foliage. Smooth gray bark peels to cinnamon in winter. There are many resistant varieties.

Betula papyrifera
SILVER BIRCH
Ⓝ ☼ ● Z2–9 H7–1 ↕90ft (25m) ↔45ft (14m)
With shining bark and light green leaves, this is often planted in small groves in island beds on lawns. More resistant to leaf miners and bark borers than *B. pendula*.

Acer griseum
PAPERBARK MAPLE
☼ ☼ ◐ ● Z4–8 H8–1
↕↔30ft (10m) ↔25ft (8m)
The young tree has pink bark that turns cinnamon and may brown with age. Also a handsome silhouette in winter and red fall foliage. Not good for deserts.

Eucalyptus pauciflora
GHOST GUM
☼ ◐◐● Z9–11 H12–10
↕60ft (18m) ↔45ft (14m)
Open growth, a good shape, and lovely bark makes this a fine specimen on a lawn and has less litter than most. Prune to shape in youth. *E. deglupta* has multicolored bark.

Melaleuca linariifolia
SNOW IN SUMMER
☼ ◐● Z8–10 H5–8
↕30ft (10m) ↔25ft (8m)
Small white flowers like snow appear in summer and cover the tree, which also has fine-leaved foliage and white shedding bark. *M. quinquenervia* is faster growing.

MORE CHOICES

- *Arbutus menziesii* Z7–9 H9–7
- *Brachychiton acerifolius* Z10–15 H12–8
- *Drimys winteri* Z8–11 H12–8
- *Eucalyptus deglupta* Z9–10 H10–9
- *Franklinia alatamaha* Z6–10 H9–6
- *Leptospermum laevigatum* Z9–10 H10–9
- *Parkinsonia aculeata* Z9–12 H12–10
- *Pinus bungeana* Z4–9 H7–1
- *Populus tremuloides* Z1–8 H8–1
- *Stewartia monadelpha* Z6–9 H9–6

Chorisia speciosa
FLOSS SILK TREE
☼ ● Z10–14 H12–10 ↕↔60ft (18m)
A fast-growing, fall-flowering tree, best after a dry summer. The thick trunk and branches have bright green bark, studded with thorns. The bark grays with age. Thornless varieties are available.

Trees for hummingbirds

Feeders help hummingbirds survive when flowers and tiny insects are less plentiful in winter, but they require regular cleaning and conscientious refilling with a refrigerated sugar formula. A safer, more reliable way to attract hummingbirds is to grow their favorite shrubs, vines, herbaceous plants, and trees. Choose carefully, so that some will bloom in each season.

Brachychiton discolor
PINK FLAME TREE
☼ ◊ Z10–11 H12–10 ‡60ft (18m) ↔30ft (10m)
Stunning when it abruptly drops its leaves and fills with bell-shaped blooms, summer to fall, this tree has a bottle-shaped trunk and attractive foliage. It needs little pruning and is drought-resistant.

Citrus limon
LEMON TREE
☼ ◊ ● Z9–11 H12–1 ‡↔20ft (6m)
Fertilize beginning late January for February flowers, sporadic later, and year-round fruit. A mature citrus needs 1lb (0.5kg) of actual nitrogen per year. Home varieties and dwarf types are available.

Aesculus californica
CALIFORNIA BUCKEYE
Ⓝ ☼ ☼ ◊ Z7–10 H8–7 ‡20ft (6m) ↔30ft (10m)
Spring blooms ornament foothills, canyons, hillside gardens, and banks with little care. The tree holds leaves until fall, given some irrigation. Large pear-shaped fruits split, showing shiny seeds.

MORE CHOICES

- *Albizia julibrissin* Z6–10 H9–6
- *Callistemon viminalis* Z9–15 H12–10
- *Erythrina coralloides* Z11–12 H12–10
- *Eucalyptus ficifolia* Z9–10 H10–9

Chorisia speciosa
FLOSS SILK TREE
☼ ◊ Z10–14 H12–10 ‡↔60ft (18m)
Hummingbirds zoom through this tree when it is covered with magenta fall blooms. Its thick green trunk and branches are covered with thorns. Large pods split open, spreading floss used in nests.

Chilopsis linearis
DESERT WILLOW
Ⓝ ☼ ◊ Z8–10 H9–8 ‡30ft (10m) ↔20ft (6m)
Varieties offer lavender, pink, white, or purple blooms, spring to fall in the desert and inland, bringing many hummingbirds. The bark turns shaggy with age, the foliage is deciduous. Prune in fall.

WOODY PLANTS

Trees for butterflies

Butterflies need leaves for larvae, flowers for nectar, and safe places for winter hibernation. They are easily harmed by pesticides or overuse of Bt (*Bacillus thuringiensis, see p. 69*). Gardeners can nurture butterflies and attract many to their gardens by refraining from spraying and by growing a wide array of shrubs, climbers, herbaceous plants, and trees favored by these colorful insects.

see p. 69

Pinus torreyana
TORREY PINE

Ⓝ ☼ ◊◊ Z9–10 H10–9 ↕80ft (25m) ↔60ft (18m)

This massive tree turns brittle if overwatered and may invade pipes. Protect it in natural gardens. Monarch butterflies hang from branches in clusters over winter.

Arbutus menziesii
MADRONE

Ⓝ ☼ ◊◊ Z7–9 H9–7 ↕↔100ft (30m)

Butterflies travel far to visit these handsome trees in spring, sipping nectar from the large clusters of pink to white flowers. Water infrequently once established.

Malus 'Snowdrift'
WHITE CRABAPPLE

☼ ◊◊ pH Z5–8 H8–5

↕↔25ft (8m)

This disease-resistant tree needs 600 hours of winter-chill. Its red buds and white spring flowers bring butterflies and bees. Small ornamental red fruits follow, attracting birds. Prune only to shape.

Aesculus x *carnea*
RED HORSE CHESTNUT

☼ ◊◊ Z7–8 H8–6 ↕40ft (12m) ↔30ft (10m)

The most beautiful of the genus, the smaller size fits better in gardens. For cooler areas only. Swallowtail butterflies, hummingbirds, and bees like its nectar-filled, showy spring flowers.

MORE CHOICES

- *Acer rubrum* 'Schlesingeri'   Z3–9 H9–1
- *Craetaegus laevigata* 'Paul's Scarlet'   Z5–8 H8–3
- *Prunus campanulata*   Z7–8 H8–7
- *Quercus engelmannii*   Z6–10 H9–6
- *Salix udensis* 'Sekka'   Z4–9 H7–1

Trees for birds

How can you turn your garden into a bird sanctuary? The first step is to provide clean moving water, from a dripper or fountain. Properly placed birdhouses and feeders can also help. Additionally, most songbirds need thick shrubs and taller trees for nesting and cover. Finally, many trees with fruits and flowers are as attractive to birds as they are to humans.

Morus alba
WHITE MULBERRY

☼ ◑ Z4–10 H8–1 ↕↔30ft (10m)

Plant this for birds and site where messy ground is no annoyance. Fruit is flavorless to us but a delight for birds. Fruitless varieties are the best ornamentals.

Pittosporum undulatum
VICTORIAN BOX

☼ ☼ ◊◑ Z9–10 H10–9 ↕↔40ft (12m)

Fragrant flowers are followed by fruits that drop seeds in the winter. Birds use the tree for cover and seed it. The tree needs water inland but only a bit on the coast.

Ficus rubiginosa
PORT JACKSON FIG

☼ ◑ Z10–12 H12–10 ↕↔50ft (15m)

The young tree is clean, but once it matures, it drops figs that stain paving. Plant with a groundcover away from the house. Birds arrive at dawn for fruit.

Acca sellowiana
PINEAPPLE GUAVA

☼ ◑ Z8–11 H12–9

↕↔25ft (8m)

Birds and people like this tree's flowers and fruit, which falls when ripe. Shake the tree weekly. Spread pollen on flowers with feather duster for a big harvest.

Acacia constricta
WHITE THORN
☼ ☼ ◐ ◐ Z9–13 H12–10
‡60ft (18m) ↔15ft (5m)
This thorny shrub or small tree has
fernlike foliage and summer-blooming yellow
flowers. Its pods provide abundant seeds for birds.

Thuja occidentalis 'Reingold'
REINGOLD AMERICAN ARBORVITAE
Ⓝ ☼ ☼ ◐ ◐ Z2–8 H8–1 ‡10ft (3m) ↔15ft (5m)
A colorful compact selection that is best in moist air, it
may have spider mites. The shrubby types are grown in
gardens and the fruits bring birds for nesting.

MORE CHOICES

- *Arbutus unedo* Z8–10 H9–6
- *Eriobotrya japonica* Z8–11 H12–8
- *Fraxinus velutina* Z6–10 H9–6
- *Grevillea robusta* Z10–11 H12–3
- *Pittosporum rhombifolium* Z9–10 H10–9
- *Prosopis velutina* Z10–11 H12–10
- *Prunus ilicifolia* Z9–10 H10–9
- *Syzygium paniculatum* Z10–11 H12–1

Juniperus chinensis 'Torulosa'
HOLLYWOOD JUNIPER
☼ ☼ ◐ ◐ Z6–10 H9–1 ‡↔20ft (6m)
This slow-growing tree hugs walls near the house.
Birds eat the fruits, peck flowers for insects, and use
the tree for cover, nesting if it is planted near shrubs.

Callistemon citrinus
LEMON BOTTLEBRUSH
☼ ◐ ◐ Z10–11 H12–10 ‡25ft (8m) ↔15ft (5m)
Plant this large shrub or small tree near taller trees to
attract mockingbirds to nest. Do not overprune the
tree, which blooms in waves throughout the year.

Trees with fantastic shapes

Trees with extraordinary shapes add excitement to gardens. Some of these plants look as if they were dreamed up by Dr. Seuss or came from another planet. Many developed in deserts, or on continents and islands where an extreme climate or long isolation resulted in a bizarre shape. These plants are survivors; many are far easier to grow than might be supposed.

Araucaria araucana
MONKEY PUZZLE TREE
☼ ◑ z7–11 H12–6 ‡90ft (25m) ↔30ft (10m)
A hardy conifer from Chile for large gardens. Do not prune as branches should cascade to the ground, offering protection from falling 15lb (7kg) cones.

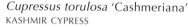

Cupressus torulosa 'Cashmeriana'
KASHMIR CYPRESS
☼ ◑ z6–10 H9–6
‡100ft (30m) ↔30ft (10m)
Never found in the wild, this may have originated in cultivation and has hanging flat sprays of branchlets and red spongy bark. Do not prune. Protect from wind.

Chorisia speciosa
FLOSS SILK TREE
☼ ◑ z10–11 H12–10 ‡↔60ft (18m)
Spectacular flowers appear in fall, especially if the tree is not irrigated in July and August. Hummingbirds love the flowers and use the floss for nests. The prehistoric trunk grows wider in age.

Carnegiea gigantea
SAGUARO
Ⓝ ☼ ◊◑ z8–10 H12–10 ‡50ft (15m) ↔10ft (3m)
A slow-growing, long-lived cactus that branches 10–15ft (3–5m) up and is a nesting place for the cactus wren. Edible fruit follows night-blooming white flowers. Water and fertilizer hastens growth.

Kigelia pinnata
SAUSAGE TREE
☼ ◑ z10–11 H12–10
‡40ft (12m) ↔30ft (10m)
Red flowers with an unpleasant night odor hang on long stems. Novel fruits, smooth when well grown, appear on this vigorous attractive tree. Plant away from the house.

Salix babylonica var. pekinensis 'Tortuosa'
CORKSCREW WILLOW
☼ ● ◐ Z5–10 H9–5 ‡50ft (15m) ↔25ft (8m)
Use this tree as a support for climbers or perennials, though it will become huge if not removed. Branches will grow if planted into the ground.

Nolina recurvata
PONYTAIL PALM
☼ ◐◐ Z10–11 H12–10
‡15ft (5m) ↔12ft (4m)
A specimen for a pot or the ground, its swollen trunk rots if hit by sprinklers. If it does not branch, cut off the top in fall; by spring it will sprout branches. Choose those you want, remove others.

Strelitzia nicolai
GIANT BIRD OF PARADISE
☼ ◐ Z10–15 H12–10 ‡40ft (12m) ↔30ft (10m)
A larger bird of paradise with less-colorful flowers, this is easy to grow and a tough, worthy tropical accent near a swimming pool or the house. Hooded orioles return each year for nectar.

Yucca brevifolia
JOSHUA TREE
Ⓝ ☼ ◐ Z9–15 H12–10
‡↔30ft (10m)
This slow-growing tree is beloved by many. Although it is difficult to find specimens with branches, this is an outstanding main accent for a dry desert garden if obtainable. Well-drained dry soil is a must. Let dry leaves hang on.

MORE CHOICES

- *Aloe bainesii* Z10–11 H12–10
- *Brachychiton populneus* Z9–11 H12–10
- *Caryota urens* Z10–12 H12–10
- *Cordyline australis* Z10–11 H12–10
- *Couroupita guianensis* Z10–15 H12–10
- *Dasylirion quadrangulatum* Z9–15 H12–10
- *Erythrina coralloides* Z10–12 H12–10
- *Fouquieria macdougalii* Z9–15 H12–1
- *Leucadendron argenteum* Z10–11 H12–10
- *Nolina longifolia* Z9–15 H12–1
- *Schefflera actinophylla* Z10–15 H12–10

WOODY PLANTS

Trees with a weeping habit

Weeping trees are effective next to water or near a house. They are thought to express sorrow, but they might just as well symbolize survival. Leaves that hang down are less prone to dehydration, and they let rain fall right through. With eucalyptus, big drops of water condense on the leaves in foggy weather and drip steadily and audibly onto the matlike surface roots.

Salix x *sepulcralis* var. *chrysocoma*
GOLDEN WEEPING WILLOW
☼ ◊ Z6–10 H9–6 ↕↔50ft (15m)
Tent caterpillars may appear in June. Break the tents with a stick and spray the tree with Bt just before the pests emerge. Good in wet spots where little grows.

Acacia pendula
WEEPING ACACIA
☼ ◊ Z10–11 H12–10 ↕25ft (8m) ↔15ft (5m)
Slow-growing for year-round beauty, not especially for its spring flowers, this is a landscape feature for a bank with good drainage. It has gray evergreen foliage and a dark trunk and needs some irrigation.

Cedrus atlantica
f. *glauca* 'Pendula'
WEEPING ATLAS CEDAR
☼ ◊ Z9–10 H10–9
↕10ft (3m) ↔30ft (10m)
A drooping tree with a limp trunk and branches, use it as a climber on a strong pergola. Let branches drip down or let it cascade over rocks.

Betula pendula 'Youngii'
YOUNG'S WEEPING BIRCH
☼ ◊ Z3–7 H7–1 ↕40ft (12m) ↔20ft (6m)
With a domed shape and white bark, this sunburns in hot dry climates and gets borers. Stake the trunk to a desired height and let it cascade or prune for shaping.

Fagus sylvatica
'Purpurea Pendula'
WEEPING COPPER BEECH
☼ ☼ ◊◊ Z5–7 H7–5
↕↔10ft (3m)
Children love to play under this tree that is also good in large tubs. Stake for shaping and pinch leader or it will become an irregular mound. Its branches trail to the ground.

MORE CHOICES

- *Acacia stenophylla* Z10–11 H12–10
- *Cedrus deodora* 'Pendula' Z7–10 H9–6
- *Eucalyptus leucoxylon* Z9–10 H10–9
- *Eucalyptus mannifera* Z9–10 H10–9
- *Maytenus boaria* Z9–10 H10–9
- *Prunus* x *subhirtella* Z6–10 H8–6
- *Pyrus salicifolia* 'Pendula' Z5–9 H9–5
- *Sophora japonica* 'Pendula' Z5–9 H9–5
- *Taxodium mucronatum* Z5–10 H10–1

Rhus lancea
AFRICAN SUMAC

☼ ◊ Z3–10 H8–1 ‡30ft (10m) ↔35ft (11m)

Dark green leaves with three long narrow leaflets cascade for a nice weeping texture. Use as a screen, hedge, or street tree in the desert. Red fruit will litter.

Juniperus scopulorum
'Tolleson's Blue Weeping'
TOLLESON'S WEEPING JUNIPER

☼ ☼ ◊ ◊◊ Z4–10 H7–1 ‡20ft (6m) ↔10ft (3m)

Adapted to the Southwest, this needs well-drained soil. Fertilizing in early spring can help ward off mites, twig borers, and juniper blight; all necessitate spraying.

Fraxinus excelsior 'Pendula'
WEEPING EUROPEAN ASH

☼ ◊ Z5–8 H8–5 ‡50ft (15m) ↔30ft (10m)

Weeping foliage touches the ground unless pruned. Other good ashes are 'Fan West' and 'Rio Grande', both tolerant of heat, drought, wind, and alkaline soil.

Trees resistant to smog

Although the Southwest is beautiful, its cities are home to some of the nation's most polluted air, due mainly to the increasing number of automobiles. This can cause leaf burn, dieback, and wilting on non-resistant trees. In the long term, we can help by driving less and using environmentally friendly vehicles, but in the meantime, try planting these resistant trees.

Liriodendron tulipifera
TULIP TREE
Ⓝ ☼ ◑ Z5–9 H9–1 ‡80ft (25m) ↔40ft (12m)
This fast-growing, upright tree from the East has wide, four-lobed leaves with lighter backs that turn yellow in fall. Yellowish flowers appear after twelve years of age.

Podopcarpus gracilior
FERN PINE
☼ ☼ ◑ Z7–11 H12–7 ‡60ft (18m) ↔20ft (6m)
With a thick trunk and branches, its soft spring gray-green foliage is densely shady unless laced out. Clean trees are seed grown; hedges are grown from cuttings.

Koelreuteria paniculata
GOLDEN RAIN TREE
☼ ◑◑ Z6–10 H9–1 ‡35ft (11m) ↔40ft (12m)
Grown inland, this takes cold, heat, drought, wind, and any soil. Leaves yellow in fall; yellow flowers appear in early summer. Prune to shape; weed out seedlings.

Lophostemon confertus
BRISBANE BOX, TRISTANIA
Z10–15 H12–10 ↕45ft (14m) ↔25ft (8m)
A clean street or lawn tree, this grows fairly fast, stiffly straight up, then spreads, becoming a good-looking, pest-free, eucalyptus look-alike. Yellow leaves from poor soil indicate chlorosis; feed with chelated iron.

Bauhinia variegata
PURPLE ORCHID TREE
Z10–15 H12–10 ↕↔35ft (11m)
A great street tree to keep away from coastal wind, this blooms from winter to spring and has heart-shaped, gray-green leaves. *B.* x *blakeana* blooms fall to spring.

Quercus ilex
HOLM OAK, HOLLY OAK
Z4–10 H9–2 ↕↔60ft (18m)
A fast-growing Mediterranean native adapted to many zones that is shrubby on the coast, larger inland. Less graceful than a native oak but more resistant to root rot, it has small round or pointed leaves.

Morus alba
WHITE MULBERRY
Z4–10 H8–1 ↕↔50ft (15m)
A deciduous shade tree from China, its fruit attracts birds but can create a mess on sidewalks. Some named varities are fruitless. Resistant to Texas root rot, desert heat, coast wind, and alkaline soil.

Agonis flexuosa
PEPPERMINT WILLOW
Z9–10 H12–6
↕35ft (11m) ↔30ft (10m)
This clean, drought-resistant, evergreen street tree with nice foliage takes pruning well but roots can push up the pavement. Bushtits may build hanging nests.

Cinnamomum camphora
CAMPHOR TREE
Z8–10 H10–8 ↕50ft (15m) ↔60ft (18m)
Camphor-scented evergreen foliage is pink-edged in spring. It has invasive roots and small fragrant flowers. It litters and needs good drainage. Fertilize when young.

MORE CHOICES

- *Brachychiton populneus* Z9–11 H12–10
- *Callistemon viminalis* 'McCaskillii' Z10–11 H12–9
- *Calocedrus decurrens* Z5–10 H8–5
- *Calodendrum capense* Z9–15 H12–10
- *Syagrus romanzoffiana* Z10–10 H12–1
- *Tipuana tipu* Z9–15 H12–10

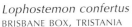

Trees resistant to oak-root fungus

Oak-root fungus (*Armillaria mellea*) is a serious condition of many western soils, especially in California. It can occur wherever oaks may have grown or where infected trees still exist. Susceptible plants catch the disease when their roots touch the roots of infected trees or rotting wood and roots from trees long since gone. The best defense is to grow resistant plants.

Pinus nigra
AUSTRIAN BLACK PINE
☼ ● Z5–9 H8–3 ‡60ft (18m) ↔30ft (10m)
A fast-growing pyramid in youth, this is wide with a flat top in age. It takes ocean wind, urban pollution, regular irrigation, and occasional fertilization.

Maclura pomifera
OSAGE ORANGE
Ⓝ ☼ ◊◊ Z5–9 H9–5 ‡60 ft (18m) ↔30ft (10m)
A coarse craggy hardwood from Texas to Oklahoma, with a messy fruit drop. Thorns may be undesireable; if so, try improved, thornless fruitless varieties.

Metasequoia glyptostroboides
DAWN REDWOOD
☼ ● Z4–11 H12–1 ‡90ft (25m) ↔20ft (6m)
A deciduous conifer that is fast-growing in youth and shapely without pruning. New foliage is feathery, light green, and burns in desert heat and coastal wind.

Gleditsia triacanthos 'Elegantissima'
ELEGANTISSIMA HONEY LOCUST
Ⓝ ☼ ◊◊ Z3–7 H7–1 ‡70ft (20m) ↔20ft (6m)
Takes heat, wind, drought, and cold. Thornless types cast a light shade and plants can grow underneath. Fernlike leaves do not litter; roots damage pavement.

MORE CHOICES

- *Abies concolor* 'Argentea' Z3–7 H7–1
- *Calocedrus decurrens* Z5–10 H8–5
- *Catalpa bignonioides* Z5–9 H9–5
- *Celtis australis* Z6–9 H8–6
- *Gymnocladus dioicus* Z5–9 H9–5
- *Ilex opaca* Z5–9 H9–5
- *Melaleuca styphelioides* Z9–11 H12–10
- *Pinus monticola* Z4–8 H8–1
- *Pinus patula* Z8–10 H9–8
- *Quercus lobata* Z7–10 H9–7
- *Sapium sebiferum* Z8–9 H10–8
- *Taxodium distichum* Z5–11 H12–5

Eucalyptus cinerea
SILVER DOLLAR TREE

☼ ◊◐ Z8–10 H10–8 ↕55ft (17m) ↔45ft (14m)

Often kept as a low plant by cutting fragrant young foliage, this matures to a bushy tree with long green leaves, reverting to round silver ones when pruned.

Quillaja sasponaria
SOAPBARK TREE

☼ ◊◐ Z8–11 H12–8 ↕45ft (14m) ↔60ft (18m)

In youth, this is a dense column with evergreen foliage to the ground. In age, it is broad with less-pendulous, leathery foliage, and star-shaped brown fruits.

Cercis siliquastrum 'Bodnant'
BODNANT JUDAS TREE

☼ ☼ ◐◐ Z6–8 H9–6 ↕↔30ft (10m)

An improved variety of a shrubby tree, this has spring pink-purple flowers straight from the branches and 4in (10cm), kidney-shaped, soft-textured leaves.

Acer tataricum subsp. ginnala
AMUR MAPLE

☼ ☼ ◊◐ Z3–7 H7–1 ↕↔25ft (8m)

'Flame' has brilliant red fall foliage, fragrant blooms in spring, and colorful red-winged seeds in summer. From Manchuria, this is best in cooler zones, in mountains.

Citrus trees

Citrus trees are heritage plants brought to the New World by Spanish conquerors. Some are regional treasures not practical as commercial fruit trees but bearing delicious homegrown fruit. In general, sour types grow in less heat and sweeter varieties need warmth to form sugars. Pink selections need heat to form color. Some types are available on dwarfing rootstock.

Citrus sinensis 'Moro'
BLOOD ORANGE
☼ ● Z9–10 H10–9 ‡↔25ft (8m)
An early ripening, Italian variety with tasty fruit – red inside and brilliant juice – that hangs in bunches outside foliage. Rind needs interior heat to turn pink.

Citrus limon 'Bearss'
BEARSS LIME
☼ ● Z9–12 H12–9 ‡15ft (5m) ↔10ft (3m)
Introduced from Tahiti in Porterville, California, this is the most valuable Western garden lime. Thorny and vigorous, it has extremely fragrant flowers and the fruit hangs until picked. Fertilize.

Citrus maxima 'Chandler'
CHANDLER PINK PUMMELO
☼ ● Z9–10 H10–9 ‡↔30ft (10m)
The huge fruit has pink flesh, many seeds, excellent flavor, and less juice in the desert (juicy in coastal zones, but not sweet). Leave them on the tree until yellow; they lack flavor when green. Needs a hot summer.

Citrus 'Oroblanco'
OROBLANCO GRAPEFRUIT
☼ ● Z9–10 H10–9
‡30ft (10m) ↔25ft (8m)
Thick-skinned, seedless, delicious fruit does not hold well on the tree. This grows best in interior California, and needs lower heat than other grapefruits. It ripens in approximately 9 to 12 months.

Citrus paradisi 'Rio Red'
RIO RED GRAPEFRUIT
☼ ● Z9–11 H12–9 ‡↔30ft (10m)
Introduced in 1984, this is excellent in Arizona and Texas, and more dependable and prolific than 'Star Ruby'. It has few seeds and sweet red flesh that fades.

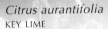

Citrus aurantifolia
KEY LIME

☼ ⬤ z10–15 H12–10 ‡15ft (5m) ↔10ft (3m)

Green or yellow, aromatic, year-round fruit has a fine flavor for pies, drinks, and Mexican foods. More acidic than lemon, it is best in tropical, subtropical climates.

Citrus x tangelo 'Minneola'
MINNEOLA TANGELO

☼ ⬤ z9–10 H10–9 ‡↔30ft (10m)

This cross between a Dancy mandarin and Duncan grapefruit is tasteless in markets but good homegrown, eaten fresh from desert trees. The neck is distinctive.

Citrus sinensis 'Valencia'
VALENCIA ORANGE

☼ ⬤ z9–12 H12–9 ‡↔25ft (8m)

Widely adapted, in the desert it begins ripening in late winter; summer on the coast. Fruit left on the tree will turn green again in winter, but will still be sweet.

Citrus sinensis 'Lane Late'
LANE LATE NAVEL ORANGE

☼ ⬤ z9–10 H10–8 ‡↔25ft (8m)

Grow with 'Valencia' and 'Robertson Navel' for year-round fruit that is good on smaller trees and perfect for eating fresh. The best flavor is in subtropical climates.

MORE CHOICES

- *Citrus limon* 'Pink Lemonade'
  z9–12 H12–9
- *Citrus maxima* 'Cocktail' z9–10 H10–9
- *Citrus medica* 'Buddha's Hand'
  z9–10 H10–9
- *Citrus meyeri* 'Improved' z9–11 H12–1
- *Citrus ponderosa* z9–10 H10–8
- *Citrus reticulata* 'Algerian' z9–11 H12–1
- *Fortunella crassifolia* 'Meiwa'
  z9–12 H12–9

WOODY PLANTS

Deciduous, interior fruit and nut trees

Each fruit and nut tree is adapted to a specific climate, and needs a certain number of hours of winter chill, below 45°F (7°C), in order to leaf out properly or bear a crop. Those shown here are generally adapted for interior zones, away from the coast. Remember to prune correctly for each type of fruit and to control overwintering pests and diseases with dormant spray.

WOODY PLANTS

MORE CHOICES

- *Ficus carica* 'Brown Turkey' z7–11 H12–7
- *Ficus carica* 'Celeste' z7–11 H12–1
- *Malus* 'Golden Delicious' z5–8 H8–1
- *Prunus armeniaca* 'Blenheim' z6–8 H9–6
- *Prunus* 'Kristin' z5–8 H8–4
- *Prunus* 'Montmorency' z4–8 H8–1
- *Prunus nucipersica* 'Mericrest' z4–8 H8–1
- *Prunus persica* 'Indian Blood Cling' z4–8 H8–1
- *Prunus salicina* 'Santa Rosa' z5–10 H8–3
- *Pyrus pyrifolia* 'Ichiban' z6–9 H9–6

Juglans regia 'Pedro'
PEDRO ENGLISH WALNUT
☼ ◐ Z3–9 H7–1 ‡↔60ft (18m)
This tree, which has a long leafless winter, may cause allergies so do not plant near the house. When nuts fall, gather daily, remove husks, and dry in shade.

Carya illinoinensis 'Western Schley'
WESTERN SCHLEY PECAN
☼ ◐ Z5–9 H9–1 ‡↔70ft (20m)
This large shade tree can be grown on a large lawn. Quality nuts appear in interior valleys with long hot summers. In fall, gather nuts daily and remove hulls.

Malus 'Dorset Golden'
LOW-CHILL GOLDEN APPLE
☼ ◐ Z5–10 H8–1
‡20ft (6m) ↔25ft (8m)
Adapted to coastal or interior climates, this has excellent summer fruit but needs regular water during fruit development. Use a light organic fertilizer just before the flower buds open, but never in fall.

Pyrus communis 'Moonglow'
MOONGLOW EUROPEAN PEAR
☼ ◐ Z5–8 H8–1
‡40ft (12m) ↔25ft (8m)
This bountiful harvest is of excellent quality in interior zones with winter chill. Plant another pear for pollination or graft on some cuttings. Pick unripe pears and store them in a cool place to ripen.

Prunus armeniaca 'Moorpark'
MOORPARK APRICOT

☼ ◐ Z6–8 H8–6 ↕↔20ft (6m)

Large fruit with excellent flavor can be eaten straight from the tree or dried. In winter, apply dormant sprays and prune to stimulate new spurs and branches. Needs winter chill.

Prunus dulcis 'All-In-One'
ALL-IN-ONE ALMOND

☼ ◐ Z5–8 H8–5 ↕↔25ft (8m)

This self-fruiting semidwarf is the best garden variety, with white spring flowers and nuts on spurs that live five years. Cut a fifth of old wood each winter to encourage growth.

Prunus x *domestica* 'Green Gage'
GREEN GAGE EUROPEAN PLUM

☼ ◐ Z5–8 H8–3 ↕60ft (18m) ↔30ft (10m)

An old variety, this tree's fruit has a tangy taste. For jam, cooking, or canning, use them ripe. This needs 700 hours of winter chill, fertilizer, dormant spray in winter, and little pruning: shape when young; remove dead wood.

Prunus 'English Morello'
SOUR CHERRY

☼ ◐ Z5–8 H8–4 ↕↔20ft (6m)

Sweet cherries need 1,000 chilling hours but cannot take too much heat or cold. This sour cherry tree has succeeded in Texas hill country, and does not need a pollinator. Prune only to train or shape.

Castanea 'Colossal'
COLOSSAL CHESTNUT

☼ ◐ 뿅 Z4–10 H8–1 ↕↔60ft (18m)

A handsome but messy tree with a low-chill requirement, but alkaline soil and water can cause problems. It has showy white flowers and aromatic pollen. Pick up its nuts when they fall and dry in the sun (or shade if hot).

WOODY PLANTS

Tropical or exotic fruit trees

Tropical and exotic fruits have a fan club called California Rare Fruit Growers, Inc. (http://www.crfg.org). Adventurous gardeners can find unique plants through this society or from specialty nurseries and botanical gardens. Many exotic fruits make handsome landscape plants and are often easier to grow in mild winter zones than their deciduous counterparts.

Carica papaya 'Sunset'
SUNSET PAPAYA
☼ ◐ Z10–12 H10–10 ‡25ft (8m) ↔6ft (2m)
This tall perennial needs to be kept frost-free on a south slope, and in a plastic tent in winter. Provide good drainage, ample water, and summer fertilizer.

Psidium cattleianum
STRAWBERRY GUAVA
☼ ◑ ◐ Z9–12 H12–10-
‡↔20ft (6m)
Hardier than *P. guajava* (common guava), this has an upright trunk with beautiful mottled bark. Fruit darkens when ripe and may ripen year round. It is flavorful fresh and can be used for juice or jelly.

Eriobotrya japonica 'Champagne'
CHAMPAGNE LOQUAT
☼ ◐◐ Z8–11 H12–8 ‡↔30ft (10m)
A small garden tree for the desert to the coast, named varieties have better fruit than the species. Use 'Champagne' for warm areas, 'Gold Nugget' for cool.

Ziziphus jujuba 'Li'
JUJUBE, CHINESE DATE
☼ ◑ ◐◐ Z5–10 H10–8 ‡20ft (6m) ↔15ft (5m)
This drought-resistant, barrier plant with prickly branches is good for a high desert. Eat fruit fresh in fall when they turn brown, or dried when fully brown.

MORE CHOICES

- *Annona cherimola* 'McPherson' Z14–15 H12–10
- *Carica* x *heilbornii* var. *pentagona* Z10–12 H12–10
- *Diospyros kaki* 'Chocolate' Z7–10 H10–7
- *Diospyros kaki* 'Hachiya' Z7–10 H10–7
- *Macadamia* 'Beaumont' Z9–15 H12–10
- *Macadamia tetraphylla* Z9–15 H12–10
- *Musa acuminata* Z10–15 H12–7
- *Persea americana* 'Pinkerton' Z9–12 H12–10
- *Pseudocydonia sinensis* Z6–8 H8–4

Cydonia oblonga 'Aromatnaya'
AROMATNAYA QUINCE
☼ ◗◖ Z6–10 H8–6 ↕↔25ft (8m)
Little winter chill is needed for this
good landscape plant. Delicious,
yellow, pineapple-flavored fruit can
be eaten fresh – and is very rare in
markets. Do not use high-nitrogen fertilizer.

Pachira aquatica
GUIANA CHESTNUT, SHAVING BRUSH TREE
☼ ◗ Z10–15 H12–1 ↕60ft (18m) ↔30ft (10m)
A gorgeous waterside tree for the tropics, its green shapely
trunk is buttressed at the bottom. Brushlike flowers are
followed by brown nuts that can be roasted.

Litchi chinensis 'Groff'
GROFF LITCHI NUT
☼ ◗ Z10–12 H12–9 ↕↔40ft (12m)
In warmer spots of California, this bears sweet, slippery, jellylike
fruit, suitable for drying. This variety has small pits inside. Harvest
when fruit peels easily. 'Kaimana' is the best Hawaiian variety.

Mangifera indica 'Keitt'
KEITT MANGO
☼ ◗ Z10–15 H12–1 ↕50ft (15m) ↔30ft (10m)
A self-fruiting, long-lived tree that is shrubby in California, this
bears ripened fruit on a warm southern hillside or in a protected
backyard. If seed-grown, cut off the top and graft with a variety.

WOODY PLANTS

Low-chill, fruit trees for mild zones

The first step in growing high-quality deciduous fruit is choosing the right variety. If you live in a mild climate, always select low-chill varieties. Some varieties needing chill might bear fruit but few leaves near the coast. Without adequate leaf cover, your fruit will turn out dry and sunburned. The trees listed here will bear bountiful crops in largely frost-free zones.

Prunus 'Bonanza II'
BONANZA II PEACH
☼ ♦ Z9–10 H10–9
↕4ft (1.2m) ↔5ft (1.5m)
Similar to 'Bonanza', which was the first dwarf, mild-climate peach, but with a better flavor, and is suitable for containers and widely available. Dormant spray at least twice in winter to prevent peach leaf curl.

Prunus glandulosa 'Floragold'
FLORAGOLD APRICOT
☼ ♦ Z9–10 H10–9 ↕↔15ft (5m)
A natural semidwarf, about two-thirds the size of a normal tree on its own roots. This needs no pollinator and is best in a cool microclimate, away from the immediate coast. Sweet fruit ripens early.

Prunus persica 'Floridaprince'
FLORDIA PRINCE PEACH
☼ ♦ Z4–10 H8–1 ↕↔25ft (8m)
Needing only 150 hours of winter chill, this bears masses of delicious juicy fruit even near the ocean. Thin in March, the tree's fruit ripens in May.

Prunus 'Flavor King'
FLAVOR KING PLUOT
☼ ♦ Z9–10 H10–9 ↕↔25ft (8m)
The best pluot (plum-apricot cross), this succeeds wherever P. salicina 'Santa Rosa' (Santa Rosa plum) does, just over the first hills from the ocean, or on a mesa top. It has delicious red fruit in May and June.

Pyrus communis 'Kieffer'
KIEFFER ASIAN PEAR
☼ ◊ Z4–10 H8–1 ‡40ft (12m) ↔25ft (8m)
Good for canning and baking, the late fruit, like that of *P. communis* 'Bartlett', is sweeter with red skins and gritty flesh. Resistant to fireblight, it bears near the coast on mesa tops.

Prunus 'Plum Parfait'
PLUM PARFAIT PLUMCOT
☼ ◊ Z9–10 H10–9 ‡↔20ft (6m)
A modern variety of an original cross between apricot and plum, this needs a pollinator. The fruit has flesh like an apricot and a plumlike flavor. Prune in winter.

MORE CHOICES

- *Ficus carica* 'Brown Turkey' Z7–11 H12–7
- *Ficus carica* 'Genoa' Z7–11 H12–1
- *Malus* 'Beverly Hills' Z5–10 H8–1
- *Malus* 'Tropical Beauty' Z5–10 H8–1
- *Prunus* x *domestica* 'Santa Rosa' Z5–10 H8–3
- *Prunus dulcis* 'All-In-One' Z5–9 H8–5
- *Prunus persica* var. *nucipersica* 'Panamint' Z4–10 H8–1
- *Pyrus communis* 'Floridahome' Z5–10 H9–1
- *Pyrus communis* 'Moonglow' Z5–9 H8–1
- *Pyrus pyrifolia* 'Ichiban' Z6–10 H9–6

Prunus 'Flavor Delight'
FLAVOR DELIGHT APRIUM
☼ ◊ Z8–9 H9–8 ‡↔25ft (8m)
Wherever *P.* 'Blenheim' (Blenheim apricot) succeeds, this will also bear excellent crops in early summer and is best with a pollinator such as apricot. Some people prefer the juicier, slightly plumlike fruit over apricots.

Prunus glandulosa 'Katy'
KATY APRICOT
☼ ◊ Z8–10 H10–8 ‡↔15ft (5m)
One of the best low-chill, home-garden apricots, this bears crops in milder zones than most and is worth a try in a cold microclimate near the coast. Early fruit has a sweet mild flavor.

Malus 'Anna'
ANNA APPLE
☼ ◊ Z9–10 H10–9 ‡20ft (6m) ↔25ft (8m)
Within sight of the sea, these delicious, juicy red apples appear in early summer and again in fall. 'Ein Shemer' is a pollinator. If no bees exist, hand-pollinate with a sable paintbrush.

WOODY PLANTS

Palms for desert gardens

Palms are so common in mild climates that many people take them for granted, perhaps never noticing that on some palms the fronds are shaped like feathers, while on others they are shaped like fans – a few varieties even have combination fronds. The trees listed here bear foliage in a wide variety of shapes and sizes, and all endure desert heat and wind.

Phoenix dactylifera
DATE PALM
☼ ◐ Z9–12 H12–10
↕80ft (25m) ↔40ft (12m)
A street or grove tree with feathery straight fronds and a thin trunk. Cut suckers from their base. 'Deglet Noor' needs desert heat and has the best fruit.

Butia capitata
PINDO PALM
☼ ◑ ◐ Z9–12 H12–10 ↕20ft (6m) ↔15ft (5m)
Small enough for home gardens, this palm has feather-shaped fronds that arch upward then down. Stubs of old leaves hang on; trim neatly to same length.

Brahea edulis
GUADALUPE PALM
Ⓝ ☼ ◊◐◐ Z9–11 H12–10 ↕30ft (10m) ↔15ft (5m)
Hardier than many palms, this is a native to an island off the California coast. Slow-growing, it can be planted from the beach to the desert. Fans fall off.

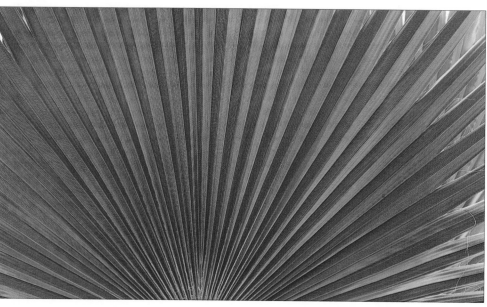

MORE CHOICES

- *Jubaea chilensis* Z8–11 H12–9
- *Yucca elata* Z7–10 H12–9

Washingtonia filifera
CALIFORNIA FAN PALM
Ⓝ ☼ ◊◐◐ Z8–11 H12–8 ↕60ft (18m) ↔20ft (6m)
A thick-trunked fan palm that originates in the desert washes of California and Arizona, this is excellent for growing in interior zones but prone to fungus along the coast. Hybridizes with *W. robusta* (Mexican fan palm). Orioles may use threads on leaves for nests.

Phoenix canariensis
CANARY ISLAND PALM
☼ ◐ Z9–15 H12–10 ↕60ft (18m) ↔50ft (15m)
For large properties near the beach or desert, pruned specimens have a "pineapple" of old frond bases topped by a head of new fronds. Water and fertilize.

Palms for tropical gardens

Can you imagine a tropical island without its fringe of coconut palms? Palms are appropriate for Hawaiian gardens, but coconuts may not be the optimum choice. Falling nuts and fronds can be lethal, needing removal every two or three years. All of the palms listed here grow outdoors in Hawaii. Most will also provide a tropical touch to mainland gardens.

Rhapis excelsa
LADY PALM
☼ ☼ ● Z10–15 H12–1 ↕↔12ft (4m)
A slow-growing, fan palm that creates a clump. Grow this outside in Hawaii, or in frost-free patios, Japanese gardens, or entryway planters on the mainland.

Ravenala madagascariensis
TRAVELER'S PALM
☼ ● Z10 H12–1 ↕50ft (15m) ↔30ft (10m)
Grow out of the wind in Hawaii or coastal California. Not a true palm, but similar to a giant *Strelitzia reginae* (bird of paradise), plant against a bare wall or building.

MORE CHOICES

- *Chrysalidocarpus lutescens* Z11–12 H12–10
- *Cocos nucifera* Z11–12 H12–10
- *Howea forsteriana* Z10–12 H12–1
- *Ravenea rivularis* Z10–11 H12–10

Roystonea regia
ROYAL PALM
☼ ● Z10–12 H12–10
↕80ft (25m) ↔30ft (10m)
This needs moist air in a frost-free location and grows well in the soils of Hawaii and the Gulf Coast. It needs a lot of irrigation in California.

Chamaedorea elegans
PARLOR PALM
☼ ☼ ● Z10–15 H12–1
↕↔25ft (8m)
Single-stemmed and sold in clumps, plant outdoors in Hawaii, or in patio beds or edges of lawns in warm coastal zones of the mainland. Feed palm food.

Pandanus tectorius
SCREW PINE
Ⓝ ☼ ● Z10–15 H12–10 ↕30ft (10m) ↔40ft (12m)
A palmlike native of Hawaii, this is rare on the mainland but grown in mild spots. Salt- and wind-tolerant, it grows on the beach with aerial roots and branches with spirals of pointed leaves. Females bear inedible fruit.

Drought-resistant palms

Palms may be an acquired taste, but they are among the most interesting of plants, with many commercial uses. The largest seeds, the most massive inflorescence, and the longest leaf of any plant are all produced by palms. As irrigation water becomes ever more expensive, drought-resistant palms are especially valuable, creating the atmosphere of a paradise with little care.

Phoenix rupicola
CLIFF DATE PALM
☼ ◑ ◑ Z9–12 H10–9 ↕25ft (8m) ↔20ft (6m)
Deserving of more planting, this relatively fast-growing feather palm is native to India. It has a thinner trunk than *P. canariensis* (Canary Island date palm), casting a lighter shade and fitting in smaller planting spaces.

Wodyetia bifurcata
FOXTAIL PALM
☼ ◑ Z9–12 H10–9
↕20ft (6m) ↔10ft (3m)
This recent Australian arrival is fast-growing from seed and already established in frost-free zones. It tolerates drought, hot sun, and wind, but may rot in cold wet soil. It has fuller fronds than *Syagrus romanzoffiana* (queen palm).

Sabal causiarum
PUERTO RICAN HAT PALM
☼ ◑ Z9–15 H12–10
↕30ft (10m) ↔15ft (5m)
Large, light green (sometimes gray) curving fans appear on a stout, light gray trunk, which is eventually tall, smooth, and white. It takes wind and salty soil and has prominent flowers.

Brahea aculeata
SINALOA HESPER PALM
☼ ◑ Z9–15 H12–10
↕25ft (8m) ↔20ft (6m)
A rare palm with gray-green leaves and spines on its leaf stalks, this is slow-growing and takes heat and wind. It grows faster with fertilizer and irrigation in well-drained soil.

Livistona mariae
CENTRAL AUSTRALIAN CABBAGE PALM
☼ ◑ Z9–11 H12–10 ↕30ft (10m) ↔10ft (3m)
A little-known fan palm with leaves 6ft (2m) wide, it is green when mature, reddish when young, including its petioles (leaf stalks). *L. rigida* is shorter-leaved.

Washingtonia robusta
MEXICAN FAN PALM

☼ ◊◊◊ z9–15 H12–10

↕100ft (30m) ↔10ft (3m)

This fast-growing palm is good for the coast and inland, and lacks the leaf threads of *W. filifera* (California fan palm) but has a taller thinner trunk. Dead fronds hang on like a skirt.

Jubaea chilensis
CHILEAN WINE PALM

☼ ◊◊◊ z8–11 H12–9 ↕60ft (18m) ↔25ft (8m)

This hardy, slow-starting palm has feather fronds and the largest trunk of any palm. Drought-resistant once established, but feed, water when young. Edible fruit.

Syagrus coronata
LICURY PALM

☼ ◊◊ z10–15 H12–10 ↕10ft (3m) ↔12ft (4m)

A rare, small, Brazilian palm with persistent leaf bases in five spiraling rows, arching blue-green fronds, and edible fruit like small coconuts that yield palm oil.

MORE CHOICES

- *Brahea brandegeei* z9–12 H12–10
- *Brahea dulcis* z10–11 H12–10
- *Brahea elegans* z9–15 H12–10
- *Chamaerops humilis* z9–14 H12–10
- *Livistona humilis* z9–15 H12–10
- *Trachycarpus wagnerianus* z8–10 H10–8

WOODY PLANTS

Palms for moist soil

The palms on this page come from subtropical climates where rains are frequent, and are highly attractive when grown in water-retentive soil with regular watering and spring feeding with palm fertilizer. They will never look good in starved sandy soil that dries out weekly between irrigations. Droughts make for uneven trunks. Some also do poorly in wind.

Archontophoenix cunninghamiana
KING PALM
☼ ☼ ◑◑ Z9–11 H12–9 ‡50ft (15m) ↔15ft (5m)
The swollen collection of smooth green leaf bases is a crownshaft. Spent fronds fall off, followed by amethyst flowers, then falling seeds that sprout on the ground.

Roystonea regia
ROYAL PALM
☼ ◑ Z10–12 H12–10 ‡80ft (25m) ↔30ft (10m)
For Hawaii or coastal Southern California, the massive white trunk is topped by a green crownshaft below arching fronds. Slow at first, growth speeds up.

MORE CHOICES

- *Acoelorraphe wrightii* Z11–15 H12–10
- *Caryota mitis* Z10–12 H12–10
- *Ravenea rivularis* Z10–11 H12–10
- *Rhapidophylum hystrix* Z6–11 H12–10
- *Rhapis excelsa* Z10–15 H12–1
- *Sabal mexicana* Z9–15 H12–10
- *Sabal palmetto* Z9–15 H12–10

Syagrus romanzoffiana
QUEEN PALM
☼ ◑ Z9–15 H10–1 ‡80ft (25m) ↔30ft (10m)
An attractive feather palm if well grown, but produces sparse, ratty-looking fronds if not fed and watered. It may bear orange dates that are decorative, not edible.

Caryota urens
FISHTAIL WINE PALM
☼ ☼ ◑ Z10–12 H12–10 ‡40ft (12m) ↔15ft (5m)
Very fast-growing, this blooms once at 20–25 years old, then dies. It is the hardiest fishtail palm. Plant in humus-rich soil, in a warm windless location.

Palms that survive frost

Hardy palms are useful in interior climates and deserts where hot summers may be followed by occasional winter frosts. Some of these palms have been found growing in remarkable spots, far from the sea on mountainsides, in canyons, even next to old mineshafts, where perhaps their seeds were deposited by birds or planted for shade by a palm-loving prospector.

Sabal palmetto
CABBAGE PALM

Ⓝ ☼ ◐ Z9–15 H12–10
↕80ft (25m) ↔10ft (3m)

A robust native to the Southeast, this grows slowly at first, then becomes faster given water. Its dark trunk is topped by a full head of fan-shaped leaves with arching tips. It grows in any soil and is much used in Texas.

MORE CHOICES

- *Butia capitata* Z9–12 H12–10
- *Jubaea chilensis* Z8–11 H12–9
- *Phoenix dactylifera* Z9–12 H12–10
- *Phoenix roebelenii* Z9–12 H12–10
- *Sabal mexicana* Z9–15 H12–10
- *Washingtonia robusta* Z8–15 H12–10

Trachycarpus fortunei
WINDMILL PALM

☼ ◐ ◑ ● Z8–11 H12–8 ↕30ft (10m) ↔10ft (3m)

A fan palm from Chinese mountain foothills, this has compact stiff fans and a black hairy trunk that is wider above as old leaf bases and black hairs fall off below.

Rhapidophyllum hystrix
NEEDLE PALM

Ⓝ ☼ ◑ ● ◐ Z6–10 H12–10
↕↔8ft (2.5m)

A clumping fan palm from the Southeast, this is the hardiest of all palms, growing where others do not. A slow-growing barrier with long black spines hidden among its frond stalks, it likes semishade and moisture.

Chamaerops humilis
MEDITERRANEAN FAN PALM

☼ ◑ ● ◐● Z9–14 H12–10 ↕↔20ft (6m)

One of the finest available fan palms for mild Mediterranean climates, this is drought-resistant once established, slow-growing, long-lived, and an eventual large handsome clump. Allow space for future growth. Old plants are transplantable.

Brahea armata
MEXICAN BLUE PALM

☼ ● Z9–12 H12–10 ↕80ft (25m) ↔30ft (10m)

A silver-blue fan palm with a trunk covered in old leaf bases, this is slow-growing. Many 15ft (5m) arching stems hold flowers that cascade 10ft (3m) downwards.

Fast-growing broadleaf trees

Many new homeowners often ask for fast-growing trees. Unfortunately, a tree that grows fast is not always the wisest choice. Some fast-growing trees are brittle while others shoot up too high. Still others are known for litter, invasive roots, or problems with pests and disease. But there are some good choices, many of which are shown here.

x *Chitalpa tashkentensis* 'Pink Dawn'
PINK DAWN CHITALPA TREE
☼ ◐ Z6–9 H8–4 ↕↔30ft (10m)
Shorter than the species and a hybrid of two native trees, this is deciduous, heat-resistant, adaptable, and drought-tolerant, with large blooms from spring to fall.

Pterocarya stenoptera
CHINESE WINGNUT
☼ ◐◐ Z7–9 H9–7 ↕90ft (25m) ↔50ft (15m)
A deciduous tree that is well shaped but very large, good for playgrounds, parks, compacted soils, and as a screen far from the house. Its winged seeds cluster.

MORE CHOICES

- *Acer saccharinum* Z4–8 H8–1
- *Agonis flexuosa* Z9–10 H12–6
- *Albizia julibrissin* Z6–10 H9–6
- *Alnus rhombifolia* Z5–9 H8–5
- *Catalpa speciosa* Z5–9 H9–5
- *Fraxinus uhdei* Z8–11 H12–8
- *Liriodendron tulipifera* 'Fastigiatum' Z5–9 H9–2
- *Metasequoia glyptostroboides* Z4–11 H12–1

Populus trichocarpa
BLACK COTTONWOOD

Ⓝ ☼ ⬤ Z4–10 H9–1
↕100ft (30m) ↔30ft (9m)
This native to streambeds from Southern California to Alaska has furrowed gray bark, brittle wood, and silver-backed leaves that turn yellow in fall. Its invasive roots are not good near the house.

Acacia longifolia
SYDNEY GOLDEN WATTLE

☼ ◊◑ Z10–11 H12–1 ↕↔20ft (6m)
Often shrublike, this is a quick screen on banks. Not for a manicured garden, but can fit into a drought-resistant landscape. Occasional pruning lengthens life.

Ulmus 'Morton'
ACCOLADE ELM

☼ ⬤ Z10–7 H9–4 ↕40ft (12m) ↔30ft (10m)
A new introduction to substitute for U. americana (American elm), this has a similar vase shape and yellow fall color. It is resistant to Dutch elm disease and elm leaf beetles.

Robinia pseudoacacia 'Frisia'
IDAHO LOCUST

☼ ◊◑ Z4–10 H9–4 ↕40ft (12m) ↔30ft (10m)
An invasive deciduous tree that takes heat, drought, and supplies nitrogen to poor soil. With lovely foliage, flowers, and fall color, it also has thorns and suckers.

Gleditsia triacanthos 'Ruby Lace'
RUBY LACE HONEY LOCUST

☼ ◊◑ Z5–9 H9–5 ↕70ft (20m) ↔35ft (11m)
With red new growth and a yellow fall color, its light filtered shade and small falling leaves allow a lawn or flowers to grow beneath. Brittle wood breaks in wind.

Eucalyptus nicholii
NICHOL'S WILLOW-LEAFED PEPPERMINT

☼ ◊ Z9–11 H10–9 ↕50ft (15m) ↔35ft (11m)
Weeping and naturally well-shaped for a garden or a street, this gets chlorosis in poorly drained soil. Do not plant until pests are controlled, but watering helps.

WOODY PLANTS

Native shrubs for desert gardens

Gardening in harmony with nature means choosing plants adapted to your soil and climate. In most interior regions of the Southwest, the climate is hot, dry, and windy, and the soil is alkaline. Fortunately, nature itself has created plants with special characteristics, such as salt-resistance or gray foliage, that enables them to survive in these difficult conditions.

Justicia californica
CHUPAROSA

Ⓝ ☼ ☼ ◊ ◑ Z8–9 H9–5 ↕↔6ft (2m)

This shrub attracts hummingbirds, fall through spring. It keeps its foliage in summer, with occasional irrigation, and can freeze in winter but bounces back.

Salvia microphylla 'Kew Red'
KEW RED DESERT SAGE

Ⓝ ☼ ☼ ◊ ◑ Z7–10 H10–8 ↕4ft (1.2m) ↔6ft (2m)

A colorful evergreen shrub from Arizona and Mexico, it is best with some irrigation. Many hybrids have red flowers, including 'Maraschino Cherry'.

Rhus trilobata
SKUNKBUSH

Ⓝ ☼ ☼ ◊ ◑ Z4–9 H6–2 ↕3ft (1m) ↔8ft (2.5m)

Do not overwater this deciduous hedge or plant it close to the house; its fuzzy fragrant foliage may cause allergic reactions. Red berries and leaves appear in fall.

Calliandra eriophylla
FAIRY DUSTER

Ⓝ ☼ ◊ ◑ Z9–15 H12–10 ↕3ft (1m) ↔5ft (1.5m)

Blossoms look like a rose-colored mist when sun shines through the plant, and mix well with cacti and agave. Site where hummingbirds can be enjoyed.

MORE CHOICES

- *Anisacanthus thurberi* Z7–11 H12–9
- *Chrysothamnus nauseosus* Z5–9 H12–3
- *Dalea frutescens* Z7–9 H12–1
- *Dalea pulchra* Z7–9 H12–9
- *Encelia farinosa* Z7–9 H9–7
- *Larrea tridentata* Z7–9 H12–8
- *Salvia greggii* Z7–10 H9–4
- *Tagetes lemmonii* Z8–10 H12–1
- *Tecoma stans* Z9–15 H12–10
- *Vauquelinia californica* Z7–8 H8–7

Calliandra californica
BAJA FAIRY DUSTER

Ⓝ ☼ ☼ ◊ ◑ Z9–15 H12–1 ↕↔4ft (1.2m)

Excellent in hot interior climates, its flowers bring hummingbirds. Flowers appear all year and seedpods follow on sparse evergreen foliage with split leaves.

Leucophyllum frutescens var. **compactum**
TEXAS RANGER
Ⓝ ☼ ◊◊ z7–9 H9–8 ↕↔5ft (1.5m)
A compact variety for shrubbery or a clipped hedge, sheared in spring. Texas humidity triggers a summer bloom; in deserts, it blooms after summer rains.

Simmondsia chinensis
JOJOBA
Ⓝ ☼☼ ◊◊ z8–15 H12–1 ↕↔6ft (2m)
A dense evergreen plant that bears nuts used for commercial oils, and are edible if roasted. Good for informal or clipped hedges and rarely needs water.

Dodonaea viscosa
HOP BUSH
Ⓝ ☼☼ ◊◊◊ z7–15 H12–10 ↕↔15ft (5m)
A fast-growing, heat-resistant, green-leaved plant like the familiar purple variety. Native to the Southwest and Hawaii, it works as a wind-break and tall hedge.

WOODY PLANTS

Fouquieria macdougalii
MEXICAN
TREE OCOTILLO

Ⓝ ☼ ◊◊

Z8–10 H12–1

↕20ft (6m) ↔4ft (1.2m)
A tree, or six-foot shrub where frosts occur, that blooms February to September, after rains. For a patio or courtyard, with well-drained soil. Water every two weeks in summer for bloom.

Dalea pulchra
INDIGO BUSH

Ⓝ ☼ ◊◊

Z7–9 H12–9

↕8ft (2.5m) ↔5ft (1.5m)
With silvery evergreen foliage and clusters of blossoms March through April, this needs cutting back by half in fall when young to encourage dense growth. Water twice monthly in summer.

Yucca rigida
BLUE YUCCA

Ⓝ ☼ ◊◊ Z8–12 H12–8 ↕12ft (4m) ↔5ft (1.5m)
Powder-blue, stiff, sharply pointed leaves hang down, forming a thatch. Two-feet high, one-foot wide clusters of white flowers appear in early summer. Keep away from walks.

Dasylirion wheeleri
DESERT SPOON, SOTOL
Ⓝ ☀ ◐ ◊ ◑ Z9–10 H10–9 ↕↔5ft (1.5m)
An easy-care plant with a sphere of leaves for many years, an eventual trunk, and some branching. Twelve-foot-high flower clusters occur from May to July.

Fallugia paradoxa
APACHE PLUME
Ⓝ ☀ ◐ ◊ Z6–9 H8–5 ↕6ft (2m) ↔5ft (1.5m)
Drifts of this plant light up mountains in high deserts and gardens. Flowers are followed by pink or purple seed capsules that create a look of pink haze.

Caesalpinia mexicana
MEXICAN BIRD OF PARADISE
Ⓝ ☀ ◊ ◑ Z9–11 H12–9 ↕↔12ft (4m)
Lemon-yellow blooms attract hummingbirds year round. Remove dead or damaged growth in late winter; water occasionally in summer.

Pachycereus schottii
SENITA
Ⓝ ☀ ◊ ◑ Z9–15 H12–10
↕↔15ft (5m)
A mature senita bears long spines, like gray hairs, on its tips. Inch-wide, pink flowers bloom at night. 'Monstrosus' has few thorns and irregular growth, like candle wax.

Leucophyllum frutescens 'Green Cloud'
GREEN CLOUD TEXAS RANGER
Ⓝ ☀ ◊ ◑ Z6–10 H10–6 ↕↔8ft (2.5m)
A compact, slow-growing plant with bright green foliage and rosy magenta flowers, it tolerates heat, drought, and alkalinity and blooms after showers.

MORE CHOICES

- *Caesalpinia californica* Z9–11 H12–9
- *Encelia farinosa* Z7–10 H10–7
- *Larrea divaricata* Z8–10 H10–8
- *Leucophyllum candidum* 'Thundercloud' Z7–10 H10–7
- *Senna pallida* Z8–11 H11–8
- *Senna polyantha* Z8–11 H11–8
- *Viguiera stenoloba* Z8–11 H12–10

WOODY PLANTS

Native shrubs for desert-style gardens

These shrubs are useful, water-thrifty plants for desert-style gardens in hot interior climates, not only in deserts. When planting, be aware that nature creates landscapes using all types of plants, including trees, climbers, and herbaceous plants. Natural landscapes use groups of plants compatible with each other and their environment.

Senna wislizenii
SHRUBBY SENNA

Ⓝ ☼ ◑ ◊ ◔ Z7–11 H12–10 ↕8ft (2.5m) ↔10ft (3m)

Deciduous in winter, with nondescript, dark bare wood. Afterwards, a clothing of gray foliage appears with flowers on its branch tips from June to September.

Fouquieria splendens
OCOTILLO

Ⓝ ☼ ◊ ◔ Z8–10 H12–1 ↕25ft (8m) ↔10ft (3m)

Leaves sprout after spring rains, drop when dry, and sprout again after summer rains. Bright red flowers on its branch tips attract hummingbirds.

Erythrina flabelliformis
SOUTHWEST CORAL BEAN

Ⓝ ☼ ◔ Z9–15 H12–10 ↕20ft (6m) ↔6ft (2m)

Flowers on bare branches, March through May, attract birds. Blooms again after summer rains. Needs a warm location, like poolside planting. Frost keeps it a shrub.

Ungnadia speciosa
MEXICAN BUCKEYE
Ⓝ ☼ ☼ ◊ ◊ Z8–11 H12–9
↕↔15ft (5m)
Deciduous in winter with fragrant spring blooms on bare wood prior to its green leaves. Poisonous black seeds come in bristly ornamental pods.

Cordia parvifolia
LITTLE-LEAF CORDIA
Ⓝ ☼ ◊ ◊ Z7–11 H12–10 ↕10ft (3m) ↔8ft (2.5m)
A splendid show of bell-shaped flowers after each watering or rainfall from late winter until late fall. Needs good drainage, little pruning. This makes an evergreen hedge with blue, pink, and yellow flowers.

Senna armata
SPINY SENNA
Ⓝ ☼ ☼ ◊ ◊ Z4–12 H7–1
↕4ft (1.2m) ↔6ft (2m)
From gravelly plains, slopes, or sandy washes, it is a deciduous plant covered with bloom March to June. Sharp spines create a good barrier. Tan seedpods hang on after bloom, and rattle in the breeze.

Chrysothamnus nauseosus
RABBIT BUSH
Ⓝ ☼ ☼ ◊ ◊ Z6–9 H12–3 ↕4ft (1.2m) ↔5ft (1.5m)
A clump-forming plant with silvery stems and foliage. In autumn, becomes an upright mound covered in masses of small, bright gold flowers, hiding foliage.

Dalea frutescens
BLACK DALEA
Ⓝ ☼ ◊ ◊ Z7–8 H12–1 ↕3ft (1m) ↔4ft (1.2m)
An evergreen with flowers from fall to spring. Cut back when young after bloom to increase bushy growth. Over- or underwatering can cause summer leaf drop.

MORE CHOICES

- *Aloysia wrightii* Z8–11 H12–8
- *Anisacanthus thurberi* Z9–11 H12–9
- *Atriplex lentiformis* Z7–9 H9–7
- *Fallugia paradoxa* Z6–9 H8–5
- *Justicia californica* Z8–9 H9–5
- *Mimosa borealis* Z9–15 H12–1
- *Psorothamnus schottii* Z9–10 H10–9
- *Psorothamnus spinosus* Z8–10 H10–8
- *Rhus microphylla* Z5–9 H9–5
- *Thamnosma montana* Z7–10 H10–7
- *Tiquilia greggii* Z8–10 H10–8
- *Zizyphus obtusifolia* var. *canescens* Z7–9 H9–7

WOODY PLANTS

Native evergreen shrubs for desert gardens

Lush lawns and tropical plants look incongruous in the desert and waste precious water. Though water may seem plentiful where there are golf courses, wasteful use saps and pollutes groundwater. It's better to create a garden that's an extension of nature. Build mounds, half-bury large rocks, and plant colorful native shrubs adapted to desert climates; water to establish.

Dasylirion longissimum
MEXICAN GRASS TREE
Ⓝ ☼ ☀ ◊◊ Z12–15
H12–10 ‡10ft (3m) ↔3ft (1m)
A dark leaved 5-foot fountain for many years, finally sends up a trunk, eventually sprouts cream-colored blooms in early summer. Other good varieties include sotol (*D. texanum*), and desert spoon (*D. wheeleri*).

Baccharis sarothroides
DESERT BROOM
Ⓝ ☼ ◊ Z6–9 H9–6 ‡↔5ft (1.5m)
Brighter green than any other desert foliage, takes desert climates with a smile. Though leaves sometimes drop, bright green stems continue. Can be sheared. Inconspicuous flowers, females bear fluffy seeds.

Berberis haematocarpa
RED BARBERRY
Ⓝ ☼ ☀ ◊◊ Z7–9 H9–7
‡↔5ft (1.5m)
Accent shrub with gray foliage resembling holly. From higher elevations, needs occasional summer irrigation in low deserts. Pretty flowers, juicy red berries relished by wildlife.

Leucophyllum laevigatum
CHIHUAHUAN SAGE
Ⓝ ☼ ◊◊ Z8–9 H9–8
‡4ft (1.2m) ↔5ft (1.5m)
Medium green leaves. Summer bloom like huge bouquet, lavender-blue spikes. No pruning, but give supplemental irrigation twice a month in hottest season. Plant like hedge, for accent, in groups, near patios.

Calliandra californica
BAJA FAIRY DUSTER
Ⓝ ☼ ◊◊ Z13–15 H12–1
‡4ft (1.2m) ↔5ft (1.5m)
Summer, fall flowers bring hummingbirds. Needs no pruning. Combine with creosote bush (*Larrea tridentate*), burro sage (*Ambrosia deltoidea*), palo verde (*Parkinsonia flordia*). Water twice a month in hottest weather.

Salvia coccinea 'Pink'
TROPICAL SAGE

Ⓝ ☼ ◐ ◗ ◖ ◗ Z11 H12–1 ‡3ft (1m) ↔30in (75cm)

Shrubby Mexican perennial. Cut old stems in February to new foliage coming from ground. May return from seeds. Stick branches in ground to hold up in wind.

MORE CHOICES

- *Acacia berlandieri* Z10–11 H12–10
- *Calliandra eriophylla* Z14–15 H12–10
- *Ceratoides lanata* Zx–x Hx–x
- *Dalea pulchra* Z9–11 H12–9
- *Dodonaea viscosa* Z12–15 H12–10
- *Ericameria laricifolia* Z8–11 H12–8
- *Eriogonum fasciculatum* var. *polifolium* H9–1
- *Larrea tridentata* Z8–11 H12–8
- *Leucophyllum candidum* 'Silver Cloud' Z8–9 H9–7
- *Ruellia peninsularis* Z13–15 H12–10
- *Simmondsia chinensis* Z10–15 H12–1

Rhus virens
EVERGREEN SUMAC

Ⓝ ☼ ◐ ◖ ◗ Z9–11 H12–9

‡8ft (2.5m) ↔10ft (3m)

Large shrub, small tree with glossy, dark-green, compound leaves. Small white flowers spring, summer, then showy red berries bringing birds. Occasional summer water.

Sophora secundiflora
TEXAS MOUNTAIN LAUREL

Ⓝ ☼ ◐ ◖ ◗ Z7–11 H12–7 ‡15ft (5m) ↔10ft (3m)

Slow growing shrub; eventually small tree. Heavy clusters of spring-blooming purple flowers with aroma of grape soda bring butterflies. Water twice a month in summer. Control pyralid moth larvae with Bt (*see p. 69*).

Encelia farinosa
BRITTLE BUSH

Ⓝ ☼ ◐ ◖ ◗ Z7–9 H9–7 ‡3ft (1m) ↔4ft (1.2m)

Profuse bloom brightens springtime deserts and gardens. Cut back by a third for second bloom. Gray foliage will stay on if watered monthly in summer, none in fall.

WOODY PLANTS

Groundcover shrubs for dry shade

No plant is perfect, as nature proves with an attractive wild shrub found in dry shade on banks, in canyons, and under trees throughout the Southwest – poison oak. Its poisonous qualities are the very features that explain its abundance. Fortunately, other plants more friendly to man and beast grow almost equally as well in dry shade; many are native.

Baccharis pilularis 'Pigeon Point'
DWARF COYOTE BUSH

Ⓝ ☼ ☀ ◊ ◑ Z6–10 H9–6
↕3ft (1m) ↔9ft (2.5m)

The best for high desert, this is fast-growing with large green leaves and can be used as a hedge. Endures heat, drought, and wind. Shear in spring, fertilize, and water.

Arctostaphylos 'Emerald Carpet'
EMERALD CARPET MANZANITA

Ⓝ ☼ ☀ ◊ ◑ Z7–10 H9–7 ↕14in (35cm) ↔5ft (1.5m)

A slow-growing mat that spreads out in a circle from a mounded center, this has attractive green leaves year-round, spring flowers, and summer berries. Mulch around plants. Needs little pruning.

Ribes sanguineum
RED FLOWERING CURRANT

Ⓝ ☼ ☀ ◊ ◑ Z6–8 H8–6 ↕↔12ft (4m)

A tall deep-rooted plant that can strike into steep ground, holding soil. Surround with shorter groundcovers. This has many good varieties, as well as blue-black fruit loved by birds. Don't grow near white pines.

Arctostaphylos densiflora 'Howard McMinn'
HOWARD MCMINN MANZANITA

Ⓝ ☼ ☀ ◊ ◑ Z7–10 H9–7 ↕4ft (1.2m) ↔5ft (1.5m)

A slow-growing shrub that thrives with little or no care, blooming for 2 or 3 months in late winter or early spring. Naturally shapely. Plant in November and remove dead wood in autumn.

Ruscus hypoglossum
BUTCHER'S BROOM
☼ ☀   ◊ ◊ ◊   Z7–9 H9–7   ↕6in (15cm) ↔2ft (60cm)
This Mediterranean native, spreading from rhizomes, makes
a small-scale groundcover under trees. Thickened stems bear
flowers in center, then berries like marbles if pollinated.

Cotoneaster dammeri 'Lowfast'
LOWFAST BEARBERRY COTONEASTER
☼ ☀   ◊ ◑   Z6–9 H8–6
↕1ft (30cm) ↔10ft (3m)
A fast-growing evergreen that roots as it
goes. Flat sheet on ground, cascades over
walls. Bright red fruits hang on for months.

Ceanothus 'Joyce Coulter'
JOYCE COULTER CALIFORNIA LILAC
Ⓝ ☼ ☀   ◊ ◑   Z9–10 H12–9
↕5ft (1.5m) ↔12ft (4m)
Given good drainage, this is among the
easiest ceanothus to grow, but 'Yankee
Point' and others are flatter. Takes shade
in hotter climates, but needs some sun.

Mahonia nervosa
LONGLEAF MAHONIA
Ⓝ ☼ ☀   ◊ ◑   Z8–10 H10–8
↕2ft (60cm) ↔3ft (1m)
An edging plant or woodland groundcover
with leaves like holly fern, spreading by
underground runners. Yellow flowers in
spring are followed by blue berries.

MORE CHOICES

- *Arctostaphylos edmundsii* 'Carmel Sur'
  Z8–10 H10–8
- *Astartea fascicularis* 'Prostrate Form'
  Z9–10 H10–9
- *Berberis haematocarpa* Z7–9 H9–7
- *Calytrix tetragona* Z9–10 H12–10
- *Ceanothus maritimus* Z9–10 H10–9
- *Coprosma repens* 'Exotica' Z8–10 H10–8
- *Cotoneaster salicifolius* Z6–8 H8–6
- *Diospyros texana* Z8–11 H12–9
- *Galvezia speciosa* Z8–11 H12–8
- *Mahonia* x *wagneri* 'Pinnacle' Z5–9 H9–1
- *Rhamnus californica* 'Sea View'
  Z7–10 H9–7
- *Ruellia californica* Z8–9 H9–8

Ceanothus griseus var. *horizontalis*
CARMEL CREEPER
Ⓝ ☼ ☀   ◊ ◑   Z9–10 H10–9   ↕30in (75cm) ↔15ft (5m)
Not good for cold climates or where deer can eat it. This
otherwise strong, fast-grower is a carpet of flowers in spring.
Ceanothus 'Hurricane Point' is sometimes sold under this name.

WOODY PLANTS

Native shrubs for dry shade

These shrubs are well-suited for growing near native oaks, which sometimes die from root rot if watered more than once or twice in summer. By planting natives, you are protecting your tree and simulating an entire ecosystem. Take care not to damage the tree's roots, and try not to plant within ten feet of the trunk. Retain the natural mulch of fallen leaves.

Agave bovicornuta
COW HORN AGAVE

Ⓝ ☼ ◑ ◊◊ Z8–12 H12–1 ‡3ft (1m) ↔6ft (2m)

A spiny but attractive plant with an eventual panicle of bloom 16–23ft (5–7m) tall, flowering on top of as many as 30 branches. Survives in low desert.

Ribes malvaceum
CHAPARRAL CURRANT

Ⓝ ☼ ◑ ◊◊ Z9–10 H9–7 ‡↔5ft (1.5m)

A deciduous shrub that may stay evergreen if watered in summer. Flowers appear in fragrant clusters through the fall and winter, followed by red fruits.

Quercus dumosa
COASTAL SCRUB OAK

Ⓝ ☼ ◑ ◊◊ Z7–10 H9–7 ‡↔10ft (3m)

A slow-growing shrub with a single or several trunks. Takes sandy soil and coastal wind. Dark evergreen leaves are curved on edges. Clean out dead wood in fall. Scrub jays bury acorns for new plants.

Epilobium canum subsp. latifolium
CALIFORNIA FUCHSIA

Ⓝ ☼ ◑ ◊◊ Z8–10 H12–8 ‡18in (45cm) ↔4ft (1.2m)

Profuse summer and fall flower shows are irresistible to hummingbirds. For informal gardens, banks, or roadsides. Cultivars have gray foliage. Clean up in fall.

MORE CHOICES

- *Choisya dumosa* Z9–10 H10–9
- *Heteromeles arbutifolia* Z9–10 H10–9
- *Justicia spicigera* Z9–11 H12–10
- *Mahonia aquifolium* Z6–10 H9–6
- *Mahonia fremontii* Z7–10 H10–9
- *Rhus integrifolia* Z9–10 H9–7
- *Rhus ovata* Z9–10 H8–1
- *Ribes indecorum* Z7–10 H9–7
- *Ribes speciosum* Z7–10 H9–7
- *Ribes viburnifolium* Z9–10 H10–9
- *Symphoricarpos albus* Z3–9 H7–1

Non-native shrubs for dry shade

Most shade plants need plentiful irrigation and acid soil. In areas where soils are poor and water is ever more scarce and expensive, it is good to know some plants that flourish in less-than-perfect conditions. Once established, most of these plants will remain attractive year-round despite soil that goes dry in summer between irrigations.

Osmanthus delavayi
DELAVAYI OSMANTHUS
☼ ☼ ◐◑ Z7–9 H9–7 ‡6ft (2m) ↔8ft (2.5m)
Its profuse fragrant blooms in spring are larger than any other osmanthus. Evergreen foliage sprawls on banks or hangs down over retaining walls. Takes clay soil.

Hypericum androsaemum
ST. JOHN'S WORT
☼ ☼ ◐ Z7–10 H8–7 ‡↔3ft (1m)
Yellow double flowers on this shrub with arching branches at top. Useful on edges of woodsy areas, as a background for more formal garden plants. Inedible fruits follow flowers.

Ilex crenata 'Helleri'
JAPANESE HOLLY
☼ ☼ ◐ ⌷ Z5–10 H7–5 ‡1ft (30cm) ↔2ft (60cm)
Small hardy plants with black berries, these are more like boxwood than holly. Use for small hedges, edgings, or rock gardens. Must have good drainage.

Pittosperum 'Garnettii'
GARNET PITTOSPORUM
☼ ☼ ◐◑ Z9–11 H12–10
‡4ft (1.2m) ↔3ft (1m)
Variegated foliage and small, bell-shaped purple flowers hang from leaf axils in summer. Rare, but many other varieties are available. All make good screens.

MORE CHOICES

- *Agave americana* Z9–11 H12–5
- *Aucuba japonica* Z6–15 H12–6
- *Callicarpa bodineiri* var. *giraldii* Z5–9 H8–3
- *Choisya ternata* Z8–10 H10–8
- *Coprosma repens* Z8–10 H10–8
- *Elaeagnus pungens* 'Maculata' Z7–10 H9–7
- *Griselinia lucida* 'Variegata' Z7–10 H9–7
- *Hypericum androsaemum* 'Albury Purple' Z6–9 H8–4
- *Ilex cornuta* 'Burfordii' Z6–9 H9–1
- *Juniperus horizontalis* 'Wiltonii' Z3–10 H9–1
- *Juniperus procumbens* Z3–10 H10–1
- *Nandina domestica* Z6–9 H9–3
- *Pittosporum eugenoides* 'Variegatum' Z9–10 H12–10

Myrtus communis
COMMON MYRTLE
☼ ☼ ◐ Z8–10 H9–8 ‡↔10ft (3m)
Formally arranged on branches, leaves release fragrance if brushed against. Flowers appear in spring or summer. An excellent hedge, clipped or not.

Shrubs for moist soil in partial shade

Partial shade can mean dappled sunshine under an open tree, shade structure, or lath house – or it can mean morning sun and afternoon shade, such as occurs on the east side of a house, a wall, or a densely foliaged tree. Beware, however, of west-facing shade. Morning shade followed by hot afternoon sun can burn or wilt the leaves and flowers of shade plants.

Azara microphylla
BOXLEAF AZARA
☼ ● Z8–11 H12–10 ↕20ft (6m) ↔12ft (4m)
A slow-growing evergreen that becomes treelike after many years. This natural espalier is good against walls with its neat foliage arranged in tiers.

Cycas revoluta
JAPANESE SAGO PALM
☼ ● Z13–15 H12–6 ↕↔10ft (3m) ↔6ft (2m)
Not a palm, but a cycad – an ancient, cone-bearing plant from the age of dinosaurs. Cut off old fronds after new ones have grown. Fertilize in spring and summer and treat scale with summer oil.

Ardisia crispa
MARLBERRY
☼ ☼ ● Z8–9 H12–10
↕5ft (1.5m) ↔2ft (60cm)
With neat evergreen foliage and white or light pink flowers, followed by clusters of berries hanging from the trunk all winter, this needs good drainage. Prune lightly in late winter.

Cornus florida 'Cloud Nine'
CLOUD NINE DOGWOOD
☼ ☼ ● Z5–8 H8–3
↕20ft (6m) ↔25ft (8m)
A deciduous, low-branching type that survives where others will not, this is best in cooler areas of the Southwest. Flowers cover the tree before leaves. String pruners damage bark.

Camellia japonica 'Guilio Nuccio'
GUILIO NUCCIO CAMELLIA
☼ ● pH Z9–10 H10–9 ↕↔12ft (4m)
Rangier in shape and not as easy to grow as some other camellias, these stunning flowers open well coastal or inland, with rabbit-ear petals in the center.

MORE CHOICES

- *Abutilon* 'Crimson Belle' Z9–10 H10–1
- *Cleyera japonica* 'Tricolor' Z8–11 H12–7
- *Rhododendron* 'Red Wing' Z6–10 H9–6

Shrubs for moist soil in deep shade

Planting in deep shade is difficult, especially under trees with invasive roots or north-facing overhangs. Such soil is cold, and often neglected or allowed to go dry. Once it gets wet, on the other hand, it may stay wet indefinitely. The best solution is to decorate deep shade with houseplants, driftwood, rocks, potted plants, and shrubs like those listed here.

Fatsia japonica
JAPANESE ARALIA

☼ ☼ ☼ ● ᵖᴴ Z8–11 H12–8 ↕↔8ft (2.5m)

An easy permanent plant for a difficult entryway, its tropical leaves cast curious shadows. Black fruits follow flowers. Cut crowded suckers with a spade.

Aucuba japonica 'Crotonifolia'
SPOTTED JAPANESE LAUREL

☼ ☼ ● ● ᵖᴴ Z6–15 H12–6 ↕↔6ft (2m)

An easy plant for under an overhang, it lights up shade with variegated foliage. 'Variegata' has smaller spots, like gold dust. Plant in a camellia-azalea mix.

MORE CHOICES

- *Eleutherococcus sieboldianus* Z7–9 H9–7
- *Skimmia japonica* Z7–9 H9–7
- *Ternstroemia gymnanthera* Z8–10 H10–8
- *Vaccinium ovatum* Z7–10 H10–7

Viburnum rhytidophyllum
LEATHERLEAF VIBURNUM

☼ ☼ ☼ ● Z5–10 H10–5

↕15ft (5m) ↔12ft (4m)

A striking plant for full shade, if artistically pruned. Strong wind tatters leaves and cold weather may make them droop. Flowers light up shade, followed by scarlet fruit aging to black.

Buxus microphylla var. *japonica* 'Green Beauty'
JAPANESE BOXWOOD

☼ ☼ ☼ ● Z7–10 H10–7

↕6ft (2m) ↔5ft (1.5m)

Taking alkaline soil, water, and hot dry summers better than *B. sempervirens*, which soon dies, this has many varieties and can be clipped into a hedge.

Sarcococca confusa
SWEET BOX

☼ ☼ ● ● Z6–10 H10–6

↕6ft (2m) ↔7ft (2.2m)

In late winter and early spring, nondescript but powerfully fragrant flowers appear with the dark green, waxy leaves. *S. ruscifolia* has red fruit. Use compost or organic fertilizer.

WOODY PLANTS

Shrubs for Zone 3 firebreaks

In the attempt to protect homes from wildfires, especially next to chaparral and forests, fire officials have devised a system wherein clearings are created around buildings and divided into zones. Zone 1 is closest to the house. Zone 3 interfaces with the wild landscape. Lists of low-fuel plants, more fire-resistant than other plants, are provided for each zone.

Myoporum parvifolium
GROUNDCOVER MYOPORUM
☼ ◐ Z9–15 H12–9 ↕6in (15cm) ↔9in (22cm)
Prostrate plant, rooting where stems touch moist ground, densely covered with water-retentive leaves. White spring flowers are followed by purple fruits.

Euonymus fortunei 'Golden Prince'
WINTERCREEPER
☼ ☼ ◐ Z5–10 H10–2 ↕↔8ft (2.5m)
Any plant will burn if hot enough, but this evergreen vining shrub creates less fuel than most. Branches trail and root in ground. Takes more sun than ivy in desert.

Portulacaria afra
ELEPHANT FOOD
☼ ☼ ☼ ◐◑ Z10–15 H10–10 ↕3ft (1m) ↔4ft (1.2m)
Similar to jade plant but with limper branches and smaller leaves. No fertilizer and slow-growing. Allow cuttings to callus overnight before planting.

Hypericum calycinum
AARON'S BEARD, CREEPING ST. JOHN'S WORT
☼ ☼ ◐◑ Z5–9 H9–4 ↕1ft (30cm) ↔2ft (60cm)
Fast-growing with underground stems sprouting into a thick carpet. Plant at 1-foot intervals. Mow in late winter every 3 or 4 years, just before growth begins.

MORE CHOICES

- *Arctostaphylos hookeri* 'Monterey Carpet' Z8–10 H10–8
- *Atriplex semibaccata* Z7–10 H10–7
- *Baccharis pilularis* 'Pigeon Point' Z6–10 H10–6
- *Callistemon citrinus* 'Compacta' Z9–11 H12–9
- *Cistus crispus* 'Descanso' Z9–10 H10–9
- *Ceanothus prostratus* Z9–10 H10–9
- *Pittosporum tobira* 'Wheelers Dwarf' Z9–11 H12–3
- *Rhamnus alaternus* 'Variegata' Z6–10 H0–6
- *Rhus integrifolia* Z7–10 H10–7

Heteromeles arbutifolia
TOYON, CALIFORNIA HOLLY
Ⓝ ☼ ☀ ◊◊ z8–10 H12–8 ↕↔10ft (3m)
This evergreen with white summer flowers provides
birds with shelter and – through its fall and winter
berries – food. In firebreaks, clean out dead twigs inside
the plant once a year if necessary.

Arctostaphylos uva-ursi 'Point Reyes'
POINT REYES PROSTRATE MANZANITA
Ⓝ ☼ ☀ ◊◊ z5–10 H10–5
↕6ft (2m) ↔15ft (5m)
Slow to establish, but eventually forms a
tidy mat of small glossy leaves, with spring
flowers and summer berries beloved by birds.
Mulch ground around plants. Many
named selections.

Prunus ilicifolia subsp. lyonii
CATALINA CHERRY
☼ ◊◊ z9–10 H10–9 ↕↔20ft (6m)
Excellent-looking shrub with green leaves like privet
and edible cherries that birds adore. Needs little
pruning, occasional deep watering in interior climates.

Carissa macrocarpa
NATAL PLUM
☼ ☀ ◊◊ ◊ z10–11 H12–1 ↕↔7in (18cm)
Many cultivars with various uses for groundcover, hedges, or
thorny barriers; one type with no thorns can be clipped as a hedge.
Easy, pest-free, with white fragrant flowers and edible fruit.

Coprosma x kirkii 'Variegata'
VARIEGATED COPROSMA
☼ ☀ ◊ z8–11 H12–8 ↕3ft (1m) ↔6ft (2m)
Tough groundcover, higher in the middle, flat on creeping edge
extending like flat fan. Keep dense by pruning. Takes coastal
wind, sun, and salt spray, but needs part-shade inland.

WOODY PLANTS

Shrubs with fragrant flowers

Fragrance may be thought of as going hand-in-hand with spectacular flowers, but aromatic blooms are often nondescript. Fragrance also varies from wafting a few feet to a block or more. Many flowers are more pungent at night, attracting insects. Placement is of paramount importance: planting roadside is pleasant for walkers; by patios or windows, a gift to yourself.

Viburnum awabuki
SWEET VIBURNUM
☼ ☼ ◐ Z9–10 H10–9 ‡12ft (4m) ↔8ft (2.5m)
Fragrant spring flowers give way to clusters of red fruit ripening to black, bringing birds. Good screen plant, glossy leaves. 'Chindo' is superior variety for hedge.

Daphne odora 'Leucanthe'
WINTER DAPHNE
☼ ◐ Z7–9 H9–7 ‡4ft (1.2m) ↔6ft (2m)
Beloved but infuriating. Pretty bunches of small flowers at branch tips beguile with intense perfume. Apparently healthy plants succumb to root rot without warning.

Chimonanthus praecox
WINTERSWEET
☼ ◐ ◐ Z7–9 H9–7
‡15ft (5m) ↔10ft (2.5m)
Late-winter-blooming, deciduous shrub with spicy fragrance. Blossoms on bare branches. Cut to ground after bloom or train as tree. Good drainage is a must.

Choisya ternata
MEXICAN ORANGE BLOSSOM
Ⓝ ☼ ◐ ◐ ᵖᴴ Z8–10 H10–8 ‡↔8ft (2.5m)
Attractive screening shrub from Mexico with glossy fans of leaves and wonderfully fragrant blooms for two months, attracting bees. Cut back old growth inside shrub after bloom, to force growth.

Clerodendrum bungei
CASHMERE BOUQUET
☼ ☼ ◐ Z8–10 H12–8 ‡↔6ft (2m)
Fast-growing, invasively suckering shrub needs full shade in desert. Resistant to oak-leaf fungus and deer. Deliciously fragrant flowers in fall and winter. Prune hard in spring.

Cestrum nocturnum
NIGHT JASMINE

☼ ◑ Z9–12 H12–9 ↕↔12ft (4m)

White berries follow creamy summer blossoms not noticeable until sundown when super-sweet fragrance hits. Often planted next to patios. Fragrance overpowering for some.

Boronia megastigma
BROWN BORONIA

☼ ◐ ◑ pH

Z9–10 H10–9 ↕↔2ft (60cm)

Fine plant to grow in light soil mix in entryway or patio. Appreciate small, bell-like, winter-blooming flowers by day, delightful fragrance morning and evening when most intense.

Jasminum sambac
ARABIAN JASMINE

☼ ◐ ◑◑ Z10–12 H12–9 ↕10ft (3m) ↔3ft (1m)

Evergreen climbing shrub with strongly perfumed flowers. Summer blooms used for perfume, jasmine tea, or leis in Hawaii. 'Grand Duke' is a double variety.

Philadelphus coronarius
SWEET MOCK ORANGE

☼ ◐ ◑◑ Z4–10 H10–4 ↕↔12ft (4m)

Fine old favorite with pretty white blooms. Fast-growing like a fountain. Heavenly perfume on good plants (check when buying). 'Aureus' has golden-yellow foliage, stays to 8 feet.

Osmanthus fragrans
SWEET OLIVE

☼ ◐ ◑◑ Z8–11 H12–8

↕10ft (3m) ↔8ft (2.5m)

Flowers are barely noticeable, but the powerful, unmistakable fruity fragrance wafts on a breeze for a block or more. Most flower in spring or summer; some year-round.

MORE CHOICES

- *Acacia constricta* Z9–12 H12–10
- *Boronia heterophylla* Z9–10 H10–9
- *Carpenteria californica* 'Elizabeth' Z8–10 H9–8
- *Clethra barbinervis* Z9–10 H10–9
- *Gardenia augusta* 'Mystery' Z9–12 H12–9
- *Rhododendron* 'Else Frye' Z9–10 H10–9
- *Rhododendron* 'Fragrantissimum' Z9–10 H10–9
- *Sarcococca humilis* Z6–9 H9–6
- *Viburnum odoratissimum* 'Chindo' Z8–10 H10–7

WOODY PLANTS

Shrubs for year-round bloom

Many tropical and subtropical plants bloom almost non-stop year-round, leaving gardeners with the question: how can you prune without losing bloom? The answer is that you may have to sacrifice some flowers. Fortunately these plants are among the easiest plants we grow. They do, however, have specific needs, so you must work to mimic their native environments.

Rhododendron 'Alaska'
ALASKA AZALEA
☼ ● pH Z9–10 H10–9 ↕↔4ft (1.2m)
Don't overwater or allow to completely dry out. Pinch back in June. Apply acid food in June and late September. Grows well in large pots under overhang facing east.

Brugmansia 'Charles Grimaldi'
CHARLES GRIMALDI ANGEL'S TRUMPET
☼ ☼ ● Z11–15 H12–1 ↕12ft (4m) ↔10ft (3m)
The most popular and vigorous hybrid to grow as a shrub or to prune as a small tree. Blooms are very fragrant, especially in evening. Fertilize in summer.

Lavatera assurgentiflora
TREE MALLOW
Ⓝ ☼ ◊● Z9–10 H10–9
↕↔12ft (4m)
From the Channel Islands, this is among the best native plants for coastal zones, with lavender flowers and maple-shaped leaves. A common roadside screen, it beautifies the landscape.

Rosa 'Iceberg'
ICEBERG ROSE
☼ ☼ ● Z5–10 H10–5
↕5ft (1.5m) ↔25ft (8m)
Even if you never prune it, all this rose requires is fertilizer and water to bloom year-round, with virtually no pests or disease, especially when grown as a standard, on a trunk.

Anisodontea x *hypomandarum* 'Tara's Wonder'
TARA'S WONDER CAPE MALLOW
☼ ☼ ● Z9–10 H10–9 ↕↔6ft (2m)
Open-growing, floriferous selection for back of flower bed. New varieties such as 'Tara's Pink' are more compact with larger flowers, for mixing in flower beds.

MORE CHOICES

- *Abutilon* 'Bartley Schwartz' Z9–10 H10–9
- *Boronia crenulata* 'Shark Bay' Z9–10 H10–9
- *Bougainvillea* 'Crimson Jewel' Z10–15 H12–1
- *Russelia equisetiformis* Z9–12 H12–9

Strelitzia reginae
BIRD OF PARADISE
☼ ◐ ◊◊◑ Z9–12 H12–9 ‡4ft (1.2m) ↔8ft (2.5m)
Thrives in vacant lots, blooms more with food and water. Pick or deadhead stems. If flowers don't open, gently cut bud, pull petals up. Attracts hummingbirds.

Euryops pectinatus 'Green Gold'
GREEN GOLD EURYOPS
☼ ◐ ◊◊ Z9–10 H10–9 ‡↔4ft (1.2m)
Compact with green foliage, blooms mostly in winter, continues year-round unless sheared in June. Equally easy, drought-resistant, long-lived as gray-foliaged type.

Fuchsia 'Gartenmeister Bonstedt'
GARTENMEISTER BONSTEDT FUCHSIA
☼ ◐ ◑ Z9–11 H12–9 ‡3ft (1m) ↔2ft (60cm)
Needs no deadheading for continued bloom. Grow in ground or large tubs. Feed with 14-14-14 monthly. Use earthworm castings to eradicate giant whitefly.

Euphorbia milii var. splendens
CROWN OF THORNS
☼ ◐ ◑ Z9–12 H12–9 ‡4ft (1.2m) ↔3ft (1m)
A fine, patio-tub plant with many varieties, all incredibly colorful. Fertilize lightly to encourage growth. Salt-tolerant for seaside; porous soil.

WOODY PLANTS

Shrubs for spring or summer bloom

More shrubs bloom in spring than at any other time of year, giving gardeners time to join with others on garden tours, drive to the desert to view the wildflowers, or hike through the burgeoning chaparral. For nature also puts on her best at this time of year. Hillsides that woke up with the first fall rains will now be in full bloom.

Mahonia aquifolium
OREGON GRAPE HOLLY
Ⓝ ☼ ☼ ◦ ◦ ◦ Z6–9 H9–6
↕6ft (2m) ↔5ft (1.5m)
Little pruning is needed other than removing damaged foliage. Yellow flowers followed by blue-black fruits with bloom on them like blueberries. Use for jelly if birds don't get them first.

Punica granatum 'Wonderful'
WONDERFUL POMEGRANATE
☼ ◦ ◦ Z8–11 H12–1 ↕↔10ft (3m)
A small patio tree bearing colorful fruit whose juice has more antioxidant power than any other drink.

Cistus 'Doris Hibberson'
DORIS HIBBERSON ROCK ROSE
☼ ◦ ◦ Z8–10 H10–8 ↕↔3ft (1m)
Improved hybrid of Mediterranean native, adapted to dry summers. Outstanding bank cover from desert to sea coast. Colorful at a distance. No pruning needed.

WOODY PLANTS

Grevillea 'Noellii'
NOEL'S GREVILLEA
☼ ◊ z8–11 H12–10 ‡4ft (1.2m) ↔5ft (1.5m)
A colorful smaller grevillea for bank cover or in a drought-tolerant flower bed. Provide good drainage, don't overwater, plant 4 feet apart, mulch ground. Fertilize lightly. No phosphorus.

Fremontodendron 'Ken Taylor'
KEN TAYLOR FLANNEL BUSH
Ⓝ ☼ ◊ z8–10 H12–8 ‡6ft (2m) ↔12ft (4m)
One of the most glorious among California's native plants. Many new selections are available with a variety of sizes and qualities. Grow on a steep bank next to ceonothus. Never water in summer.

MORE CHOICES
- *Camellia japonica* 'Debutante' z7–10 H8–7
- *Ceanothus* 'Concha' z9–10 H12–9
- *Leucospermum reflexum* z10–11 H12–10
- *Nerium oleander* 'Hawaii' z9–11 H12–1
- *Ochna serrulata* z9–11 H12–9
- *Punica* 'Chico' z8–11 H11–8
- *Rhaphiolepis indica* 'Spring Fire' z9–10 H10–9
- *Sollya heterophylla* z9–12 H12–6
- *Tibouchina urvilleana* z10–15 H12–10

Ceanothus maritimus
CALIFORNIA LILAC
Ⓝ ☼ ☼ ◊ ◊ z9–10 H10–9
‡3ft (1m) ↔5ft (1.5m)
Bank cover for drought-resistant gardens, little water or care needed once established. Best in coastal zones. 'Frosty Dawn' has blue flowers. 'Point Sierra' endures summer heat better.

Hebe 'Purple Queen'
PURPLE QUEEN HEBE
☼ ☼ ◊ z9–10 H12–9 ‡↔5ft (1.5m)
Fast-growing, summer-flowering, some year-round. Best in cool moist climates, good on coast. Bad drainage kills. After bloom, cut back stems that have bloomed by half their length.

Polygala x dalmaisiana
SWEET PEA SHRUB
☼ ☼ ◊ z9–10 H10–9 ‡4ft (1.2m) ↔5ft (1.5m)
Nonstop blooms completely cover gray foliage from midsummer until fall. Cut back in late winter or early spring. Short-lived but eye-catching with good drainage and sufficient moisture.

Shrubs for fall and winter bloom

By choosing plants that bloom at various seasons of the year, gardeners can enjoy year-round color. Whether you plant all the colors of the rainbow or restrict your choices to specific color schemes, the More Choices box can increase your palette. Most plants that bloom in fall and winter should never be pruned in fall or you'll have no flowers.

Euryops pectinatus
GRAY EURYOPS

☼ ◊ Z9–10 H10–9 ‡↔6ft (2m)

A permanent, drought-tolerant, easy-to-grow shrub covered with lemon-yellow daisies all winter long. Shear annually in June after main flowering has finished to control growth and strengthen plant.

Kunzea baxteri
SCARLET KUNZEA

☼ ◊◊ Z9–10 H10–9

‡8ft (2.5m) ↔20ft (6m)

A fast-growing, open shrub for bank cover, or to prune as a small tree. The flowers are like large rounded bottlebrushes and attract mockingbirds and hummingbirds. This tree prefers sandy soil.

Cantua buxifolia
SACRED FLOWER OF THE INCAS

☼ ◊ Z10–11 H12–10 ‡15ft (5m) ↔8ft (2.5m)

A rangy plant for marking a turn in a wandering path, but gets mildew and spider mites if shaded. White, pink, red, or striped flowers. Fertilize in fall.

Leptospermum scoparium 'Ruby Glow'
NEW ZEALAND TEA TREE

☼ ◊◊ Z9–10 H10–9 ‡6–8ft (2–2.5m) ↔10ft (3m)

A spectacular shrub or small tree with a twisted trunk. The foliage will be completely blanketed in flowers throughout winter if not pruned incorrectly in fall.

Escallonia 'Langleyensis'
DONARD HYBRID ESCALLONIA

☼ ☼ ◊ Z9–10 H10–9 ‡↔15ft (5m)

The best known variety, called 'Apple Blossom', is a dense spreading shrub for screen, or a small tree with red buds and pink flowers. Best in coastal zones. Burning sun disfigures foliage.

Rhododendron 'Phoenicia'
PHOENICIA RHODODENDRON

☀ ◑ ⌂ Z9–10 H10–9 ↕↔4ft (1.2m)

'Phoenicia' and 'Duc de Rohan' (in background) are easy-to-grow hybrids that have vigor and the ability to withstand morning sun. Do not let roots dry out.

Protea cynaroides
KING PROTEA

☀ ◑ ⌂ Z10–11 H12–9

↕↔5ft (1.5m)

Flowers are a foot across. Best on banks where water can travel through root zone, never standing still. Bad drainage kills. Fertilize lightly, no phosphorus.

Tagetes lemmonii
COPPER CANYON DAISY

Ⓝ ☀ ◑ Z9–10 H10–9

↕↔4ft (1.2m)

Easy shrub for roadside or banks, stunning next to Mexican sage that blooms at the same time. Blooms again in spring. Cut back hard after each bloom for most massive show.

Salvia leucantha
MEXICAN BUSH SAGE

Ⓝ ☀ ◑ Z9–10 H12–4 ↕4ft (1.2m) ↔6ft (2m)

Outstanding color, especially in fall. Renews itself each winter with fresh growth from ground. Needs little care other than cutting off dead growth.

Camellia sasanqua 'Yuletide'
YULETIDE CAMELLIA

☀ ◑ ⌂ Z9–10 H10–9 ↕4ft (1.2m) ↔3ft (1m)

Still one of the finest sasanquas that blooms for the holidays, now joined by many more. Fertilize after bloom, prune to shape, if necessary, immediately after bloom. Sasanquas do not get blossom blight.

MORE CHOICES

- *Acacia podalyriaefolia* Z9–12 H12–10
- *Aloe arborescens* 'Variegata' Z10–12 H12–10
- *Arbutus unedo* 'Octoberfest' Z9–10 H10–9
- *Astartea fascicularis* 'Braemer Bay' Z9–10 H10–9
- *Euphorbia pulcherrima* 'Hollywood' Z9–10 H10–9
- *Leonotis leonurus* Z9–10 H10–9
- *Leptospermum scoparium* 'Red Damask' Z9–10 H10–9
- *Melaleuca fulgens* Z9–11 H11–9
- *Michelia doltsopa* Z9–11 H12–1
- *Senna artemisioides* Z9–11 H9–9

WOODY PLANTS

Shrubs for tropical gardens

Many plants that grow in coastal Hawaii also thrive outdoors in mild coastal zones of California and in the southern tip of Texas. Do not try them in the desert; it is too hot and dry. The plants listed here are easy to grow in Hawaii, but need extra care in California. Most have colorful leaves or flowers year round, and respond well to frequent light pruning.

Codiaeum variegatum 'Pictum'
CROTON
☼ ☼ ◑ Z10–15 H15–10
↕6ft (2m) ↔5ft (1.5m)
A houseplant in most areas, a garden plant in Hawaii for edging lawns. This will not color up in solid shade and needs well-drained soil. Many named varieties with multicolored leaves are available.

Monstera deliciosa
SPLIT-LEAVED PHILODENDRON
☼ ☼ ◑◑ Z10–12 H12–10 ↕60ft (18m) ↔5ft (1.5m)
A big-leaved climber with fruit that is edible only when very ripe. Can keep short for years by taking tip cuttings in summer, rooting back in a pot or ground.

Gunnera manicata
GIANT RHUBARB
☼ ◑ Z10–15 H15–10 ↕↔8ft (2.5m)
An astounding shrubby perennial with huge leaves, 5ft (1.5m) wide or more, on stems up to 6ft (2m) long that sprout anew each spring. Evergreen in mild climates, plant in a wet spot by a stream or pond. Protect from snails.

Ochna serrulata
MICKEY MOUSE PLANT
☼ ◑ ᵖᴴ Z9–11 H11–9 ↕↔8ft (2.5m)
Yellow buttercup-like flowers in early summer, followed by seed capsules opening to look like Mickey Mouse. Birds love the seeds. Grows in a pot or in the ground.

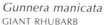

Clerodendrum myricoides var. *ugandense*
BLUE BUTTERFLY BUSH
☼ ☼ ◑ ᵖᴴ Z9–11 H12–3 ↕10ft (3m) ↔5ft (1.5m)
Blossoms with one large violet petal, four smaller light blue petals, arching blue pistils and stamens, suggest flock of butterflies. Full sun in Hawaii, part shade in California.

Philodendron bipinnatifidum
SELLOUM PHILODENDRON

☀ ☀ ◐ ◐ ◑ Z9–15 H15–0

↕15ft (5m) ↔10ft (3m)

A big shrub that may climb; at 30 years of age, it may grow up a support with large treelike trunks. In north-facing shade, it will stay shrubby for many years. Aerial roots to 50ft (15m) or more will find their own water.

Brunfelsia pauciflora
YESTERDAY, TODAY, AND TOMORROW

☀ ☀ ◑ Z10–15 H15–10

↕↔5ft (1.5m)

A colorful tropical shrub with three flower colors at once: purple for yesterday, lavender today, white tomorrow. 'Macrantha' is smaller, with larger purple blooms.

Hibiscus schizopetalis
JAPANESE LANTERN

☀ ◑ Z10–15 H15–10 ↕10ft (3m)

↔3–5ft (1–1.5m)

A common shrub in Hawaii, this is rangy unless pruned, with a weeping habit and year-round bloom. Cut back a third of one or two of the longest branches each month.

MORE CHOICES

- *Abutilon megapotamicum* Z9–12 H12–9
- *Alberta magna* Z10–12 H12–10
- *Burchellia bubalina* Z10–12 H12–10
- *Carica quercifolia* Z10–12 H12–10
- *Carissa macrocarpa* Z9–11 H12–9
- *Cestrum fasciculatum* Z9–11 H10–9
- *Dammaropsis kingiana* Z10–12 H12–10
- *Drepanostachyum falcatum* Z10–12 H12–10
- *Justicia brandegeeana* Z10–12 H12–10
- *Meryta sinclairii* Z10–15 H12–10
- *Mitraria coccinea* Z10–15 H15–10
- *Murraya paniculata* Z9–12 H12–9
- *Pisonia umbellifera* Z10–12 H12–10
- *Rothmannia globosa* Z10–12 H12–10
- *Schizolobium parahybum* Z10–12 H12–10
- *Streptosolen jamesonii* Z9–12 H12–10

Russelia equisetiformis
CORAL PLANT

☀ ☀ ◐ ◑ Z9–12 H12–1 ↕↔5ft (1.5m)

A shrub in Hawaii, in California, this is a drought-resistant, good bank cover that brings hummingbirds. Plant stems in the ground. Blooms year round if fed.

Shrubs for subtropical gardens

The subtropics of the world border on the tropics and may be either wet or dry. The term "subtropical garden," as used here, means a garden growing in a mild, frost-free climate, concentrating on plants with luxuriant foliage and colorful flowers from warm subtropical regions of the world. There are many subtropical gardens in Hawaii, Southern California, and South Texas.

Ruellia macrantha
RUELLIA

☼ ☀ ◐ ◐ ◐ Z9–12 H12–10

↕↔3ft (1m)

A Brazilian plant with bunches of rose-pink, darker-veined flowers all winter long on tips of deep green foliage from early fall to spring. Grow in a tub, bring under cover if frost is expected.

Ixora coccinea
FLAME OF THE WOODS

☼ ☀ ◐ ⌐ pH Z10–15 H12–10

↕10ft (3m) ↔6ft (2m)

A jungle plant from India for Hawaii or a warm spot on the California coast. Pinch tips to increase bloom and bushiness. Luxurious green leaves and showy flowers appear year-round in pink, red, yellow, or orange.

Iochroma cyanea
VIOLET BELLS

☼ ☀ ◐ Z10–12 H12–10 ↕8ft (2.5m) ↔6ft (2m)

A rangy shrub, more luxuriant in tropical climates, that flowers throughout warm weather in California and year-round in Hawaii. Prune for bushiness, fertilize for flowers and growth. Few pests or problems.

Abutilon megapotamicum
CHINESE LANTERN

☼ ☀ ◐ Z10–12 H12–10 ↕↔10ft (3m)

Spring and summer flowers (year-round in Hawaii) appear on this vigorous climbing shrub, for espalier, trellis, hanging baskets, patio, or edging a path. Prune to shape. Control whiteflies with earthworm castings on ground.

Solanum ratonnettii 'Royal Robe'
BLUE POTATO BUSH
☀ ◐ ◊ ◗ Z9–12 H12–6 ↕↔8ft (2.5m)
This easy garden plant has year-round color in California and Hawaii. Grow it on a single trunk as a patio tree, prune as a big shrub, or let it scramble into larger shrubs or lean over walls or fences.

Cestrum elegans var. smithii
PINK-FLOWERED CESTRUM
☀ ◗ Z10–12 H12–10 ↕↔10ft (3m)
Hanging pink flowers attract hummingbirds all summer, followed by berries, on this climbing shrub for espalier, or for leaning on walls or other plants. Evergreen in frost-free climates. Use organic fertilizer.

Justicia brandegeeana 'Yellow Queen'
YELLOW SHRIMP BUSH
☀ ◐ ◗ Z10–12 H12–10 ↕↔4ft (1.2m)
This hybrid form of a Mexican native can be a garden shrub in Hawaii, or a potted plant on the mainland. It attracts hummingbirds and blooms all summer. "Flowers" are actually bracts; cut some for branching.

Streptosolen jamesonii
MARMELADE BUSH
☀ ◐ ◗ Z10–12 H12–10 ↕↔6ft (2m)
An intense mix of yellow and orange that blooms from spring to fall. Adds spark to a flower border or cascading over a retaining wall. Give it full sun on the coast, part-shade inland, water, fertilizer, and good drainage.

MORE CHOICES

- *Aloe thraskii* Z10–12 H12–10
- *Aloe x salm-dyckiana* Z10–12 H12–10
- *Bambusa gracilis* Z8–15 H10–1
- *Begonia luxurians* Z10–12 H12–1
- *Clianthus puniceus* Z7–11 H12–1
- *Cussonia spicata* Z10–11 H12–10
- *Cyathea medullaris* Z10–11 H12–10
- *Dahlia imperialis* Z8–11 H11–8
- *Dracaena fragrans* 'Lemon and Lime' Z9–12 H12–9
- *Gunnera manicata* Z9–12 H12–7
- *Jatropha multifida* Z9–12 H9–5
- *Metrosideros polymorpha* Z10–11 H12–1
- *Monstera deliciosa* Z10–12 H12–10
- *Musa velutina* Z10–12 H12–10
- *Pentas lanceolata* Z9–12 H12–9
- *Puya alpestris* Z9–11 H12–1
- *Tetrapanax papyrifer* Z9–10 H12–6

Shrubs with flowers for tropical effects

Tropical shrubs look good with white-walled modern or Spanish architecture. It is not necessary to water or feed them wastefully as gardeners did years ago. Many jungles live on their own refuse in old gardens or canyons where water seeps from higher ground. The shrubs listed here look best when combined with palms, bamboos, and big leafy plants like rice paper plant (*Tetrapanax papyriferus*).

Justicia carnea
BRAZILIAN PLUME
☼ ☼ ● Z10–12 H12–10
↕6ft (2m) ↔3ft (1m)
Correct legginess by hiding bare stems with ferns, double-potting in a tall container. Move inside for winter to keep leaves. Cut back in spring, pot to larger size, fertilize.

Tibouchina urvilleana
PRINCESS FLOWER
☼ ☼ ● ᵖᴴ Z10–12 H12–10   ↕8–18ft (2.5–5.5m)   ↔10ft (3m)
Most bloom summer, fall, and winter, and can grow to 18ft in Hawaii, 8ft in California. Needs sun on the coast, half shade inland. Fill planting hole with camellia-azalea mix, provide drainage and constant food and water.

Hibiscus rosa-sinensis
CHINESE HIBISCUS
☼ ● Z10–12 H12–1
↕15ft (5m) ↔5–10ft (1.5–3m)
Strong old varieties 'Angel Wings' and 'Agnes Galt' become small trees, pop flower on every branch tip. A good informal hedge but don't shear. To prune, pinch back or reach inside here and there.

Senna alata
POPCORN PLANT
☼ ● Z10–12 H12–10
↕8ft (2.5m) ↔12ft (4m)
A large shrub with large leaves and flowers in late summer and fall. Drought-resistant once established. Cut back a few branches at a time for growth.

Hibiscus schizopetalus
CORAL HIBISCUS
☼ ● Z10–12 H12–10   ↕to 10ft (3m)   ↔5ft (1.5m)
Not often grown as a shrub but excellent in hanging baskets where charming hanging flowers can be fully appreciated. Fertilize and keep moist on a drip system.

Hedychium gardnerianum
KAHILI GINGER
☼ ● Z10–12 H12–9   ↕6ft (2m)   ↔3ft (1m)
Grow in a tub or in the ground. Fragrant flowers appear in August but old stems won't bloom again. Cut to ground in spring and fertilize for new stalks.

Solanum laciniatum
LARGE KANGAROO APPLE
☼ ⬤ Z10–12 H12–10 ↕6ft (2m) ↔5ft (1.5m)
A tropical nightshade from Australia and New Zealand, with larger flowers than the blue potato bush that last all summer, followed by large yellow fruits.

Pentas lanceolata
STAR CLUSTERS
☼ ⬤ Z9–12 H12–10 ↕6ft (2m) ↔3ft (1m)
Year-round bloom, easy to grow. Useful for edging paths. Grows bigger in Hawaii. Needs frequent grooming to cut faded flowers and damaged foliage.

MORE CHOICES

- *Iochroma cyanea* Z10–12 H12–10
- *Luculia grandifolia* Z10–12 H9–7
- *Mackaya bella* Z10–12 H12–10
- *Metrosideros villosa* 'Tahiti' Z9–11 H12–1
- *Senecio grandifolius* Z10–12 H12–1
- *Tibouchina granulosa* Z10–12 H12–10
- *Vireya* 'Tropic Glow' Z9–12 H12–9
- *Wigandia caracasana* Z10–12 H12–10

Justicia brandegeeana
'Yellow Queen'
YELLOW SHRIMP PLANT
☼ ☼ ⬤ Z10–12 H12–10
↕↔4ft (1.2m)
A container plant with summer flowers. Keep on dry side in winter. Cut back in early spring. Fertilize during growth.

Shrubs for the oceanfront

Shrubs that stand up to salt spray, strong winds, and salty alkaline soils, while maintaining a decent appearance, are worthy of our respect. Like people who face adversity with strength of character, these shrubs often become more beautiful when buffeted by ocean winds. The wind rounds them off into interesting shapes, a sort of natural pinching back.

Rosa 'Frau Dagmar Hartopp'
RAMANA'S ROSE, SEA TOMATO
☼ ◊ ◑ Z3–10 H9–1 ↕↔6ft (2m)
A great barrier plant even on beach front. Branches root in ground. Blooms spring, summer, and fall, followed by edible, seedy ornamental hips that bring birds.

Pittosporum crassifolium
SEASIDE PITTOSPORUM
☼ ☼ ◊ ◑ Z9–11 H12–10 ↕25ft (8m) ↔20ft (6m)
Easy shrub for a beach front or coastal garden, eventual tree with small, fragrant, wine-colored flowers in spring. 'Compactum' grows to 3ft(1m), seldom blooms.

Phlomis fruticosa
JERUSALEM SAGE
☼ ☼ ◊ ◑ Z8–10 H9–8 ↕↔4ft (1.2m)
Flowers in waves throughout summer if cut back after each flowering. If not cut back, will flower only once and become leggy. Follow up with light feeding.

Lantana montevidensis
LILAC-FLOWERED LANTANA
☼ ◊ Z9–10 H12–9 ↕2ft (60cm) ↔6ft (2m)
Most elegant lantana for large gardens, tops of walls, or banks. Year-round bloom. To renew, cut to ground in spring or fall, fertilize organically, and water.

Rosmarinus officinalis
ROSEMARY
☼ ◊ Z7–12 H12–8 ↕↔6ft (2m)
Useful as edible herb, drought-resistant shrub, or flowering groundcover. This type is the best plant for sheared hedges in coastal gardens; simply forgo flowers.

MORE CHOICES
- *Artemisia australis* Z4–8 H8–1
- *Artemisia pycnocephala* Z4–8 H8–1
- *Cistus crispus* 'Santa Cruz' Z9–10 H10–9
- *Cytisus* x *spachianus* Z9–11 H12–9
- *Eriogonum arborescens* Z12–15 H12–9
- *Escallonia* x *exoniensis* 'Balfouri'
  Z7–9 H9–5
- *Hakea laurina* Z10–11 H12–10
- *Halimium lasianthum* Z9–11 H12–9
- *Lavandula canariensis* Z5–8 H8–5
- *Rhaphiolepis indica* 'Springtime'
  Z7–11 H12–7
- *Rhus integrifolia* Z7–9 H9–7
- *Westringia fruticosa* Z13–15 H12–9

Rhamnus californica
COFFEEBERRY
Ⓝ ☼ ☀ ◊◗ Z7–10
H9–7 ↕15ft (5m) ↔8ft (2.5m)
Upright in woodland, prostrate along coast. 'Mound San Bruno' is the best known, with smaller leaves and a compact shape. Do not water once established.

Galvezia speciosa
ISLAND BUSH SNAPDRAGON
Ⓝ ☼ ☀ ◊◗ Z8–10 H12–8 ↕3ft (1m) ↔5ft (1.5m)
Allow to twine among open structured shrubs, or grow as groundcover. Long-blooming flowers at branch tips bring hummingbirds. 'Firecracker' is more compact.

Aloe arborescens
TREE ALOE
☼ ☀ ◊◗ Z10–11 H12–10 ↕10ft (3m) ↔6ft (2m)
Long-lasting flowers brighten winter, bring hummers. If desired, prune into stunning formal shape, such as roadside triangle, pruned flat on top. Whole top blooms.

Roses for foggy coastal gardens

Despite thorny, disease-prone dispositions, roses have so much charm and fragrance that even gardeners along the beach may yearn to grow one or two. Beware of cabbage-shaped roses with many petals; they often won't open near the sea. Here are some that shrug off rust and mildew and usually can open petals in the face of foggy days.

Rosa 'Evelyn'
EVELYN ROSE
☼ ◑ Z5–10 H10–5 ↕6ft (2m) ↔4ft (1.2m)
An intensely fragrant, fast-growing David Austin rose that needs deadheading to maintain bloom. Train like a shrub or upright like a climber. Ruby thorns on new mahogany canes sparkle in sun.

Rosa banksiae 'Lutea'
YELLOW LADY BANKS ROSE
☼ ◑ ◊◑ Z7–10 H9–8 ↕30ft (10m) ↔20ft (6m)
No thorns, pests, or diseases, but if pruned in winter, this rose will have no spring flowers either. Train when young, then prune lightly after bloom for second wave. Prune more heavily after second bloom.

Rosa 'Iceberg'
ICEBERG ROSE
☼ ◑ ◑ Z5–10 H9–5 ↕4ft (1.2m) ↔3ft (1m)
Easiest rose for coastal gardens, lightly fragrant, blooms year-round, even in shade, non-stop unless pruned. Very successful, hopefully a harbinger of roses to come.

Rosa MARY ROSE ('Ausmary')
MARY ROSE ROSE
☼ ◑ Z6–10 H9–6 ↕4ft (1.2m) ↔3ft (1m)
Among a handful of most successful Austin roses, this has a damask shape and a light fragrance and flowers from the ground up with dark green foliage resistant to mildew in most areas. May get rust.

MORE CHOICES

- *Rosa* 'Apricot Nectar' z4–10 H12–1
- *Rosa banksiae* z7–10 H10–7
- *Rosa* 'Bonica' z4–10 H10–1
- *Rosa* 'Brass Band' z4–10 H12–1
- *Rosa* 'Gruss en Aachen' z4–10 H12–1
- *Rosa* 'Hansa' z3–9 H9–1
- *Rosa* 'Intrigue' z4–10 H12–1
- *Rosa* 'Joseph's Coat' z5–10 H10–5
- *Rosa* 'Sally Holmes' z5–10 H10–3
- *Rosa* 'Scentimental' z4–10 H10–1
- *Rosa* 'Simplicity' z4–10 H12–1
- *Rosa* 'Singin' in the Rain' z4–10 H12–1
- *Rosa* 'Sun Flare' z5–10 H10–1
- *Rosa* TRUMPETER ('Mactru') z5–9 H9–5

Rosa 'Duchesse de Brabant'
DUCHESS OF BRABANT ROSE
☼ ◕◕ z7–10 H10–7 ↕6ft (2m) ↔3ft (1m)
A heavily perfumed, old tea rose that Teddy Roosevelt
wore in his lapel. Sometimes found in deserted
gardens. Cupped blooms need some sun to open.

Rosa 'Abraham Darby'
ABRAHAM DARBY ROSE
☼ ◕ z5–10 H10–3 ↕6ft (2m) ↔3ft (1m)
A great David Austin English rose with little
disease. Very fragrant flowers open well and
hang down, making this a good choice for
growing upright on an obelisk. Do
not prune hard when young.

Rosa 'Golden Showers'
GOLDEN SHOWERS ROSE
☼ ◕ z5–10 H10–5 ↕10ft (3m) ↔6ft (2m)
Lammerts climber with self-standing canes to train as
pillar or big shrub. Won't bend onto fence. Fragrant,
with 25–30 loose petals opening easily, blooming early.

Rosa 'Amber Queen'
AMBER QUEEN ROSE
☼ ◕ z5–10 H10–5 ↕↔3ft (1m)
An award-winner from England, this wonderfully fragrant rose double blooms, with many
petals still opening well along the coast. A bushy rounded plant with shiny green foliage.

WOODY PLANTS

Shrubs for thorny barriers

Settlers in the Southwest often bordered vegetable patches and ornamental gardens with hedges of opuntia cactus or with ocotillo branches thrust into the ground to create a living prickly fence. It's an equally good idea today to use well-chosen and attractive, though thorny, shrubs to deter unwanted visitors, keep dogs off lawns, or wild animals out of flowerbeds.

WOODY PLANTS

Agave americana 'Media Picta'
CENTURY PLANT
Ⓝ ☼ ☼ ◊ ◑ Z10–12 H12–10   ‡6ft (2m) ↔10ft (3m)
Once thought to live 100 years, this agave may live up to 30 before sending up a 15- to 40-foot bloom spike, like a giant asparagus, opening into flowers and followed by seeds.

Sabal minor
SABAL PALM
Ⓝ ☼ ◑ Z12–15 H12–10
‡6ft (2m) ↔10ft (3m)
An impenetrable, trunkless palm that can take drought, alkaline soil, saltwater, and wind. Not often seen in California, adapted ocean to desert and thrives on Texas' coast.

MORE CHOICES

- *Acacia smallii* z10–11 H12–10
- *Berberis* x *hybrido* z7–9 H9–7
- *Carissa macrocarpa* 'Green Carpet' z10–11 H12–1
- *Chaenomeles japonica* 'Super Red' z6–9 H9–1
- *Duranta erecta* z9–12 H12–9
- *Euphorbia milii* z10–12 H12–1
- *Fouquieria splendens* z8–9 H12–1
- *Hakea suaveolens* z10–11 H12–10
- *Ilex cornuta* 'Berries Jubilee' z7–10 H9–1
- *Opuntia ficus-indica* z9–12 H12–9
- *Osmanthus heterophyllus* z7–9 H9–7
- *Prosopis pubescens* z9–11 H12–1
- *Pyracantha angustifolia* 'Yukon Belle' z4–10 H12–1
- *Pyracantha* 'Ruby Mound' z7–10 H10–1

Ilex aquifolium 'Gold Coast'
VARIEGATED ENGLISH HOLLY
☼ ☼ ◑ ⵗ Z7–10 H10–7
‡↔6ft (2m)
'Gold Coast' has dense foliage that lights up in shade, but colors better in sun. 'Ferox', also known as hedgehog or porcupine holly, is the best one to plant under a window – you won't need bars.

Berberis wilsoniae
WILSON BARBERRY
☼ ☼ ◊ ◑ Z6–9 H9–4
‡↔6ft (2m)
Deciduous to semi-evergreen foliage is attractive and compact, creating a handsome barrier even if all colorful berries are eaten by birds. Wear leather gloves when pruning to shape.

Rosa 'Frau Dagmar Hartopp'
FRAU DAGMAR HARTOPP ROSE

☼ ◊ ◐ z2–10 H10–1 ↕↔6ft (2m)

Rugosa rose with spring-blooming, single pink flowers followed by orange hips. Dark green foliage has green apple aroma after rain. To control aphids, sprinkle with water and apply pre-chilled ladybugs.

Rosa 'Lady Penzance'
LADY PENZANCE ROSE

☼ ◑ ◐ z5–10 H10–5 ↕↔6ft (2m)

Broadens scope of rugosa roses with hybrid vigor, stronger color, longer bloom (all summer), and more compact shape. No pests or diseases. Adapted to many zones, but best along coast, in mountains.

Rhapidophyllum hystrix
NEEDLE PALM

Ⓝ ☼ ◑ ◑ ◊ ◊ ◐ z6–10 H12–10 ↕↔8ft (2.5m)

Slow-growing, trunkless Southeast native thought to be hardiest of palms. Long black spines at base of highly attractive, cascading leaves make it a formidable barrier.

Carissa macrocarpa 'Fancy'
FANCY NATAL PLUM

☼ ◑ ◊◊◐ z10–11 H12–1 ↕↔7ft (2.2m)

Fragrant white flowers bloom year-round, followed by edible fruits, larger and better flavored on this variety than others. Ripe, bright red or purple fruit makes good jam.

Chorizema ilicifolium
HOLLY FLAME PEA

☼ ◑ ◊ z9–11 H12–10 ↕↔3ft (1m)

An Australian shrub with prickly leaves and showy flowers in fall and again in late winter through spring. Grow on banks, cascading over a wall, or in a hanging basket.

WOODY PLANTS

Shrubs for sandy soil

Why struggle to grow plants that need moist soil if your garden has sandy or gravelly soil that dries out quickly? It is far wiser to choose plants adapted to the conditions you already have, such as South African proteas and their Australian relatives, the banksias and grevilleas. No more exciting plants can be found for full sun and fast-draining soils.

Chamelaucium unicinatum
GERALTON WAX FLOWER
☼ ◐ ◊ Z9–10 H10–9 ↕↔8ft (2.5m)
Long winter season of pink, lavender, or white bloom. Long-lasting cut flower. Cut to ground annually or allow to grow twisted trunk. No phosphorus fertilizer.

Grevillea juniperina
JUNIPER-FOLIAGED GREVILLEA
☼ ☼ ◊ ◊ Z9–10 H10–9 ↕1ft (30cm) ↔6ft (2m)
Groundcover with spring and summer flowers that need little care once established. Search nurseries for superior named selections of various heights and sizes.

Leucospermum cordifolium
PINCUSHION PROTEA
☼ ◊ Z10–11 H12–1 ↕↔4ft (1.2m)
Best grown with drip system on higher side of bank so that water flows through root zone and never stands still. Light organic fertilizer. No phosphorus.

MORE CHOICES

- *Banksia speciosa* Z10–11 H12–10
- *Calytrix tetragona* Z10–11 H12–10
- *Grevillea alpina* Z9–11 H10–9
- *Kunzea baxteri* Z9–11 H12–1
- *Monardella villosa* Z9–10 H10–9
- *Protea cynaroides* Z10–11 H12–9

Banksia ericifolia
AUSTRALIAN HONEYSUCKLE
☼ ◊ Z10–11 H12–10 ↕20ft (6m) ↔12ft (4m)
Fragrant, 6- to 8-inch flowers appear on open shrub, sometimes treelike, and attract birds. Interesting seed capsules. Good coastal plant. No phosphorus fertilizer.

Evergreen shrubs for informal screens

When shrubs are chosen for their eventual height and width, you don't have to continually shear them. Many can be left to grow naturally. Pruning can be confined to removal of dead growth and occasional shaping by reaching in and cutting branches back to a shorter cross branch that becomes the new tip. After pruning, the plant should look as natural as it was before.

Myoporum laetum 'Carsonii'
CARSON'S MYOPORUM
☼ ◐ ◊ ◑ Z9–11 H12–9 ‡30ft (9m) ↔20ft (6m)
A fast-growing variety with larger, darker green leaves and no bare stems below. Mature, windblown specimens are good climbing trees for children.

Acacia longifolia
SYDNEY GOLDEN WATTLE
☼ ◊ ◑ Z9–11 H12–1 ‡20ft (6m) ↔10ft (3m)
A fast-growing screen that brightens the landscape for weeks in spring. An eventual leaning tree that can live 100 years, leaving many seedlings. Brings birds.

Berberis x *gladwynensis* 'William Penn'
WILLIAM PENN BARBERRY
☼ ◐ ◊ ◑ Z6–9 H9–4 ‡4ft (1.2m) ↔5ft (1.5m)
Good floral display of yellow spring flowers followed by dark purple berries on dense glossy evergreen foliage. A great informal screen that attracts birds.

Westringia fruticosa
COAST ROSEMARY
☼ ◊ ◑ Z9–11 H12–9 ‡8ft (2.5m) ↔10ft (3m)
Often sold with perennials to unsuspecting gardeners. Large, moderately fast-growing screen plant or hedge. Dense coastal windbreak. Compact varieties available.

MORE CHOICES

- *Berberis* 'Chenaultii' Z6–9 H9–6
- *Juniperus virginiana* 'Cupressifolia' Z3–9 H9–1
- *Ozothamnus rosmarinifolius* Z8–9 H9–8
- *Pittosporum rhombifolium* Z9–10 H10–9
- *Vaccinium ovatum* Z7–10 H10–7

Ilex cornuta 'Burfordii'
BURFORD'S HOLLY
☼ ◐ ◑ pH Z7–10 H10–7
‡15ft (5m) ↔10ft (3m)
A widely planted and successful holly, not noticeably spiny. Leaves cup downward, creating a softer-looking, dark-green hedge or screen with red berries.

WOODY PLANTS

Flowering shrubs for informal screens

The most important thing to understand about flowering shrubs is how and when to prune. Otherwise, you may cut off the flowers or prevent them from blooming. Our flowering shrubs come from many areas of the world. Some bloom on new wood, others on old wood that has hardened off, and their flowers brighten our gardens at various times of year.

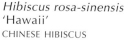

Hibiscus rosa-sinensis 'Hawaii'
CHINESE HIBISCUS
☼ ◊ Z14–15 H12–1
↕30ft (10m) ↔8ft (2.5m)
Blooms on this year's new wood. Pinch tips to increase bloom. In warm weather, cut 1/3 of branch for growth.

Berberis darwinii
DARWIN'S BARBERRY
☼ ☼ ◊◊ Z7–9 H9–4 ↕10ft (3m) ↔7ft
Very colorful evergreen barberry with orange-yellow flowers followed by blue berries, growing on last year's wood. Prune after bloom, never in spring or fall.

MORE CHOICES

- *Callistemon citrinus* 'Violaceus' Z10–12 H12–9
- *Clerodendrum paniculata* Z10–11 H10–1
- *Duranta stenostachya* Z11–12 H12–10
- *Escallonia* x *exoniensis* 'Frades' Z7–9 H9–5
- *Garrya elliptica* 'James Roof' Z8–10 H10–8
- *Grevillea* 'Ivanhoe' Z9–11 H12–10
- *Lavatera* 'Rosea' Z8–11 H12–8
- *Leucophyllum frutescens* 'Green Cloud' Z7–12 H10–8
- *Photinia* x *fraseri* 'Birmingham' Z8–10 H9–8
- *Pittosporum eugenioides* 'Variegatum' Z9–10 H12–10
- *Rhaphiolepis indica* 'Springtime' Z7–11 H12–7
- *Rosa* MARY ROSE ('Ausmary') Z6–10 H10–6
- *Syringa vulgaris* 'Lavender Lady' Z4–10 H8–1
- *Tecoma capensis* Z9–12 H12–10

Leptospermum scoparium 'Snow White'
NEW ZEALAND TEA TREE
☼ ◊◊ Z9–12 H12–3 ↕4ft (1.2m) ↔5ft (1.5m)
A compact shrub that flowers all winter. Reach into the shrub for long-stemmed cut flowers. Avoid shearing like a blob as you will never see the glory of it.

Callistemon citrinus 'Compacta'
COMPACT BOTTLEBRUSH
☼ ◊◊ Z10–12 H12–9 ↕↔15ft (5m)
Flowers year-round in waves of bloom, unlike large types, seldom needing pruning except to remove dead or discolored foliage lying on ground. Fine bank cover.

Lavatera thuringiaca 'Barnsley'
BARNSLEY TREE MALLOW
☼ ● Z6–10 H8–6 ↕↔6ft (2m)
Blooms on new wood, year-round in mild zones. Easy
to grow; prune lightly at intervals throughout the year.
Blooms best when not over-fertilized.

Abelia x grandiflora
GLOSSY ABELIA
☼ ◐ ● Z6–10 H10–1 ↕8ft (2.5m) ↔5ft (1.5m)
Bell-shaped blooms all summer long. 'Edward Goucher'
is more compact. 'Prostrata' makes groundcover. Take
out unwanted branches fall or spring. Never shear.

Metrosideros excelsa 'Spring Fire'
NEW ZEALAND CHRISTMAS SHRUB
☼ ◐ ◐ Z9–11 H12–1 ↕8ft (2.5m) ↔4ft (1.2m)
Outstanding shrub for hedge, better than escallonia.
Plentiful rose-red blossoms are very showy against
gray foliage. Tolerates shade but flowers more in sun.

Garrya elliptica
COAST SILK TASSEL
Ⓝ ☼ ◐ ◐ Z8–11
H12–8 ↕↔20ft (6m)
From the northern
California coast, male
and female plants
have cascading
catkins in spring.
Male plants are
showier, while
females bear
purple fruit. A
male variety,
'James Roof',
has foot-long
catkins.

Shrubs for espalier

Espaliers are plants trained to grow flat against a support or wall. They answer difficult questions, such as: What should I plant in that narrow bed next to the front door? What should I put along that bare fence in the side yard? How do I hide that ugly dog run? Though they may not be as colorful or exciting as climbers, most tend to be neater, cleaner, and narrower.

Punica granatum 'Nana'
DWARF POMEGRANATE
☼ ◊ ◊ Z7–12 H12–7 ↕3ft (30cm) ↔6ft (60cm)
Blooms at a foot tall or less. For espalier, cut out unwanted branches, tie others to trellis, wires, or wall-ties. Almost evergreen, its fruit hangs on for months.

Kerria japonica 'Golden Guinea'
GOLDEN GUINEA PLANT
☼ ☀ ◊ ◊ Z5–10 H10–1 ↕6ft (2m) ↔8ft (2.5m)
A deciduous shrub with summer to early-fall bloom, and yellow leaves in autumn. This can be a free-standing fountain, or espalier by cutting off branches that have bloomed in fall, tying new growth to a support.

Camellia japonica 'Elegans'
ELEGANS CAMELLIA
☼ ◊ ◊ pH Z9–11 H10–7 ↕↔12ft (4m)
For espalier, remove jutting branches. Cut winter flowers with a bit of stem and a leaf or two to take as gifts wherever you go. Feed acid food after bloom, and twice in summer.

Pyracantha 'Santa Cruz'
SANTA CRUZ FIRETHORN
☼ ◊ Z7–10 H10–7 ↕↔12ft (4m)
Easily maintained at a lower height. Spring flowers are followed by berries. Leave some new growth, which will bear the following year. Wear thick leather gloves to prune and train.

MORE CHOICES

- *Camellia sasanqua* 'Hana Jiman' z9–11 H8–7
- *Carissa macrocarpa* 'Prostrata'
  z10–12 H12–9
- *Cotoneaster lacteus* z7–9 H9–4
- *Duranta stenostachya* z10–12 H12–10
- *Eucalyptus macrocarpa* z9–11 H12–1
- *Eucalyptus rhodantha* z9–12 H10–9
- *Eriobotrya deflexa* z8–11 H12–8
- *Gardenia augusta* z9–11 H12–8
- *Magnolia grandiflora* 'San Marino'
  z6–10 H10–7
- *Pyrus kawakamii* z9–11 H12–9
- *Viburnum macrocephalum* z7–10 H10–7

Grewia occidentalis
LAVENDER STAR FLOWER
☼ ◊ ◑ z9–12 H12–9
↕↔10ft (3m)
Wind-resistant, natural espalier with open growth, or use as a bank cover or clipped hedge. Charming flowers can be appreciated up close, mostly in spring and fall. Pinch to thicken growth and prune after bloom.

Calliandra tweedii
BRAZILIAN FLAME BUSH
☼ ◊ ◑ z9–10 H12–10
↕↔8ft (2.5m)
Fernlike leaves with stunning flowers. A magnet to hummingbirds all winter in the desert; elsewhere mostly spring and fall. Espaliers easily, or grow as a free-standing shrub. Prune off lower branches for artistic flat-topped tree.

Calliandra haematocephala
PINK POWDER PUFF
☼ ◑ z10–12 H12–10 ↕↔10ft (3m)
A natural espalier for an entryway with divided leaves and flowers like shocking pink powder puffs. Faded flowers go dark. Daily deadheading keeps it elegant.

Xylosma congestum
GLOSSY XYLOSMA
☼ ◑ z9–10 H10–9 ↕↔10ft (3m)
A tidy-looking, heat-resistant evergreen that sheds leaves in spring as young bronze ones grow. A single spring feeding wards off problems from mites or scale.

Shrubs with variegated foliage

Variegated shrubs add elegance to gardens. Some do well in shade; others need sunshine to maintain colors. Few wild species are variegated. Most garden selections came about when a plant sported some variegated foliage, and an observant person rooted a cutting. The finest variegated flowering shrubs have leaf colors that enhance flower color.

Bougainvillea 'Hawaii'
HAWAII BOUGAINVILLEA
☼ ◐◑ Z10–12 H12–1 ↕↔3ft (1m)
Shrubby and great in containers or hanging baskets, this has red flowers and leaves with golden yellow margins. Flowers on new wood so cut bloomed-out branches and fertilize. Often sold as 'Raspberry Ice.'

Abutilon pictum var. *thompsonii*
THOMPSON'S VARIEGATED ABUTILON
☼ ☼ ◐◑ Z9–12 H12–8
↕8ft (2.5m) ↔5ft (1.5m)
Continual bloom is good in tropical gardens, next to a path, patio, or swimming pool. Needs drainage. Spread earthworm castings to control whiteflies. Use ladybugs.

Cotoneaster atropurpureus
COTONEASTER
☼ ◐ Z5–7 H7–5 ↕10ft (3m) ↔15ft (5m)
A variegated form of a deciduous, tall treelike variety. Reddish pink berries follow white flowers. *C. horizontalis* 'Variegatus' has same look, but shorter.

Westringia fruticosa 'Morning Light'
COAST ROSEMARY
☼ ◐ Z9–10 H10–9 ↕↔3ft (1m)
White-edged foliage with grayish leaves shines in morning or evening light. This shrub stays compact without pruning, a great advantage over the species.

MORE CHOICES

- *Acca sellowiana* Z9–12 H12–9
- *Coprosma repens* Z8–11 H11–8
- *Fatsia japonica* Z8–11 H12–8
- *Pittosporum tobira* Z9–10 H10–9
- *Hydrangea macrophylla* 'Tricolor' Z6–10 H10–6

Shrubs with colorful foliage

Colorful foliage can take the place of flowers or increase their visibility. Purple-leaved shrubs enhance the greens around them. Shrubs with gray foliage are magic in a garden. Place gray foliage next to pink, orange, or purple flowers, and see how those colors sing. Also use gray foliage to separate flowers with colors that clash, like orange and magenta.

Juniperus squamata 'Blue Star'
BLUE STAR JUNIPER
☼ ◐ ◐ ◑ z4–10 H10–1 ↕3ft (1m) ↔4ft (1.2m)
This long-lived groundcover has a strong blue color and is elegant beneath plants with plum-colored or pink foliage, or surrounding Japanese maples.

Loropetalum chinense 'Razzleberri'
RAZZLEBERRI LOROPETALUM
☼ ◐ ◑ z8–10 H10–8 ↕↔10ft (3m)
Waves of fringed red blooms year-round on variegated leaves when young, turns greener with age. Many new varieties have more leaf color. Takes well to pruning.

Prunus x *cistena*
PURPLE-LEAVED SAND CHERRY
☼ ◐◑ z3–8 H8–1 ↕↔5ft (1.5m)
A slow-growing deciduous shrub grown in cold-winter climates for dark foliage and spring flowers. In warm-winter areas, try *P. campanulata* (Taiwan cherry).

Leptospermum scoparium 'Ruby Glow'
NEW ZEALAND TEA TREE
☼ ◐◑ z9–12 H12–9 ↕8ft (2.5m) ↔5ft (1.5m)
Foliage works with flowers as the shrub looks solidly red, fall through spring. Prune sprays inside the plant for cut flowers. Don't shear. Trainable as a small tree.

MORE CHOICES

- *Coprosma* 'Coppershine' z8–11 H11–8
- *Cotinus coggygria* 'Royal Purple' z5–8 H8–1
- *Juniperus* x *pfitzeriana* 'Gold Coast' z4–9 H9–1
- *Leucadendron argenteum* z10–11 H12–10

Shrubs for cottage gardens

Savvy gardeners know the style of the garden should blend with the style of the house. Cottage gardens are in harmony with any house, new or old, that has design elements reminiscent of cottages – wooden shutters, for example, a front porch, or Dutch doors. Cottage gardens are colorful and blowsy, mixing annual and perennial flowers with informal old-fashioned shrubs.

Lavandula dentata
FRENCH LAVENDER
☼ ◊ Z5–10 H9–4 ↕4ft (1.2m) ↔6ft (2m)
Lavenders are short-lived shrubs, often succumbing to root rot in summer. This one is the most durable. Extend its life by shearing the plant after spring bloom.

Alyogyne huegelii
BLUE HIBISCUS
☼ ◊ Z9–11 H12–1 ↕↔8ft (2.5m)
Charming over a wall or picket fence, year-round flowers appear in full sun, one on each branch tip. Cut a few back every few weeks for extended bloom.

MORE CHOICES

- *Argyranthemum frutescens* 'Cobbity Daisy' Z9–11 H11–9
- *Argyranthemum frutescens* Elfin Series Z10–11 H12–1
- *Buddleia davidii* 'Empire Blue' Z6–10 H10–1
- *Rosa* 'Iceberg' Z5–10 H10–5

Perovskia atriplicifolia 'Blue Spire'
BLUE SPIRE RUSSIAN SAGE
☼ ☼ ◊◊ Z7–10 H10–7 ↕↔4ft (1.2m)
Many thin stems bear a cloud of deep violet blossoms on feathery gray foliage from late spring through summer, into fall. Deadheading lengthens bloom.

Rosa 'Gertrude Jekyll'
GERTRUDE JEKYLL ROSE
☼ ◊ z5–11 H11–5 ‡8ft (2.5m) ↔3ft (1m)
Grow this David Austin rose, named for an English garden doyenne, upright on an obelisk. Blooms to ground. Never cut Austins back hard when young.

Salvia leucantha
MEXICAN BUSH SAGE
☼ ◊◊ z9–12 H12–4 ‡4ft (1.2m) ↔6ft (2m)
Although shrublike, this is actually a perennial that sends up fresh basal growth from the ground each spring. After these shoots are one foot tall, cut down last year's stems, resulting in a new plant.

Rosa 'The Prince'
THE PRINCE ROSE
☼ ◊ z5–10 H12–1 ‡6ft (2m) ↔3ft (1m)
A modern David Austin English rose prized for its musk aroma, deep red color, and as a cut flower. Grow next to *Lavatera sylvestris* 'Magic Merlin'.

Fuchsia arborescens
TREE FUCHSIA
☼ ◊ z9–10 H10–9
‡6ft (2m) ↔5ft (1.5m)
Feed in warm months with balanced fertilizer for growth and bloom. Cut back in fall or spring, never all at once, pinch to increase bushiness. Allow to overhang wandering path.

Rosa gallica 'Versicolor'
ROSA MUNDI ROSE
☼ ◊ z3–10 H10–1
‡4ft (1.2m) ↔3ft (1m)
Related to the 16th-century Gallica rose used on floors during ancient Roman orgies. Blooms once a year in spring or early summer. Drop-dead fragrance. Use for potpourri.

Artemisia 'Powis Castle'
POWIS CASTLE WORMWOOD
☼ ◊◊ z7–10 H10–7 ‡3ft (1m) ↔6ft (2m)
This has silver foliage that is particularly attractive next to a pink or orange rose – if the rose's water can be kept from it. Shear or cut back long branches to stop it from splitting open in the middle.

WOODY PLANTS

Shrubs for butterflies

Most gardeners think of butterflies as floating flowers deserving protection, but they pick and choose. They may love monarchs, painted ladies, and swallowtails, but detest European cabbage butterflies and moths that lay eggs on geraniums. You can control these troublesome creatures while protecting native butterflies by spraying affected plants only with Bt.

Calycanthus occidentalis
SPICE BUSH

Ⓝ ☼ ◑ ◊ Z6–10 H10–6 ↕↔12ft (4m)
Easy to grow from seed, native to coastal ranges and the foothills of California, this blooms like tiny waterlilies. The flowers and leaves smell a bit like empty wine barrels. Use as a screen or bank cover.

Hebe 'Purple Queen'
PURPLE QUEEN HEBE

☼ ◑ ◊ Z9–11 H12–9 ↕↔5ft (1.5m)
This is a large cultivar of a New Zealand native, like veronica. Flowers bring butterflies. Can be used as a hedge, screen, shrubbery, or bank. Best near the coast. Not for hot dry summers or poor drainage.

Viburnum carlesii
KOREAN SPICE VIBURNUM

☼ ◑ ◊ Z8–10 H10–8 ↕↔8ft (2.5m)
Butterflies like these sweetly fragrant flowers. The deciduous foliage may go red before falling. Prune to keep compact. Fruits aren't showy but birds like them.

Ligustrum ovalifolium
CALIFORNIA PRIVET

☼ ◑ ◊ Z6–10 H10–6 ↕15ft (5m) ↔10ft (3m)
Butterflies float over these leaves, visiting summer-blooming flowers for nectar. Deciduous except in warm climates, this is from Japan. Birds spread seeds.

Salix caprea 'Kilmarnock'
PINK PUSSY WILLOW
☀ ◑ z6–10 H10–6 ↕8ft (2.5m) ↔6ft (2m)
A weeping form often labeled as 'Pendula', the male bears fat pink catkins in spring prior to leafing out. Leaves attract butterflies. Control caterpillars with Bt.

Hibiscus syriacus
'Minerva'
MINERVA ROSE OF SHARON
☀ ◑ z9–11 H11–9
↕12ft (4m) ↔6ft (2m)
One of the longest blooming varieties of this deciduous shrub. For cold winters and hot summers. Shines where a tropical hibiscus is not the best choice but has same effect on butterflies.

Ceanothus 'Blue Mound'
CALIFORNIA LILAC
Ⓝ ☀ ◐ ◊◑ z9–10 H10–8
↕5ft (1.5m) ↔6ft (2m)
An evergreen shrub, mounded in the middle, that covers itself in spring bloom. Butterflies float above and alight to sip nectar. Larvae never damage foliage. Many fine horticultural varieties.

Aesculus californica
CALIFORNIA BUCKEYE
Ⓝ ☀ ◑ z7–10 H10–7 ↕20ft (6m) ↔30ft (9m)
A slow-growing, deciduous, long-term shrub that can be a tree. The spring bloom attracts butterflies; foliage is rarely damaged. Plant in canyons or on dry banks.

MORE CHOICES

- *Abutilon megapotamicum* 'Marianne' z10–12 H12–1
- *Buddleja marrubiifolia* z9–10 H9–6
- *Grewia occidentalis* z9–12 H12–9
- *Hibiscus syriacus* 'Woodbridge' z9–11 H11–9
- *Lantana camara* 'Feston Rose' z9–12 H12–1
- *Lavandula angustifolia* 'Hidcote' z5–10 H8–5
- *Lavatera assurgentiflora* z9–10 H12–9
- *Philadelphus lewisii* z6–10 H8–5
- *Rhamnus ilicifolia* z9–10 H10–9
- *Ribes malvaceum* z9–10 H10–9
- *Syringa chinensis* 'Alba' z6–10 H8–1

WOODY PLANTS

Shrubs for hummingbirds

When plants are blooming, hummingbirds prefer the plants to feeders. Feeders that aren't cleaned and refilled can be injurious to the health of birds, so grow the flowers. These shrubs, when chosen to provide year-round bloom, will keep a population of happy hummers in your garden, especially if you also have a fountain or another source of moving water.

Buddleia davidii 'Harlequin'
HARLEQUIN BUTTERFLY BUSH
☼ ☼ ◐ Z6–10 H10–4 ↕↔10ft (3m)
Cut back woody branches in fall or spring to encourage fresh green growth. Take soft cuttings from tips in March, root in potting mix for new plants. Needs good drainage.

Hibiscus rosa-sinensis 'Agnes Galt'
AGNES GALT CHINESE HIBISCUS
☼ ◐ Z9–12 H12–9 ↕↔10ft (3m)
A fine small tree unless controlled by progressive pruning. (Don't shear it!) Fertilize in summer. Control giant white fly with earthworm castings beneath plant.

Arctostaphylos pumila
DUNE MANZANITA
Ⓝ ☼ ☼ ◐◐ Z9–10 H10–8 ↕2ft (60cm) ↔6ft (2m)
Coastal groundcover, branches will root in ground. Needs good drainage. Plant in November, mulch ground. Prune only to remove dead growth in fall.

Lantana camara 'Radiation'
RADIATION LANTANA
☼ ◐ Z9–12 H12–1 ↕3ft (1m) ↔6ft (2m)
Most colorful of lantanas, year-round when in full sun. Excellent bank cover, roadside plant, but overwhelming in small spaces. Renew by cutting to ground.

Correa 'Dusky Bells'
AUSTRALIAN FUCHSIA
☼ ☼ ◐ Z9–10 H10–9 ↕3ft (1m) ↔6ft (2m)
Blooms from late fall into spring, sporadically in summer. Needs good drainage and little fertilizer. When container-grown, protect the pot from sun or reflected heat.

Lavandula angustifolia 'Hidcote'
ENGLISH LAVENDER

☼ ◊ Z5–10 H10–5

↕↔2ft (60cm)

Although not as easy to grow as French lavender, this is worth growing for its superior fragrance and flowers. Cut the flowers for bouquets and shear after bloom. As you brush past the plant, it releases fragrance.

Leucophyllum frutescens 'Compactum'
TEXAS RANGER

☼ ◊◊ Z8–10 H10–8 ↕3ft (1m) ↔4ft (1.2m)

One of the finest plants for banks and roadsides in hot-interior climates. Its bright color shows for long distances against small-leaved, gray foliage. Summer-deciduous if not watered.

Tecoma capensis
CAPE HONEYSUCKLE

☼☼ ◊ Z9–12 H12–9 ↕30ft (10m) ↔12ft (4m)

An almost indestructible shrub or climber that turns into a larger shrub or tree. Prune occasionally to shape and encourage branching. Year-round bloom in sun.

Acacia baileyana
COOTAMUNDRA WATTLE

☼ ◊◊ Z9–10 H12–10 ↕30ft (10m) ↔40ft (12m)

Late winter or early spring flowers completely cover shrub, usually grown on one trunk as tree. Well-drained soil, on banks. Pinch back growth tip when planting.

Heteromeles arbutifolia
TOYON, CALIFORNIA HOLLY

Ⓝ ☼☼ ◊◊ Z8–10 H12–8 ↕↔10ft (3m)

White flowers on branch tips followed by red berries in winter, "apples" for birds. Settlers named Hollywood for this plant. Needs good drainage and little care.

MORE CHOICES

- *Abelia* 'Edward Goucher' Z6–10 H10–1
- *Abutilon* x *hybridum* 'Moonchimes' Z9–11 H12–1
- *Acca sellowiana* Z8–11 H12–9
- *Bouvardia glaberrima* Z9–10 H12–1
- *Fuchsia* 'Gartenmeister Bonstedt' Z9–11 H12–9
- *Grevillea* 'Poorinda Constance' Z9–10 H12–10
- *Grevillea thelemanniana* Z9–10 H12–10
- *Justicia californica* Z9–10 H9–5
- *Leucophyllum frutescens* 'Green Cloud' Z7–12 H12–7
- *Ribes speciosum* Z9–10 H10–9
- *Salvia canariensis* Z9–10 H12–1
- *Sambucus mexicana* Z7–11 H11–7
- *Syringa vulgaris* 'Lavender Lady' Z4–8 H8–1

WOODY PLANTS

Hedges for birds

A great garden pleases all five senses. It gives us textures to touch, colors and shapes to see, fragrances to smell, fruit or herbs to taste, and sounds of water and birds to hear. Some gardens are great stage sets, but if they have no fountain or birds, they lack the orchestra. Gardens with moving water and fruit-bearing hedges have songbirds galore.

Pyracantha 'Mohave'
MOHAVE FIRETHORN
☼ ◐ Z6–10 H10–6 ↕↔12ft (4m)
Named varieties are best but plants are often mislabeled. Choose in winter when berries are on plants. Grow as a hedge to attract mockingbirds.

Prunus laurocerasus
ENGLISH LAUREL
☼ ☼ ◐◐ Z6–9 H9–6 ↕↔30ft (10m)
A tree or tall unclipped hedge with small black fruits relished by birds. To prune, reach into the plant; the leaves are too large for shearing. Many smaller named varieties are available.

Berberis thunbergii var. *atropurpurea* 'Rose Glow'
ROSE GLOW JAPANESE BARBERRY
☼ ☼ ◐◐ Z5–10 H10–5 ↕↔6ft (2m)
A spiny, deciduous bank cover, screen, or barrier plant. Spring foliage is marbled, then red, later bronze. Red berries appear in fall.

MORE CHOICES

- *Cotoneaster lacteus* Z7–9 H9–4
- *Elaeagnus multiflora* 'Red King' Z5–7 H7–5
- *Ilex* x *altacarensis* 'Wilsonii' Z7–9 H9–7
- *Luma apiculata* Z9–11 H12–10
- *Mahonia lomariifolia* Z8–10 H9–5
- *Photinia glabra* 'Rubens' Z7–10 H9–7
- *Rosa rubiginosa* Z4–10 H10–1

Prunus caroliniana
CAROLINA CHERRY LAUREL
Ⓝ ☼ ◐◐ Z8–10 H10–1 ↕↔20ft (6m)
A choice replacement for psyllid-ridden *Syzygium*, this needs irrigation in hot weather. Dense branching grows from its base. Fruit grows to ½in (30cm) and is hidden in foliage.

Native shrubs for birds

A live garden is an extension of nature and can be a home for the creatures native to each region. One of the many advantages of growing native plants is that they have evolved along with animal species. As a bonus, wild plants are perfectly adapted to our climate. Plant these and attract wildlife without even trying.

Prunus ilicifolia subsp. *lyonii*
CATALINA CHERRY
Ⓝ ☼ ◐ ◊ ◑ Z9–10 H10–9
↕↔20ft (6m)
Catalina Island has many gifts for gardens, including this screening plant that looks presentable with little water or pruning.

Rhus ovata
SUGAR BUSH
Ⓝ ☼ ◐ ◊ ◑ Z9–10 H10–9 ↕↔10ft (3m)
Similar to *R. integrifolia* but for hot interior, this can be pruned or espaliered or a bank cover. Less water is better. The fruit is enjoyed by many birds, including California towhees whose scratchings plant seeds.

Rhus integrifolia
LEMONADE BERRY
Ⓝ ☼ ◐ ◊ ◑ Z9–10 H10–9 ↕↔10ft (3m)
Like *R. ovata* but coastal, this is a good plant for banks and outer edges. It is better without irrigation and takes clipping well. Edible berries are loved by birds.

Mahonia fremontii
DESERT MAHONIA
Ⓝ ☼ ◐ ◊ ◑ Z7–10 H10–7 ↕1ft (30cm) ↔6ft (2m)
An evergreen groundcover, native to deserts. Spring flowers are followed by brown-blue fruits. The foliage is spiny so use gloves for planting and late-fall cleanup.

MORE CHOICES

- *Atriplex lentiformis* Z7–9 H9–7
- *Berberis haematocarpa* Z7–9 H9–7
- *Heteromeles arbutifolia* Z9–10 H10–8
- *Rhamnus californica* Z9–12 H12–9
- *Ribes malvaceum* Z9–10 H10–9

Shrubs with fantastic shapes

First-time visitors to the Southwest often remark on the amazing shapes of many of the plants that grow here. Intriguing shapes can result from strong winds or careful pruning, but certain plants are naturally mind-boggling. Incorporating a few showstoppers into the landscape can add excitement and humor to your garden.

Euphorbia characias subsp. *wulfenii* 'John Tomlinson'
JOHN TOMLINSON SPURGE
☼ ◐ Z6–10 H10–6 ‡↔4ft (1.2m)
This shrubby perennial needs little irrigation. In February, cut stems that have bloomed after new growth is 8in (2.5cm) long. 'Humpty Dumpty' is short and vigorous.

Euphorbia milii
CROWN OF THORNS
☼ ◑ ◐ Z10–12 H12–10 ‡4ft (1.2m) ↔3ft (1m)
This spiny shrub from Madagascar has tangled branches that build into a thicket and year-round, red flowers, even on beachfront. Needs drained soil.

Adenium obesum
DESERT ROSE
☼ ◑ ◐ ◐ Z10–12 H12–10 ‡9ft (3m) ↔3ft (1m)
Twisted branches that rise from a huge swollen trunk have sparse foliage and pink flowers. In a pot or in the ground, this needs warmth, light, and a dry winter.

Erythrina x *bidwillii*
CORAL SHRUB
☼ ◐ Z9–10 H10–9 ‡↔8ft (2.5m)
A deciduous, extremely thorny shrub with spectacular summer flowers on long branches. Use loppers to cut back each flowering branch after bloom.

Opuntia microdasys
BUNNY EARS
☼ ◐ ◐ Z9–10 H10–9 ‡3ft (1m) ↔5ft (1.5m)
Flat, round, soft green pads, with woolly polka dots bear smaller pads, like ears. This grows fast unless planted in pots. In the desert, it bears spring flowers and fruit. Do not touch.

MORE CHOICES

- *Adansonia grandidieri* z10–12 H12–10
- *Brugmansia arborea* 'Knightii' z10–12 H12–10
- *Echium wildpretii* z9–10 H10–9
- *Eucalyptus kruseana* z9–12 H12–9
- *Eucalyptus macrocarpa* z9–12 H12–9
- *Fouquieria splendens* z8–10 H12–1
- *Hesperaloe parviflora* z8–10 H10–8
- *Kalanchoe beharensis* z10–12 H12–10
- *Nolina parryi* z7–10 H10–7
- *Pachypodium lamerei* z10–12 H12–6
- *Plumeria alba* z10–12 H12–10
- *Xanthorrhoea preissii* z9–10 H10–9
- *Yucca brevifolia* z8–9 H9–8
- *Yucca recurvifolia* z8–10 H10–8
- *Yucca whipplei* z8–10 H10–8

Acacia cultriformis
KNIFE ACACIA

☼ ◊◊ z9–10 H10–9 ↕↔15ft (5m)

With fragrant spring flowers, triangular phyllodes (thickened stalks) sprout straight from branches. Plant by a path or on a patio or banks.

Jatropha podagrica
MINI BAOBAB

☼ ◊ z10–12 H12–10 ↕20in (50cm) ↔10in (25cm)

A succulent for pots or a dry garden, its trunk grows straight up from a swollen bulblike base that is warty with age. Branches bear maple-shaped leaves and red flowers on bright red bracts.

Agave attenuata
FOXTAIL AGAVE

☼ ☼ ◊◊ z10–11 H11–10 ↕3ft (1m) ↔5ft (1.5m)

A Mexican succulent that looks like a giant gray-green rose, its suckers eventually make it a clump. When many arching bloom stalks appear in fall, it means rains are coming in spring to sprout seeds.

Melianthus major
HONEY BUSH

☼ ☼ ◊◊ z9–12 H12–9 ↕12ft (4m) ↔10ft (3m)

A fast-growing, long-lived plant with a statuesque form, lush gray-green foliage, a leaning trunk, and attractive spikes of red-brown spring flowers. Prune to shape.

Native shrubs resistant to deer

An eight-foot fence may protect your garden plants from deer but it can also destroy your views. In England and Europe, animals are kept from gardens with a clifflike terrace, or a ditch in which one side is higher than the other, called a "ha-ha," because people often fall into them. Hungry deer will eat anything, but these plants are less frequently damaged.

Trichostema lanatum
WOOLLY BLUE CURLS
Ⓝ ☀ ☀ ◊　Z9–10 H10–9　↕5ft (1.5m) ↔8ft (2.5m)
Attractive flowers need little care once established. No summer irrigation; best with good soil on sloping ground. Deadheading prolongs spring bloom to fall.

Fremontodendron 'California Glory'
CALIFORNIA GLORY FLANNEL BUSH
Ⓝ ☀ ◊　Z9–10 H10–9　↕20ft (6m) ↔12ft (4m)
Plant in November next to ceanothus on a steep bank. Spring bloom covers foliage. No summer water. Prune to remove dead wood, if necessary, in fall or winter.

Ribes speciosum
FUCHSIA FLOWERING GOOSEBERRY
Ⓝ ☀ ☀ ◊◊◊　Z9–10 H10–9　↕8ft (2.5m) ↔10ft (3m)
This prickly barrier plant takes heat, drought, and neglect with a neat year-round appearance. Winter and spring flowers attract hummingbirds.

Heteromeles arbutifolia var. *macrocarpa*
TOYON, CALIFORNIA HOLLY
Ⓝ ☀ ☀ ◊◊　Z8–10 H10–8　↕↔10ft (3m)
With larger berries than the species, this is liked by birds. Use on a bank cover. Water to thicken growth and improve appearance and berry crop.

MORE CHOICES

- *Calycanthus occidentalis* Z8–10 H9–6
- *Carpenteria californica* Z9–10 H9–8
- *Ceanothus* 'Blue Mound' Z9–10 H10–8
- *Dendromecon harfordii* Z9–10 H10–9
- *Lavatera assurgentiflora* Z9–10 H10–9
- *Senna wislizenii* Z8–9 H9–8

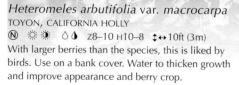
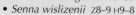

Non-native shrubs resistant to deer

When planting a garden where deer abound, concentrate on choosing plants that deer like less than others. Use shrubbery, such as bamboo, as barriers with wandering paths, rocks, and deer-resistant selections planted in drifts for a bigger effect. Though a deer does eat anything if hungry enough, the plants shown here often go untouched.

Bambusa multiplex 'Alphonse Karr'
ALPHONSE KARR BAMBOO
☼ ◐ ◧ ◧ Z9–12 H10–1 ‡10ft (3m) ↔8ft (2.5m)
A dense screen, branching from bottom to top as a hedge, this is less likely to invade streets or a neighbor's property. Attractive on its own as a standing shrub.

Coleonema pulchrum 'Golden Sunset'
BREATH OF HEAVEN
☼ ◐ ◧ Z8–10 H10–8 ‡18in (45cm) ↔4ft (1.2m)
Formerly called *Diosma*, this variety with yellow foliage and tiny pink flowers in winter and spring is shorter than the type most commonly sold. Good in drifts of 5 to 7.

Cotoneaster lacteus
MILKFLOWER COTONEASTER
☼ ◐ ◧ Z9–10 H10–9 ‡8ft (2.5m) ↔10ft (3m)
An arching, graceful informal hedge or screen has neat, attractive evergreen foliage and clusters of white flowers followed by red fruits that last long if birds don't get them.

MORE CHOICES

- *Anisodontea* x *hypomandarum* 'Tara's Wonder' Z9–10 H10–9
- *Grevillea* 'Red Hooks' Z9–10 H10–9
- *Phlomis fruticosa* Z7–10 H10–7
- *Sollya heterophylla* Z9–12 H12–9
- *Westringia fruticosa* Z9–10 H10–9

Correa pulchella
AUSTRALIAN FUCHSIA
☼ ◐ ◧ Z9–10 H10–9
‡30in (75cm) ↔8ft (2.5m)
Its long winter bloom lasts from fall to late spring with little hanging flowers that are attractive up close. Do not overwater or overfertilize.

Shrubs to plant under windows

Shrubs planted beneath windows can eventually obstruct views and make windows hard to reach for cleaning. To avoid these problems, here are some choices that are attractive year-round, stay relatively low, and are not thorny or difficult to work around. You can place small stepping stones between the plants to keep your feet clean.

Grevillea juniperina
GREVILLEA
☼ ◊ ◑ Z9–10 H10–9 ↕↔6ft (2m)
Many compact types, such as 'Noellii', have been developed from this Australian native, making better choices under windows. Attractive foliage and spring flowers on branch tips.

Ceratostigma plumbaginoides
DWARF PLUMBAGO
☼ ◊ ◑ Z7–10 H10–7
↕12in (30cm) ↔18in (45cm)
Shear in early spring, then fertilize and water. After 10 years, take tip cuttings in March, dig up and discard old plants, and replace with rooted stems. Flowers summer and fall.

Punica granatum 'Nana'
DWARF POMEGRANATE
☼ ◊ ◑ Z8–12 H12–8 ↕3ft (1m) ↔6ft (2m)
Dense growth, colorful ruffled petals, small ornamental fruits. Deciduous and bright yellow in fall; evergreen in mild climates. Similar named varieties are available.

Escallonia x exoniensis 'Frades'
ESCALLONIA
☼ ☼ ◊ ◑ Z9–10 H10–9 ↕3ft (1m) ↔6ft (2m)
A wind-tolerant evergreen shrub with summer and fall flowers. Good as a hedge, this can be sheared or pinched. A dwarf form, 'Compakta', stays low for good placement beneath windows.

Pittosporum tobira 'Wheeler's Dwarf'
WHEELER'S DWARF MOCK ORANGE
☼ ☼ ◊ ◑ Z9–10 H10–9 ↕↔2–3ft (0.6–1m)
More compact than the species, this is widely available at nurseries and is the perfect green hedge beneath windows. Stays 2 or 3 feet high, and bears fragrant flowers in spring.

Gardenia jasminoides 'Veitchii'
VEITCHII CAPE JASMINE
☼ ◐ ◔ Z9–11 H11–9
↕3ft (1m) ↔6ft (2m)
Many fragrant blooms appear a few miles from the coast, but not on the coast itself. This needs a night temperature 20 degrees colder than day or buds drop off unopened.

Abelia 'Edward Goucher'
EDWARD GOUCHER ABELIA
☼ ◐ ◔ Z9–10 H10–9 ↕3ft (1m) ↔5ft (1.5m)
An easy plant that grows well near houses. Pinch the tips and prune selectively to control size. Shearing destroys its graceful form. Lacy foliage flowers throughout the summer and fall.

Abelia x grandiflora 'Prostrata'
GLOSSY ABELIA
☼ ◐ ◔ ◔ Z9–12 H12–9 ↕2ft (60cm) ↔5ft (1.5m)
This is also good as a groundcover on a bank or as foreground in a shrub bed. Hard frosts freeze it to ground but it recovers and blooms the same year.

MORE CHOICES

- *Carissa macrocarpa* 'Tuttlei' Z10–11 H12–1
- *Cistus* x *dansereaui* Z9–10 H10–9
- *Correa backhouseana* Z9–10 H10–9
- *Ilex cornuta* 'Rotunda' Z9–10 H10–9
- *Leptospermum scoparium* 'Snow White' Z9–10 H10–9
- *Myrsine africana* Z9–10 H10–9
- *Nandina domestica* 'Harbor Dwarf' Z9–12 H12–4
- *Rhaphiolepis indica* 'Ballerina' Z9–12 H12–7
- *Rosmarinus officinalis* 'Santa Barbara' Z9–12 H12–9
- *Santolina chamaecyparissus* Z6–12 H12–6

Calliandra tweedii
BRAZILIAN FLAME BUSH
☼ ◐ ◔ Z9–10 H10–9 ↕↔8ft (2.5m)
Use for framing a window, enjoying the sight of hummingbirds visiting flowers or nesting in a tree. The three-foot-high *C. eriophylla* or dwarf type, *C. emarginata*, are better choices for beneath windows.

Lantana camara 'Feston Rose'
LANTANA
☼ ◐ ◔ Z10–12 H12–10 ↕3ft (1m) ↔6ft (2m)
Its constant bloom brings hummingbirds and butterflies. Compact varieties such as 'Gold Rush' and 'Dwarf White' are great under windows. Clipping keeps it tidy and encourages growth and flowers.

WOODY PLANTS

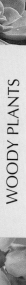

Small shrubs for herb gardens

In botany, the word "herb" means a plant that is soft-bodied and may die to the ground in winter. In common parlance, an herb is a plant that has been treasured by humans since ancient times for fragrance, flavoring, medicine, or dyeing cloth. Even planting just a few of those shown here will lend historic impact and a peaceful, healing atmosphere to any garden.

Pelargonium graveolens
ROSE GERANIUM
☼ ☼ ◊ ◊   Z9–10 H10–9   ‡3ft (1m) ↔4ft (1.2m)
Its spring flowers are edible but it is grown for its fragrant foliage. An easy-care hedge for a fence or to grow next to a path or a scentless rose to waft scent as you pass. Flavor yellow cake batter with leaves.

Lavandula angustifolia 'Hidcote'
HIDCOTE ENGLISH LAVENDER
☼ ◊   Z8–10 H10–8   ‡↔2ft (60cm)
Pick its summer flowers for use in bouquets, scenting linens and drawers, as garnishes for food or light flavoring in tea or sugar cookies. Then shear into a neat rounded shape and fertilize lightly.

MORE CHOICES

- *Aloysia triphylla* z7–10 H10–7
- *Aloysia wrightii* z8–10 H10–8
- *Artemisia ludoviciana* var. *albula* z5–10 H10–5
- *Jasminum sambac* z9–12 H12–9
- *Laurus nobilis* z9–12 H12–9
- *Lavandula heterophylla* z9–10 H10–9
- *Lavandula intermedia* 'Super' z8–10 H10–8
- *Ocimum basilicum* 'African Blue' z9–11 H10–1
- *Origanum marjorana* z9–10 H10–9
- *Pelargonium crispum* z9–10 H10–9
- *Pelargonium tomentosum* z9–10 H10–9
- *Poliomintha longiflora* z9–10 H10–9
- *Rosmarinus officinalis* z9–12 H12–9
- *Salvia officinalis* z6–12 H12–6
- *Teucrium marum* z9–10 H10–9
- *Teucrium x lucidrys* z6–10 H10–6

Thymus vulgaris
COMMON THYME
☼ ☼ ◐ Z4–10 H9–1
↕1ft (30cm) ↔2ft (60cm)
Grow on the edge of a vegetable garden or in a container by the kitchen door. Can be a permanent shrub when using a light fertilizer, but better to use for seasoning food and to replant each year in spring.

Satureja montana
WINTER SAVORY
☼ ◐ Z6–10 H10–6 ↕15in (38cm) ↔2ft (60cm)
Its profuse summer bloom attracts bees. Hardier in winter than summer savory (S. hortensis). Grow summer savory for cooking and this one as ornamental.

Satureja hortensis
SUMMER SAVORY
☼ ◐◐ Z1–12 H12–1 ↕18in (38cm) ↔9in (60cm)
Plant from seeds above drip line in potager or use in a border. It has an aromatic, milder flavor than S. montana and needs richer soil. The peppery flavor is good for salads, soups, stew, and chicken. Purplish pink flowers appear midsummer to fall.

Salvia officinalis 'Tricolor'
VARIEGATED SAGE
☼ ☼ ◐ Z6–12 H8–1 ↕↔2ft (60cm)
In cool climates, prune to keep going for three years. In the Southwest, it is best to replace each year. Highly ornamental; the gray-green kind tastes better.

Melissa officinalis
LEMON BALM
☼ ☼ ◐ Z6–10 H10–6 ↕3ft (1m) ↔18in (45cm)
An invasive perennial to grow in a tub. Use dried leaves in potpourri or fresh in iced tea, a fruit cup, salads, and fish.

Santolina pinnata
GREEN SANTOLINA
☼ ◐◐ Z8–10 H10–8 ↕2ft (60cm) ↔3ft (1m)
The gray-foliaged S. chamaecyparissus can be used for dyeing. This has green foliage and lighter flowers. Pinch back in early spring, shear after bloom. If killed in cold winter, it will resprout from the ground.

Origanum vulgare 'Roseum'
OREGANO
☼ ◐ Z6–10 H10–6 ↕30in (75cm) ↔3ft (1m)
More a perennial than a shrub, oregano is vigorous and long-lived in pots and rock gardens. Some make matlike groundcovers, but the erect types are best for cooking.

WOODY PLANTS

Shrubs for use near swimming pools

Swimming pools built in small backyards are inevitably close to plants. Plants growing near pools need to be adapted to reflected light. The best choices are those that have no sharp leaves or spines, stay attractive year round without much pruning, have few or no falling leaves, and don't attract bees. If they're also tropical looking, so much the better.

Griselinia littoralis 'Variegata'
VARIEGATED GRISELINIA
☼ ☀ ◊ ◖ Z9–10 H10–9 ‡↔10ft (3m)
Tropical-looking foliage has 4-inch leathery leaves with little leaf drop so it always looks good. The variegated type is attractive with other foliage plants, colors best with good light.

Sparmannia africana
AFRICAN LINDEN
☼ ☀ ◊ ◖ Z9–12 H12–9 ‡20ft (6m) ↔12ft (4m)
A multitrunked tree or big shrub has a tropical look, wih clusters of small flowers midwinter to spring. Cut back to control and more arises.

Camellia sasanqua 'Yuletide'
YULETIDE CAMELLIA
☼ ◖ pH Z9–10 H10–9 ‡5ft (1.5m) ↔3ft (1m)
Sasanquas bloom earlier than large-flowered types and are easy-care, long-lived, slow-growing plants with no petal blight. Takes considerable sun without burning.

Viburnum davidii
PERE DAVID VIBURNUM
☼ ◖ pH Z9–10 H10–9 ‡↔4ft (1.2m)
This Chinese native has dark green leaves in a tidy mound. Its pink buds and white flowers are followed by a dazzling display of metallic turquoise berries.

Crassula ovata
SILVER JADE PLANT
☼ ◐ ◊ ◊ Z10–12 H12–10
↕↔4ft (1.2m)
Winter flowers last for a month or two in sun. Cut off after bloom. In frost-free zones, this is a good filler for bare stems of hedge plants that have lost low leaves.

Schefflera arboricola
VARIEGATED UMBRELLA PLANT
☼ ◐ ◊ ◊ Z10–12 H12–10 ↕↔20ft (6m)
A variegated form of a dense, shrubby, dark green species. Eventually bears yellow flowers in foot-wide spheres, bronzing with age. Plant at an angle, for permanently leaning trunks.

Hydrangea macrophylla
BIG-LEAF HYDRANGEA
☼ ◐ ◊ ◊ Z6–11 H11–6 ↕↔8ft (2.5m)
Feed with aluminum sulfate or special hydrangea food to maintain blue color. Grows best when east-facing. Spring and summer bloom; new varieties have more.

MORE CHOICES

- *Agave attenuata* Z10–11 H11–10
- *Cussonia paniculata* Z10–12 H12–10
- *Fatsia japonica* Z9–12 H12–8
- *Griselinia lucida* Z9–10 H9–7
- *Hibiscus rosa-sinensis* 'All Aglow' Z9–12 H12–9
- *Phlomis fruticosa* Z9–10 H10–9
- *Pittosporum tobira* 'Variegatum' Z9–11 H12–3
- *Polyscias fruticosa* Z10–12 H12–10
- *Rhaphiolepis indica* 'Ballerina' Z9–10 H10–9
- *Ternstroemia gymnanthera* Z8–10 H10–8

Jatropha integerrima
PEREGRINA, SPICY JATROPHA
☼ ◐ ◊ ◊ Z10–11 H11–10 ↕↔20ft (6m)
A big shrub or tree with fragrant summer flowers and poisonous seeds and sap. Best in warm, humid locations, like Hawaii. Flowers last all year if warm.

Shrubs for containers

Plant patio beds with tall shrubs or climbers cascading over walls. For seasonal color, rely on pots that can be easily changed for something else or taken under cover during frosts. Beware of sheltering tender plants under eaves within a walled patio. In the evening, as warm air escapes, cold air builds up like water in a swimming pool and freezes plants under eaves.

Plumeria auriculata var. *alba*
WHITE FRANGIPANI
☼ ☼ ◑ Z10–12 H12–10 ↕20ft (6m) ↔10ft (3m)
The quintessential Hawaiian plant also grows successfully in warm micro-climates of coastal California and Texas, planted in spring, not fall.

Rhododendron 'Red Wing'
RED WING AZALEA
☼ ◑ pH Z9–10 H10–9 ↕3ft (1m) ↔4ft (1.2m)
A long-lived, easy, evergreen Brooks hybrid. Among the finest of warm-winter azaleas, its roots must never dry out, but can survive with weekly irrigation. Feed after bloom and in late September.

Leptospermum scoparium 'Nanum Tui'
NEW ZEALAND TEA TREE
☼ ◑ Z9–11 H11–9 ↕2ft (60cm) ↔3ft (1m)
Long-lasting flowers smother foliage fall through spring. This low rounded shrub is good in a ceramic tub. Shear after bloom, or prune selectively.

Argyranthemum frutescens
MARGUERITE
☼ ☼ ◑ Z9–10 H10–9 ↕2ft (60cm) ↔3ft (1m)
Improved, heat-resistant hybrids are available. Shear lightly in June. Fertilize regularly. Year-round blooms in white, pink, yellow, double or single flowers.

Streptosolen jamesonii
MARMALADE BUSH

☼ ☼ ● Z9–12 H12–9 ↕↔6ft (2m)

Great cascading over a terrace, in pots, or hanging baskets, this needs a warm spot, fast drainage, a drip system, regular fertilizer, and frost protection.

Fuchsia 'Swingtime'
SWINGTIME FUCHSIA

☼ ☼ ● Z9–10 H10–9

↕2ft (60cm) ↔3ft (1m)

Grow in a hanging basket or in the ground to five feet high. Cut back old standards one-third at a time, allow to re-grow before cutting more. Hanging plants are best in their second year, then start anew.

Mandevilla sanderi 'Red Riding Hood'
RED RIDING HOOD MANDEVILLA

☼ ☼ ● Z10–12 H12–10 ↕2ft (60cm) ↔3ft (1m)

Prune in spring. Pinch back twining growth, fertilize monthly with slow-release, and keep moist for constant bloom. Loves east-facing patios and big tubs.

MORE CHOICES

- *Arbutus unedo* 'Elfin King' Z9–10 H9–6
- *Boronia crenulata* 'Shark Bay' Z9–10 H10–9
- *Brunfelsia pauciflora* Z9–12 H12–9
- *Correa* 'Dusky Bells' Z9–10 H10–9
- *Gardenia augusta* Z9–11 H11–9
- *Iochroma cyanea* Z10–12 H12–10
- *Justicia carnea* Z9–12 H12–9
- *Pachystachys lutea* Z10–12 H12–10
- *Pelargonium* 'Ann Hoysted' Z9–10 H10–9
- *Hydrangea macrophylla* Z8–11 H11–8
- *Tibouchina urvilleana* Z10–12 H12–10

Cuphea ignea
CIGAR PLANT

☼ ☼ ● Z9–12 H12–6 ↕↔1ft (3m)

Good for pots, hanging baskets, or edging borders, its small flowers bring hummingbirds. Cut back old plants in fall or spring and pinch to make bushy.

Camellia 'Dr. Clifford Parks'
DR. CLIFFORD PARKS CAMELLIA

☼ ● pH Z9–10 H10–9 ↕12ft (4m) ↔8ft (2.5m)

This camellia may need root pruning in the fall: slide out of tub, use knife to slice off quarter of root ball, top to bottom, on opposite sides; replace, add fresh soil.

WOODY PLANTS

Shrubby succulents for containers

Succulents are like people who triumph over adversity. When climates changed from wet to dry over the course of earth's history, they coped by storing water in thickened stems or leaves. In the process they developed an exciting array of shapes and colors, even more so since gardeners adopted and took an interest in them as hobby plants.

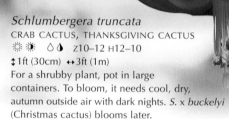

Crassula arborescens
JADE TREE
☼ ☀ ◊ ◊ Z9–10 H10–9
↕4ft (1.2m) ↔3ft (1m)
A houseplant in cold climates and a ground plant in frost-free climates. To make new plants, break off branches, allow to callus (make skin) overnight, and plant. White flowers appear in December and January.

MORE CHOICES

- Aloe arborescens Z10–12 H12–10
- Aeonium arboreum Z9–10 H10–9
- Agave americana Z9–12 H12–9
- Agave attenuata Z10–12 H12–10
- Cotyledon ladismithinsis Z10–11 H12–10
- Crassula ovata 'Sunset' Z11–15 H12–1
- Kalanchoe beharensis Z10–12 H12–10
- Portulacaria afra Z10–12 H12–10

Aloe aristata
DWARF ALOE
☼ ☀ ◊ ◊ Z10–11 H11–10 ↕↔1ft (30cm)
Useful as a spiny barrier or low groundcover, this cannot be walked over; a wide band planted next to sidewalks keeps out dogs or people. Stays attractive for years with little or no care.

Aeonium arboreum 'Zwartkop'
BLACK AEONIUM
☼ ☀ ◊ ◊ Z10–11 H11–10 ↕↔3ft (1m)
For pots or ground. Yellow blooms appear on strong stems and are good cut flowers. When stems grow too tall in pots, break them off, let callus, and replant. Increase drifts with cuttings.

Schlumbergera truncata
CRAB CACTUS, THANKSGIVING CACTUS
☼ ☀ ◊ ◊ Z10–12 H12–10
↕1ft (30cm) ↔3ft (1m)
For a shrubby plant, pot in large containers. To bloom, it needs cool, dry, autumn outside air with dark nights. S. x buckelyi (Christmas cactus) blooms later.

Cotyledon orbiculata var. oblonga
FANCY-LEAVED COTYLEDON
☼ ☀ ◊ ◊ Z9–10 H12–10 ↕4ft (1.2m) ↔3ft (1m)
A wavy-leaved variety of a common bank cover for largely frost-free zones. An easy pot plant that can survive in the ground for a hundred years or more.

Shrubs for hanging baskets

Hanging baskets keep plants safely above playful dogs and children, and away from destructive slugs and snails. Hang them from trees or create a special lath-house with wood slats running north and south so shadows continually move. A drip system with a timer, pipes hidden on top, and emitters to water individual plants, makes for easy care.

Camellia sasanqua 'Mine-No-Yuki'
MINE-NO-YUKI CAMELLIA

☼ ● Z9–10 H10–9 ↕6ft (2m) ↔3ft (1m)

This plant grows tall in the ground but can be kept small for a basket by pruning its roots. Remove from container annually after bloom, slice off some roots. Replace in fresh soil mix.

Abutilon megapotanicum
MAGIC LANTERN

☼ ☼ ● Z10–12 H12–10 ↕↔10in (25cm)

A tall plant in the ground, smaller in baskets. Prune roots annually as described above or plant from cuttings in spring. Pinch, prune, and feed to increase bloom.

MORE CHOICES

- *Abutilon* 'Moonchimes' Z9–12 H12–9
- *Brunfelsia pauciflora* 'Macrantha' Z10–12 H12–10
- *Mandevilla splendens* Z10–12 H12–10
- *Streptosolen jamesonii* Z9–12 H12–9

Fuchsia 'Marinka'
MARINKA FUCHSIA

☼ ● Z9–11 H11–9 ↕1ft (30cm) ↔2ft (60cm)

Like most trailing fuchsias, this is ideal for hanging baskets and takes more heat than most. Cut back in fall or spring, fertilize, pinch until bushy, then let bloom. Remove berries weekly.

Fuchsia 'Lena'
LENA FUCHSIA

☼ ● Z9–11 H11–9 ↕1ft (30cm) ↔2ft (60cm)

An easy trailing fuchsia variety. Treat the same as 'Marinka'. Cut all fuchsias back lightly in August. Fertilize monthly with 14-14-14 on top of soil. Do not let them dry out.

Tall cacti for dramatic effects

Cacti are the New World's answer to drought, heat, and poor soil. Not all the cacti on this page are native, but all eventually became large, dramatic, and statuesque plants. They make excellent specimens in dry gardens when planted with other succulents, including aloes, euphorbias, and agaves. Note the zones for each selection and plant accordingly.

Cephalocereus senilis
OLD MAN CACTUS
Ⓝ ☼ ☼ ◊◊
Z10–11 H12–10 ‡40ft (12m)
↔6ft (2m)
Remarkably tall in age, it needs water and fertilizer to speed growth. Two-inch-long, rose-colored, nocturnal flowers appear in spring. Yellow spines are hidden under grayish white hairs. Separate from paths with rocks.

Cereus uruguayanus
APPLE CACTUS
Ⓝ ☼ ☼ ◊◊ Z10–12 H12–10
‡10ft (3m) ↔15ft (5m)
This has a striking shape and gray color, and branches from the base to form a big clump, eventually looking even treelike. The crested form, often sold as *C. peruvianus* 'Monstrosus', is not as tall. Protect from frost.

Opuntia robusta
PRICKLY PEAR
Ⓝ ☼ ◊◊ Z9–12 H12–10 ‡8ft (2.5m) ↔6ft (2m)
A large prickly pear with yellow spring flowers and red fruits; becomes treelike in age. Use as a protective hedge or background plant in dry-garden arrangements.

Espostoa lanata
PERUVIAN OLD MAN CACTUS
☼ ☼ ◊◊ Z9–10 H12–10 ‡8ft (2.5m) ↔2ft (60cm)
Branching columns are covered with spines and long white hairs. Grows much faster in the ground than in pots. Tubular pink blooms appear in spring.

MORE CHOICES

- *Echinopsis candicans* Z9–10 H12–10
- *Echinopsis huascha* Z10–11 H12–10
- *Myrtillocactus geometrizans* Z10–11 H12–10
- *Pachycereus marginatus* Z10–11 H12–10
- *Pachycereus schotti* 'Monstrosus' Z10–11 H12–10

Small cacti for garden accents

These smaller native cacti grow well in desert gardens. Like the ones on the opposite page, many are also useful for dry-garden arrangements in coastal zones. Opuntia or prickly pear is one of the most noticeable plants in desert landscapes and comes in many playful forms, not all of which have flat pads. This list includes two colorful species.

Echinocactus grusonii
GOLDEN BARREL CACTUS
Ⓝ ☼ ☼ ◊ Z9–10 H10–8 ↕4ft (1.2m) ↔6ft (2m)
Many barrel cacti are native to the Southwest. This one, with yellow spines, is the most available. Easy to grow, it needs water once a week in summer.

Opuntia violacea
SANTA RITA PRICKLY PEAR
Ⓝ ☼ ◊◊ Z9–10 H12–1 ↕4ft (1.2m) ↔6ft (2m)
In winter, pads turn bright purple or pink. Yellow and red flowers appear in spring. Outstanding in a mixed succulent garden. 'Tubac' has color year round.

MORE CHOICES

- *Echinocereus engelmannii* Z8–10 H12–10
- *Opuntia acanthocarpa* Z10–12 H12–1
- *Opuntia echinocarpa* Z10–12 H12–1
- *Opuntia ficus-indica* Z9–12 H12–9
- *Opuntia fulgida* Z10–12 H12–1
- *Opuntia leptocaulis* Z9–10 H12–1

Ferocactus cylindraceus
COMPASS BARREL CACTUS
Ⓝ ☼ ◊◊ Z9–10 H12–10 ↕9ft (2.5m) ↔3ft (1m)
This leans southward because its shaded north side grows faster. Slow-growing with bell-like orange or yellow flowers in spring and summer.

Opuntia basilaris
BEAVER-TAIL CACTUS
Ⓝ ☼ ◊◊ Z9–10 H12–1 ↕1ft (3m) ↔4ft (1.2m)
Magenta flowers appear on rosy purplish pads, common in the low desert. A good groundcover for undulating berms, it catches light well.

WOODY PLANTS

Shrubby succulents for rocky landscapes

Smooth-leaved succulents are familiar plants in frost-free zones, treasured for their beauty and durability. Old cottages in coastal towns often are surrounded by charming gardens created entirely with these easy-care plants, sometimes partially shaded by twisting trees, and interspersed with driftwood, rocks, and found objects.

Aeonium arboreum
AEONIUM
☼ ☀   ◊ ◐   Z10–11 H9–4   ↕↔3ft (1m)
Green rosettes with long-lasting yellow blooms appear on stout stems in late winter and early spring in full sun; it will not bloom in shade. Good on ocean cliffs.

Aeonium haworthii
PINWHEEL PLANT
☼ ☀   ◊ ◐   Z9–10 H12–10
↕2ft (6m)   ↔3ft (10m)
A woody-based shrub that stays neat with no attention. A piece stuck in the ground eventually becomes a large shrub. Bare stems are hidden by rosettes of leaves.

MORE CHOICES

- *Cotyledon tomentosa* Z9–10 H12–10
- *Dudleya brittonii* Z9–10 H12–10
- *Echeveria agavoides* Z9–10 H12–1
- *Echeveria* 'Violet Queen' Z9–10 H12–10
- *Euphorbia burmannii* Z10–12 H12–10
- *Senecio mandraliscae* Z9–12 H12–10
- *Senecio serpens* Z9–10 H12–10
- *Sempervivum tectorum* Z6–10 H11–6

Kalanchoe pumila
PUMILA KALANCHOE
☼ ◊ Z10–12 H12–1 ↕8in (20cm) ↔18in (45cm)
For pots, hanging baskets, or in the ground as a small groundcover held in by rocks or other plants, this has scalloped foliage, pink-gray leaves, and spring flowers.

Kalanchoe beharensis
FELT BUSH
☼ ☼ ◊ ◊
Z10–12 H12–1
↕8ft (2.5m) ↔5ft (1.5m)
An exciting accent shrub that adds character to a walled corner behind a mixed arrangement of succulents, this can grow 20ft (6m) tall in the wild, usually less in Southwestern gardens.

Crassula perfoliata var. minor
PROPELLER PLANT
☼ ☼ ◊ ◊ Z9–12 H12–10 ↕↔3ft (1m)
Formerly called *C. falcata*, this patio tub plant has large, orange-red flowers that appear in late August. Cut off heavy pieces and stick back in the pot.

Cotyledon orbiculata var. oblonga
FANCY-LEAVED COTYLEDON
☼ ◊ ◊ Z9–10 H12–10 ↕3ft (1m) ↔2ft (60cm)
A green-leaved form of the gray type shared by gardeners. If it gets leggy, take a cutting, callus off, and stick it back in a pot. A bare stem may sprout again.

Portulacaria afra
ELEPHANT FOOD
☼ ☼ ◊ ◊ Z9–12 H12–10 ↕↔4ft (1.2m)
Similar to *Crassula argentea,* with smaller leaves and longer uneven branches. Pruning and growing in sun can improve its messy appearance. Use in wreaths.

Climbers for desert gardens

Climbers add a special magic to desert gardens. They can drape over structures, clamber into trees, bathe walls in color, or wind around posts. They make people look up instead of just gazing at the ground, and can be used to create walls between garden rooms. Some climbers give a filmy, see-through effect, while others are thick privacy screens.

Antigonon leptopus
CORAL VINE
Ⓝ ☼ ◑◐ Z9–12 H12–10 ↕↔20ft (6m)
From Mexico, this is at its best in the low desert. Fast-growing with tuberous roots, it is evergreen in mild climates and blooms late summer through fall.

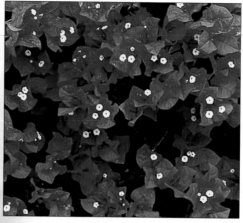

Bougainvillea 'Barbara Karst'
RED BOUGAINVILLEA
☼ ◑◐ Z9–12 H12–1 ↕40ft (12m) ↔20ft (6m)
Among the best for the desert, this bounces back after frost. Cut damaged portions off after growth begins. On the coast, plant in the hottest spot.

Beaumontia grandiflora
EASTER LILY VINE
☼ ☼ ◑ Z9–12 H12–10 ↕↔30ft (10m)
Fragrant 5in (1.5cm) blooms appear in spring and summer on two-year-old wood. Prune afterwards. Needs drainage, humus-rich soil, fertilizer, and warmth.

Pyrostegia venusta
FLAME VINE
☼ ◑ Z9–12 H12–10 ↕40ft (12m) ↔20ft (6m)
From the desert to the beach, this is a sheet of color in winter and filmy shade in summer. Lies on tile roofs or a pergola and spills over the edge of fences and walls.

Podranea ricasoliana
PINK TRUMPET VINE
☼ ☼ ◑◐ Z11–12 H12–9 ↕↔20ft (6m)
Loose generous clusters of pink, veined, trumpet-shaped flowers appear on growth tips in spring and summer. Needs heat, good drainage, and a support.

MORE CHOICES

- *Campsis grandiflora* 'Morning Charm' Z9–10 H9–6
- *Macfadyena unguis-cati* Z9–12 H12–10
- *Merremia aurea* Z9–10 H12–1
- *Wisteria floribunda* 'Texas Purple' Z6–10 H9–5

Drought-resistant climbers

Climbers that can withstand periods of drought are a boon in the Southwest, and those pictured here have the additional advantage of being easy to grow. The only slightly tricky one is the wisteria, which, like all members of the genus, must be tied loosely onto a support for two or three years. Once it has covered its support, cut new sprouts back to two buds in summer.

Rosa banksiae 'Alba Plena'
LADY BANKS ROSE

☼ ◑ Z7–12 H9–4 ↕↔20ft (6m)

Exactly like *R. banksiae* 'Lutea' (yellow Lady Banks rose) but with white flowers – whose fragrance is similar to that of violets – this is evergreen in mild zones. Cut back lightly after spring bloom for an encore performance.

Campsis radicans
COMMON TRUMPET CREEPER

☼ ☼ ◑◑ Z6–9 H9–3 ↕40ft (12m) ↔20ft (6m)

A large invasive climber with many suckers, for climates with hot summers and cold winters. This may freeze to the ground during winter, but will leap back. Fast-growing, it blooms all through the summer.

Solanum wendlandii
COSTA RICAN NIGHTSHADE

☼ ☼ ◑◑ Z9–12 H12–10 ↕20ft (6m) ↔10ft (3m)

Blooming year round in Hawaii, and in summer on the mainland, this dies back in cold winter and is slow to restart. Climbs with spines onto trees, pergolas, walls.

Wisteria floribunda 'Macrobotrys'
JAPANESE WISTERIA

☼ ☼ ◑◑ Z6–10 H8–3
↕20ft (6m) ↔30ft (10m)

Blooms as long as 18in (45cm) need strong support. Leaves sprout in spring along with blossoms that open top to bottom, lasting longer than *W. sinensis*.

Fallopia baldschuanica
SILVER LACE VINE

Ⓝ ☼ ◑◑ Z6–10 H9–5 ↕↔40ft (12m)

A vigorous, sprawling, fast cover for an arbor, fence, tool shed, or bank. Deciduous in colder parts of its range, it is best inland but needs water in the desert.

MORE CHOICES

- *Clematis lasiantha* Z9–10 H9–1
- *Hardenbergia comptoniana* Z9–10 H12–6
- *Ipomoea indica* Z9–12 H12–9
- *Macfadyena unguis-cati* Z9–12 H12–10
- *Wisteria* 'Cooke's Special' Z7–10 H10–7

Climbers for subtropical gardens

All of these climbers will do well in a warm, subtropical garden, and two can even be grown in cold-winter climates: orange clock vine freezes in cold winters, but is often grown as a summer annual, and Chinese wisteria is reliably hardy, easily enduring Southwest winters. The rest of these vines are for warm zones only. Some do well in Hawaii, and all provide glorious color.

Wisteria sinensis
CHINESE WISTERIA
☼ ☼ ◐ ◑ Z5–10 H8–5 ‡↔30ft (10m)
Blooming all at once on bare wood, followed by leaves, this twines counterclockwise. In summer, cut unwanted twiners, leaving stubs with two buds.

Distictis buccinatoria
BLOOD RED TRUMPET VINE
☼ ☼ ◐ Z9–11 H12–9 ‡30ft (10m) ↔80ft (25m)
A Mexican climber, clinging with tendrils, that flowers mainly in summer, but year round near the coast. Provide good drainage, a sturdy shade structure, and hard pruning in winter.

Ipomoea indica
BLUE DAWN FLOWER
☼ ☼ ◐ ◑ Z9–12 H12–9
‡30ft (10m) ↔80ft (25m)
Sheets of bloom appear spring through fall, from dawn to dusk. Grow on banks, fences, and shrubs. Control in a special bed; stems root into moist ground. Brings bumblebees.

Solanum jasminoides
POTATO VINE
☼ ☼ ◐ ◑ Z9–11 H12–3
‡30ft (10m) ↔15ft (5m)
A clean, non-invasive, tangled growth near a swimming pool, for hiding an ugly fence, or to provide dappled shade, with year-round white bloom. Cut back any time.

Passiflora x alato-caerulea
PASSION FLOWER
☼ ☼ ◐ ◑ Z10–12 H12–7 ‡15ft (5m) ↔3ft (1m)
Grow on a post. Fuzzy black caterpillars eat all the leaves but not the flowers or other garden plants. Many Gulf Fritillary butterflies will hatch.

MORE CHOICES
- Beaumontia grandiflora Z10–12 H12–10
- Gelsemium sempervirens Z8–10 H9–7
- Macfadyena unguis-cati Z9–11 H12–10
- Hibbertia scandens Z10–11 H12–10
- Jasminum polyanthum Z9–10 H10–8
- Stephanotis floribunda Z10–12 H12–10

Pandorea jasminoides
BOWER VINE
☼ ☀ ⬤ Z10–11 H12–8 ↕↔20ft (6m)
Unscented flowers on white or light pink types, fragrant on deep pink, appear spring through fall. Then cut back for new growth the following year. Keep from wind.

Clytostoma callistegioides
VIOLET TRUMPET VINE
☼ ☀ ⬤⬤ Z10–12 H12–9 ↕↔20ft (6m)
Blooms cover a sunny wall in spring, but are less plentiful in fall. Good afternoon shade. Climbs by tendrils. Prune in early spring; deadhead in summer.

Solandra maxima
CUP OF GOLD VINE
☼ ⬤ Z10–12 H12–6 ↕40ft (12m) ↔30ft (10m)
On a foggy beach, face this west or south; in hot interior, face east. Needing fertilizer, drainage, and support, this can be an edging on a balcony or wall.

Thunbergia alata
BLACK-EYED SUSAN VINE
☼ ☀ ⬤ Z10–12 H12–10 ↕↔10ft (3m)
A twining vine for banks and arches, grow this in full sun on the coast. Evergreen in mild climates, grow this as a summer annual from seeds or plants in spring.

WOODY PLANTS

Climbers for tropical gardens

These climbers are excitingly colorful, tender plants, native to the tropics or subtropics. Some bloom year round in Hawaii, while several grow well in mainland gardens, mostly in coastal zones. Some are drought-resistant and others need much irrigation, depending on their place of origin, be it dry, misty, or alternating from dry to wet.

Bougainvillea 'Orange King'
ORANGE KING BOUGAINVILLEA
☀ ◑◐ Z10–12 H12–1 ‡↔20ft (6m)
Do not break roots when planting, feed and water to establish. Prune lightly year round for new blooming wood. Needs a hot spot on a patio or near a sunny road.

Petrea volubilis
QUEEN'S WREATH
☀ ◐ Z10–12 H12–6 ‡↔20ft (6m)
Mildewing in coastal wind and shade, it blooms in winter and spring in Hawaii; spring and summer in California. Mix with other climbers and prune in winter.

Mucuna bennettii
RED JADE VINE
☀ ◐ Z12 H9–5 ‡50ft (15m) ↔20ft (6m)
This massive tropical for rainy parts of Hawaii needs strong support, a warm moist climate, and ample water during its summer bloom. Thin in spring.

Clerodendrum thomsoniae
GLORY BOWER
☀ ◐ Z10–12 H12–1 ‡12ft (4m) ↔5ft (1.5m)
This blooms on new wood in summer and fall in a partially shaded, warm protected spot, such as a patio post or wall, in a well-drained container.

WOODY PLANTS

Stigmaphyllon ciliatum
ORCHID VINE

☼ ☼ ● Z10–12 H12–10 ‡↔20ft (6m)

This lightweight twiner for moist organic soil has profuse summer bloom, some flowers year round in mild zones, and is good for mixing with other plants. Prune in during summer and fertilize in spring.

Strongylodon macrobotrys
JADE VINE

☼ ☼ ● Z12 H12–10 ‡↔20ft (6m)

Twining stems 1in (2.5cm) thick need strong support. Luminescent aqua flowers appear spring to summer. Much water is needed during its growth and bloom.

MORE CHOICES

- *Allamanda blanchetii* z10–12 H12–10
- *Allamanda cathartica* z10–12 H12–10
- *Aristolochia grandiflora* z10–12 H12–10
- *Bauhinia corymbosa* z10–12 H12–10
- *Distictis laxiflora* z10–12 H12–10
- *Ipomoea horsfalliae* z10–12 H12–6
- *Jasminum nitidum* z9–12 H12–7
- *Mandevilla boliviensis* z10–12 H12–1
- *Pandorea jasminoides* z10–12 H12–8
- *Pandorea pandorana* 'Golden Showers' z10–12 H12–9
- *Passiflora jamesonii* z9–12 H9–6
- *Podranea ricasoliana* 'Deep Pink Form' z10–12 H12–9
- *Securidaca diversifolia* z11–12 H7–5
- *Thunbergia erecta* z10–12 H12–1
- *Thunbergia mysorensis* z10–12 H12–6

Antigonon leptopus
CORAL VINE

Ⓝ ☼ ●● Z9–12 H12–10 ‡↔20ft (6m)

A Mexican plant adapted to warm coasts, inland heat, low desert, and Hawaii, this is a good choice for the dry sides of islands. Grow for lacy shade on a pergola or over a hot wall.

Senecio confusus
MEXICAN FLAME VINE

☼ ☼ ●● Z10–12 H12–10 ‡40ft (12m) ↔30ft (10m)

This creates a great display climbing into an open tree, and likes moist air, no frost, shaded roots, and a partially shaded top. Shear off dead flowers and cut back hard after bloom.

Climbers for Mediterranean-style gardens

Gardeners living in Mediterranean climates have grown grape vines and other climbers for shade since ancient times. Leafy evergreens are old-style Southwestern plants, providing cool havens for outdoor eating or lounging. Smaller climbers with colorful flowers are useful for growing up posts or over walls. All these plants grow well in Mediterranean climate zones.

Vitis vinifera 'Purpurea'
PURPLELEAF GRAPE
☼ ☼ ◐ ◑ Z8–10 H9–6 ↕↔10ft (3m)
An ornamental grape for its foliage, leaves change from green to purple, with a deeper color in fall. This climbs by tendrils, provides summer shade, a Mediterranean atmosphere, and no messy grapes.

Clematis 'Polish Spirit'
POLISH SPIRIT CLEMATIS
☼ ☼ ◐ Z9–10 H9–1 ↕15ft (5m) ↔6ft (2m)
A deciduous climber for a sunny patio away from the coast, this needs some winter chill, shade for roots, and moist, richly organic soil. Pruning varies according to each group, but plants are forgiving.

Rosa 'Mermaid'
MERMAID CLIMBING ROSE
☼ ☼ ◐ Z6–10 H9–5 ↕30ft (10m) ↔8ft (2.5m)
This tough clind thorny rose is deep rooted for covering a shade structure. To climb it into a tree, plant it 10ft (3m) away on a windward side. Fragrant yellow blooms open spring through fall.

Lagenaria siceraria
TRUMPET GOURD
☼ ☼ ◐ Z1–12 H9–1
↕↔10ft (3m)
These gourds of many sizes and shapes have been grown for shade, ornamentation, and usefulness by southwestern gardeners for centuries. Use for birdhouses as well.

Lonicera x brownii 'Dropmore Scarlet'
SCARLET TRUMPET HONEYSUCKLE
☼ ☼ ◐ ◑ Z5–9 H9–1 ↕10ft (4m) ↔8ft (2.5m)
Evergreen in mild climates, this hybrid of an East Coast native is less invasive than *L. japonica*. Unscented spring and summer flowers bring hummingbrids.

MORE CHOICES

- *Bougainvillea spectabilis* Z9–12 H12–1
- *Cissus rhombifolia* Z9–12 H12–10
- *Hedera helix* var. *baltica* Z7–11 H12–6
- *Ipomoea indica* Z9–12 H12–9
- *Plumbago auriculata* Z9–12 H12–10
- *Tecoma capensis* Z9–12 H12–10
- *Wisteria floribunda* 'Macrobotrys' Z5–10 H8–3

Humulus lupulus 'Aureus'
GOLDEN HOPS

☼ ● Z7–10 H8–1 ↕15ft (5m) ↔10ft (3m)

A quick shade over an archway, this has fragrant bracts and edible foliage tips. Plant roots in fertile soil in spring. Use earthworm castings to control whiteflies.

Sollya heterophylla var. parvifolia
AUSTRALIAN BLUEBELL CREEPER

☼ ☼ ●● Z9–12 H12–6 ↕10ft (3m) ↔6ft (2m)

More of a true climber than its parent species, with deeper blue flowers, this is good for covering the bare stems of a climbing rose and twines onto a support.

Jasminum angulare
SOUTH AFRICAN JASMINE

☼ ☼ ●● Z9–11 H12–9 ↕20ft (6m) ↔5ft (1.5m)

A fast-growing shrub with tall stems that climbs into other plants, lean this on a trellis or arbor. White flowers have a pleasant light fragrance in the evening.

Ampelopsis brevipedunculata
PORCELAIN VINE

☼ ☼ ●● Z5–10 H8–2 ↕20ft (6m) ↔10ft (3m)

A vigorous climber for growing on a strong support, its handsome leaves are rampant, like a grape gone wild, climbing by tendrils. Leaves go red in fall, then drop; more grow later. Berries turn bright blue.

Climbers for cottage gardens

The term "cottage garden" has many meanings. It could mean a moist coastal plot surrounded by a picket fence, a mass of dry-garden flowers next to an adobe wall, or simply a patch of wildflowers, like an embroidered apron, for a mountain cottage. Cottage gardens are whimsical. Climbers that grow in them often have old-fashioned names and fairy-tale shapes.

Eccremocarpus scaber
CHILEAN GLORY FLOWER
☼ ◐ Z8–10 H12–10 ↕15ft (5m) ↔6ft (2m)
A fast-growing annual in cold climates, this blooms year round in frost-free zones. Seeds sprout at 60°F (15°C). Grow on a trellis or put twigs in the ground.

Ipomoea tricolor 'Heavenly Blue'
HEAVENLY BLUE MORNING GLORY
☼ ◐◐ Z1–12 H12–1
↕6ft (2m) ↔2ft (60cm)
This vigorous annual opens in the morning and closes in the afternoon. Nick seeds before planting in the garden (mild zones) or in indoor pots (colder zones.)

Cobaea scandens
CUP AND SAUCER VINE
Ⓝ ☼ ◐ Z7–12 H12–10
↕40ft (12m) ↔15ft (5m)
This vigorous Mexican perennial grows as an annual in cold zones and clings to rough walls and fences. Plant indoors, nick seeds, push lightly into moist soil mix.

Rhodochiton atrosanguineus
PURPLE BELL VINE
Ⓝ ☼ ◐ Z9–11 H8–2
↕10ft (3m) ↔3ft (1m)
Grown from seeds in fall or spring at 60–65°F (15–18°C), this takes 12–40 days to sprout. Plant in a hanging basket, on an obelisk, or on sticks after the last frost.

Gloriosa superba 'Rothschildiana'
GLORY LILY
☼ ☼ ◐ Z10–12 H12–7 ↕6ft (2m) ↔2ft (60cm)
A bulb climber, in spring, plant several in a large shaded patio pot, with tops of plants in the sun. In mild zones, leave in the pot over winter so they come back.

Rosa 'Dorothy Perkins'
DOROTHY PERKINS ROSE

☼ ● z12 H9–5 ‡↔10ft (3m)

A tough rambler, this cross of *R. wichuriana* is a good screen that needs light shade in the hottest climates, but it may mildew. June and July brings many flowers.

Rosa 'Climbing Cécile Brunner'
SWEETHEART ROSE

☼ ● z5–10 H9–5 ‡↔12ft (4m)

Masses of tiny fragrant roses appear in spring, or all year on an ever-blooming type. Ideal for covering an arch, it is evergreen in mild climates. Prune in winter.

Lathyrus odoratus 'Cupani'
CUPANI SWEET PEA

☼ ● z1–12 H10–1 ‡↔5ft (1.5m)

Before planting, pour boiling water on its seeds and soak for 24 hours; or freeze in moist peat moss for two nights, plant seeds, and pour boiling water over them.

Cardiospermum halicacabum
BALLOON VINE

☼ ● z10–12 H12–1 ‡12ft (4m) ↔10ft (3m)

This fast-growing cover self-seeds, or plant it in spring. Summer flowers are followed by seed pods that turn orange before releasing winged seeds.

MORE CHOICES

- *Clematis* 'Jackmanii Superba' z5–10 H9–1
- *Clerodendrum thomsoniae* z10–12 H12–1
- *Clianthus puniceus* z9–11 H12–1
- *Humulus japonicus* 'Variegatus' z7–10 H8–1
- *Lagenaria siceraria* z8–10 H9–1
- *Lapageria rosea* z9–10 H12–10
- *Lathyrus odoratus* 'Old Spice Mix' z1–12 H10–1
- *Lonicera* x *heckrottii* 'Gold Flame' z5–12 H9–6
- *Passiflora caerulea* z9–12 H9–6
- *Tropaeolum majus* 'Jewel of Africa' z1–12 H12–1
- *Tropaeolum peregrinum* z9–12 H10–9
- *Tropaeolum tricolorum* z8–10 H12–10
- *Vigna caracalla* z10–11 H12–10

WOODY PLANTS

Climbers for groundcover

Many climbers make outstanding groundcovers. They can stabilize loose earth with their deep roots and be combined with shrubs and perennial groundcovers for a more interesting look. Red bougainvillea, planted with orange lantana and yellow gazania, can hold steep ground in full sun and provide drought-resistant, year-round color, given appropriate irrigation.

Jasminum laurifolium
ANGEL WING JASMINE
☼ ☼ ◐ ◑ Z9–12 H10–8 ‡20ft (6m) ↔10ft (3m)
Liking long warm summers or a Hawaiian climate, its fragrant flowers appear in bunches in spring and summer. The mounds can be cut back in spring.

Bougainvillea 'La Jolla'
LA JOLLA BOUGAINVILLEA
☼ ◐ ◑ Z10–12 H12–1 ‡↔10ft (3m)
This shrubby bougainvillea is ideal for growing on a bank, mixing in with other plants. 'San Diego' is a deeper red, bigger, and thrives without care or water.

Hibbertia scandens
GUINEA GOLD VINE
☼ ☼ ◐ Z9–10 H12–10 ‡↔10ft (3m)
Fast-growing and evergreen in mild zones, this returns after a frost and blooms from spring to fall. Use for a bank, fence, or near a swimming pool. Prune in fall.

Plumbago auriculata
CAPE LEADWORT
☼ ◐ ◑ Z9–11 H12–10 ‡15ft (5m) ↔20ft (6m)
An invasive, deep-rooted, but colorful climbing shrub that sends up many stems from the ground. New forms are less invasive with darker blue flowers.

Macfadyena unguis-cati
CAT'S CLAW
☼ ◐ Z9–12 H12–10 ‡40ft (12m) ↔10ft (3m)
Fast-growing with a spring bloom on upper portions inland, its stems root on banks, controlling erosion. Cut some low stems after bloom, forcing lower bloom.

MORE CHOICES

- Hedera helix 'Variegata' z5–11 H12–6
- Lonicera japonicum 'Halliana' z4–11 H12–1
- Muehlenbeckia complexa z8–10 H10–8
- Rosa 'Flower Carpet' z5–10 H9–5
- Trachelospermum jasminoides z8–11 H12–6

Climbers for groundcover in shade

These climbers are among the best plants for creating a flat green look on large or small expanses of shaded or partially shaded ground. In addition, some provide seasonal flowers or colorful leaves. Some of these selections are deciduous in cold-winter climates, but most are evergreen. All except aralia ivy are useful for controlling erosion on banks.

x *Fatshedera lizei*
ARALIA IVY
☼ ◐ ● Z7–11 H12–8 ‡↔10ft (3m)
A hybrid of *Hedera helix* and *Fatsia japonica* that grows upright. For a groundcover, cut back every few weeks and pinch tips. Protect this from snails.

Hedera canariensis
var. *algeriensis*
ALGERIAN IVY
☼ ◐ ◑ ◐ ● Z8–11 H12–6
‡↔10ft (3m)
Fast-growing and large-leaved, old plants become upright fruiting trees. Cut to ground in late winter every few years to prevent buildup, otherwise this is an easy-care ivy.

Akebia quinata
CHOCOLATE VINE
☼ ◐ ◑ ● ● Z5–9 H9–5 ‡30ft (10m) ↔6ft (2m)
The vanilla-scented flowers that appear in spring are less important than the attractive foliage. This is a fast-growing, semi-evergreen, large-scale bank cover in mild zones; deciduous and easy to control in cold winters.

Lonicera periclymenum 'Serotina'
LATE DUTCH HONEYSUCKLE
☼ ◐ ◐ ● Z4–10 H9–5 ‡20ft (6m) ↔10ft (3m)
Purple and yellow flowers in summer. Quick evergreen groundcover on coast, deciduous in cold winters. Less invasive than *L. japonica*. Cut back after bloom.

MORE CHOICES

- *Cissus hypoglauca* Z9–10 H12–10
- *Cissus rhombifolia* Z10–12 H12–10
- *Gelsemium sempervirens* Z7–10 H9–7
- *Lonicera japonica* 'Halliana' Z4–10 H12–1
- *Philodendron scandens* var. *oxycardium* Z10–12 H12–1

Rhoicissus capensis
EVERGREEN GRAPE
☼ ◐ ◑ ● ● Z9–12 H12–10 ‡20ft (6m) ↔10ft (3m)
Trained flat on arbors, its tuberous roots like shade, its tops like sun. A bronze-green groundcover out of sun, this needs occasional pruning and spring fertilizer.

Parthenocissus quinquefolia
VIRGINIA CREEPER
Ⓝ ☼ ◐ ● Z3–9 H9–1 ‡50ft (15m) ↔15ft (5m)
From the eastern US, this has red or orange fall color. On a north- or east-facing bare wall, it will be filled with singing nesting birds.

Climbers for butterflies

Some gardens, and not always the tidiest, are graced with colorful butterflies resting on flowers or swooping lazily over foliage. Other gardens have none. The reason is the choice of plants. A gardener who pulls out an invasive honeysuckle without replacing it with another butterfly-attracting plant may unintentionally lose an important ingredient of a garden's charm.

Senecio confusus
MEXICAN FLAME VINE
☼ ☀ ◑ ◔ Z10–12 H12–10 ‡40ft (12m) ↔30ft (10m)
Messy in winter, this is worth growing for its summer color, masses of daisy flowers bringing butterflies. Let climb into an open tree, but cut back after bloom.

Passiflora caerulea
BLUE CROWN PASSION VINE
☼ ☀ ◑ ◔ Z7–10 H9–6
‡20ft (6m) ↔10ft (3m)
Grow in a pot or in the ground with support. Enjoy summer bloom and Gulf Fritillary butterflies. Caterpillars will eat the foliage.

Wisteria brachybotrys
SILKY WISTERIA
☼ ☀ ◔ ◑ ◔ Z5–10 H8–5 ‡20ft (6m) ↔10ft (3m)
The most fragrant of wisterias, this also takes more water and can grow on a patio post or by a lawn. Sometimes sold as *W. venusta* 'Alba', its fat clusters of bloom bring butterflies.

Passiflora 'Amethyst'
AMETHYST PASSION VINE
☼ ☀ ◑ ◔ Z10–12 H12–10 ‡↔20ft (6m)
With large flowers, its foliage brings Gulf Fritillary caterpillars. To get the butterflies, just let them eat it. Vigorous for a fence, trellis, or growing into shrubs, cut out tangled growth.

Lonicera japonica 'Halliana'
JAPANESE HONEYSUCKLE
☼ ☀ ◔ ◑ Z4–10 H12–1
‡30ft (10m) ↔10ft (3m)
Invasive, tough, and drought-resistant, without vigilance this may sprout in unwanted spaces from seeds dropped by birds.

MORE CHOICES

- *Aristolochia californica* Z5–12 H9–5
- *Campsis radicans* Z4–10 H9–3
- *Clematis ligusticifolia* Z9–10 H9–6
- *Humulus japonicus* 'Variegatus' Z5–10 H8–1
- *Lathyrus odoratus* 'America' Z1–12 H8–1

Climbers for hummingbirds

One factor to consider when choosing plants is the hummingbirds they will bring. For example, giant Burmese honeysuckle may not be as elegant as some climbers, but it is an easy way to fill a patio with colorful guests. And, although scarlet runner beans may not suit everyone's palate, hummingbirds have never been heard to complain about the nectar of their blooms.

Ipomoea lobata
SPANISH FLAG
☼ ☼ ◐ ◑ Z8–12 H12–10 ‡15ft (5m) ↔6ft (2m)
A fast-growing, short-lived tropical or annual that shades a porch or grows up stems of *Verbena bonariensis*. Presoak seeds for 48 hours in warm water.

Lonicera hildebrandiana
GIANT BURMESE HONEYSUCKLE
☼ ☼ ◐ ◑ Z9–11 H8–6 ‡30ft (10m) ↔3ft (1m)
An evergreen with a tropical air, train this fast-growing climber on a strong trellis, on wires on a wall, or along eaves. Cut off unwanted portions and tie up.

MORE CHOICES

- *Ipomoea quamoclit* Z8–12 H12–6
- *Ipomoea* x *multifida* Z9–12 H12–1
- *Lathyrus odoratus* 'Jayne Amanda' Z1–12 H8–1
- *Lonicera sempervirens* 'Cedar Lane' Z4–10 H9–1
- *Pyrostegia venusta* Z9–12 H12–10
- *Tecomaria capensis* Z9–11 H12–10

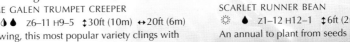

Campsis x *tagliabuana* 'Madame Galen'
MADAME GALEN TRUMPET CREEPER
☼ ☼ ◐ ◑ Z6–11 H9–5 ‡30ft (10m) ↔20ft (6m)
Fast-growing, this most popular variety clings with aerial roots to walls, and bears salmon-red flowers. Shorten some branches, pinch tips, and pull suckers.

Lapageria rosea
CHILEAN BELL FLOWER
☼ ◐ Z9–10 H12–10 ‡20ft (6m) ↔6ft (2m)
Chile's national flower is long-lasting if cut. It twines up posts and onto trellises. Protect from wind, slugs, and snails, and provide ample moisture, humus-rich soil, and good drainage.

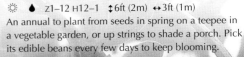

Phaseolus 'Scarlet Runner'
SCARLET RUNNER BEAN
☼ ◐ Z1–12 H12–1 ‡6ft (2m) ↔3ft (1m)
An annual to plant from seeds in spring on a teepee in a vegetable garden, or up strings to shade a porch. Pick its edible beans every few days to keep blooming.

Climbers with fragrant flowers

Fragrant plants are mysterious – they can be sensed without being seen. Visitors often hunt for the source of the aroma or ask garden owners where the perfume is coming from. An easy way to add this magic element to your home is to plant a fragrant climber. Many take up little space, spreading aboveground on to walls, fences, posts, and overhead structures.

Passiflora incarnata 'Incense'
INCENSE PASSION VINE

☼ ☀ ◑◐ Z7–10 H12–1
‡20ft (6m) ↔10ft (3m)
A tender untidy climber that is worth growing for butterflies and its summer flowers that are 5in (13cm) wide and smell like sweet peas, followed by sweet, fragrant, yellow, egg-sized fruit.

Trachelospermum jasminoides
STAR JASMINE

☼ ☀ ◑◐ Z9–10 H12–6
‡30ft (10m) ↔10ft (3m)
Choose plants already climbing onto sticks or a trellis to quickly cover a fence or wall as low ones take years to climb. Feed before late spring flowers.

Stephanotis floribunda
MADAGASCAR JASMINE

☼ ◑◐ Z14–15 H12–10 ‡30ft (10m) ↔10ft (3m)
Perfect for a patio post, facing south in a coastal zone, or in partial shade in hot interior, this needs warmth, drainage, fertilizer in summer, and pinching back.

Gelsemium sempervirens
CAROLINA YELLOW JESSAMINE

Ⓝ ☼ ◑◐ Z7–9 H9–7 ‡20ft (6m) ↔10ft (3m)
A southern native that blooms dramatically in spring, lightly in summer, and into winter in Hawaii. Face south on a wall, trellis, arbor, or as a groundcover.

MORE CHOICES

- Beaumontia grandiflora Z13–15 H12–10
- Ipomoea alba Z12–15 H12–10
- Jasminum officinale f. affine Z9–11 H12–9
- Mandevilla laxa Z12–15 H12–1
- Wisteria brachybotrys Z5–8 H8–5

Clematis armandii
EVERGREEN CLEMATIS

☼ ☀ ◐ Z7–9 H9–7 ‡35ft (11m) ↔10ft (3m)
The easiest clematis for mild climates, grow it in a spot where its roots are in shade and the top of the plant in the sun. Needs protected warmth, no wind, and cutting back. In clay soils, apply gysum to leach out salts.

Climbers with edible fruit

Most climbers grown for fruit require special pruning and training – they must not run wild. Spur-type grapevines, for example, need to be trained onto wires or fences, while cane types will grow high enough to cover a pergola if their branches are cut back annually. It is also important to remember that some climbers need a pollinator in order to bear fruit.

Passiflora edulis 'Frederick'
FREDERICK PASSION FRUIT
☀ ● Z6–9 H9–6 ‡20ft (6m) ↔10ft (3m)
This vigorous climber climbs by tendrils and has summer flowers and fall fruit that falls off if not picked ripe. Use for juice or eat with a spoon, including seeds. Earthworm castings control ants.

Actinidia deliciosa
KIWI, CHINESE GOOSEBERRY
☀ ☀ ● Z7–9 H9–7 ‡10ft (3m) ↔20ft (6m)
Fast growing, this needs pruning and a sturdy trellis or low pergola. One male pollinates seven females, or grow a self-fruiting type that bears after a year.

Vitis vinifera 'Thompson Seedless'
THOMPSON SEEDLESS GRAPE
☀ ☀ ●● Z5–9 H9–1 ‡20ft (6m) ↔10ft (3m)
Best in a hot dry interior, this may mildew near the coast but bears good fruit facing south on a fence, wall, or wind-protected, patio shade structure.

MORE CHOICES

- *Actinidia arguta* 'Issai' Z3–8 H8–1
- *Actinidia kolomikta* 'September' Z3–11 H12–1
- *Hylocereus undatus* Z11 H12–10
- *Rubus loganbaccus* 'Tayberry' Z5–9 H9–5
- *Vitis labrasca* 'California Concord' Z5–9 H9–1

Rubus 'Bababerry'
RASPBERRY
☀ ● Z4–9 H9–1 ‡↔5ft (1.5m)
A top-quality, flavorful, ever-bearing climber. Upper stems bears fruit in winter, lower stems in spring. Remove each part of the plant after it has borne fruit, or simply cut all stems down in fall.

Climbers for chain-link fences

Chain link is a practical, though inelegant, way to keep young children or dogs safely inside a garden, and large animals or unwanted visitors out. You can beautify chain link by attaching redwood lath panels and training climbing roses or slower-growing climbers onto the lath. Or for a less formal look, you can let one of these climbers grow directly on the fence.

Bougainvillea x *buttiana* 'Golden Glow'
GOLDEN GLOW BOUGAINVILLEA
☀ ◊ ◊ Z10–12 H12–1
‡30ft (10m) ↔10ft (3m)
A thorny impenetrable barrier with masses of solid color, year round in mild zones, the largest and hardiest is *B. spectabilis*, with purple flowers. Choose a mix of varieties.

Tecoma capensis
CAPE HONEYSUCKLE
☀ ☀ ◊ ◊ Z9–12 H12–10 ‡30ft (10m) ↔8ft (2.5m)
A rank but trouble-free climbing shrub, tied to a support. Prune hard on front and top to force bushiness. It has fall to spring bloom; year-round in Hawaii or mild zones.

Ipomoea indica
BLUE DAWN FLOWER
☀ ◊ ◊ Z10–12 H12–9
‡30ft (10m) ↔8ft (2.5m)
A quick twining cover from mature plants or rooted cuttings, not seeds, purchase this in summer, when it is in bloom. A thrilling informal addition to big spaces, not elegant gardens, let this climb or cascade over a boring tree.

Thunbergia gregorii
ORANGE CLOCK VINE
☀ ☀ ◊ Z9–11 H12–10 ‡12ft (4m) ↔8ft (2.5m)
A quick easy cover with eye-catching color, year round in mild zones or in summer in interior. Plant 3ft (1m) apart on a fence, 6ft (2m) apart as a bank cover.

MORE CHOICES

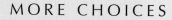

- *Lonicera japonica* 'Halliana' Z4–11 H12–1
- *Pelargonium peltatum* 'Cesar Franck' Z10–11 H12–1
- *Plumbago auriculata* Z12–15 H12–10
- *Senecio confusus* 'Sao Paulo' Z13–15 H12–1
- *Solanum jasminoides* Z9–11 H12–3
- *Trachelospermum jasminoides* Z9–10 H12–6

Pyrostegia venusta
FLAME VINE
☀ ◊ Z9–11 H12–10
‡40ft (12m) ↔10ft (3m)
From coastal zones to the desert, this grows quickly by twining and tendrils, spilling off edges and hanging down like a flat curtain of solid bloom. Plant facing south or east near a beach.

Climbing roses for fences and arbors

Climbing roses bloom most abundantly when trained horizontally on a fence. It is the same principle as an espaliered fruit tree – the plant naturally produces more budding wood. Fortunately, however, some modern climbers have also been especially bred to grow as pillars. These types cover their canes with ample flowers almost to the ground.

Rosa 'Dortmund'
DORTMUND ROSE
☼ ☀ ◗ z5–10 h9–5 ‡8ft (2.5m) ↔4ft (1.2m)
The hardiest climbing rose, except for 'John Davis', this is better inland than on the coast. Its fragrant repeat blooms come in bunches. Disease-resistant.

Rosa 'Handel'
HANDEL ROSE
☼ ◗ z5–10 h9–5
‡15ft (5m) ↔7ft (2.2m)
Train on a fence or trellis for fast growth. Profuse, rapid, repeat blooms of slightly fragrant, single or small bunches of flowers appear with disease-resistant foliage.

MORE CHOICES

- *Rosa* 'Altissimo' z5–10 h9–1
- *Rosa* 'America' z5–10 h9–1
- *Rosa* 'Don Juan' z5–10 h9–1
- *Rosa* 'Eden Rose' z5–10 h9–5
- *Rosa* 'Fourth of July' z5–10 h9–5
- *Rosa* 'Golden Showers' z5–10 h9–5
- *Rosa* 'Joseph's Coat' z5–10 h9–5
- *Rosa* 'Royal Sunset' z4–10 h9–1

Rosa 'Golden Celebration'
GOLDEN CELEBRATION ROSE
☼ ◗ z6–10 h9–6 ‡8ft (2.5m) ↔4ft (1.2m)
This David Austin rose is a shrub in cold climates, a climber for an arch or obelisk in mild. Fragrant, old-fashioned, nodding flowers are long blooming. Its flexible canes are easily trained.

Rosa 'Dublin Bay'
DUBLIN BAY ROSE
☼ ◗ z5–10 h9–5
‡12ft (4m) ↔8ft (2.5m)
A modern, large-flowered, red climber with fragrant, hardy, disease-resistant waves of bloom. Grown on an arbor, the blooms will appear all over the canes.

Rosa 'New Dawn'
NEW DAWN ROSE
☼ ☀ ◗ z5–10 h9–5 ‡20ft (6m) ↔10ft (3m)
The first patented rose (in 1930) is a hardy, repeat-blooming modern climber that will flower on the same canes on a fence for years before they need replacement. Cut back the laterals.

Drought-resistant climbing roses

No plants lend greater romance to gardens than climbing roses. While most roses need plentiful irrigation, climbers can be an exception, sending roots deep until they hit water. Hence, they have long enjoyed a role in Southwest gardens, especially the yellow or white form of Lady Banks. All of the taller roses named here are suitable for climbing into trees or on large pergolas.

Rosa banksiae 'Lutea'
YELLOW LADY BANKS ROSE
☼ ☀ ◊ ◊ Z7–10 H9–8 ‡20ft (6m) ↔50ft (15m)
Evergreen in mild areas. Train onto support. Blooms profusely in spring, cut back lightly for rebloom. May show mildew first year; disease free after that.

Rosa laevigata
CHEROKEE ROSE
☼ ☀ ◊ ◊ Z8–10 H9–7 ‡↔10–20ft (3–6m)
Stiff base, flaky bark in age. Attractive orange thorns. Disease-free and nearly evergreen. Fragrant flowers, even in shade. Once established, thrives on neglect.

Rosa 'Ramona'
RAMONA ROSE
☼ ◊ ◊ Z7–10 H9–1
‡8ft (2.5m) ↔10ft (3m)
Combines tough characteristics of Cherokee with dramatic color, anemone shape, longer bloom. Most flowers in spring but can bloom throughout year.

Rosa 'Climbing Mrs. Sam McGredy'
CLIMBING MRS. SAM MCGREDY ROSE
☼ ◊ ◊ Z5–10 H9–5 ‡20ft (6m) ↔15ft (4.5m)
Repeat-blooming. Good for sunny dry climates, air-drained slopes. Foliage plum-colored when young. The profuse first bloom is stunning against adobe wall.

Rosa 'Mermaid'
CLIMBING MERMAID ROSE
☼ ☀ ◊ ◊ Z6–10 H9–5 ‡20–30ft (6–10m) ↔20ft (6m)
Plant 10 feet from trunk on windward side of tree. Beware of thorns. Blooms non-stop, spring to fall. Disease-resistant and evergreen in mild climates.

Rosa 'Climbing Cécile Brünner'
CLIMBING CÉCILE BRUNNER ROSE
☼ ◐ ◊ ◔ Z5–10 H9–1 ↕30in (75cm) ↔24in (60cm)
Popular in the Southwest and largely spring-blooming. Vigorous, easy to grow, and almost indestructible once established. Buds are famous for button holes.

Rosa 'Climbing Iceberg'
ICEBERG CLIMBING ROSE
☼ ◐ ◊ Z5–10 H9–5 ↕↔10ft (3m)
Sweet fragrance, lasting color, long bloom, and glossy, dark green, disease-resistant foliage. Easy to train and control. Will bloom in partial shade, but best in sun.

Rosa 'Scabrosa'
SCABROSA ROSE
☼ ◊ ◊ ◔ Z7–10 H9–1 ↕8ft (2.5m) ↔10ft (3m)
An easy-care shrub or short climber with wrinkled foliage. Tomato-red edible hips follow cupped mauve blossoms. Needs no spraying but prone to aphids.

Rosa 'Dorothy Perkins'
DOROTHY PERKINS ROSE
☼ ◊ ◊ Z5–10 H9–5 ↕13ft (4m) ↔6ft (2m)
The longer this rambler grows the tougher it gets. Not good for walls because of mildew, but great for pergolas and screens. Blooms in late spring and early summer.

Rosa 'Climbing Queen Elizabeth'
CLIMBING QUEEN ELIZABETH ROSE
☼ ◊ Z5–10 H9–5 ↕↔10ft (3m)
Flowers held high above foliage on good stems for cutting. Flowers singly or in groups, resistant to wind and rain. Strong summer and fall bloom.

Rosa banksiae
WHITE LADY BANKS ROSE
☼ ☼ ◊ ◊ Z7–10 H9–8 ↕↔to 20ft (6–10m)
Somewhat hardier than the yellow type, and differs in that its canes are thorny and its flowers are larger and borne singly. Its fragrance is similar to violets.

MORE CHOICES

- *Rosa* 'Albéric Barbier' Z5–10 H9–7
- *Rosa banksiae* 'Alba Plena' Z7–10 H9–4
- *Rosa* 'Belle Portugaise' Z8–9 H9–8
- *Rosa bracteata* Z4–10 H9–1
- *Rosa* 'First Prize' Z5–10 H9–1
- *Rosa* 'Cluticote' Z5–10 H10–5
- *Rosa* 'Gardenia' Z5–10 H9–5
- *Rosa* 'Juane Deprés' Z6–10 H10–6
- *Rosa* 'Paul's Himalayan Musk' Z6–10 H9–6
- *Rosa* 'Paul's Scarlet Climber' Z5–12 H9–5
- *Rosa* 'Paul Transon' Z5–9 H9–1
- *Rosa* 'Sanders White Rambler' Z5–9 H9–5
- *Rosa* 'Veilchenbrau Climbing' Z6–10 H9–5
- *Rosa wichuraiana* Z5–10 H9–5

WOODY PLANTS

Climbing roses for mild coastal zones

Roses along the coast are often plagued with mildew and rust. If you live near the sea, choose roses with few petals and disease-resistant foliage. Roses with many petals, especially old-fashioned cabbage roses with incurving petals, need ample sunshine and heat to open. The climbers listed here open well even on foggy days and get little, if any, mildew.

Rosa 'Altissimo'
ALTISSIMO ROSE
☼ ◐ Z5–10 H9–1 ↕12ft (4m) ↔4m (1.2m)
Single blooms appear almost year-round, and on an arbor, this blooms almost to the ground. Canes are easy to train; dark green foliage is disease-resistant.

Rosa 'Joseph's Coat'
JOSEPH'S COAT ROSE
☼ ◐ Z5–10 H9–5 ↕12ft (4m) ↔6ft (2m)
A large-flowered climber for an arbor, against the house, or on an obelisk on own roots, it blooms early with constant flowers if picked. Keep from wind; gets rust.

Rosa 'Sally Holmes'
SALLY HOLMES ROSE
☼ ◐ Z5–10 H9–3 ↕12ft (4m) ↔8ft (2.5m)
A large shrub in cold climates, this is a vigorous climber with many succulent canes (low ones do not bloom). Train horizontally on a fence or arbor.

Rosa 'Fourth of July'
FOURTH OF JULY ROSE
☼ ◐ Z5–10 H9–5 ↕12ft (4m) ↔6ft (2m)
Tough with a constant bloom, this AARS winner has no disease problems, even in wind. The easiest climber ever developed may be a sign of future roses.

MORE CHOICES

- *Rosa* 'Berries N Cream' Z5–10 H9–5
- *Rosa* 'Cécile Brünner' Z5–10 H9–5
- *Rosa* 'Iceberg' Z5–10 H9–5
- *Rosa* 'Dortmund' Z5–10 H9–5
- *Rosa* 'Golden Showers' Z5–10 H9–5
- *Rosa* 'Sombreuil' Z4–10 H9–3

Climbing roses for hot interior zones

Some roses are better away from the immediate coast. These types love sunshine and can take heat. In mild-winter climates, most climbing roses should be pruned in January, but roses that flower only once should be pruned after they bloom. Prune mature modern climbing roses by cutting out one or two old woody canes and cutting laterals back to two buds.

Rosa 'Jeanne Lajoie'
JEANNE LAJOIE ROSE
☼ ● Z5–10 H9–5 ↕8ft (2.5m) ↔4ft (1.2m)
A disease-resistant, miniature climbing rose with masses of blossoms, from spring to fall. Upright and vigorous, grow as a hedge or cascade over a fence.

Rosa 'America'
AMERICA ROSE
☼ ● Z5–10 H9–1 ↕8ft (2.5m) ↔4ft (1.2m)
Fragrant clusters of bloom, nodding from an arbor, are constant but mainly in spring and fall. Mildews and rusts near the coast, except in a warm sheltered spot.

Rosa 'Royal Sunset'
ROYAL SUNSET ROSE
☼ ● Z4–10 H9–1 ↕8ft (2.5m) ↔4ft (1.2m)
Blooms on old and new wood, with elegant buds and fragrant bunches. Good for picking stems, this has a stiff, disease-resistant growth for an obelisk or pillar.

MORE CHOICES

- *Rosa banksiae* 'Lutea' Z8–10 H9–8
- *Rosa* 'Blaze' Z5–11 H11–5
- *Rosa* 'Climbing Queen Elizabeth' Z5–10 H9–5
- *Rosa* 'Dublin Bay' Z5–10 H9–5
- *Rosa* 'Lace Cascade' Z5–10 H9–5
- *Rosa* 'Lawrence Johnston' Z5–10 H9–5
- *Rosa* 'Meg' Z5–10 H9–5
- *Rosa* 'Mermaid' Z5–10 H9–5

Durable shrub roses

Roses in the Southwest have to put up with many climate extremes, from foggy coasts to short-summer mountains, and from dry heat of deserts to the moist heat in south Texas. Fortunately, hybridizers are developing new varieties resistant to pests, disease, and drought. Here are some easy-care roses, both old and new, that flourish in many difficult climates.

Rosa 'Betty Boop'
BETTY BOOP ROSE
☼ ◗ Z4–10 H10–4 ↕↔4ft (1.2m)
Plant by gray and purple perennials, not roses. Heat- and disease-resistant. Recut stems under water and add a few drops of bleach for a long-lasting cut flower.

Rosa 'Livin' Easy'
LIVIN' EASY ROSE
☼ ◗ Z5–10 H12–1 ↕6ft (2m) ↔3ft (1m)
A semidouble English Legend rose with a fruity fragrance, disease-free foliage, and masses of bloom with weather-proof color. An All America Rose winner.

Rosa 'Ballerina'
BALLERINA ROSE
☼ ◗ Z4–10 H9–6 ↕4ft (1.2m) ↔3ft (1m)
A disease-resistant, charming and trendy rose that is covered with masses of small spring flowers. It continues with fewer, but steady, blooms through fall.

Rosa 'Country Dancer'
COUNTRY DANCER ROSE
☼ ◗ Z3–10 H9–1 ↕↔3ft (1m)
Long-lasting, perfumed double flowers appear on this disease-free Griffith Buck rose. So hardy it can live through an Iowa winter, yet stand up to summer heat.

Rosa 'Carefree Beauty'
CAREFREE BEAUTY ROSE
☼ ◗ Z4–10 H9–1 ↕5ft (1.5m) ↔3ft (1m)
Vigorous in difficult climates, it comes from the Iowa breeder, Griffin Buck. Do not confuse with 'Carefree Wonder' or 'Carefree Delight', both by Meilland.

Rosa 'Carefree Sunshine'
CAREFREE SUNSHINE ROSE
☼ ◗ Z5–10 H10–5 ↕4ft (1.2m) ↔3ft (1m)
A disease-resistant bushy shrub or hedge with informal semidouble blooms from June to October. Flowers through the hottest summers without wilting or burning.

Rosa 'Outta the Blue'
OUTTA THE BLUE ROSE
☼ ◑ Z5–10 H10–5 ↕↔3ft (1m)
Blue highlights appear on this 2002 magenta rose by Tom Carruth of Weeks Roses that is already a favorite for its old-fashioned shape, aroma, and tough constitution.

Rosa 'The Fairy'
THE FAIRY ROSE
☼ ◑ Z4–10 H9–5
↕↔42in (1m)
An irresistible healthy Polyantha packed with cottage-garden charm, this rose has been grown and loved in the Southwest for many years. Plant in a perennial border.

Rosa 'Belle Story'
BELLE STORY ROSE
☼ ◑ Z4–10 H9–1 ↕4ft (1.2m) ↔3ft (1m)
Semidouble cupped blooms stand up in hot climates and open along the coast. Grows tall in the Southwest.

Rosa 'Tamora'
TAMORA ROSE
☼ ◑ Z5–10 H9–5 ↕↔3ft (1m)
A short David Austin, this fits into small gardens and borders and smells like lilac in the evening. Disease-resistant, it stays unblemished in heat, smog, and fog.

Rosa 'Souvenir de la Malmaison'
SOUVENIR DE LA MALMAISON ROSE
☼ ◑ Z6–10 H9–6
↕↔3ft (1m)
This Old Bourbon rose survives in neglected gardens. If you live in a hot interior climate, this rose is for you. Not good on coast.

Rosa 'Rose de Rescht'
ROSE DE RESCHT ROSE
☼ ◑ Z5–10 H9–1
↕↔3ft (1m)
This ancient rose from Persia is favored for its color, fragrance, gemlike form, and healthy green foliage. It blooms in spring and fall, and summer once established.

MORE CHOICES

- *Rosa* 'Apricot Nectar' Z4–11 H12–1
- *Rosa* 'Belinda's Dream' Z5–10 H9–5
- *Rosa* 'Betty Prior' Z5–10 H10–5
- *Rosa* BONICA ('Meidomonac') Z4–10 H9–1
- *Rosa* 'Escapade' Z5–10 H9–5
- *Rosa* 'Red Meidiland' Z4–10 H9–1
- *Rosa* 'Star of the Republic' Z7–10 H10–7

WOODY PLANTS

Climbing and trailing succulents

A collection of these succulents arranged at various heights, cascading from hanging baskets, or even naturalized into the crotches of trees provides charm in small gardens, patios, and hidden retreats. Some bear stunning blooms, but it is their unique shapes that really grab us. Occasional watering and infrequent spraying with diluted fish emulsion is all they require.

Epiphyllum crenatum
ORCHID CACTUS
☀ ◊ Z10–12 H12–1
↕3ft (1m) ↔2ft (60cm)
Plant a staked cutting in a 4-inch plastic pot with a well-drained soil mix. Water once, cover, then let dry. Once rooted, water weekly or less, switch to larger pot. Stunning bloom in May and June.

Sedum morganianum
DONKEY TAIL
☀ ◊ Z10–12 H12–1
↕4ft (1.2m) ↔1ft (30cm)
Grow in a round terracotta pot with holes for wires. Fragile, so hang back from paths; otherwise easy. Water enough so leaves don't shrivel, fertilize occasionally. Possible bloom.

Bowiea volubilis
CLIMBING ONION
☀ ☀ ◊ Z10–15 H12–10
↕3ft (1m) ↔1ft (30cm)
Plant roots in pot, bulb sitting exposed on top. Keep on the dry side, hang from tree in partial shade. Train up bamboo or allow to cascade. When growth dies back, cut off.

Aporocactus flagelliformis
RATTAIL CACTUS
☀ ☀ ◊ Z10–12 H12–10
↕3ft (1m) ↔1ft (30cm)
Fertilize lightly for easy growth. Needs well-drained soil and ample water during growth and bloom, slight moisture in winter. Protect from rain and midday sun.

Hoya carnosa
WAX PLANT

☀ ☀ ◊ ◊ z10–15 H12–8

↕10–20ft (3–6m) ↔10ft (3m)

Waxy evergreen foliage with very fragrant summer flowers, especially at night. Needs reflected light in full shade. Grow in rich, well-drained soil. Blooms better when pot-bound. Leave flower stems for repeat bloom.

Rhipsalis capilliformis
BUNDLE OF STRINGS

☀ ☀ ◊ ◊ z10–11 H11–10

↕3ft (1m) ↔2ft (60cm)

The only genus from the Old World, this undemanding cactus can perch in leaf mold in trees and in hanging baskets. Beware of tiny spines at spine cushions. Attracts birds.

Senecio rowleyanus
STRING OF BEADS

☀ ☀ ◊ z10–15 H12–10

↕4ft (1.2m) ↔1ft (30cm)

Great for hanging baskets in well-drained potting mix. Fertilizer occasionally during warm months. Stems root when they hit soil. Fun to grow spilling over or from rocks.

MORE CHOICES

• *Aloe tenuior* z10–15 H12–10
• *Crassula perforata* z10–15 H12–1
• *Dioscorea elephantipes* z9–15 H12–10
• *Epiphyllum oxypetalum* z10–12 H12–1
• *Hylocereus polyrhizus* z10–15 H12–10
• *Hylocereus undatus* z10 H12–10
• *Senecio herreianus* z10–11 H11–10
• *Senecio radicans* z8–10 H10–8

Ceropegia linearis subsp. *woodii*
HEARTS ON A STRING

☀ ☀ ◊ z10–15 H12–10 ↕3ft (1m) ↔8ft (2.5m)

Leaves provide the appeal. Purple or dull pink flowers aren't showy, but add a nice surprise. Grows from tubers that sprout on stems. Many types are available.

Aloe ciliaris
CLIMBING ALOE

☀ ☀ ☀ ◊ ◊ z10–11 H12–10

↕4ft (1.2m) ↔5ft (1.5m)

A scrambling climber with bright orange flowers that can survive on rainfall alone. Plant around Washingtonia fan palm. Climbs up trunk 3 feet, providing a long season of flowers in winter.

WOODY PLANTS

HERBACEOUS PLANTS

HERBACEOUS PLANTS – by definition, those that die down to ground level each year – are the multifaceted components of almost every gardener's palette. Whatever the size of your garden, you can use them to produce infinite combinations of colors, textures, scents, and shapes and to provide interest throughout most of the year (all year round, in the case of evergreen herbaceous plants). They often require more time investment than woody plants but repay rich dividends.

The backbone of the herbaceous garden is often a drift of bulbs – babianas, narcissus, iris, or alstroemerias, just to name a few. Among the earliest harbingers of spring in cold-winter climates, bulbs bloom in all seasons in the warm Southwest.

Verbascum 'Banana Custard'
Mullein is an old-fashioned European biennial or perennial with spring and summer bloom. It is well adapted to irrigated gardens with well-drained soil.

Sphaeralcea ambigua
Apricot mallow is native to hot, dry interior regions and deserts. Numerous straight stems angle out from the crown of the plant, each bearing many flowers in spring, with additional blooms in summer, and again in fall.

Many bulbous plants last for years, often naturalizing and, in many cases, spreading well beyond the area where they were originally planted.

At the other end of the spectrum are the decorative grasses, whose leaves and seedheads remain until they are pruned back in fall in mild zones or spring in cold-winter climates. Some grasses and grasslike plants can be grown in ponds. A few are drought-tolerant.

Another group of perennials well suited to difficult growing conditions are the natives adapted to deserts, hillsides, or savannahs. They stand up to drying winds and are often used in rock gardens because of their preference for well-drained soil.

Many of our garden plants come from other dry climates around the world. These further broaden the gardener's palette and help to conserve water in regions where summers are hot and winters are mild.

Garden ponds are becoming increasingly popular and give the opportunity to grow an entirely new range of plants, like waterlilies and water iris in submerged containers, with goldfish, koi, or mosquito fish policing all parts of the pond.

Regardless of any limitations your garden might possess, you will be able to find many herbaceous plants to provide a kaleidoscope of color and texture.

Miscanthus sinensis 'Morning Light'
The white leaf margin of this compact maiden grass give a silvery effect in the sunlight. In autumn, tall flower spikes arch downward from the crown.

Anigozanthos 'Bush Gold'
Bush Hybrids are compact, long-blooming varieties of the Australian kangaroo paws. They are available in a range of colors, from pink to chartreuse.

Perennials for hot interior gardens

Many perennials that enjoy full sun along the coast need partial shade in hot-interior climates. You can provide this by planting open, deep-rooted trees in the middle of beds, or on the northern edge, so your plants will receive sun in the morning and afternoon, and shade in the middle of the day. Another way is to plant flowerbeds on the east side of a house or wall.

Erigeron karvinskianus
SANTA BARBARA DAISY
Ⓝ ☼ ◔ ◊   Z7–11 H7–5
↕20in (50cm) ↔3ft (1m)
Mounding growth with small blooms year round, mainly in spring, larger-flowered varieties are available. Control caterpillars with Bt (*see p. 69*) and pull unwanted seedlings.

Verbena bonariensis
BUTTERFLY VERBENA
☼ ◔ ◊ ◐   Z7–10 H12–7   ↕6ft (2m) ↔3ft (1m)
This seeds itself in hot climates, so it can be invasive, naturalizing in some areas. A good combination with roses, it has tall stems with puffs of bloom that appear to float. Cut faded stems to ground.

Gaura lindheimeri 'Whirling Butterflies'
WHIRLING BUTTERFLIES GAURA
Ⓝ ☼ ◔ ◊   Z5–10 H9–6   ↕4ft (1.2m) ↔3ft (1m)
This long-lived, self-seeding plant grows a long tap root, making a clump, and has spring to fall blooms. Cut spent stems and pull unwanted young plants.

MORE CHOICES

- *Agapanthus* 'Rancho White' Z8–11 H12–1
- *Agastache* 'Apricot Sunrise' Z5–10 H12–5
- *Amaryllis belladonna* Z8–11 H12–7
- *Artemisia* 'Huntington' Z6–10 H9–6
- *Asclepias tuberosa* Z4–10 H9–2
- *Centranthus ruber* Z5–10 H8–5
- *Echium fastuosum* Z10 H10–9
- *Heuchera* 'Santa Ana Cardinal' Z3–10 H8–1
- *Narcissus papyraceus* Z7–10 H9–7
- *Phormium* 'Rainbow Warrior' Z9–10 H10–9
- *Salvia greggii* 'Desert Blaze' Z7–10 H9–7
- *Stachys byzantina* Z8–10 H8–1
- *Tithonia rotundifolia* Z8–11 H12–1
- *Zinnia grandiflora* Z4–11 H12–1

Phormium 'Apricot Queen'
NEW ZEALAND FLAX
☼ ◔ ◊   Z8–11 H10–9   ↕3ft (1m) ↔5ft (1.5m)
Large, coarse bloom spikes appear in spring. Plant where sun can shine through the leaves in morning or evening, and combine with ornamental grasses.

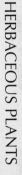

Coreopsis grandiflora 'Early Sunrise'
EARLY SUNRISE TICKSEED

Ⓝ ☼ ☀ ◊ Z6–10 H9–1 ↕2ft (60cm) ↔3ft (1m)

This trouble-free, long-lived plant blooms from earliest spring to fall. Divide in late winter for more plants and groom by cutting handfuls of spent flowers.

Ballota pseudodictamnus
FALSE DITTANY

☼ ◊ Z8–10 H9–7 ↕18in (45cm) ↔3ft (1m)

A Mediterranean native with fuzzy leaves, this is a good background plant for brightly colored perennials and attracts butterflies. Beloved by flower arrangers.

Rehmannia elata
CHINESE FOXGLOVE

☼ ☀ ☀ ◊ Z9–10 H12–10 ↕3ft (10m) ↔2ft (60cm)

Easy to grow from cuttings in spring, this needs moist, rich organic soil in order to flourish. With a summer bloom in cold climates, and spring to fall blooms in mild-winter zones, this has long-lasting cut flowers.

Achillea millefolium
Summer Shades
SUMMER SHADES YARROW

☼ ◊ Z3–10 H9–2

↕↔2ft (60cm)

A tough groundcover for the front of a bed, plant in a flat bed in fall, and set out in spring for blooms the following year. Or purchase mature plants. Mow off spent flowers.

Perennials for hot dry shade

Dry soil can result from dry air, rapid drainage, or invasive roots. Even clay soil may become desiccated in old gardens with many trees, and plants growing beneath these trees must also cope with shade. Here are some shade-tolerant perennials that have developed fleshy or tuberous roots and other devices that help them survive through hot dry summers.

Acanthus mollis
BEAR'S BREECHES

☀ ☀ ◊   Z7–10 H12–7
↕5ft (1.5m) ↔3ft (10m)
Remove stems after bloom and confine roots to prevent a spread. Water deeply in summer to keep leaves green. Attracts butterflies.

Iris foetidissima
GLADWIN IRIS

☀ ☀ ◊◊   Z7–9 H9–2   ↕5ft (1.5m)   ↔3ft (10m)
A European native with glossy leaves, this tolerates severe drought. After bloom, seed capsules open in fall to show orange-red seeds. The stems are nice in dry arrangements.

Crassula multicava
PRIDE OF LONDON

☀ ☀ ◊◊   Z9–11 H12–10
↕1ft (30cm) ↔3ft (1m)
As their blooms fade, baby plants will fall and grow, and are easy to weed out. Shake stems if more plants are desired.

Billbergia nutans
QUEEN'S TEARS

☀ ☀ ◊◊   Z10–12 H12–1   ↕↔3ft (1m)
A bromeliad grown from the desert to the ocean, and in Hawaii since the 1900s, this is spiny and long-lived in big pots, or as a groundcover under trees in desert.

Helleborus argutifolius
CORSICAN HELLEBORE

☀ ☀ ☀ ◊   Z6–10 H9–6   ↕↔3ft (1m)
This shrubby hellebore is the best for Mediterranean climates. Sun-tolerant, it blooms winter to spring. Water every two weeks in summer; mulch with manure.

MORE CHOICES

- *Asparagus densiflorus* 'Sprengeri' Z9–12 H12–1
- *Aspidistra elatior* Z8–11 H12–4
- *Chasmanthe aethiopica* Z8–10 H10–8
- *Cissus antarctica* Z9–11 H12–10
- *Heuchera* 'Santa Ana Cardinal' Z5–10 H8–1
- *Ophiopogon japonicus* Z8–11 H12–1
- *Oxalis crassipes* Z9–10 H10–8

Asparagus densiflorus 'Myersii'
MYERS ASPARAGUS FERN
☼ ☼ ☼ ◐ ◑ Z9–12 H12–1
↕2ft (60cm) ↔4ft (1.2m)
Non-invasive with no seeds, this cascades from hanging baskets or is a drought-resistant groundcover, and is attractive year round with little care. 'Sprengeri' is hardier but less tidy.

Nephrolepis cordifolia
SOUTHERN SWORD FERN
☼ ☼ ◐ ◑ Z10–12 H12–1 ↕3ft (1m) ↔5ft (1.5m)
An invasive, drought-resistant tropical that spreads by fuzzy runners in sun or shade. Looks ratty in sun if not watered. Keep in a shady bed or use for groundcover.

Clivia miniata
KAFFIR LILY
☼ ☼ ◐ ◑ Z10–11 H12–10 ↕↔3ft (1m)
This blooms in full shade with reflected light but sun burns its leaves. Put a drop of liquid snail killer on the base of flower stems prior to bloom; apply 14-14-14.

Liriope muscari
BIG BLUE LILYTURF
☼ ☼ ☼ ◑ Z6–10 H21–1 ↕↔18in (45cm)
A clumping, not running, type, plant this singly or 1ft (30cm) apart. Fertilize in spring and protect from slugs and snails. Cut back leaves when new foliage emerges.

HERBACEOUS PLANTS

Perennial groundcovers for Zone 2 firebreaks

The government has created a system of firebreaks for areas prone to wildfires, which are separated into concentric zones surrounding buildings. The plants listed here are recommended for Zone 2, the second away from the house. These low-level groundcovers provide little fuel and are useful in many gardens. Fertilize them lightly in early spring.

Echinocactus grusonii
GOLDEN BARREL CACTUS
Ⓝ ☼ ☀   ◊ ◊   Z9–12 H10–8   ↕4ft (1.2m)   ↔30in (75cm)
Slow-growing with eventual clumps, surround this with groundcovers or a circle of gravel, or grow it in pots. Water every two weeks in summer. It needs part-shade inland.

Thymus serpyllum
CREEPING THYME
☼ ☀   ◊   Z3–9 H9–1   ↕3in (8cm)   ↔1ft (30cm)
Plant around rocks or between stepping stones in well-drained soil. Use as a seasoning. Summer flowers bring bees. *T. pseudolanuginosis* (woolly thyme) is more vigorous.

Vinca minor 'Variegata'
VARIEGATED PERIWINKLE
☼ ☀ ☀   ◊◊ ◊   Z4–10 H9–1
↕2ft (60cm)   ↔10ft (3m)
Aggressively invasive, confine this to a rock-bound raised bed, surrounded with path. Runners extend under mulch and emerge as rooted plants. Also good in hanging baskets.

Potentilla neumanniana
CINQUEFOIL
☼ ☀   ◊ ◊◊   Z5–9 H8–5
↕6in (15cm)   ↔3ft (1m)
An evergreen creeper with spring and summer flowers, this is tougher than it looks and takes light foot traffic. Plant in well-drained soil at 1ft (30cm) intervals; plant bulbs to grow up through foliage.

Santolina rosmarinifolia
GREEN LAVENDER COTTON

☼ ◊◑ Z7–10 H9–6 ‡2ft (60cm) ↔3ft (90cm)

Cut back in early spring to shape, or cut closer to the ground to renew. Shear after summer bloom, removing spent flowers and rounding the plant, which needs good drainage.

Amaryllis belladonna
NAKED LADIES

☼ ◊ Z8–11 H12–7

‡1ft (30cm) ↔2ft (60cm)

Plant or transplant in the fall; this becomes a clump if left alone for many years. Winter rains cause green leaves. In late summer, 3ft (1m) tall, fragrant flowers arise from bare bulbs.

Eschscholzia californica
CALIFORNIA POPPY

☼ ◊◑ Z6–11 H9–2

‡1ft (30cm) ↔3ft (1m)

Rake seeds lightly into a prepared bed in fall. Sprinkle daily to germinate seeds, then let rains take over. Thin to 8in (20cm) apart and deadhead for a longer bloom.

Fragaria chiloensis
BEACH STRAWBERRY

Ⓝ ☼ ◔ ● Z4–10 H9–1 ‡8in (20cm) ↔1ft (30cm)

A thick green mat with rooting runners, this is one parent of modern hybrid strawberries. Sprinkled with flowers in summer, this has seedy fruit birds enjoy. Mow in early spring.

MORE CHOICES

- Achillea tomentosa Z4–10 H8–1
- Ajuga reptans 'Catlin's Giant' Z3–10 H9–1
- Artemisia caucasica Z5–9 H9–1
- Cerastium tomentosum Z3–10 H7–1
- Duchesnea indica Z5–11 H8–6
- Dymondia margaretae Z8–11 H12–10
- Gazania rigens 'Sunglow' Z9–11 H12–1
- Osteospermum fruticosum Z9–11 H6–1
- Phyla nodiflora Z8–12 H12–10
- Salvia sonomensis Z9–10 H9–5
- Thymus pseudo-lanuginosus Z3–9 H9–1
- Verbena peruviana Z9–11 H12–9

Rosmarinus officinalis 'Prostratus'
CREEPING ROSEMARY

☼ ◊◑ Z6–11 H12–8 ‡2ft (60cm) ↔8in (20cm)

An edible creeping form of a Mediterranean shrub that pours off edges of walls and spreads on the ground. Provide good drainage; add organics before planting.

HERBACEOUS PLANTS

Mild-zone perennials: spring

Over the next six pages, perennials for mild climates are arranged according to seasons of bloom. Those listed here bloom mainly in spring, though some, such as the pelargoniums, will have lesser displays year round. Some of these plants may be grown as summer annuals in cold-winter climates, where they are not hardy.

Pelargonium graveolens
ROSE GERANIUM
☼ ☼ ◊ Z9–11 H12–1
↕↔3ft (1m)
A shrubby evergreen with only a spring bloom, this has compact selections. Plant near non-fragrant roses for scent as you prune; cut back often to force branching.

Pelargonium 'Amethyst'
IVY GERANIUM
☼ ◊◊ Z9–11 H12–1
↕18in (45cm) ↔5ft (1.5m)
For pots or as a groundcover, new varieties are heat-resistant and bloom year round with no rust or mildew, and few budworms. Remove faded blooms; feed and pinch all year.

Romneya 'White Cloud'
MATILIJA POPPY
Ⓝ ☼ ◊◊ Z7–10 H9–2 ↕8ft (2.5m) ↔10ft (3m)
A tall shrubby perennial that spreads by runners and holds ground on big banks. Burn the stems of cut flowers for durability. Plant and prune in November. New shoots come from the ground.

Gaura lindheimeri 'Whirling Butterflies'
WHIRLING BUTTERFLIES GAURA
Ⓝ ☼ ◊ Z5–10 H9–6
↕↔3ft (1m)
The continual bloom, mostly in spring, of flowers (larger than the species) drops off, leaving bare stems; cut off to groom. Weed out seedlings.

Bulbine frutescens
BULBINE
☼ ☼ ◊◊ Z10 H12–10
↕1ft (30cm) ↔3ft (1m)
This small perennial expands rapidly to a big drift covered with flowers in spring, a few year round in full sun. When flowers are spent, cut back with grass shears.

Felicia amelloides 'Santa Anita'
VARIEGATED BLUE MARGUERITE

☀ ◐ ◑ Z9–11 H12–1 ↕↔2ft (60cm)

A low shrubby perennial from South Africa with succulent stems, this has a massive spring bloom. When faded, shear off, then feed and water for a quick repeat show.

Osteospermum 'Whirligig'
WHIRLIGIG FREEWAY DAISY

☀ ◐ ◑ ◑ Z8–10 H6–1

↕2ft (60cm) ↔3ft (1m)

Eye-catching, this short-lived hybrid can be viewed up close in the ground or in pots with a darker background. It needs some shade inland and stretches to sun. Feed lightly; pinch back.

Convolvulus cneorum
BUSH MORNING GLORY

☀ ◐ ◑ ◑ Z8–10 H12–8 ↕↔3ft (1m)

An evergreen Mediterranean shrub to grow with perennials in a well-drained soil, with noon or afternoon shade inland. Gray foliage appears when it is out of bloom. Prune hard in fall.

Limonium perezii
SEA LAVENDER

☀ ◐ ◑ Z9–11 H12–1 ↕↔3ft (1m)

Naturalized on coastal cliffs and in canyons, this gets mites when crowded. Its massive spring bloom has flowers lasting until winter, spreading seeds. Cut the blooms to make fresh ones arise.

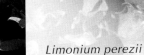

MORE CHOICES

- *Acanthus mollis* Z7–10 H12–7
- *Agapanthus* 'Storm Cloud' Z7–11 H12–1
- *Arctotis* 'Magenta' Z9–11 H9–1
- *Beschorneria yuccoides* Z9–12 H12–10
- *Clivia miniata* 'Aurea' Z10–11 H12–10
- *Erigeron karvinskianus* 'Moerheimii' Z7–11 H7–4
- *Euphorbia characias* 'Humpty Dumpty' Z8–10 H12–7
- *Leonotis leonurus* Z9–11 H12–6
- *Phormium* 'Monrovia Red' Z8–11 H10–9
- *Puya berteroniana* Z9–10 H12–1

Achillea 'Moonshine'
MOONSHINE YARROW

☀ ◑ Z3–10 H9–1 ↕2ft (60cm) ↔18in (45cm)

An undemanding hybrid with fernlike gray foliage and large, soft yellow blooms, mainly spring to summer, that last long if not overwatered.

Mild-zone perennials: summer

These perennials bloom best in summer and come from our own and other Mediterranean climates throughout the world. Though the best time to plant is fall, plants sell better while they are in bloom, so that is when you are likely to find them. Some Mediterranean plants do not look their best in nursery containers, but once in the ground, they explode with growth.

Salvia azurea 'Nekan'
PRAIRIE SAGE
Ⓝ ☼ ☀ ◊ ◗ ● Z4–10 H10–9 ‡↔3ft (1m)
Passed around by gardeners for 100 years or more, these are widely adapted and easy to grow from cuttings. Masses of cerulean blue flowers on lax stems need twiggy support.

Penstemon heterophyllus
MOUNTAIN PENSTEMON
Ⓝ ☼ ☀ ◊ ◗ Z7–10 H10–7 ‡2ft (60cm) ↔3ft (1m)
A clumping, drought-resistant, long-lived bird magnet, the hybrid 'Marguerita B.O.P.', discovered "back of porch," has green foliage and iridescent flowers.

Iris pallida
BEARDED IRIS
☼ ☀ ● Z4–10 H9–1 ‡4ft (1.2m) ↔2ft (60cm)
Non-blooming if overshaded, crowded, or not fed, it needs half shade in hottest climates. Divide every three years, toss woody center, cut leaves, replant tubers.

°*Salvia spathacea*
HUMMINGBIRD SAGE
Ⓝ ☼ ☀ ◊ Z9–10 H9–5 ‡2ft (60cm) ↔4ft (1.2m)
June-blooming flowers return in fall. 'Powderline Pink' has blooms 3ft (1m) tall, the same height as the plant. Colonize in humus-rich soil; water every two weeks.

Anigozanthos Bush Gem Hyrbids
KANGAROO PAW

☼ ◐◑ Z9–10 H12–10 ↕↔3ft (1m)

Compact varieties of this Australian perennial are available in a range of colors. For a cut flower, recut stems under water; add a few drops of bleach to vase.

Hemerocallis 'Betty Woods'
BETTY WOODS DAYLILY

☼ ◐ ◐◑ Z5–11 H12–1 ↕2ft (60cm) ↔3ft (1m)

An evergreen daylily, appropriate for a mild-winter climate. In cold-winter climates, plant hardy deciduous daylilies, choosing rust-free types only.

MORE CHOICES

- *Achillea ageratifolia* Z6–10 H9–1
- *Amaryllis belladonna* Z7–11 H12–7
- *Aristea major* Z8–10 H12–1
- *Crinum asiaticum* Z10–12 H12–8
- *Eryngium amethystinum* Z7–10 H8–1
- *Hesperaloe parviflora* Z7–11 H12–6
- *Ipomopsis rubra* Z7–10 H9–5
- *Lychnis coronaria* Z4–10 H8–1
- *Pelargonium sidoides* Z9–11 H12–1
- *Veronica prostrata* Z5–9 H8–4
- *Zantedeschia aethiopica* 'Green Goddess' Z8–11 H10–4

Foeniculum vulgare
COMMON FENNEL

☼ ◐ ☼ ◐◐◑ Z5–10 H9–1 ↕5ft (1.5m) ↔3ft (1m)

A Mediterranean native to be used as a winter annual in the desert. 'Purpurescens' and 'Smokey' are 6ft (2m) ornamentals with purple foliage that take summer heat.

Mild-zone perennials: fall and winter

In mild climates, gardeners work year-round, even in winter. Some favorite garden plants bloom mainly in fall or winter and may need to be fertilized and groomed during this time. Most Mediterranean (mild-zone) perennials are best divided in February, whereas overall clean-up and planting should generally take place during the fall and late winter.

Rhodanthe chlorocephala subsp. *rosea*
PINK AND WHITE EVERLASTING
☼ ● Z9–11 H12–1 ↕↔2ft (60cm)
A late-blooming Australian annual that looks drought-resistant but is not. Good for garden color and arrangements. The perennial form, *R. anthemoides,* is gray foliaged, mounded.

Alpinia zerumbet
PINK PORCELAIN LILY
☼ ●● Z10–12 H12–10 ↕↔6ft (2m)
This tropical lily creates large clumps of blooms year round, mostly in fall and winter. Cut every blooming stem after flowers fade or blooms will stop.

Aechmea gamosepala
BOTTLEBRUSH BROMELIAD
☼ ● Z8–10 H12–1 ↕↔2ft (60cm)
A South American bromeliad with no thorns, long-lasting inflorescences, and a late summer and fall bloom. Usually a pink clump with blue flowers on tips, it has poisonous seeds.

Cymbidium 'Thurso'
LARGE-FLOWERED CYMBIDIUM
☼ ●● Z10–11 H12–1
↕2ft (60cm) ↔3ft (1m)
To bloom, this needs 60°F (15°C) nights and 80°F (26°C) days in August, morning sun, good drainage, slow-release fertilizer, and frequent water.

MORE CHOICES

- *Aloe saponaria* Z9–11 H12–10
- *Aloe vera* Z8–11 H12–3
- *Dahlia imperialis* Z8–10 H12–5
- *Echeveria gibbiflora* 'Carunculata' Z9–11 H12–10
- *Helleborus argutifolius* 'Janet Starnes' Z6–9 H9–6
- *Kalanchoe blossfeldiana* Z10–12 H12–1
- *Salvia dorisiana* Z10–12 H10–9
- *Trachelium caeruleum* Z9–11 H12–1

Aechmea fasciata
URN PLANT
☼ ◐ ☀ ● Z10–12 H12–1 ↕↔2ft (60cm)
Small blue flowers on pink bracts emerge in late August and September; inflorescence lasts all winter. Cut down the mother plant. Good for tubs, baskets, and trees.

Cynara cardunculus
CARDOON
☼ ☼ ◑ ◑ ◑ Z6–10 H9–7 ↕5ft (1.5m) ↔4ft (1.2m)
Similar to an artichoke with edible stalks but non-edible flowers, grow this as a vegetable for its summer foliage and fall flowers in back of a perennial bed.

Hypoestes aristata
RIBBON BUSH
☼ ◑ ◑ Z10–11 H12–1 ↕6ft (2m) ↔4ft (1.2m)
Masses of flowers appear in November. Cut back after bloom for new growth, and by one-third in late spring to force branching. Seedlings appear away from coast.

Pelargonium 'Rica'
RICA GERANIUM
☼ ☼ ◑ Z9–11 H12–1 ↕15ft (5m) ↔8ft (2.5m)
A South African native with year-round bloom, mostly in spring and fall. Winter color comes if pinched, fed year round, and kept in full sun. No budworm.

Urginea maritima
SIBERIAN SQUILL
☼ ◑ ◑ Z8–10 H12–10 ↕5ft (1.5m) ↔10ft (3m)
A giant bulb that sends up an enormous vertical flower in fall, and has leaves in winter. Allow open space around it or grow it in a pot. Mix with yuccas or cacti.

Dietes grandiflora
FORTNIGHT LILY
☼ ☼ ◑ ◑ Z9–11 H12–10 ↕↔3ft (1m)
Large-flowered with brown blotches outlined in bearded yellow, these are tough and weedy but lovely in winter bloom. Remove seedpods but leave stems.

Perennials for tropical gardens

Tropical plants are native to regions where rains occur on and off year round, or as seasonal monsoons. They need warmth and more irrigation than Mediterranean or subtropical plants, although some have water storage systems to help them through dry times. Most tropical plants need shallow, humus-rich soil, but some are epiphytes and grow clinging to trees.

Streptocarpus 'Constant Nymph'
CAPE PRIMROSE
☼ ● Z10–11 H12–10 ↕1ft (30cm) ↔2ft (60cm)
Grow in a humus-rich ground, tubs, or large hanging baskets. Give a balanced, low-nitrogen fertilizer or leaves grow too big, hiding year-round blue flowers.

Scadoxus multiflorus
subsp. *katherinae*
BLOOD LILY
☼ ☼ ●● Z10–12 H12–10
↕15ft (5m) ↔8ft (2.5m)
Plant just below ground or in pots in moist, humus-rich soil with undisturbed roots. Scarlet seed capsules appear after bloom.

Vanda 'Miss Joaquim'
MISS JOAQUIM VANDA
☼ ◊●● Z12 H12–10
↕4ft (1.2m) ↔2ft (60cm)
Plant in a wood basket with slow-release fertilizer or fish emulsion. Do not cut off roots or overwater; wet leaf joints may rot. This likes moist air.

Pteris cretica 'Albolineata'
SILVER RIBBON FERN
☼ ☼ ● pH Z10–12 H12–10 ↕↔2ft (60cm)
A fine garden fern for moist Hawaiian climates or as a houseplant elsewhere, this bright stripe lightens shade. Its short creeping rhizomes are suitable for the ground, however, not baskets.

Aechmea Foster's Favorite Group
LACQUERED WINE CUP
☼ ● Z10–12 H12–1 ↕↔2ft (60cm)
A tender tropical bromeliad attractive to birds and bees. Water in the rosette, but dry it out occasionally. Turn container upside down to drain. Wear gloves to protect hands from nasty thorns.

Asplenium nidus
BIRD'S NEST FERN
☼ ☼ ◐ ◑ ⌂ z10–12 H12–3 ↕5ft (1.5m) ↔3ft (1m)
Grow outside in Hawaii year round. On the mainland, grow in containers and leave outside in summer. Take inside in winter, withhold fertilizer, and reduce water.

Columnea x banksii
COLUMN PLANT
☼ ◐ z10–11 H12–10
↕6ft (2m) ↔4ft (1.2m)
This thick-leaved, cascading plant needs humidity, crowded roots, organic soil, 70–80°F (21–26°C) days and 50–60°F (10–15°C) nights for a long, all-over bloom.

Vriesea hieroglyphica
HIEROGLYPHIC VASE PLANT
☼ ◐ ◑ z10–12 H12–1 ↕3ft (1m) ↔4ft (1.2m)
A large-scale bromeliad with tall dramatic inflorescence, this is tricky on the mainland and needs moist air. Water with rainwater or drinking water, but dry out occasionally. Feed it fish emulsion.

Zantedeschia aethiopica 'Green Goddess'
GREEN GODDESS CALA LILY
☼ ☼ ◐ z8–11 H10–4
↕3ft (1m) ↔2ft (60cm)
This can take full sun in moist air, morning sun in mild-winter zones, and blooms in shade inland. The common type has gone wild in moist coastal canyons.

MORE CHOICES

- *Alocasia odora* z10–12 H12–10
- *Alocasia* x *amazonica* z10–12 H12–10
- *Asplenium bulbiferum* z9–11 H12–8
- *Begonia floccifera* z10–12 H12–1
- *Datura meteloides* z9–11 H12–1
- *Eucomis pole-evansii* z9–10 H10–7
- *Guzmania* 'Cherry' z10–12 H12–1
- *Hippeastrum hybridis* z10–11 H12–1
- *Setaria palmifolia* z9–11 H12–9
- *Tillandsia usneoides* z9–12 H12–1
- *Vriesia fosteriana* 'Rubra' z11–12 H12–1
- *Xeronema callistemon* z10–11 H12–10

Crinum asiaticum
SPIDER LILY
☼ ☼ ◐ ◑ z10–12 H12–8 ↕6ft (2m) ↔7ft (2.2m)
A bulb with evergreen leaves, flowers year round in Hawaii, summer in California. Protect from snails. Can go dry occasionally. Any soil. Leaves burn in wind.

HERBACEOUS PLANTS

Hardy perennials

The hardiness of a plant is its ability to survive winter conditions in a given location. For specific details on the hardiness of individual plants, check the zone ranges given in each entry (*see p. 22 for details*). The perennials listed here may die to the ground in winter, but their roots can survive under snow and sprout again in spring. All are drought-resistant.

Alyssum montanum 'Berggold'
CREEPING BASKET OF GOLD
☀ ☀ ◑ Z6–9 H9–1 ‡8in (20cm) ↔18in (45cm)
A Mediterranean plant with spring flowers and gray foliage that survives in poor soil if well drained. Needs some chill. Use in rock gardens or to spill over walls.

Linum lewisii 'Appar'
BLUE FLAX
Ⓝ ☀ ☀ ◑ ◑ ◑ Z3–9 H8–5 ‡↔18in (45cm)
Plant patches of seeds in fall to create clumps. Rake in lightly and do not crowd. Seeds germinate all over, with the best show inland. Water deeply periodically.

Erodium chrysanthum
YELLOW STORK'S BILL
☀ ☀ ☀ ◑ Z6–9 H8–7 ‡6in (15cm) ↔16in (40cm)
With a similar growth to *Geranium spp.* but with pale yellow flowers and gray foliage, this is best with some winter chill. Nestle around rocks or edges of pots.

Salvia x sylvestris 'Mainacht'
MAY NIGHT SAGE

☼ ◊ Z5–10 H9–4 ‡↔18in (45cm)

This European and Asian native blooms spring to fall through hottest weather. Pinch in early spring and support with twiggy branches. Water deeply once established and deadhead to keep blooming.

Agastache aurantiaca 'Shades of Orange[R]'
HUMMINGBIRD MINT

Ⓝ ☼ ◊ Z6–10 H10–7 ‡2ft (60cm) ↔18in (45cm)

One of best agastaches for the Southwest, from northern Mexico, needs good soil and occasional deep watering. Summer to winter blooms bring birds.

Stachys albotomentosa 'Hot Spot Coral'
HIDALGO

Ⓝ ☼ ☼ ◊ Z7–10 H10–7
‡6in (15cm) ↔6ft (2m)

A heat-loving Mexican native for an average, well-drained soil. The heart-shaped leaves have a soft texture and pleasant fragrance. Use as bookmarks.

Salvia daghestanica
DWARF SILVER LEAF SAGE

☼ ◊ Z5–8 H12–1 ‡↔1ft (30cm)

This Asian native is at home in a rock garden, anywhere Lavandula will grow. It prefers to be grown in well-drained, gravelly or sandy soil. This small plant is a good companion for Penstemon pinifolius.

Stanleya pinnata
PRINCE'S PLUM

Ⓝ ☼ ◊ Z4–9 H9–7 ‡3ft (1m) ↔18in (45cm)

An easy-care native to Colorado and the Chihuahuan desert, this blooms in heat and dry winds. Deadhead after flowering. Mix with pink Penstemon palmeri.

MORE CHOICES

- Aethionema schistosum Z4–8 H8–6
- Calylophus lavandulifolius Z5–9 H12–1
- Eriogonum umbellatum 'Shasta Sulfur'
  Z5–8 H8–1
- Hymenoxys scaposa Z4–9 H9–1
- Rabia albipuncta Z4–9 H9–4
- Salvia jurisicii 'Blue' Z4–8 H8–4
- Salvia nemerosa 'May Night' Z4–9 H9–4
- Scutellaria resinosa Z4–8 H9–1

HERBACEOUS PLANTS

Perennials for cottage gardens

Traditionally, cottage gardens are filled to overflowing with old-fashioned flowers beloved by gardeners for generations. In the Southwest, some of these require heavy irrigation, but if you like, you can use them in conjunction with other perennials from this book to create a Southwest-style cottage garden, incorporating plants adapted to hot dry climates.

Centranthus ruber
JUPITER'S BEARD, RED VALERIAN
☼ ☼ ◊ ◑ Z5–10 H8–5 ↕↔3ft (1m)
Weedy in irrigated gardens, but can be easily pulled out. Naturalized in coastal areas, this fine groundcover needs light shade in sun in the greatest heat.

Argyranthemum frutescens
MARGUERITE DAISY
☼ ☼ ◑ Z8–10 H12–1 ↕↔3ft (1m)
From the Canary Islands, hybrids are heat-resistant, live years in pots or the ground, and bloom year round if deadheaded, watered, and fertilized. Shear in June.

Heliotropium arborescens
COMMON HELIOTROPE
☼ ☼ ◑ Z9–11 H12–9 ↕↔3ft (1m)
A small plant in fall, the following year it is shrubby. Give fertilizer and drainage or it dies. Cut dead flowers and leaves. People love or hate its vanilla fragrance.

Stokesia laevis
STOKES' ASTER
Ⓝ ☼ ◑ Z7–10 H9–5
↕2ft (60cm) ↔18in (45cm)
Evergreen in mild climates, semi-evergreen in cold, this southeastern native must have sun, as it languishes in cool fog. Use compact varieties for pots; tall varieties for cut flowers.

Verbena bonariensis
BUTTERFLY VERBENA
☼ ◑◑ Z7–10 H12–7
↕6ft (2m) ↔3ft (1m)
A South American plant, naturalized in some areas, that seeds massively but not on the coast. Cut stems to bottom as flowers fade. Impervious to rabbits and squirrels, it dies if shaded.

Aster x *frikartii* 'Wunder von Stäfa'
MICHAELMAS DAISY
☼ ◑ Z5–10 H8–1 ↕28in (70cm) ↔16in (40cm)
One of few asters to thrive in mild climates, this is long-blooming, spring through fall. Clip to force bushiness and deadhead often. This plant flops in shade. Feed it and prop it up with twiggy sticks.

MORE CHOICES

- *Campanula glomerata* 'Alba' Z3–9 H9–1
- *Delphinium* Summer Skies Group Z7–10 H6–1
- *Delphinium* Pacific Hybrids Z7–10 H6–1
- *Dierama grandiflorum* Z8–10 H9–8
- *Iberis* spp. Z7–11 H9–1
- *Monarda didyma* 'Croftway Pink' Z4–10 H9–2
- *Nigella damascena* Persian Jewels Series Z6–10 H10–1
- *Ocimum basilicum* 'African Blue' Z10–12 H10–1
- *Pelargonium* spp. Z9–12 H12–1

Achillea ptarmica 'The Pearl'
PEARL YARROW

☼ ◊ Z3–10 H8–1 ↕↔30in (75cm)

From Europe and Asia, this likes some heat, plenty of sun, and no shade. Good for a rock garden or in front of a dry border. Shear off flowers or use in arrangements.

Filipendula rubra 'Venusta'
QUEEN OF THE PRAIRIE

Ⓝ ☼ ☼ ◊ Z3–9 H9–1 ↕6ft (2m) ↔4ft (1.2m)

A tall flower for humid parts of Oklahoma and Texas, this needs constant moisture and rich soil. Grow by a pond, lake, streambed, or next to a fence.

Gypsophila paniculata 'Bristol Fairy'
BABY'S BREATH

☼ ◊ Z4–9 H9–1 ↕4ft (1.2m) ↔3ft (1m)

A tall, large-flowered, bushy variety of a hardy Asian species. Not for mildest zones as frosts are needed for winter dormancy. Arrange with roses as a cut flower.

Linum perenne
PERENNIAL FLAX

Ⓝ ☼ ☼ ◊◊ Z7–10 H8–5
↕2ft (60cm) ↔18in (45cm)

Do not crowd; grow in front of bed with space around. Plant a patch with seeds in fall where you want it to grow, or add to wildflower mixes. Mildews on coast.

Aquilegia McKana Hybrids
MCKANA COLUMBINE

☼ ◊ Z3–10 H7–1
↕30in (75cm) ↔2ft (60cm)

This may die in hot summers or wet winters. Seedlings sprout in spring, but will differ from parent. Long-spurred flowers come in a choice of colors.

Salvia 'Indigo Spires'
INDIGO SPIRES SAGE

☼ ☼ ◊◊ Z8–11 H12–7 ↕6ft (2m) ↔12in (30cm)

A shrubby perennial with 8in (2.5cm) blooms, summer through fall, that attract hummingbirds. Pinch and prop up early in the season. May climb on other plants.

Perennials for full sun

Many flowering plants require full sun in mild coastal zones in order to bloom, but need some shade inland. All the plants on these pages fall into this category. A little splash of shade in the middle of the afternoon will keep them alive and kicking in the hottest zones. The east side of a house, wall, or open tree is ideal for these selections.

Belamcanda chinensis
BLACKBERRY LILY

☼ ☀ ● Z8–11 H9–5 ‡4ft (1.2m) ↔2ft (60cm)
With pointed leaves in fans, like an iris, tall flower stems appear in summer. Blossoms open for only a day, but many follow. Plant in fall and water in spring and summer.

Geranium 'Ann Folkard'
ANN FOLKARD HARDY GERANIUM

☼ ☀ ● ● Z6–9 H9–3 ‡20in (50cm) ↔3ft (1m)
Chartreuse leaves that darken with age are dotted with dark magenta blooms on mounded growth, spring to fall. Use in the front of a border or over a wall.

Euphorbia characias subsp. wulfenii
WULFEN'S SPURGE

☼ ☀ ◐ ● Z8–10 H12–7 ‡↔4ft (1.2m)
This has a late winter chartreuse bloom and bracts, and flops in shade or heavy rain. Needs little irrigation on the coast. Cut old stems when 8in (20cm) high.

Epilobium angustifolium f. album
WHITE FIREWEED

Ⓝ ☼ ☀ ◐ ● Z2–9 H7–1 ‡5ft (1.5m) ↔3ft (1m)
A North American native, the red form seeds itself after fires in northern zones, becoming a noxious weed in some areas and should not be planted near waterways. This white form is better behaved.

Centaurea pulcherrima
KNAPWEED

☼ ☀ ● ● Z4–8 H8–1 ‡16in (40cm) ↔2ft (60cm)
This clump-forming centaurea is best adapted to moist interior zones. C. hypoleuca 'John Coutts' is similar but with deeply lobed leaves, deep rose flowers, and adapted to most zones.

Eremurus robustus
FOXTAIL LILY

☼ ◐ Z6–10 H8–5 ↕9ft (2.5m) ↔3ft (1m)

This needs winter chill; moist, well-amended soil; and light afternoon shade in high heat. Early summer bloom. Plant gently in back of flower bed; do not disturb roots.

MORE CHOICES

- *Achillea filipendulina* Z3–10 H9–1
- *Campanula collina* Z5–9 H9–5
- *Chamaemelum nobile* Z5–10 H9–6
- *Geranium clarkei* Z7–9 H8–5
- *Geum* 'Starker's Magnificum' Z6–9 H9–5
- *Helenium autumnale* Z3–9 H8–1
- *Linum perenne* Z7–10 H8–5
- *Phlomis cashmeriana* Z8–11 H9–8
- *Phlox carolina* Z5–8 H8–5
- *Scabiosa caucasica* Z4–10 H9–1
- *Stachys byzantina* Z5–10 H8–1
- *Verbena* x *hybrida* 'Imagination' Z6–8 H12–1

Artemisia ludoviciana
WHITE SAGE

Ⓝ ☼ ◐ ◊ ◐ Z4–10 H9–1 ↕3ft (1m) ↔2ft (60cm)

This desert and mountain native needs water during drought and afternoon shade in the hottest deserts. Creeping roots control erosion. Its foliage is aromatic.

Penstemon barbatus
BEARDTONGUE

Ⓝ ☼ ◐ ◐ Z3–10 H9–2 ↕3ft (1m) ↔18in (45cm)

This long-bloomer from the Rockies to Mexico is best adapted to mountains and the moist areas of Texas and Oklahoma but needs winter chill. 'Elfin Pink' is compact.

Nepeta x faassenii
CATMINT

☼ ◐ ◊ ◐ Z3–10 H8–1
↕1ft (30cm) ↔2ft (60cm)
A mounded growth that is aromatic when stepped on, cats love rolling in it. 'Six Hills Giant' is taller and floppy in bloom. Plant with roses to hide their thorny stems.

Alstroemeria 'Parigo Charm'
PERUVIAN LILY

☼ ◊ ◐ Z9–10 H10–8 ↕5ft (1.5m) ↔3ft (1m)

A fine variety, this has summer flowers. Meyer hybrids make good cut flowers, blooming spring to fall in mild zones, compact, and non-invasive. Ligtu hybrids are June-blooming, taller, hardy, and invasive.

HERBACEOUS PLANTS

Perennials for butterflies

These perennials and the annuals on the opposite page attract butterflies, which will travel long distances to obtain nectar from their blooms. When they arrive, they swoop over the area, alighting on flowers to feed. If appropriate foliage for larvae exists, they may stay to mate. Planting for butterflies helps replace natural habitats that have been destroyed.

Scabiosa columbaria 'Butterfly Blue'
PINCUSHION FLOWER

☼ ☼ ◊ ◑   Z6–10 H8–1
↕18in (45cm) ↔3ft (1m)
A winter annual in the desert with year-round blooms in mild zones, mildews on the coast, and needs light shade in hottest areas.

Asclepias tuberosa
BUTTERFLY WEED

Ⓝ ☼ ◊ ◑   Z3–9 H9–2
↕3ft (1m) ↔1ft (30cm)
From the eastern US, this weedy but attractive evergreen in mild zones brings dozens of butterflies. This self-seeds easily with light winter chill, or start as a plant.

Lobelia cardinalis
CARDINAL FLOWER

Ⓝ ☼ ☼ ◑   Z3–10 H8–1   ↕4ft (1.2m) ↔1ft (30cm)
A bog plant in the wild, this needs well-amended soil in an irrigated garden or pond edge. In interior, it blooms in morning or afternoon sun, or with midday shade.

Echinacea purpurea 'Bright Star'
PURPLE CONEFLOWER

Ⓝ ☼ ◊ ◑   Z3–10 H9–1   ↕4ft (1.2m) ↔12ft (4m)
A form of the tall prairie native, seeds do not sprout easily in mild zones, but it has long summer bloom. Needs heat on the edge of gardens, but not for deserts.

MORE CHOICES

- *Eupatorium greggii* 'Boothill'   Z3–9 H9–1
- *Origanum libanoticum*   Z8–10 H12–1
- *Verbena* Tapien Hybrids   Z7–10 H12–1

Annuals for butterflies

An annual is a plant that blooms, sets seeds, and dies all in one season. Open-pollinated annuals may leave many seedlings to come up the following year. Like the perennial plants on the opposite page, the annuals listed here will attract butterflies, which will also appreciate an area of wet sand or soil from which they can drink after finishing their meal of nectar.

Gomphrena globosa
GLOBE AMARANTH
Ⓝ ☼ ☼ ◐ Z9–12 H12–1 ↕2ft (60cm) ↔1ft (30cm)
A tough plant for hot-interior gardens, its wilt-proof, papery blooms sail through smog and drought. Easy to grow from seed, new varieties are available in a range of colors and sizes. Plant next to paths.

Zinnia elegans 'Peter Pan Gold'
PETER PAN GOLD ZINNIA
Ⓝ ☼ ◐ Z8–11 H12–1
↕4ft (1.2m) ↔2ft (60cm)
A compact, small-flowered hybrid of an African plant for filling beds, plant this in warm weather. It grows well in all zones. Water it on the ground or it will mildew.

Tithonia rotundifolia 'Torch'
TORCH MEXICAN SUNFLOWER
Ⓝ ☼ ◐◐ Z8–11 H12–1
↕6ft (2m) ↔4ft (1.2m)
This Mexican, tall, informal flower endures intense heat inland. Mix with fall-planted wildflowers or plant in drifts. Colorful but smelly, it returns from seed with some chill.

Lobularia maritima 'Snow Crystals'
SWEET ALYSSUM
☼ ☼ ◐◐ Z7–10 H12–1 ↕↔1ft (3m)
A widely adapted, useful edging plant, this needs moisture but less so when self-seeded. Its pollen attracts beneficials. On granitic soil, it acts like a lawn.

MORE CHOICES

- *Ageratum houstonianum* 'Adriatic' Z9–12 H12–1
- *Euphorbia marginata* Z4–10 H12–1
- *Malva sylvestris* 'Primley Blue' Z5–10 H8–1
- *Tagetes lucida* Z9–11 H12–1

Annual wildflowers for desert gardens

Except for the types germinated only by fires, wildflower seeds will sprout in the zones where they grow in nature. Wildflowers planted in the wrong zones sometimes need special treatment, such as freezing. This is why commercial mixes include only specific seeds, and in some cases encompass non-native Mediterranean or South African seeds that sprout easily.

Lupinus arizonicus
ARIZONA LUPINE

Ⓝ ☼ ◊◑ Z7–9 H9–8 ↕2ft (60cm) ↔18in (45cm)

For gardens, save seeds. In November, nick each seed with a sharp knife and soak overnight. Rake into a prepared bed, keep moist until sprouted, then water only if wilted. Allow space for growth.

Oenothera deltoides
BIRDCAGE PRIMROSE

Ⓝ ☼◔ ◊◑ Z9–10 H10–9
↕8in (20cm) ↔1ft (30cm)

A short-lived perennial, with some sprinkling in summer, that grows well in gardens. Buy seeds from a botanic garden or save your own. Plant in November.

Eschscholzia mexicana
MEXICAN POPPY

Ⓝ ☼ ◊◑◑ Z9–10 H8–1
↕8in (20cm) ↔6in (15cm)

An annual or perennial from West Texas and Arizona, this is smaller than *E. californica,* with less divided leaves. Water and deadhead to keep blooming.

Phacelia campanularia
CALIFORNIA DESERT BLUEBELLS

Ⓝ ☼ ◑◑ Z8–10 H9–1 ↕↔18in (45cm)

A spring-blooming annual easily grown in a warm open spot from seeds planted in fall; it will die if crowded or in part shade. Sow on the front edge of a bed.

Phacelia distans
WILD HELIOTROPE

Ⓝ ☼◔ ◊◑ Z7–10 H12–1 ↕8in (20cm) ↔1ft (30cm)

Sprouting under burned shrubs, this likes light shade. Plant in November and water occasionally. It blooms in spring, even if crowded. Comes in wildflower mixes.

MORE CHOICES

- *Coreopsis bigelovii* Z5–11 H12–1
- *Eriophyllum lanosum* Z7–10 H8–5
- *Lasthenia chrysostoma* Z8–9 H9–8
- *Mimulus bigelovii* Z7–10 H12–1
- *Monoptilon bellioides* Z8–10 H12–9
- *Oenothera primiveris* Z5–10 H8–5
- *Platystemon californicus* Z7–10 H12–7
- *Rafinesquia neomexicana* Z7–10 H12–10
- *Sphaeralcea coulteri* Z7–10 H9–5
- *Xylorhiza tortifolia* Z7–10 H9–5

Geraea canescens
DESERT SUNFLOWER
Ⓝ ☀ ◊◗ Z8–10 H9–8
↕2ft (60cm) ↔1ft (30cm)
Save seeds in summer. Keep them dry and cool with desiccant in a jar or paper bag – not plastic. From Arizona, Colorado, and Utah's desert floor, it needs chill to sprout.

Abronia villosa
SAND VERBENA
Ⓝ ☀ ☀ ◊◗ Z8–10 H12–1 ↕8in (20cm) ↔2ft (60cm)
In nature, it blooms in March and April. Plant in a well-drained, desert garden in November. Irrigate it for a longer bloom and thicker growth.

Malacothrix glabrata
DESERT DANDELION
Ⓝ ☀ ◊◗ Z8–10 H10–1 ↕2ft (60cm) ↔1ft (30cm)
Save seeds from four o'clock seedheads as this is not easy to transplant. In fall, plant seeds in well-drained soil, allowing space away from other plants. Some water prolongs bloom.

HERBACEOUS PLANTS

Wildflowers for mountain zones

All these wildflowers are easy to grow at higher elevations, and many also do well in other zones. Some are annuals, others are perennials. All germinate in spring and die down in fall, leaving seeds. Some are native to moist meadows and prefer damp soil. Few like shade. Wildflowers often sprout after fires because that is when they have room to grow.

Coreopsis lanceolata
LANCE-LEAVED COREOPSIS
Ⓝ ☼ ◊◑ Z4–10 H9–1
↕2ft (60cm) ↔18in (45cm)
This southeastern perennial, often planted as an annual, is naturalized in Hawaii. Once established in interior zones, it returns annually unless shaded. A good cut flower.

Silene armeria
CATCHFLY
Ⓝ ☼ ☼ ◑ Z5–9 H8–1
↕1ft (30cm) ↔6in (15cm)
With foolproof prolific blooms in first-year meadows, this is available in many mixes and is loved by children. Seeds need light to bloom. Sprinkle on prepared ground and press down. In a mix, rake lightly.

Centaurea cyanus
BACHELOR'S BUTTONS
☼ ◑ Z5–10 H7–1 ↕18in (45cm) ↔1ft (30cm)
This European annual is a weed in the Northwest, but a garden wildflower in the Southwest, and included in wildflower mixes. Needs good drainage. Do not crowd or shade. Plant in fall.

Dodecatheon meadia
SHOOTING STARS
Ⓝ ☼ ☼ ◑ Z4–10 H8–1 ↕1ft (30cm)
↔4in (10cm)
Adapted to moist shaded woodlands and open meadows, this creates a big effect en masse. A good cut flower, this is better outdoors; leave wild stands untouched.

Penstemon strictus
ROCKY MOUNTAIN PENSTEMON

Ⓝ ☼ ◊◊ Z5–8 H8–1 ‡3ft (1m) ↔2ft (60cm)

From the Southwest, early summer blooms are showy in cultivated areas and wild gardens. Easy from seeds or plants, stolons make a big clump. Thrives in Santa Fe.

MORE CHOICES

- *Achillea filipendulina* Z5–10 H9–1
- *Clarkia unguiculata* Z5–10 H9–1
- *Consolida ajacis* Z5–10 H12–1
- *Dracopis amplexicaulis* Z4–10 H10–4
- *Hesperis matronalis* Z5–10 H9–1
- *Linum lewisii* Z5–10 H8–1
- *Lupinus perennis* Z7–9 H9–1
- *Machaeranthera tanacetifolia* Z7–9 H9–5
- *Mertensia ciliata* Z3–9 H8–1
- *Papaver rhoeas* Z5–10 H12–1
- *Ratibida columnifera* Z3–10 H10–1

Gaillardia aristata
PERENNIAL BLANKET FLOWER

Ⓝ ☼ ◊ Z5–10 H8–1

‡30in (75cm) ↔2ft (60cm)

An easy-to-grow perennial, native to prairies and the West, improved forms are common garden plants; wild forms are usually striped like a Navajo blanket and will reseed. Takes heat.

Erysimum x allionii
SIBERIAN WALLFLOWER

☼ ◊ Z4–8 H7–1 ‡18in (45cm) ↔2ft (60cm)

This biennial or perennial wildflower is a weed in some areas, or an ingredient of meadow mixes. Seeds sprout easily. Plant in fall in mild climates; plant in spring elsewhere. It has fragrant flowers.

Gaillardia pulchella
'Red Plume'
DOUBLE BLANKET FLOWER

Ⓝ ☼ ◊ Z6–10 H12–1

‡2ft (60cm) ↔1ft (30cm)

A double selection of an easy-to-grow annual, this is native to prairie and western states. Plant from seeds in fall or spring for summer bloom. Single forms reseed readily, attract butterflies.

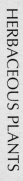

HERBACEOUS PLANTS

Wildflowers for Texas

Some of the world's most splendid wildflower displays are in Texas. Home gardeners can grow these famous flowers on banks flanking driveways or in island beds, parking strips, informal borders, or meadows. Although wildflowers find their own spots in nature, they need prepared ground in gardens. Till the earth and add organic amendment, but no fertilizer.

Layia platyglossa
TIDYTIPS

Ⓝ ☼ ◊◑ Z7–9 H12–6 ↕↔16in (40cm)

This California native is a common ingredient in mixes for Texas gardens. Very drought-tolerant, it naturalizes on banks and sprouts from seeds sown in fall or spring.

Ratibida columnifera
MEXICAN HAT

Ⓝ ☼ ◊◑ Z6–10 H10–1 ↕30in (75cm) ↔6in (15cm)

This perennial native to Texas and plains states returns yearly where established, with summer blooms in heat and wind. Mix with annual coreopsis, rudbeckias.

Echinacea purpurea
PURPLE CONEFLOWER

Ⓝ ☼ ◑ Z6–9 H9–1 ↕4ft (1.2m) ↔2ft (60cm)

A perennial prairie flower, propagate by division. Good for garden edges and as a cut flower. Finches love its seeds and it brings many kinds of butterflies.

MORE CHOICES

- *Callirhoe involucrata*
  Z6–9 H7–1
- *Callirhoe leiocarpa* Z7–8 H7–1
- *Coreopsis tinctoria*
  Z5–10 H12–1
- *Dalea purpurea* Z7–8 H12–9
- *Geum triflorum* Z6–9 H9–5
- *Ipomopsis rubra* Z7–8 H9–5
- *Lychnis coronaria* 'Oculata'
  Z5–10 H8–1
- *Machaeranthera tanacetifolia*
  Z7–9 H9–5
- *Oenothera speciosa* Z5–9 H8–1
- *Oenothera triloba* Z7–9 H8–5
- *Phlox drummondii*
  'African Sunset' Z6–9 H12–1
- *Salvia carduacea* Z6–9 H10–8
- *Tradescantia virginiana*
  Z5–9 H9–5

Tradescantia andersoniana
SPIDERWORT

Ⓝ ☼ ☼ ☼ ● Z5–9 H9–5
↕↔18in (45cm)
An east coast native, adapted
to moist humid climates, making
a clump of arching leaves. Many
varieties in blue, pink, or white
are sold. Self-seeds in some areas.

Lupinus texensis
TEXAS BLUEBONNET

Ⓝ ☼ ☼ ☼ ◊●● Z7–9 H9–5 ↕14in (35cm) ↔9in (23cm)
A beloved state flower, seen by sides of highways, it is picky as to where
it will grow – it is difficult or impossible away from Texas. *L. succulentis*
is easier. Always nick seeds and presoak when planting in gardens.

Eustoma grandiflorum
TEXAS BLUEBELL

Ⓝ ☼ ☼ ◊●● Z8–11 H12–1 ↕15ft (5m) ↔8ft (2.5m)
Delicate-looking but a tough prairie plant. Compact
forms are sold in nurseries but you can achieve a
leggier display from seeds.

Castilleja indivisa
TEXAS INDIAN PAINTBRUSH

Ⓝ ☼ ☼ ◊●● Z7–9 H12–9
↕16in (40cm) ↔1ft (30cm)
Popular, easy, attracts hummingbirds. Plant seeds in
spring or summer; germinate in fall for a spring bloom.

Salvia coccinea 'Lady in Red'
TROPICAL SAGE

Ⓝ ☼ ● Z7–11 H12–1 ↕3ft (1m) ↔30in (75cm)
A variety of a Mexican native, this is a weed in Hawaii,
an annual in all zones, a perennial in mild zones. Cut
back to basal foliage in spring. Use as filler in a border.

HERBACEOUS PLANTS

Wildflowers for summer and fall

One of the profound joys of gardening is growing wildflowers. Along the coast, the main show is in spring, with a few species blooming later. In interior zones, the show is spread more evenly. By mixing types that flower in spring with ones, such as those shown here, that flower in summer and fall, gardeners in mild but sunny zones can have bloom almost year-round.

Papaver rhoeas
CORN POPPY
☼ ◊◊ Z6–10 H12–1
↕12–18in (30–45cm)
↔1ft (30cm)
Grows well with irrigation. Plant in fall. Blooms in spring along the coast, then pull out. Summer bloom in cold-winter climates.

Coreopsis tinctoria
CALLIOPSIS, GOLDEN TICKSEED
Ⓝ ☼☼ ◊◊ Z4–10 H12–1 ↕3ft (1m) ↔2ft (60cm)
A delightful annual that provides a long season of color, into fall if you water and deadhead. Better inland than coastal. Good cut flower for arrangements. Will grow in clay soil and may come back every year.

Ammi majus
BISHOP'S FLOWER
☼☼ ◊ Z5–10 H9–1 ↕3–4ft (1–1.2m) ↔2ft (60cm)
Equally happy coastal or inland. In mild zones, plant in fall on spaded ground, rake level, sprinkle seeds, pour boiling water, cover lightly with potting soil, and keep damp. They will sprout all at once.

Cosmos sulphureus Ladybird Series
DWARF COSMOS
☼ ◊◊ Z5–10 H12–1
↕12–16in (30–40cm) ↔8in (20cm)
Use on the edges of beds. For larger areas, mix with other seeds and choose a seven-foot-tall species. When flowers fade, pull them out but leave a few for seeds.

Helianthus maximiliani
MAXIMILLIAN SUNFLOWER
Ⓝ ☼ ◊◊ Z5–10 H9–1 ↕10ft (3m) ↔3ft (1m)
Fall bloom for larger or dry gardens. Equally adapted throughout Southwest. Fun to grow, but difficult to get rid of. Even small hunks of root sprout the next year.

MORE CHOICES

- *Asclepias tuberosa* Z4–10 H9–2
- *Cosmos bipinnatus* Z5–10 H12–1
- *Hesperis matronalis* Z4–9 H9–1
- *Petalostemum purpureum* Z6–11 H12–9
- *Penstemon strictus* Z3–10 H8–1
- *Phlox drummondii* Z5–10 H12–1
- *Rudbeckia amplexicaulis* Z5–10 H10–4
- *Rudbeckia hirta* Z5–10 H7–1
- *Silene armeria* Z5–9 H8–1
- *Tanacetum coccineum* Z5–10 H9–5
- *Tanacetum parthenium* Z5–10 H9–1
- *Verbena tenuisecta* Z7–10 H12–8

HERBACEOUS PLANTS

Tithonia rotundifolia 'Torch'
TORCH MEXICAN SUNFLOWER

☀ ◍ Z6–10 H12–1

↕ to 6ft (2m)   ↔ 12in (30cm)

A perennial usually planted as an annual. Plant in tilled ground, but the next year it will return in untilled. Best in warm zones. Attracts hummingbirds and butterflies.

Gaillardia aristata
BLANKET FLOWER

Ⓝ ☀ ◍ Z3–10 H8–1   ↕ 24in (60cm)   ↔ 20in (50cm)

A perennial, easy to grow from seeds and often reseeds itself. There are many hybrids. Better inland than coastal, and a good cut flower. Blooms early summer through fall if you deadhead.

Oenothera macrocarpa
OZARK SUNDROPS

Ⓝ ☀ ◐ ◊ ◊ Z5–8 H8–3

↕ 6in (15cm)   ↔ 2ft (60cm)

Flowers open every day from spring to fall. Good in rock gardens or on planted banks. This plant survives in difficult places, but needs shade midday in hottest areas.

Linum perenne
PERENNIAL BLUE FLAX

☀ ◍ Z5–10 H8–5   ↕ 3ft (1m)   ↔ 2ft (60cm)

Easy to grow from seeds, then self-sows freely. Best away from cool foggy coast. Given room, makes a big display, spring to fall, on top third of plant, with bare stems below. Flowers close on cloudy days.

Helenium 'Wyndley'
WYNDLEY SNEEZEWEED

☀ ◍ Z4–8 H8–1   ↕ 32in (80cm)   ↔ 2ft (60cm)

Compact hybrid variety of tall weedy species. Best in hot regions, with regular irrigation. Remove faded flowers to keep them blooming. Perennial. Comes back yearly where adapted.

HERBACEOUS PLANTS

Cool-season annual wildflowers

These winter, spring, and early summer wildflowers from our own and other Mediterranean climates are easy to grow in mild-winter gardens from seeds planted in fall. Prepare the soil in full sun by turning it spade-length deep, breaking up any clods, and mixing in compost but no fertilizer. Then, sprinkle the seeds evenly, rake them in lightly, and water them until they sprout.

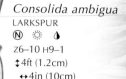

Eschscholzia californica
CALIFORNIA POPPY
Ⓝ ☼ ◊◑ Z8–10 H9–2 ↕2ft (60cm) ↔6in (15cm)
The spring bloom attracts bumblebees. Do not confuse long seed pods with buds. Clip off seed pods and give occasional water to keep it blooming into summer.

Linaria maroccana
TOADFLAX, BABY SNAPDRAGON
☼ ☼ ◑◑ H9–1 ↕2ft (60cm) ↔6in (15cm)
Mix seeds with dry sand in your palm and sprinkle close to the ground so they do not blow away. Use on edges of beds, above walls, or in a wildflower bed.

Consolida ambigua
LARKSPUR
Ⓝ ☼ ◑
Z6–10 H9–1
↕4ft (1.2cm)
↔4in (10cm)
Plant doubles from seed racks (blue forms stronger than pink) in sandy soil or well-amended clay. Seeds must have light to germinate. Broadcast in drifts and do not rake them in.

Linum grandiflorum 'Rubrum'
SCARLET FLAX
☼ ◑ Z6–10 H8–1 ↕30in (75cm) ↔1ft (30cm)
North African, well-adapted, non-invasive, and easy-to grow, plant it annually in drifts and patches with other wildflowers. Display may vary depending on weather.

MORE CHOICES

- *Anagallis monelli* 'Pacific Blue' Z7–10 H8–7
- *Calendula officinalis* Z5–10 H6–1
- *Castilleja affinis* Z7–9 H12–9
- *Cerinthe major* 'Purpurescens' Z7–10 H9–7
- *Chrysanthemum coronarium* Z5–10 H12–1
- *Cichorium intybus* Z4–9 H8–1
- *Clarkia amoena* Z5–10 H7–1
- *Clarkia unguiculata* Z5–10 H9–1
- *Collinsia bicolor* Z8–10 H12–1
- *Cynoglossum amabile* Z5–10 H8–1
- *Dodecatheon hendersonii* Z5–10 H7–5
- *Lavatera trimestris* 'Mont Rose' H9–1
- *Lupinus texensis* 'Alamo Fire' H9–5
- *Papaver rhoeas* Z6–10 H12–1
- *Papaver rhoeas* Shirley Series Z6–10 H12–1
- *Phacelia crenulata* Z8–10 H12–1
- *Phacelia tanacetifolia* Z6–10 H9–1
- *Tropaeolum majus* Z6–10 H12–1

Nemophila menziesii
BABY BLUE EYES
Ⓝ ☼ ☼ ◑◑ Z7–10 H12–2 ↕2ft (60cm) ↔3ft (1m)
Sprinkle seeds around edges of beds. The tiny flowers are best massed with others they can lean on. Showier than white *N. maculata*, cut flowers last a week.

Centaurea cyanus
CORNFLOWER
☼ ◑ Z5–10 H7–1 ↕18in (45cm) ↔10in (25cm)
Grows in wheat fields in Europe, though more rare than in former times. Mix tall varieties with other wildflowers. Weedy in cold moist climates, not in the Southwest.

Dimorphotheca sinuata
ANNUAL AFRICAN DAISY

Ⓝ ☼ ◊◊ Z9–10 H12–10 ↕↔1ft (30cm)

Miles of roadside bloom of brilliant yellow, gold, and orange in March. Shorter than *Escholscholzia californica*, it blooms earlier. Plant alone in open area.

Phacelia ramosissima
FIDDLENECK PHACELIA

Ⓝ ☼ ◊◊ Z5–10 H9–1 ↕18in (45cm) ↔2ft (60cm)

Several species are found in wildflower mixes. Easy to grow, they bring bees and butterflies. Plant this one at the back of bed. *P. campanulata* is best in hot interiors.

Malva sylvestris 'Zebrina'
ANNUAL MALLOW

☼ ◊◊◊ Z3–10 H8–1 ↕↔4ft (1.2m)

Plant seeds in fall where you want them to grow; thin to allow room for a large plant. Plant *M. trimestris* 'Magic Merlin' next to *Rosa*, 'The Prince' when young.

HERBACEOUS PLANTS

Herbaceous plants with fragrant flowers

Fragrance is defined as a pleasing or sweet scent, but some plant odors are offensive. Names like skunk cabbage are a strong hint to keep your distance. Also, individual people are variously affected by fragrance. For some, a distant whiff of a paper white daffodil outdoors is pleasant, but up close, the scent becomes disagreeable. Use fragrance with care.

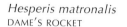

Hesperis matronalis
DAME'S ROCKET

☼ ☀ ◑ ●   Z4–9 H9–1   ↕↔3ft (1m)

Old-fashioned with a night fragrance, near the coast its seeds will not germinate unless they are frozen two nights prior to planting. Sprinkle on prepared soil and rake lightly to cover.

Lilium regale
REGAL LILY

☼ ●   Z3–9 H8–1   ↕6ft (2m) ↔3ft (1m)

Like camellias and azaleas, but with more moisture, these are easy in the right spot, with 25 huge flowers from one bulb. Plant facing east and shade roots.

Hedychium coronarium
WHITE GINGER LILY

☼ ☀ ●   Z9–11 H12–7

↕7ft (2.2m) ↔3ft (1m)

A naturalized lei flower in Hawaii, a cut flower on the mainland, use for edges of tropical gardens. Cut faded stems, feed in spring, divide rhizomes with spade, replant.

Convallaria majalis
LILY OF THE VALLEY

☼ ●   Z2–7 H7–1

↕8in (20cm) ↔2in (5cm)

Grow inland around camellias, azaleas, and pieris. In mild-winter and dry zones, buy pre-chilled "pips" in spring, plant in containers, and enjoy six weeks of nostalgic bloom indoors.

Dianthus caryophyllus Hanging Mixed
CASCADING CARNATION

☼ ☀ ●   Z7–10 H10–7   ↕↔1ft (30cm)

These heat-resistant, hanging-basket hybrids are easy, with a long summer bloom and no propping up. Water daily, feed, and deadhead. Beware of slugs and snails.

Matthiola Trisomic Hybrids
TRISOMIC HYBRID STOCK

☼ ◗ Z6–10 H9–1 ‡2ft (60cm)
↔6ft (2m)

This is an early seven-week type sold by nurseries. For a huge show, plant Trisomic Ten Week Giants in flats from seeds in August. Plant in September, in good drainage, feed, and rotate.

Nicotiana sylvestris
TOBACCO OF THE WOODS

☼ ☼ ◗ Z9–11 H12–1 ‡5ft (1.5m) ↔2ft (60cm)

Plant from seeds in fall. Near the coast, freeze seeds for two nights in a plastic bag, rake in lightly, and keep moist for tall flowers and deep night fragrance. Needs space.

MORE CHOICES

- *Amaryllis belladonna* Z7–11 H12–7
- *Cosmos atrosanguineus* Z5–11 H12–1
- *Cyclamen purpurascens* Z5–10 H9–4
- *Heliotropium arborescens* 'Marine' Z9–11 H12–1
- *Hosta plantaginea* Z3–9 H9–1
- *Iberis amara* 'Pinnacle' Z8–10 H10–1
- *Narcissus papyraceus* Z7–10 H9–7
- *Paeonia lactiflora* 'Duchesse de Nemours' Z3–9 H8–1
- *Phlox paniculata* 'Eva Cullum' Z4–9 H8–1

Nelumbo 'Mrs. Perry D. Slocum'
MRS. SLOCUM AMERICAN LOTUS

☼ ◗ Z4–11 H12–3 ‡4ft (1.2m) ↔6ft (2m)

A large lotus for ponds that has exotic summer flowers and seed pods. Its 2ft (60cm) deep sides keep raccoons away. Feed pellets annually. Grow smaller lotus in tubs.

HERBACEOUS PLANTS

Border perennials: spring

Creating a flower border is an art, requiring skill and trial and error. Great gardeners consider the heights, shapes, colors, and bloom times of thousands of plants and then combine them for a continual succession of bloom. This can often be a tough order in mild climates. To help you get started, here are some flowers that bloom in spring.

HERBACEOUS PLANTS

Thalictrum aquilegifolium
MEADOW RUE
☼ ♦ Z5–10 H9–5
↕3ft (1m) ↔1ft (30cm)
A heat-loving plant for Japanese-style arrangements with airy, columbine-like foliage. Seed pods follow a brief pink, white, or purple bloom. Give wind protection and light shade.

Delphinium elatum
CANDLE LARKSPUR
Ⓝ ☼ ♦ Z3–10 H7–3
↕6ft (2m) ↔2ft (60cm)
A perennial, grow as an annual. In a hole under the plant, put compost, chopped papaya and banana peels, slow-release 14-14-14, and potting mix. Stake well. 'Pacific Giant' is a superior strain.

Heuchera micrantha 'Palace Purple'
CORAL BELLS
Ⓝ ☼ ♦ ♦ Z4–10 H8–1 ↕↔18in (45cm)
A western perennial grown from seeds, with year-round, bronze-purple, maplelike foliage, that grows in desert shade for a rock garden or groundcover.

Iberis sempervirens 'Schneeflocke'
SNOWFLAKE CANDYTUFT
☼ ♦ Z5–10 H9–5 ↕1ft (30cm) ↔3ft (1m)
Use as a tidy green border year round in mild climates. Plant in fall for showy white spring flowers. Shear them off after bloom to round out the plant. It needs plenty of water.

Papaver orientale 'Degas'
DEGAS ORIENTAL POPPY

☼ ◊◊◊ Z3–9 H9–1 ↕3ft (1m) ↔2ft (60cm)

Outstanding for interior gardens, this will not grow in mildest zones. Plant gypsophila to hide it through summer. Superpoppy hybrids, developed for California, take summer heat.

Saponaria ocymoides
ROCK SOAPWORT

☼ ☼ ◊◊ Z4–10 H8–1
↕1ft (30cm) ↔3ft (1m)

The long bloom spills over edges. Easy and attractive, it thrives 8 miles (13km) inland in many interior zones and is not for the coast. Cut back in early or late winter.

Aquilegia Dragonfly Hybrids
COLUMBINE

Ⓝ ☼ ☼ ◊◊◊ Z4–10 H7–1
↕1ft (30cm) ↔2ft (60cm)

A compact hybrid with many beloved types, some native, sold in spring. May die in hot summer, but seedlings sprout in early spring with adequate chill. Plant where you want them to grow.

Polemonium caeruleum
JACOB'S LADDER

☼ ☼ ◊ Z4–9 H9–1 ↕3ft (1m) ↔18in (45cm)

One of the best plants for blooming under trees and in heat of interior summers, its flowers hang like bells into summer. 'Brise d'Anjou' has variegated leaves.

Iris 'Beverley Sills'
BEVERLEY SILLS IRIS

☼ ☼ ◊◊ Z3–10 H9–1 ↕↔3ft (1m)

Choose remounting types to plant in fall, three in a group, pointing out, in well-drained soil. If bloom stops, reduce shade and divide plants. Plant in June on coast.

MORE CHOICES

- *Agapanthus* 'Peter Pan' Z8–11 H12–1
- *Alstroemeria* Meyer Hybrids Z8–11 H12–7
- *Armeria maritima* Z3–10 H9–1
- *Aubrieta deltoidea* 'Novalis Blue' Z5–9 H7–5
- *Bergenia* 'Bressingham Salmon' Z4–10 H8–1
- *Delphinium* 'Summer Skies' Z3–10 H6–1
- *Dianthus chinensis* 'Telstar Picotee' Z6–10 H12–1
- *Lamium maculatum* 'White Nancy' 4–10 H8–1
- *Nepeta* x *faassenii* 'Six Hills Giant' Z3–10 H8–1
- *Salvia coccinea* 'Brenthurst' Z7–10 H12–1
- *Scabiosa columbaria* 'Pink Mist' Z5–10 H8–1
- *Silene californica* Z8–11 H12–9

HERBACEOUS PLANTS

Border perennials: summer

All of these perennials bloom well in hot summers. Many are informal types, excellent for wilder borders, but inappropriate if a manicured atmosphere is desired. If you find that these plants are too casual, try filling gaps in the border with summer-blooming annuals or shrubs. Many southwestern gardeners find that the best border is not strictly herbaceous.

Hemerocallis 'Cat's Cradle'
CAT'S CRADLE DAYLILY
☼ ☼   ◐ ◑   Z3–10 H12–2   ‡3ft (1m)
You must water for bloom. For easier summer flowers, choose a heat-resistant, remounting variety. Insist on rust-resistance – many old types get daylily rust.

Dicentra spectabilis
COMMON BLEEDING HEART
☼   ◐   Z3–9 H9–1   ‡↔3ft (1m)
A Japanese plant for savoring up close that needs moist, humus-rich soil. It blooms all summer in cooler zones but dies down in hot climates, leaving an ugly gap. Plant lobelia to cover it.

Rudbeckia fulgida var. *sullivantii* 'Goldsturm'
BLACK-EYED SUSAN
Ⓝ ☼ ☼   ◐ ◑   Z4–10 H9–1
‡3ft (1m) ↔2ft (60cm)
A non-stop, heat-resistant bloom, summer through fall, needs a bit of shade midday in hottest zones. Not as good on the coast. Forms clumps.

Ricinus communis 'Carmencita Pink'
CASTOR BEAN
☼   ◐   Z7–10 H12–1
‡15ft (5m) ↔8ft (2.5m)
An African plant used in English flower beds, it survives southwestern gardens with little care, naturalized in drainage ditches. Keep children from poisonous seeds in colorful pods.

Thalictrum delavayi 'Album'
WHITE CHINESE MEADOW RUE
☼   ◐   Z4–10 H7–1   ‡6ft (2m) ↔2ft (60cm)
A lilac-colored, summer bloom lasts two months in the right climates. Stake with a long thin bamboo at back. Use purple-stemmed, lacy foliage for arrangements.

MORE CHOICES

- *Achillea* 'Moonshine' Z3–10 H8–1
- *Coreopsis basalis* 'Sunshine' Z4–10 H9–1
- *Dictamnus albus* Z3–10 H8–1
- *Kniphofia* 'Border Ballet' Z5–9 H9–1
- *Monarda* 'Cambridge Scarlet' Z4–9 H9–1
- *Perovskia atriplicifolia* 'Blue Mist' Z6–10 H9–6
- *Verbascum* 'Helen Johnson' Z6–9 H9–5
- *Verbena* 'Quartz Burgundy' Z9–11 H12–1

HERBACEOUS PLANTS

HERBACEOUS PLANTS

Phormium tenax 'Monrovia Red'
NEW ZEALAND FLAX

☼ ☀ ◑◐ Z9–10 H10–9 ↕↔5ft (1.5m)

Tough and drought-resistant, this is a landscaper's standby with stiff leaves for banks, commercial plantings, and roadsides. Many colors and sizes are available. Statuesque, tubular summer flowers appear on tall stems.

Cuphea x *purpurea*
BAT FLOWER

Ⓝ ☼ ☀ ◑◐ Z10–11 H12–1 ↕↔3ft (1m)

A shrubby perennial that produces purple-centered flowers that resemble bats' faces and are loved by hummingbirds. Pinch to keep a compact shape. Cut old plants back hard in late fall or early spring.

Phlox paniculata 'Eva Cullum'
SUMMER PHLOX

Ⓝ ☼ ☀ ◑ Z4–9 H8–1 ↕5ft (1.5m) ↔2ft (60cm)

A fragrant native of the eastern US, with a long bloom, this gets severe mildew on the coast so grow it 5 miles (8km) inland. The flowers bleach in hottest climates; they hold up better in light shade and cooler temperatures.

Border perennials: fall and winter

Autumn is warm and sunny in the Southwest, but as the weather begins to cool down, you may see some of the year's best flowers. Take advantage of this by filling your border with perennials, which come into bloom as temperatures grow colder. Combined with native landscapes that often green up with the first rains, this will make fall feel almost like spring.

Solidago sphacelata 'Golden Fleece'
GOLDENROD
Ⓝ ☀ ◐ ◊ Z7–9 H9–1 ↕18in (45cm) ↔2ft (60cm)
A groundcover when not in bloom, this wild plant, tamed for gardens, has a long fall bloom, is unjustly blamed for allergies, and has hybrids for other colors.

Helleborus niger
CHRISTMAS ROSE
☀ ◐ ◊ Z3–9 H8–1 ↕1ft (30cm) ↔18in (45cm)
With an elegant growth habit, this flowers at Christmas and lasts into spring, but often dies without winter chill. *H. argutifolius* is a better choice for mild zones.

Anemone x *hybrida*
JAPANESE ANEMONE
☀ ◊ Z4–10 H8–5
↕4ft (1.2m) ↔1ft (30cm)
This aggressive re-seeder thrives in north-facing shade, just a few miles from the coast in many interior zones. Not for the desert, it needs winter chill and blooms in winter.

Chrysanthemum 'Clara Curtis'
CLARA CURTIS CHRYSANTHEMUM
☀ ◊ Z5–9 H9–1 ↕↔2ft (60cm)
A great variety that brings flocks of butterflies and grows in interior southwestern zones. The main show is in fall, but it begins blooming in hot summers where similar *Leucanthemum vulgare* could not survive.

Viola x *wittrockiana*
'Jolly Joker'
JOLLY JOKER PANSY
☼ ◑ ● Z5–10 H9–1
↕10in (25cm) ↔1ft (30cm)
Grow this perennial as an annual; plant in fall in mild zones. Small, heat-resistant flowers may cover foliage; larger flowers have less color.

Anchusa azurea 'Loddon Royalist'
ITALIAN BUGLOSS
☼ ● Z3–10 H8–1 ↕5ft (1.5m) ↔2ft (60cm)
This Mediterranean plant's tall stems bear flowers similar to those of *Myosotis*. Blooms persist between summer and fall when some flowers quit. Deadhead.

MORE CHOICES

- *Crocus sativus* Z5–10 H8–1
- *Cyclamen persicum* Z9–10 H6–1
- *Cymbidium* 'Lisa Rose' Z10–11 H12–1
- *Gaillardia* x *grandiflora* 'Dazzler' Z3–10 H8–1
- *Helianthus maximiliani* Z4–10 H9–1
- *Narcissus* 'Grand Soleil d'Or' Z7–10 H9–7
- *Primula polyantha* Z4–10 H8–1
- *Rudbeckia hirta* 'Prairie Sun' Z3–10 H7–1
- *Sedum* 'Ruby Glow' Z5–9 H9–1
- *Silene schafta* Z4–9 H9–3
- x *Solidaster luteus* Z5–9 H8–5
- *Sternbergia lutea* Z7–10 H9–6

Lampranthus spectabilis
TRAILING ICEPLANT
☼ ◊ Z9–12 H12–10 ↕1ft (30cm) ↔indefinite
Pink, red, orange, purple blooms cover foliage all at once. A good, drought-resistant, spreading bank cover or rock-garden plant with winter and spring color for mild zones.

Oxalis obtusa
OBTUSA OXALIS
☼ ◑ ◊● Z9–10 H6–1 ↕4ft (1.2m) ↔6ft (2m)
An African perennial that spreads from bulbs and rhizomatous roots and springs up in fall, blooming fall through spring in mild zones. Selections are available in pink, white, yellow, mauve, and purple. The best-known is 'Grand Duchess'.

HERBACEOUS PLANTS

Drought-resistant perennials for hummingbirds

Perennials that bring hummingbirds are always a delight, and ones that grow with little irrigation are a particular boon to southwestern gardens. Most of these are native plants with bright flower colors. As with almost all drought-resistant plants, good drainage is of utmost importance to these colorful specimens. Natives should be planted in groups in November.

Leonotis leonurus
LION'S TAIL
☼ ◊◑ Z9–12 H12–6 ↕↔6ft (2m)
Clumping with a year-round bloom in mild zones, cut branches to renew young plants. Old plants: cut one-third to ground, allow to re-grow, then cut next third.

Heuchera 'Firefly'
FIREFLY CORAL BELLS
☼ ◐ ◑ Z4–10 H8–1 ↕30in (75cm) ↔18in (45cm)
Hummingbirds love this, but it needs sun and moist organic soil. Native and drought-resistant, these are among the best shade plants for under native oaks.

Mimulus bifidus Verity Hybrids
STICKY MONKEY FLOWER
Ⓝ ☼◐ ◊◑ Z7–11 H12–7 ↕↔5ft (1.5m)
Grows wild on north-facing hillsides, blooms almost year round in coastal zones, and comes in yellow, orange, purple. Prune before and after spring bloom.

Asclepias tuberosa
BUTTERFLY WEED

Ⓝ ☼ ◊ ◊ Z4–10 H9–2
↕3ft (1m) ↔4ft (1.2cm)
Grow 'Gay Butterflies' or 'Hello Yellow' from seeds. Remove seed pods to prevent weedy spreading. The long bloom brings flocks of butterflies as well as hummingbirds.

Zauschneria californica
CALIFORNIA FUCHSIA

Ⓝ ☼ ◊ ◊ Z10–11 H12–8 ↕2ft (60cm) ↔20in (50cm)
These wild plants choose a sloping ground, arching from banks and are difficult on a flat clay ground. When conditions are right, it spreads by aggressive roots and seeds, and has many flowers in fall.

Salvia greggii
AUTUMN SAGE

Ⓝ ☼ ☼ ◊ ◊ Z7–10 H9–4 ↕↔4ft (1.2m)
A small shrub from Texas and Mexico with small tidy flowers on a long summer and fall bloom, it needs little care or water. Shear lightly after bloom.

MORE CHOICES

- *Agastache* 'Desert Sunrise' Z7–10 H10–7
- *Agastache mexicana* Z7–11 H12–7
- *Aloe aristata* Z9–11 H12–10
- *Crocosmia* 'Lucifer' Z6–10 H9–6
- *Penstemon* x *mexicali* 'Pikes Peak Purple' Z4–10 H8–1
- *Penstemon strictus* Z3–10 H8–1
- *Penstemon utahensis* Z4–9 H9–1
- *Russelia equisetiformis* Z9–12 H12–1
- *Silene laciniata* Z6–10 H9–5
- *Stachys albotomentosa* 'Hot Spot Coral' Z7–10 H10–7
- *Zauschneria arizonica* Z7–9 H12–8

Hesperaloe parviflora
RED YUCCA

Ⓝ ☼ ◊ ◊ Z7–11 H12–6 ↕↔4ft (1.2m)
Very heat-tolerant, taking full sun even in desert, it has narrow spiky leaves and flowers in spring, summer, even fall with occasional water. Place near patios.

Lupinus succulentus
ARROYO LUPINE

Ⓝ ☼ ☼ ◊ ◊ Z7–10 H9–1 ↕↔3ft (1m)
Large with showy flowers for erosion control, as a quick cover after fires or on disturbed land. Easier than most lupines with succulent foliage. Plant inoculated seeds.

HERBACEOUS PLANTS

Plants between stepping stones

Some plants live most comfortably with their roots squished into the cracks between stepping stones, often becoming so tightly imbedded it is almost impossible to weed them out. In moist countries, such as England, this can be a nuisance. In the Southwest we don't have that problem; the tougher the plant is, the more we love it. Here are a few that are tried and true.

Anacyclus pyrethrum var. *depressus*
MOUNT ATLAS DAISY
☼ ◊ Z4–10 H8–6 ‡1in (2.5cm) ↔1ft (30cm)
A rugged plant for hot dry places. Wet soil and harsh winters may kill it. Spreads slowly to form a dense mat, flowers in summer with bright red buds.

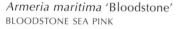

Armeria maritima 'Bloodstone'
BLOODSTONE SEA PINK
☼ ◊ Z4–10 H9–1 ‡4in (10cm) ↔6in (15cm)
Mounds of late spring flowers on long stems. (Shear when faded; they might bloom again.) Best on paths for strolling. Needs sharp drainage and a little moisture, which space between stepping stones provides.

Chamaemelum nobile 'Treneague'
TRENEAGUE LAWN CHAMOMILE
☼ ☼ ◊ Z5–10 H9–6 ‡↔12in (30cm)
Soft texture, but tougher than it looks. Delightful fragrance released when stepped on. Shear occasionally to keep neat and compact. 'Treneague' has no flowers and can sometimes be purchased in flats.

Sagina subulata
SCOTCH MOSS
☼ ☼ ◊ Z4–10 H9–6
‡½in (1.5cm) ↔8in (20cm)
Texture like miniature grass. If it dislikes a spot, it dies, seeds itself in a better location, then lives for years. Lovely in hanging baskets or containers, watered by drip system.

Raoulia australis
RAOULIA
☼ ◊ Z7–10 H9–8 ‡½in (1.5cm) ↔1ft (30cm)
Rubbery texture, mounded shape. Good for edges of gravel paths, bonsai pots, and sandy soil. Needs good drainage, little moisture for roots. Mulch can kill it.

Pratia pedunculata

BLUE STAR CREEPER

☼ ☀ ◐ ◊ Z7–11 H7–5 ‡3in (1cm) ↔1ft (30cm)

A popular, long-lived, and soft-textured groundcover with a lush appearance for small raised beds. Flowers from late spring to fall, with full sun along the coast, part-shade inland.

MORE CHOICES

- *Antennaria parvifolia* 'McClintock' Z3–9 H9–5
- *Cerastium tomentosum* Z3–10 H7–1
- *Dianthus gratianopolitanus* Z6–10 H9–1
- *Dichondra micrantha* Z9–11 H12–9
- *Dymondia margaretae* Z8–11 H12–10
- *Ophiopogon japonicus* 'Compactus' Z4–10 H12–1
- *Soleirolia soleirolii* Z9–11 H12–1
- *Teucrium cossonii* 'Majoricum' Z8–11 H9–5
- *Thymus serpyllum* 'Minus' Z3–10 H9–1
- *Veronica oltensis* Z6–10 H8–6

Ajuga reptans

CARPET BUGLEWEED

☼ ☀ ◐ ◊ Z5–10 H9–1

‡6in (15cm) ↔36in (90cm)

A tenacious plant that spreads rapidly by runners in moist soil. Flowers in spring or early summer. Improved varieties have colored leaves or larger flowers.

Herniaria glabra

GREEN CARPET, RUPTURE WORT

☼ ☀ ◐ ◊◊ Z7–10 H12–8

‡3in (1cm) ↔1ft (30cm)

An evergreen perennial that is bronze red in fall. An easily controlled, flat, green creeping mat that roots as it goes. Best where there is little foot traffic.

Iberis sempervirens

EVERGREEN CANDYTUFT

☼ ◐ ◊ Z4–11 H9–3 ‡12in (30cm) ↔24in (60cm)

White flowers in spring, similar in shape to sweet alyssum, cover the bushy little perennial. After bloom, shear off, and you'll have a neat green plant that can take heat for the rest of the year.

Succulents for dry landscaping or containers

Succulents, the ideal plants for collectors, never cease to amuse and amaze. Beloved by children, they are perfect for patios, and need little care. Plant them in well-drained soil or bagged cacti mix and arrange artistically on mounds with rocks or driftwood or in well-chosen pots. Ideal for side yards or entries in partial shade. Water a little in summer.

Kalanchoe tomentosa
PANDA PLANT
☀ ☼ ◊ ◊ Z10–11 H12–1 ‡3ft (1m) ↔8in (20cm)
Plays well against more angular plants and as a good ingredient for succulent wreaths. Only needs occasional water in summer. Good drainage a must.

Kalanchoe fedtschenkoi
LAVENDER-GRAY KALANCHOE
☀ ◊ ◊ Z10–11 H12–10 ‡20in (50cm) ↔10in (25cm)
A houseplant that can be grown outdoors in mild climates. Good for fronts of borders and in hanging baskets. Break off leaves to plant. Blooms in winter.

Crassula perfoliata var. *minor*
PROPELLER PLANT
☀ ◊ Z10–12 H12–10 ‡3ft (1m) ↔30in (75cm)
A stunning flower display in late summer or early fall of large dense clusters of orange-red flowers that sometimes cascade from weight. Pruning after bloom encourages growth and provides plants for rooting.

Agave parryi
PARRY AGAVE

☼ ☼ ◊ Z9–11 H12–5 ‡20in (50cm) ↔36in (90cm)
Fierce spines on leaf tips. Needs excellent drainage and a little shade in desert. When mature, it sends up a bloom stalk with flowers attractive to birds and bees.

Euphorbia obesa
GLOBE EUPHORIA

☼ ◊ Z9–11 H12–10 ‡8in (2.5m) ↔5in (13cm)
A fun shape, but poisonous, giving some people a rash if touched. Plant where it can be enjoyed but is unlikely to be handled. Needs good drainage.

Echeveria elegans
MEXICAN GEM, PEARL ECHEVERIA

☼ ☼ ◊ Z9–11 H12–10 ‡2in (5cm) ↔20 in (50cm)
A waxy-leaved groundcover. Many hybrids are available with different colors and textures. Small types make clumps; bigger ones are usually solitary.

Sedum spathulifolium 'Purpureum'
PURPLE MAT PLANT

☼ ☼ ◊ Z5–10 H9–5
‡4in (10cm) ↔18in (45cm)
Dense groundcover for small areas. Grow on top of pot or mound, or nestled between rocks, next to contrasting colored succulent, but up front so it's not shaded out.

Sedum spectabile 'Brilliant'
BRILLIANT STONECROP

☼ ☼ ◊ ◊ Z4–9 H9–1 ‡↔12–18in (30–45cm)
A perennial grown for its attractive pinkish, gray-green foliage spring to fall and dramatic display of fall flowers. Good as edging plant or in big drift. Flowers fade quickly after bloom – they hang on but are brown. Dies down in winter. Good inland.

Kalanchoe blossfeldiana
CHRISTMAS KALANCHOE

☼ ◊ Z9–12 H12–1 ‡↔to 16 in (40cm)
A good plant for border edging or to mix with other succulents. To increase size of clump, break off bits for planting. Long winter bloom. Many colored forms.

Agave victoriae-reginae
QUEEN VICTORIA AGAVE

Ⓝ ☼ ☼ ◊ Z9–11 H12–5 ‡20in (50cm) ↔1ft (30cm)
A stunning example of artistic designs that nature creates. Will survive in a pot for many years with little care or change. Seldom do these bloom. Well-drained soil is a must; occasional water in summer.

MORE CHOICES

- *Aeonium tabuliforme* Z9–11 H9–4
- *Aloe brevifolia* Z10–11 H12–3
- *Crassula perfoliata* var. *minor* Z9–11 H12–10
- *Crassula multicava* Z9–10 H12–10
- *Dudleya brittonii* Z9–10 H12–10
- *Echeveria agavoides* Z10–11 H12–1
- *Echeveria* 'Violet Queen' Z10–11 H12–10
- *Euphorbia characias* subsp. *wulfenii* 'John Tomlinson' Z7–11 H12–7
- *Kalanchoe pumila* Z10–11 H12–1
- *Portulacaria afra* Z10–11 H12–10
- *Sedum rubrotinctum* Z9–10 H10–9
- *Sedum telephium* subsp. *maximum* Z4–10 H9–1
- *Sempervivum tectorum* Z4–9 H8–1
- *Senecio serpens* Z9–11 H12–10

HERBACEOUS PLANTS

Perennials for hanging baskets

Swing hanging baskets from the branches of open trees, use them to bring flowers up to eye level, to keep plants above frolicking dogs and children, and to protect them from slugs and snails. Many cascading plants look far better in baskets than at ground level. For easy care, water with a drip system on a timer, and feed monthly with slow-release 14-14-14 fertilizer.

Pelargonium peltatum 'Balcon'
IVY GERANIUM
☼ ◐ ◊ ● Z9–11 H12–1 ‡3ft (1m) ↔5ft (1.5m)
Old, spring-blooming types climb high enough to cover chain-link fence. New hybrids are everblooming, compact, heat-resistant. Deadhead, feed.

Lotus berthelotii
PARROT'S BEAK
☼ ◐ ◊ Z9–11 H12–10 ‡1ft (30cm) ↔3ft (1m)
In a container or the ground, it needs good drainage. If a basket plant fails to have a bloom, move it away from the house for cooler nights, a natural day-length.

Begonia 'Orange Rubra'
CANE BEGONIA
☼ ◐ ◊ ● Z9–11 H12–1 ‡↔2ft (60cm)
Lax-stemmed types cascade from baskets or climb into shrubs. Others with bamboolike stems live 50 years in tubs. Cut a few old stems to the ground in spring.

Sedum morganianum
DONKEY TAIL

☼ ☼ ◐ ◑ Z10–11 H12–1
↕5ft (1.5m) ↔3ft (1m)
Fragile, this needs bright light,
filtered shade, wind cover, and
light food. To transplant from pot,
place it in a basket, hammer,
remove shards, and add soil.

Campanula isophylla 'Alba'
ITALIAN BELLFLOWER

☼ ☼ ◐ ◑ Z5–10 H7–5 ↕8in (20cm) ↔2ft (60cm)
Trailing stems produce flowers in spring, summer, and fall. Grow as a
basket plant in a tree stump, around stepping-stones, in pockets of soil
among rocks, or above stone walls.

Platycerium bifurcatum
STAGHORN FERN

☼ ☼ ◑ Z10–11 H12–10 ↕↔3ft (1m)
An easy-to-grow epiphyte, feed it fish emulsion and
banana peels tucked behind fronds. Do the same with
P. grande and P. superbum. Increase by division.

Calibrachoa hybrids
MILLION BELLS

☼ ☼ ◑ Z7–10 H12–1 ↕↔3ft (1m)
Popular for pots, baskets, and windowboxes, with
many colors available. This has constant bloom in
mild zones but is a summer annual in cold-winter
climates. Feed it slow-release.

Epiphyllum hybrids
ORCHID CACTUS

☼ ☼ ◐ ◑ Z10–12 H12–1 ↕3ft (1m) ↔2ft (60cm)
Fleshy, green wavy leaves grow from each other,
cascading from containers. Spectacular iridescent
flowers appear in May and June in a range of colors.

MORE CHOICES

- *Davallia trichomanoides* Z9–11 H12–1
- *Lobelia richardsonii* Z9–11 H9–1
- *Scaevola aemula* 'New Wonder'
  Z7–11 H12–1
- *Streptocarpus saxorum* 'Concord Blue'
  Z9–11 H12–10
- *Verbena* Tapien Hybrids Z8–10 H12–1
- *Xerochrysum bracteatum* 'Sundaze
  Golden Yellow' Z7–11 H12–1

Nephrolepis exaltata 'Bostoniensis'
BOSTON FERN

Ⓝ ☼ ☼ ◐ ◑ Z8–11 H12–1 ↕↔3ft (1m)
Grow this tropical under a tree near the house, or as
a groundcover; cover during frosts. Hang indoor plant
out in shade during weekdays; in at night, weekends.

HERBACEOUS PLANTS

Succulent groundcovers for Zone 1 firebreaks

These low groundcovers are recommended for Zone 1, the area closest to the house within a zoned firebreak. If a fire is hot enough, just about anything will burn, but these plants provide less fuel than taller plants, and their moist succulent leaves are fire resistant. They are also fine groundcovers for other uses, especially erosion control on banks.

Drosanthemum floribundum
ROSEA ICEPLANT
☼ ◊ Z9–11 H12–10 ‡6in (15cm) ↔1ft (30cm)
A hybrid form sold in flats as a groundcover, the old variety is shared by gardeners as a flatter carpet, with less vivid magenta flowers and tight gray foliage.

Crassula multicava
PRIDE OF LONDON
☼ ☼ ☼ ◊ ◊ Z9–11 H12–10
‡18in (45cm) ↔3ft (1m)
Shared by gardeners, not in nurseries, this self-sustaining plant is for covering shady ground and holding banks. It has spring flowers and invasive plantlets, easily pulled out.

Sedum acre
GOLD MOSS STONECROP
☼ ☼ ◊ ◊ Z5–9 H8–1 ‡5in (13cm) ↔5ft (1.5m)
A hardy creeping plant that roots as it goes. Rampant growth can become weedy. Use on banks, between paving stones, or to stop erosion on sides of a path.

Sedum spurium 'Bronze Carpet'
BRONZE CARPET STONECROP
☼ ☼ ◊ ◊ Z3–10 H9–1 ‡4in (10cm) ↔1ft (30cm)
Useful on slopes, this spreads and has trailing runners and small pink flowers. It is artistic in patches with other gray, red, or maroon-foliaged varieties and rocks.

Lampranthus aurantiacus
ORANGE ICEPLANT

Ⓝ ☼ ◑ ◐ Z9–11 H12–10 ‡16in (40cm) ↔2ft (60cm)

A spreading South African native that can grow on an oceanfront or inland, with three-sided, pointed gray leaves and flowers that can be also yellow or gold. Combine with other iceplants, succulents, rocks.

Lampranthus spectabilis
TRAILING ICEPLANT

☼ ◑ ◐ Z9–11 H12–10 ‡1ft (30cm) ↔2ft (60cm)

The most colorful iceplant with gray foliage, then a show-stopping winter-spring display of bright pink, red, or purple blooms, spilled on ground. Use by rocks.

Lampranthus deltoides
ICEPLANT

☼ ☼ ◑ ◐ Z9–11 H12–10
‡1ft (30cm) ↔2ft (60cm)

South African with pink flowers and oddly shaped, gray leaves on woody stems growing up, then trailing onto the ground. For pots or cascading around rocks and over walls.

Aptenia cordifolia
RED APPLE ICEPLANT

☼ ☼ ◐ ◐ Z9–11 H12–10 ‡2ft (60cm) ↔1ft (30cm)

A South African native that has small, red, daisylike flowers from summer to fall, and needs lots of water and fertilizing with calcium nitrate to keep it green.

MORE CHOICES

- *Aeonium simsii* Z9–11 H12–10
- *Calandrinia spectabilis* Z9–11 H12–1
- *Cephalophyllum speciosum* 'Red Spike' Z9–10 H12–10
- *Lampranthus filicaulis* Z9–10 H12–1
- *Malephora lutea* Z9–10 H12–10
- *Sedum album* 'Coral Carpet' Z5–10 H9–4
- *Sempervivum arachnoideum* Z5–9 H8–5

Carpobrotus edulis
HOTTENTOT FIG

☼ ☼ ◑ ◐ Z9–11 H12–10 ‡1ft (30cm) ↔8ft (2.5m)

Spreading and invasive in wild zones, it is used as a quick cover for slopes but can pull down a cliff if hanging over. It grows in beach sand, discouraging foot erosion, and has edible but tasteless fruit.

Senecio mandraliscae
GRAY FINGERS

☼ ☼ ◑ ◐ Z9–11 H11–9
‡18in (45cm) ↔2ft (60cm)

Grow as a groundcover, edging paths, in combination with other succulents. Prized for its gray-blue foliage, not its daisylike flowers, it needs half sun in the desert, full sun elsewhere.

HERBACEOUS PLANTS

Herbaceous groundcovers for full sun

Green lawns provide the best play space for children and dogs, but patios, mulched areas, and groundcovers can take the place of lawn grass and require less water and care. Many of these herbaceous groundcovers are drought resistant, and thrive from hot interiors to beachfronts. Some, such as yarrow, can even be walked or run upon without ill effect.

Aegopodium podagraria 'Variegatum'
VARIEGATED GOUTWEED
☼ ☼ ☼ ◐ Z4–10 H9–1
↕6in (15cm) ↔1ft (30cm)
An aggressive groundcover for full sun in mild climates. It lightens up dry shade in hot interior. If bedraggled by summer's end, mow and water; it will bounce back.

Achillea tomentosa
WOOLLY YARROW
☼ ◐◐ Z4–10 H8–1 ↕10in (25cm) ↔18in (45cm)
Groundcover for small areas with gray-green, fernlike foliage and white or yellow summer flowers. Plant *A. millefolium* seeds for a lawn and mow off flowers.

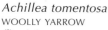

Polygonum capitatum
KNOTWEED
☼ ☼ ◐ Z8–9 H9–8 ↕3in (8cm) ↔1ft (30cm)
A flat everblooming Himalayan that can be weedy with too much water. Use it to cover ground, spill over the edge of a raised bed, or under a small specimen tree.

Carex comans
NEW ZEALAND HAIR SEDGE
☼ ☼ ◐◐ Z6–10 H9–7 ↕18in (45cm) ↔30in (75cm)
Very popular but invasive, this is easy to grow and spreads by seeds. Muted brown flower spikes appear in summer. Variants come with warm brown foliage.

Arabis x *arendsii* 'Rosabella'
ROSABELLA ROCK CRESS
☼ ◐ Z5–10 H8–5
↕4in (10cm) ↔1ft (30cm)
A compact selection with a spring
bloom, excellent for bulb cover or
tucking into crevices of dry
walks, walls, steps, and rock
gardens. Often sold as *A.
caucasica* 'Rosabella'.

Dymondia margaretae
SILVER CARPET
☼ ◐ ◐◐ Z8–11 H12–10 ↕3in (8cm) ↔20in (50cm)
A flat South African mat, with tiny, yellow spring flowers,
used as a lawn substitute that survives children, dogs, and
less water than grass. Plant between stepping stones.

Cerastium tomentosum
SNOW IN SUMMER
☼ ◐ ◐◐ Z3–10 H7–1 ↕8ft (2.5m) ↔25ft (8m)
Good but short-lived so replace it after it dies.
Grown from the desert to coastal zones in most
western climates, it cannot take shade on the
coast, but needs partial shade in the desert.
Use on slopes, level ground, and rock gardens.

MORE CHOICES

- *Ajuga reptans* Z3–10 H9–1
- *Antennaria dioica* var. *rosea* Z5–9 H9–4
- *Arctotheca calendula* Z8–11 H12–10
- *Artemisia caucasica* Z5–9 H9–1
- *Carex flacca* Z5–10 H9–5
- *Dampiera diversifolia* Z9–10 H12–10
- *Drosanthemum floribundum*
  Z9–11 H12–10
- *Erodium reichardi* Z7–10 H9–8
- *Osteospermum* 'Brightside' Z8–10 H6–1
- *Phyla nodiflora* Z8–12 H12–10
- *Plecostachys serpyllifolia* Z9–10 H12–10
- *Thymus pseudo-lanuginosus* Z3–10 H9–1

Pelargonium peltatum
'Balcon'
IVY GERANIUM
☼ ◐ ◐◐ Z9–11 H12–1
↕18in (45cm) ↔3ft (1m)
A single-flowered variety sold in
flats, that looks better planted
than in nurseries. Covers ground
in California with solid color.
Spills from balconies in Europe.

Leptinella squalida
NEW ZEALAND BRASS BUTTONS
☼ ◐ ◐◐ Z5–10 H7–1
↕6in (15cm) ↔12ft (4m)
Evergreen, feathery gray foliage
spreads aggressively and roots as
it goes. Cut edges and share
with others. It cascades over
walls, covers ground under open
trees, and has spring flowers.

HERBACEOUS PLANTS

Perennial groundcovers for full shade

The most difficult shade area for planting is under a north-facing overhang next to a front door. The space may be cold, damp, and drafty, or it may tend toward the other extreme: hot, dry, and windy. Transform deep shade into a welcoming space by improving the soil, arranging a fountain with rocks and a dry streambed, and surrounding these features with plants.

Opiophogon jaburan
JABURAN LILY
☼ ◐ ◑ ● Z7–8 H10–7
↕↔1ft (30cm)
This goundcover and accent plant does not creep. Late summer flowers are followed by attractive violet fruits on stems to use for arrangements. 'Vittatus' is a variegated form that lightens shade.

Liriope spicata 'Silver Dragon'
SILVER DRAGON LILYTURF
☼ ◐ ◑ ● Z4–10 H12–1 ↕10in (25cm) ↔18in (45cm)
Quick-spreading, rhizomatous, and grasslike, this needs moist, fertile, and well-drained soil. Confine invasiveness with path or edging; mow in early spring.

Ophiopogon planiscapus 'Nigrescens'
BLACK MONDO GRASS
☼ ◑ ● Z5–10 H12–1 ↕8in (20cm) ↔12in (30cm)
A choice selection for Japanese gardens, arrange it as an accent with *Liriope muscari*, *O. japonicus* 'Nana', and others. A dwarf form is also available.

Ophiopogon japonicus
MONDO GRASS
☼ ◐ ◑ ● Z7–9 H12–1 ↕↔1ft (30cm)
Slow-spreading, this becomes a dense cover. Small white flowers are hidden by foliage. Shear or mow in early spring before new growth. Also dwarf varieties.

Cyrtomium falcatum
JAPANESE HOLLY FERN
☼ ◐ ● Z9–11 H12–10 ↕2ft (60cm) ↔4ft (1.2m)
Easy in shade with bright light, this likes organic soil, gets mites if neglected in darkest shade, gets crown rot if planted too deeply, and naturalizes in mild zones.

Plectranthus verticillatus
CREEPING CHARLIE
☼ ☀ ◑ ◑ z10–12 H12–1 ↕8in (20cm) ↔6ft (2m)
A common houseplant or groundcover for an informal
feel near the house in mild zones. For quick cover,
plant cuttings 1–2ft (30–60cm) apart in moist soil.

Rumohra adiantiformis
LEATHERLEAF FERN
☼ ☼ ☀ ◑ ◑ z9–12 H12–8 ↕↔3ft (1m)
Coarse, drought-resistant, and easy in any soil with
attractive leaves on tall strong stems for arrangements.
Cut old spent fronds down as new ones arise.

Adiantum aleuticum
FIVE FINGER FERN
Ⓝ ☼ ☼ ☀ ◑ z3–9 H8–1 ↕↔3ft (1m)
It gives a refreshing, airy woodland atmosphere when
mixed with a fountain, dry stream bed, or other ferns.
Feed with fish emulsion; protect from slugs and snails.

Maranta leuconeura var. *kerchoviana*
PRAYER PLANT
☼ ☀ ◑ z10–11 H12–1 ↕↔1ft (30cm)
A groundcover close to the house or in an entryway
or atrium in mild zones; a houseplant in all zones.
Leaves close at night. Cut back and feed in spring.

MORE CHOICES

- *Acanthus mollis* Latifolius Group z6–10 H12–7
- *Ajuga reptans* 'Jungle Green' z5–10 H9–1
- *Aspidistra elatior* 'Variegata' z8–11 H12–1
- *Cyrtomium falcatum* 'Rochfordianum'
  z9–11 H12–10
- *Davallia trichomanoides* z10–12 H12–1
- *Ligularia dentata* 'Gregynog Gold' z5–8 H8–1
- *Liriope muscari* 'Big Blue' z6–10 H12–1
- *Liriope muscari* 'Monroe White' z6–10 H12–1
- *Nephrolepis cordifolia* z10–12 H12–1
- *Pleioblastus pygmaeus* z5–10 H10–5
- *Soleirolia soleirolii* z9–11 H12–1

HERBACEOUS PLANTS

Native perennial groundcovers: dry shade

A few native plants have become common garden plants, but not many. Most are interdependent and like being planted with the same neighbors they have in nature. It is better to designate an entire portion of your garden to native plants than to mix them with non-natives. Except for the columbine, all plants listed here could grow near native oaks.

Mahonia repens
CREEPING BARBERRY
Ⓝ ☀ ☀ ◊ ◊ Z5–10 H8–3
↕1ft (30cm) ↔3ft (1m)
A creeping native to the Pacific Northwest with yellow flowers, blue fruits, blue-green foliage – or pinkish bronze in cool weather. Plant it in fall; its roots spread in winter.

Aquilegia formosa
SCARLET COLUMBINE
Ⓝ ☀ ☀ ◊ Z4–9 H7–1
↕3ft (1m) ↔18in (45cm)
One of several native columbines grown in gardens, it needs moist soil and good drainage. Cut back stems after bloom for repeat show. Let seed capsules mature and save seeds.

Dudleya edulis
SANTA CATALINA DUDLEYA
Ⓝ ☀ ☀ ◊ ◊ Z10 H12–10 ↕4in (10cm) ↔2ft (60cm)
From the Catalina Island coast this was eaten by Native Americans. Use for fire breaks, dry rock gardens, next to steps and paths, and on steep banks.

Heuchera 'Wendy'
WENDY CORAL BELLS
Ⓝ ☀ ◊ Z7–10 H8–1 ↕2ft (60cm) ↔1ft (30cm)
This hybrid variety survives with less water than most. Charming in drifts under oaks and loved by hummingbirds, it needs good drainage, light shade, and is best with some winter chill.

MORE CHOICES

- *Asarum caudatum* Z8–10 H8–1
- *Dudleya caespitosa* Z9–10 H12–10
- *Festuca californica* Z9–10 H8–1
- *Pellaea andromedifolia* Z9–10 H10–8
- *Salvia spathacea* Z5–10 H9–5

Native perennial groundcovers: hot interiors

People have designed houses to keep themselves cool through hot summer days. Plants have developed their own ways to deal with heat, such as flowers that close up during the day, woolly hairs that shade their leaves, and water-storage systems in their stems or roots. Flowers will bloom longer on these desert-dwelling plants with occasional irrigation.

Bouteloua curtipendula
SIDE OATS GRAMA
Ⓝ ☼ ◊◊ Z6–9 H9–6 ↕↔2ft (60cm)
A native grass with large, purple-green flowers that hang on one side only from leaning stems. The whole plant turns yellow or red in fall and white in winter.

Oenothera stubbei
SALTILLO EVENING PRIMROSE
Ⓝ ☼◐ ◊◊ Z9–10 H10–7 ↕5in (13cm) ↔4in (10cm)
Blooms open in the evening on this matlike, creeping Mexican plant with large flat clumps of gray foliage. It endures intense heat and drought. The spring bloom lasts longer with irrigation.

Baileya multiradiata
DESERT MARIGOLD
Ⓝ ☼◐ ◊◊ Z7–9 H10–6
↕↔18in (45cm)
A native to deserts where summer rains keep it blooming. With irrigation it blooms year round in low deserts. Sow seeds in fall and keep moist. Thin to 18in (45cm) intervals.

Berlandiera lyrata
CHOCOLATE FLOWER
Ⓝ ☼ ◊◊ Z7–9 H9–7 ↕↔3ft (1m)
Native from Arizona to Arkansas, its yellow flowers have a strong chocolate fragrance when new. It has pale green leaves and waves of bloom from spring to fall after southwestern monsoons. Shear occasionally. Attracts butterflies.

Bahia absinthifolia
BAHIA
Ⓝ ☼ ◊◊ Z8–9 H12–9 ↕↔1ft (30cm)
This has yellow flowers spring and fall, silvery foliage, and a tidy habit. It grows rapidly in alkaline, shallow hardpan soils and takes temperatures to 15°F (-9°C).

MORE CHOICES

- *Asclepias subulata* Z3–10 H8–1
- *Dalea greggii* Z6–9 H10–8
- *Dyssodia acerosa* Z5–9 H9–6
- *Eriogonum wrightii* Z6–10 H12–1
- *Gutierrezia sarothrae* Z6–9 H12–10
- *Phlox tenuifolia* Z6–10 H9–7
- *Plumbago scandens* Z12–15 H12–10
- *Salazaria mexicana* Z7–9 H9–7
- *Tequilia greggii* Z7–9 H9–7
- *Thymophylla pentachaeta* Z7–9 H12–1
- *Verbena rigida* Z7–10 H12–1

Groundcovers for light foot traffic

The plants shown on these pages are matlike groundcovers you can walk on while pruning, cleaning, or deadheading other plants. Use them for covering banks or flat ground between taller specimens. Some of these groundcovers are best for the edges of paths or stepping stones, while others can be used in place of lawns, usually requiring less water than grass.

Origanum vulgare 'Compactum'
CREEPING OREGANO

☼ ◐ Z4–10 H10–2 ↕3in (8cm) ↔1ft (30cm)

Delightfully fragrant when stepped on, this is dense, flat, and spreads vigorously by runners between stepping stones or on informal risers. Cut off the occasional upright flower stem and use for flavoring.

Verbena peruviana 'Alba'
WHITE PERUVIAN VERBENA

☼ ◐ Z9–11 H12–9 ↕3in (8cm) ↔3ft (30cm)

Popular in hot-interior, desert zones, flat species or billowing hybrids sail through hot summers with nonstop color in a variety of shades. Mildews on coast.

Chamaemelum nobile 'Treneague'
TRENEAGUE CHAMOMILE

☼ ☼ ◐ Z6–10 H9–6 ↕↔1ft (30cm)

A flat selection for a lawn with a soft texture. No mowing is needed and it stands up well to foot traffic. To use other types as lawns, or on paths, plant at 1ft (30cm) intervals, and mow off summer flowers.

Bouteloua gracilis
BLUE GRAMA

Ⓝ ☼ ◐◐ Z6–9 H9–5 ↕2ft (60cm) ↔1ft (30cm)

Mow this drought-resistant lawn to 18in (45cm), for the high plains, Rocky Mountains, and hot interior. It takes heat, drought, and alkalinity. Plant seeds in fall with deep irrigation until established, then none.

Phyla nodiflora
LIPPIA

☼ ◐◐ Z9–11 H12–10

↕2in (5cm) ↔2ft (60cm)

Heat-resistant, this brings bees. For dogs and children, mow off flowers in June. It holds ground on a beachfront with little water. Nematodes can weaken it in desert.

Arctotheca calendula
CAPE WEED
☀ ☀ ◐◑ Z9–12 H12–10 ↕1ft (30cm) ↔18in (45cm)
Do not plant near wild lands: this spreads by runners and seeds, crowding out natives in any moist soil. Otherwise it is an easy, flat persistent groundcover that survives fifty years in parking strips.

0Thymus pseudo-lanuginosus
WOOLLY THYME
☀ ☀ ◑ Z4–10 H9–1
↕3in (8cm) ↔1ft (30cm)
The best thyme for a groundcover with a great look; plant several. Use as a filler or bank cover on well-drained soil. Must have full sun on coast. Blooms in June.

MORE CHOICES

- *Achillea tomentosa* Z3–10 H8–1
- *Ajuga reptans* 'Purpurea' Z3–10 H9–1
- *Dichondra micrantha* Z9–11 H12–9
- *Duchesnia indica* Z6–10 H8–6
- *Dymondia margaretae* Z9–12 H12–10
- *Festuca rubra* Z6–10 H9–1
- *Herniaria glabra* Z10 H12–8
- *Persicaria capitatum* Z9–10 H9–8
- *Teucrium chamaedrys* 'Prostratum' Z4–10 H9–1
- *Zoysia tenuifolia* Z8–11 H12–8

HERBACEOUS PLANTS

Ornamental grasses

Many grasses, sedges, and rushes can be charming additions to gardens. However, not all are drought resistant, as commonly supposed. Additionally, some of the most beautiful, including pampas grass, fountain grasses, and Natal ruby grass are invading wild lands at a frightening rate. Selections should therefore be chosen with care, to avoid problems.

Pennisetum setaceum 'Rubrum'
PURPLE FOUNTAIN GRASS
☼ ◊◊◊ Z9–12 H12–8 ↕↔5ft (1.5m)
A colorful hybrid form with no viable seeds. Cut to ground in fall with first rains. Follow with lawn fertilizer and water. Ratty unless cut back.

Panicum virgatum 'Heavy Metal'
HEAVY METAL SWITCH GRASS
Ⓝ ☼ ☼ ◊◊◊ Z5–10 H9–4
↕5ft (1.5m) ↔4ft (1.2m)
Stiff metallic blue, this turns yellow in fall. Native, but not to western deserts or seashores, it may crowd out shorter seashore natives. Use in cold-winter climates for winter color.

Miscanthus sinensis
'Morning light'
JAPANESE SILVER GRASS
☼ ☼ ◊ Z4–10 H9–1 ↕↔4ft (1.2m)
Extremely attractive in gardens, deadhead when flowers become ratty in mild zones, prior to new growth. Invasive, seeds dropped by birds will sprout, given adequate chill.

Calamagrostis x *acutiflora* 'Karl Foerster'
FOERSTER'S FEATHER REED GRASS
☼ ◊ Z6–10 H9–5 ↕3ft (1m) ↔4ft (1.2m)
A tall, cool-season grass that forms a big clump and may invade wild wetlands. Like other grasses, it can be cut to ground to renew, in fall or spring.

MORE CHOICES

- *Achnatherum speciosum* Z7–9 H10–8
- *Muhlenbergia rigida* 'Nashville' Z8–10 H12–10
- *Stipa tenuissima* 'Pony Tails' Z8–10 H12–7

Bamboos

Bamboos are giant grasses and among the world's most useful plants, providing food, shelter, animal fodder, and habitat. In moist climates like Hawaii, running bamboos can be invasive interlopers. All bamboos are monocarpic, meaning each species lives to its mature age – in some cases hundreds of years – then blooms and dies, to begin again from seeds.

Bambusa multiplex 'Golden Goddess'
GOLDEN GODDESS BAMBOO
☼ ☼ ◊ ◐ Z9–12 H10–1 ‡↔10ft (3m)
Clumping, not running, with a graceful, dense arching growth. Plant several for a big screen. Allow room for tops to spread. Can grow 6ft (2m) high in a tub.

Otatea acuminata var. *aztecorum*
Ⓝ MEXICAN WEEPING BAMBOO
Ⓝ ☼ ☼ ◊ ◐ Z8–12 H12–8 ‡↔20ft (6m)
Mexico's native bamboo has hollow canes used for baskets. New ones will live to be 35. Textural and animal-like, stake up one side to shade a bench.

Bambusa oldhamii
GIANT TIMBER BAMBOO
☼ ☼ ◊ ◐ Z9–12 H12–8
‡55ft (17m) ↔100ft (30m)
A clumping useful specimen for large or botanical gardens. Hollow timber is often used for construction of buildings, bridges, fences, floor planks.

Phyllostachys aureosulcata
YELLOW GROOVE BAMBOO
☼ ☼ ◊ ◐ Z6–11 H12–3 ‡20ft (6m) ↔100ft (30m)
This hardy running bamboo spreads indefinitely if not confined by an underground barrier. Young culms are green with yellow grooves. A good screen plant.

Bambusa tuldoides
BUDDHA'S BELLY BAMBOO
☼ ☼ ◊ ◐ Z8–11 H12–9 ‡30ft (10m) ↔20ft (6m)
This clumping bamboo grows tall and straight unless confined in a container. For swollen corms, plant a crowded specimen in poor soil in a Chinese pot.

MORE CHOICES

- *Chusquea coronalis* Z9–11 H12–8
- *Phyllostachys nigra* Z6–11 H12–4
- *Semiarundinaria fastuosa* Z6–9 H9–6
- *Sinarundinaria nitida* Z6–9 H9–5

Hardy bulbs

If you live in a mild climate, choose bulbs carefully. The bulbs on these pages grow well in the Southwest, but most of them need some winter chill to bloom. They can all survive snowy winters in mountainous zones, but most will refuse to flower in frost-free climates no matter how much you coax them.

Calochortus superbus
MARIPOSA LILY
Ⓝ ☼ ◐ ◊◊◗ Z5–9 H10–6
↕↔6in (15cm)
For a rock garden or grassy hillside, this needs a long, hot dry summer and mild winter. Or plant in buried pots, lift, store outdoors in hot dry shade.

Asphodeline lutea
YELLOW ASPHODEL
☼ ☼ ◗ Z6–9 H9–6 ↕5ft (1.5m) ↔1ft (30cm)
Good in mountains and interior, not coasts, it has grassy leaves, rhizomatous roots, and a fragrant spring bloom on stalks 3ft (1m) high. Needs regular irrigation.

Lilium pardalinum
LEOPARD LILY
Ⓝ ☼ ☼ ◗ Z5–8 H8–5 ↕10ft (3m) ↔3ft (1m)
Native to moist meadows and streambeds, plant from seeds in moist garden beds or streamside, anywhere in California or higher elevations in the Southwest.

MORE CHOICES

- *Allium* 'Globemaster' Z4–8 H8–1
- *Camassia cusickii* 'Zwanenburg' Z3–9 H12–1
- *Crocus imperati* 'De Jager' Z3–8 H8–1
- *Hyacinthus orientalis* 'Queen of the Pinks' Z5–10 H9–5
- *Lilium columbianum* Z6–8 H8–6
- *Narcissus* 'Actaea' Z3–10 H9–1
- *Narcissus* 'Fortissimo' Z3–10 H9–1

Chionodoxa luciliae
GLORY OF THE SNOW
☼ ☀ ● Z3–9 H9–1 ↕6in (15cm) ↔4in (10cm)
This needs winter chill, but not necessarily snow, and water for growth and bloom. Plant under a deciduous tree for sun during bloom, semishade in summer.

Cyclamen coum f. albissimum
HARDY CYCLAMEN
☼ ☀ ◊●◊● Z5–9 H9–5 ↕↔6in (15cm)
A fragrant Mediterranean with small flowers, this grows excellently in mild climates. In cold-winter climates, plant C. hederifolium, which is similar but more reliably hardy.

Muscari armeniacum
GRAPE HYACINTH
☼ ☀ ● Z4–8 H8–1
↕8in (20cm) ↔3in (8cm)
This hardy bulb multiplies and returns yearly in moist gardens with winter chill. It will not bloom on Southern California coast, except in cold pockets. Not adapted to pre-chilling.

Anemone blanda
GRECIAN WINDFLOWER
☼ ● Z4–8 H8–1 ↕8in (20cm) ↔6in (15cm)
Plant with tulips, in short lawns, under deciduous trees. They spread and return annually with cold winters. They will not bloom in frost-free climates.

Fritillaria camtschatcensis
CHOCOLATE LILY
Ⓝ ☼ ☀ ☀ ◊●◊●
Z4–9 H8–2
↕18in (45cm) ↔5in (13cm)
Native to moist, cool climates, this grows wild in mountains near Santa Barbara. F. biflora (mission bells) is easier to grow, with spotted flowers.

Leucojum vernum
SPRING SNOWFLAKE
☼ ☀ ● Z4–8 H9–3 ↕1ft (30cm) ↔3in (8cm)
Needs winter chill below 20°F (-7°C), sun during bloom, light shade, and water in summer. Spreads readily in orchards, under deciduous trees and shrubs.

HERBACEOUS PLANTS

Bulbs for winter and spring bloom

The plants listed here are European bulbs for winter and spring bloom in pots or the ground. In frost-free climates, Darwin tulips, hyacinths, and Dutch crocuses must be pre-chilled: place the bulbs in a paper bag in the refrigerator for six weeks, then plant them immediately. Daffodils, however, need no pre-chilling in mild zones and will naturalize in cold-winter climates.

Narcissus 'Tahiti'
TAHITI DAFFODIL
☼ ☼ ● Z3–10 H9–1 ‡18in (45cm) ↔6in (15cm)
Choose large firm bulbs with 2 or 3 "noses." Buy early and plant in cool fall. Do not divide; each nose will send up flowers. Keep pots cool, moist, and dark until leaves are up 4in (10cm).

Scilla peruviana
PERUVIAN SQUILL
☼ ☼ ● Z8–10 H9–8 ‡1ft (30cm) ↔5in (13cm)
Well adapted to dry summers, in coastal gardens they bloom once but they may return annually inland. Each bulb can produce several blooms.

Anemone fulgens
SCARLET WINDFLOWER
☼ ● Z7–9 H12–8 ‡1ft (30cm) ↔6in (15cm)
In dry climates, presoak tubers in fall, scar-side up; plant in a well-drained loam. Short-lived, it grows in mild climates, but is best with some winter chill.

Anemone coronaria 'The Bride'
THE BRIDE ANEMONE
☼ ☼ ● Z7–9 H12–8 ‡18in (45cm) ↔6in (15cm)
Presoak bulb and plant as *A. x fulgens*. White and blue varieties mix well with *Ranunculus* Tecolote Giants, which are easy in well-drained soil in mild climates.

HERBACEOUS PLANTS

Muscari botryoides 'Album'
WHITE GRAPE HYACINTH
☼ ☀ ◊ Z2–9 H8–1 ‡1ft (30cm) ↔3in (8cm)
Hardy bulbs with a shorter growth in mild climates, they return annually in moist gardens, 10 miles (6km) or more from the coast, and need some winter chill to bloom.

Crocus vernus 'Purpureus Grandiflorus'
DUTCH CROCUS
☼ ◊ Z3–8 H8–1 ‡5in (13cm) ↔3in (8cm)
Good in cold-winter climates where they multiply and return annually – not for mild-winter climates as they are hard to pre-chill and blooms damage in heat.

Cyclamen persicum 'Sierra White'
FLORIST'S CYCLAMEN
☼ ◊◊ Z9–10 H6–1
‡9in (23cm) ↔1ft (30cm)
In cold winter, grow in a cool atrium; in mild winter, fall-purchased plants bloom all winter in hanging baskets or pots. Do not overwater. Control snails. Pull off faded blooms; do not cut them off.

Hyacinthus orientalis 'Ostara'
DUTCH HYACINTH
☼ ◊ Z5–10 H9–5
‡1ft (30cm) ↔8in (20cm)
A fragrant bulb for either mild-winter or snowy-winter climates. In mild zones, bulbs should be pre-chilled before planting. Plant in pots or the ground, or grow in a bulb vase with water. It may return as a single.

Ornithogalum umbellatum
STAR OF BETHLEHEM
☼ ☀ ◊ Z7–11 H12–7 ‡1ft (30cm) ↔6in (15cm)
Mediterranean for mild or cold winters, it naturalizes in some gardens, including high elevations in Hawaii. O. arabicum has white flowers with black shiny centers.

MORE CHOICES

- Cyclamen pupurascens Z5–9 H9–4
- Hippeastrum papilio Z9–11 H12–1
- Muscari azureum Z5–9 H9–1
- Ornithogalum arabicum Z9–11 H12–9
- Ornithogalum saundersiae Z7–10 H10–7
- Ornithogalum thyrsoides Z7–10 H10–7
- Ranunculus asiaticus Tecolote Hybrids Z9–11 H8–2
- Tulipa Darwin Hybrids Z3–10 H8–1

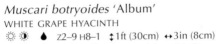

Bulbs for summer and fall bloom

A true bulb has a basal plate and rudimentary leaves surrounding a bud with the magic makings of a plant, but we often lump together under this term all plants that arise from thickened or bulbous storage units. The plants described here arise from bulbs, corms, tubers, rhizomes or tuberous roots, and give colorful shows in summer and fall.

Crinum x *powellii*
CAPE LILY
☼ ☼ ● Z9–12 H12–8 ↕↔3ft (1m)
A huge bulb with straplike leaves. A big groundcover that is foolproof, but takes much water. Excellent in Hawaii and in large landscapes. Protect from snails. Strongly fragrant, it also comes in pink.

Tigridia pavonia
TIGER FLOWER
Ⓝ ☼ ● Z7–10 H12–3
↕18in (45cm) ↔1ft (30cm)
Easy, bright bold flowers show up well in sunny climates. Irrigate only during growth and bloom and give light shade in hot zones. Plant in spring; divide in three years.

Caladium bicolor
FANCY-LEAVED CALADIUM
☼ ☼ ● z10–12 H12–4
↕30in (75cm) ↔18in (45cm)
A tropical foliage plant, purchase full-grown or grow from tubers. Plant in Hawaii and mild zones in spring. Needs rich, moist soil, fertilizer, and water. Protect from slugs and snails.

Dahlia 'Hayley Jane'
HAYLEY JANE DAHLIA
☼ ☼ ● Z9–11 H12–5
↕5ft (1.5m) ↔2ft (60cm)
Dig deeply in good drainage and add organics. Plant roots deeply in holes. Fill in as sprout grows. Stake, water, and feed.

Liatris spicata
DENSE GAYFEATHER
Ⓝ ☼ ◊●● Z4–9 H9–1 ↕4ft (1.2m) ↔18in (45cm)
For hot summers, cold winters, and some rain, and great in Texas, New Mexico, and Oklahoma, it takes poor arid soil, heat, and chill. Not for mild climates.

MORE CHOICES

- *Begonia* Nonstop[R] Z9–10 H12–1
- *Galtonia candicans* Z7–10 H10–7
- *Gladiolus* spp. Z8–10 H9–1
- *Hymenocallis* x *festalis* Z8–10 H10–8
- *Lycoris aurea* Z8–10 H10–8
- *Polianthes tuberosa* Z7–12 H11–7

Sternbergia lutea
WINTER DAFFODIL

☼ ◊ ◊ ◊ Z7–10 H9–6 ↕9in (23cm) ↔1ft (30cm)

Crocuslike bulb. Buy bulbs in summer, plant immediately in crevices, by steps, in rock gardens. Needs excellent drainage. Don't disturb once planted.

Sprekelia formosissima
AZTEC LILY

Ⓝ ☼ ☼ ◊ Z9–10 H12–10 ↕1ft (30cm) ↔6in (15cm)

An elongated Mexican bulb, slowly clumping, that blooms in summer in mild zones, and successively in sandy soil that goes dry between irrigations or rains.

Schizostylis coccinea 'Sunrise'
CRIMSON FLAG

☼ ☼ ◊ Z9–10 H9–7 ↕2ft (60cm) ↔1ft (30cm)

South African, it grows from rhizomes in moist soil. Native to moist streamsides with star-shaped flowers in red, pink, and white. Plant in spring for fall bloom.

Gladiolus communis
BYZANTINE GLADIOLUS

☼ ◊ Z8–10 H9–1

↕3ft (1m) ↔10in (25cm)

Long-lived and vigorous, this needs good drainage and no special care. Summer blooms are maroon, reddish, and coppery. Can take heat.

Iris 'Dusky Challenger'
DUSKY CHALLENGER IRIS

☼ ☼ ◊ Z3–10 H9–1 ↕3ft (1m) ↔1ft (30cm)

This gradually moves outward and eventually stops blooming if too shaded or not divided. It needs fertilizer, good drainage, and division of crowded clumps. Give light shade only in hottest zones.

Nerine sarniensis
GUERNSEY LILY

☼ ☼ ◊ Z8–10 H10–8

↕2ft (60cm) ↔6in (15cm)

South African with iridescent flowers, this needs water during growth and bloom, but dry dormant summers. Good in pots with well-drained, loamy soil.

Bulbs for naturalizing in mild-winter zones

The bulbs listed here will die in harsh winters, but naturalize easily in mild, frost-free climates with no winter chill. Many are happy in soil that goes dry in summer; others like irrigated ground. All prefer good drainage. Their native countries range from the US to South Africa and the Mediterranean. They bloom at various times of the year, but mostly in spring.

Iris innominata
DEL NORTE COUNTY IRIS
Ⓝ ☼ ☼ ◊ ◑   Z8–10 H9–7
↕10in (25cm) ↔8in (20cm)
A species adapted to winter rains and dry summers, the plants in nurseries are hybrid forms. Grow in rock gardens. *I. douglasiana* is also grown in native gardens.

Crocosmia 'Lucifer'
LUCIFER MONTBRETIA
☼ ☼ ◑   Z8–11 H9–6
↕↔4ft (1.2m)
This South African corm makes big drifts in moist soil and blooms in summer. In dry soil, it needs weekly irrigation, but clumps are smaller. Needs staking in shade.

Leucojum aestivum 'Gravetye Giant'
GRAVETYE GIANT SNOWFLAKE
☼ ☼ ◑   Z4–10 H9–1   ↕3ft (1m)   ↔4ft (1.2m)
A big leafy clump next to paths, it blooms fall through spring, and can dry in summer. Leaves die but return in fall. If it stops blooming, divide bulbs while dormant.

Sparaxis tricolor
HARLEQUIN FLOWER
☼ ◑◑   Z9–10 H10–7   ↕↔1ft (30cm)
Needing moisture during growth and spring bloom, it then can go dry. Combine with freesias and iris. If it fails to return and bloom, reduce crowding or shade.

MORE CHOICES

- *Amaryllis belladonna* z8–11 H12–7
- *Brodiaea elegans* z8–10 H10–8
- *Chasmanthe aethiopica* z9–11 H10–8
- *Crocosmia* x *crocosmiiflora* z7–11 H9–3
- *Freesia* 'Oberon' z9–11 H12–6
- *Freesia lactea* z9–11 H12–6
- *Homeria collina* z9–10 H10–9
- *Hyacinthoides hispanica* z5–10 H9–1
- *Ipheion uniflorum* z6–10 H9–6
- *Ixia* hybrids z10–11 H12–10
- *Oxalis obtusa* z9–10 H6–1

Triteleia hyacinthina
WHITE BRODIAEA
Ⓝ ☼ ◊ z4–10 H12–7
↕2ft (60cm) ↔1ft 30cm)
For open spaces and dry rock gardens, it grows with winter rains, blooming in spring. After fires, the previously dormant species carpet hillsides.

Watsonia 'Stanford Scarlet'
SCARLET WATSONIA
☼ ◗ z9–10 H10–9
↕3ft (1m) ↔6in (15cm)
An easy-to-grow South African corm. In mild climates, red, pink, lavender, or white (which may take over) spring blooms make big clumps, then die back. Cut dry foliage.

Babiana rubrocyanea
BABOON FLOWER
☼☼ ◗◗ z9–10 H12–10 ↕8in (20cm) ↔5in (13cm)
This South African corm needs water during growth and spring bloom. Liking well-drained soil with or without summer water, it is a carpet under open trees.

Tulipa bakeri 'Lilac Wonder'
LILAC WONDER TULIP
☼☼ ◊◊◗ z5–10 H8–1 ↕10in (25cm) ↔4in (10cm)
A wild tulip from the island of Crete, grow this in pots of potting mix, rock gardens, or poor, well-drained soil. It multiplies by runners, making little bulbs, and likes mild winters and hot summers.

HERBACEOUS PLANTS

Orchids for mild zones

In order to bloom, orchids need fertilizer, sunshine or very bright light, and constant moisture, but they must never be soggy. To protect them from slugs and snails, put one drop of liquid snail bait on the base of each bloom spike as soon as they emerge. Except for cascading or strongly upright types, stake your orchids to protect them against breakage.

Bletilla striata
CHINESE GROUND ORCHID
☀ ◊ ◑ ◑ Z7–10 H8–5 ↕↔2ft (60cm)
A hardy orchid for semishaded beds or pots. Water during growth and bloom. Spring and summer flowers last six weeks. Plant dormant, divide in early spring.

Coelogyne cristata
ANGEL ORCHID
☀ ◑ Z10–11 H12–6 ↕↔2ft (60cm)
With a fragrant winter bloom, it thrives outdoors with cybidiums, and is less fussy about temperature (but no wind). Can plant in hanging baskets in filtered shade.

Epidendrum x *obrienianum*
REED ORCHID
☀ ◑◑ Z9–12 H12–9 ↕↔2ft (60cm)
Easy in well-drained soil or large pots of bark, stick prunings in the pot or ground. Fertilize with 15-15-15. East-facing sun is perfect. Other heights and colors.

Cymbidium hookerianum
HOOKER'S CYMBIDIUM
☀ ◑ Z9–11 H12–6 ↕↔4ft (1.2m)
Used by hybridizers, a range of colors and sizes are sold. Choose those with flowers held above the foliage, not hidden in it. Grow cascading types in baskets.

Cattleya aurantiaca
SMALL-FLOWERED CATTLEYA
☀ ◑ Z10–12 H12–10 ↕↔1ft (30cm)
Easy to grow at 60–90°F (15–32°C) in wood baskets or slabs of bark naturalized into open trees. Blooms young; old plants may bear ten flowers. Many colors.

MORE CHOICES

- *Cymbidium* Strathbraan Z9–11 H12–6
- *Dendrobium* Spiral Gem 'Universal Topaz' Z10–12 H12–1
- *Laelia anceps* Z10–12 H12–6
- *Oncidium cavendishianum* Z10–11 H12–1
- *Sobralia macrantha* Z10–12 H12–1

Daffodils for mild zones

Daffodils are hardy, spring-blooming bulbs, surviving freezing winters in the ground and blooming naturally in spring. They can also be planted in Mediterranean climates in pots or the ground, blooming in spring with no pre-chilling. Most varieties, however, will only flower the first year. Fortunately, those listed here are exceptions: they naturalize in mild zones.

Narcissus 'February Gold'
FEBRUARY GOLD DAFFODIL
☼ ☼ ● Z6–10 H9–1 ‡1ft (30cm) ↔5in (13cm)
A small-flowered variety to grow in a short, cool- or warm-season lawn. It will form big drifts flowering in late winter in Bermuda grass cut short under tall trees.

Narcissus 'Fortune'
FORTUNE DAFFODIL
☼ ● Z4–10 H9–1 ‡18in (45cm) ↔8in (20cm)
A large-cupped daffodil to plant in pots or the ground. Keep pots moist, dark, and cool after planting until sprouts are 4in (10cm); then give bright light and sunshine for bloom. Flowers face sun.

Narcissus 'Cragford'
CRAGFORD DAFFODIL
☼ ☼ ● Z4–10 H9–1
‡20in (50cm)
↔6in (15cm)
For the ground or forcing in water indoors: layer in a bowl a little charcoal, pebbles, bulbs, more pebbles, and water. Keep dark until 4in (10cm), then give it sun.

Narcissus 'Ice Follies'
ICE FOLLIES DAFFODIL
☼ ● Z4–10 H9–1 ‡18in (45cm) ↔8in (20cm)
A large-cupped daffodil for the ground or pots. After pot plants have bloomed, transplant into a hole in a flower bed and fertilize for possible bloom next year.

Narcissus 'Grand Soleil d'Or'
GRAND SOLEIL D'OR DAFFODIL
☼ ☼ ● ● Z8–10 H9–7 ‡18in (45cm) ↔1ft (30cm)
Easy to grow, it returns annually in big fragrant drifts. Long-blooming fall to spring in mild zones, underplant beds for winter color when other blooms are gone.

MORE CHOICES

- *Narcissus* 'Avalanche' z5–10 H9–1
- *Narcissus* 'Geranium' z8–10 H9–1
- *Narcissus* 'Minnow' z8–10 H9–1
- *Narcissus papyraceus* z8–10 H9–7
- *Narcissus* 'Trevithian' z4–10 H9–1
- *Narcissus* 'Yellow Cheerfulness' z5–10 H9–1

Aquatic plants

In hot sunny climates, ornamental ponds need to be large enough to prevent the water from becoming too warm. Most of the plants listed here will shade the water's surface or help aerate it. Some aquatics live underwater, while others float on top. Most bear leaves and flowers above the water's surface, and grow from roots fully submerged in pots of soil.

Cabomba caroliniana
CAROLINA WATER SHIELD

Ⓝ ☼ ● Z8–11 H12–6
↕12ft (4m) ↔6ft (2m)
A submerged weed partially above the surface with feathery foliage bearing flowers. It emits tiny bubbles of oxygen and fish hide in it.

Ranunculus aquatilis
WATER CROWFOOT

☼ ● Z5–8 H8–5 ↕8in (20cm) ↔1ft (30cm)
A floating and rooting plant with floating leaves and flowers. Roots need to be submerged deeper than 3ft (1m) in order for the stems to bear oxygenating, threadlike underwater leaves.

Marsilea quadrifolia
WATER CLOVER

☼ ☀ ● Z9–11 H12–9
↕6in (15cm) ↔1ft (30cm)
A hardy creeping fern with clover-like leaves, floating on or growing thickly above water on thin stems from a submerged pot; it becomes terrestrial on surrounding ground.

Myriophyllum aquaticum
DIAMOND MILFOIL

☼ ● Z10–12 H12–6 ↕6in (15cm) ↔12ft (4m)
This oxygenating pond weed grows partially above the surface, partially below it. Grow in pots submerged 6in (15cm). Invasive in bogs. Young fish hide in stems.

Pontederia cordata
PICKEREL WEED

Ⓝ ☼ ☀ ● Z3–11 H12–1
↕4ft (1.2m) ↔30in (75cm)
A pond-edge plant blooming spring to fall, it is good for a tub water garden too. Plant in a pot submerged up to 5in (13cm); it needs division when crowded.

Nymphaea tetragona
PYGMY WATERLILY

☼ ◐ Z7–10 H12–1 ↕↔16in (40cm)

Hardy, slightly fragrant flowers float on water, or rise slightly above it. The right size for a small water garden, it must have sun to bloom.

Nymphaea 'Panama Pacific'
PANAMA PACIFIC WATERLILY

☼ ☼ ◐ Z10–12 H12–1 ↕16in (40cm) ↔3ft (1m)

A tropical, day-blooming waterlily suitable for containers. Tropical lilies are more difficult to grow than hardy ones, but wherever oranges grow, tropical lilies will survive.

Nymphaea odorata 'Sulfurea Grandiflora'
AMERICAN WHITE WATERLILY

Ⓝ ☼ ◐ Z3–11 H12–1 ↕16in (40cm) ↔8in (20cm)

Hardy fragrant flowers appear above water or float open in daytime. Grow from a submerged container for shade for pond water. Fertilize annually in spring.

MORE CHOICES

- *Eichhornia crassipes* Z9–12 H12–1
- *Hottonia palustris* Z6–9 H12–4
- *Nelumbo lutea* Z6–11 H12–1
- *Nelumbo nucifera* 'Alba Grandiflora' Z8–12 H12–3
- *Nelumbo nucifera* 'Speciosum' Z8–12 H12–3
- *Nymphaea capensis* Z9–11 H12–1
- *Sagittaria sinensis* Z4–11 H12–3

Trapa natans
WATER CHESTNUT

☼ ◐ Z5–10 H12–1 ↔indefinite

A floating plant grown in shallow water with a muddy bottom in a protected position, or contain invasive roots in pots. In warm climates, it bears large, black spiny seeds, traditionally used in Chinese cooking.

Petasites japonicus
FUKI

☼ ☼ ☼ ◐ Z5–10 H9–5 ↕3ft (1m) ↔5ft (1.5m)

A hardy accent, grow at pond edges in a container, otherwise rhizomatous roots are invasive. Yellow flowers on tall stalks are beloved by flower arrangers and appear before large leaves emerge.

Perennials for shallow water

Some water and bog plants have grasslike foliage, including water iris and many rushes and sedges. Sedges can be distinguished from grasses by their solid triangular stems, while rushes have round segmented stems topped by brown flowers. If you live near wetlands, choose non-invasive plants with seeds that are not spread by wind or birds.

Cyperus papyrus
PAPYRUS
☼ ☼ ● Z10–12 H12–6
↕10ft (3m) ↔4ft (1.2m)
A historic African sedge for ponds and flower arrangers. Short bunches of leaves send up tall stems with round broomlike heads that curl gracefully outward as they mature.

Iris pseudacorus
YELLOW FLAG
☼ ☼ ● pH Z5–10 H8–3 ↕5ft (1.5m) ↔3ft (1m)
A hardy, European streamside plant with floating seeds responsible for its worldwide spread. Easy to grow in garden ponds, do not plant in natural running water.

Iris laevigata
JAPANESE WATER IRIS
☼ ● pH Z4–10 H9–1 ↕3ft (1m) ↔18in (30cm)
A hardy bog plant, it blooms after the bearded iris. Grow in pots immersed on pond edges. A variegated variety is interesting even when out of bloom.

Juncus effusus 'Spiralis'
CORKSCREW RUSH
☼ ☼ ● Z4–10 H9–6 ↕↔30in (75cm)
Spiraling stems like corkscrews cascade outward above a submerged pot. Use in straight-sided ponds with modern architecture like white walls, plate glass.

Schoenoplectus lacustris
subsp. tabernaemontani 'Zebrinus'
ZEBRA RUSH
☼ ☼ ● Z4–10 H9–6 ↕↔4ft (1.2m)
Hollow stems grow straight up and look best when confined in a pot. Place close to the water's edge to permit grooming.

MORE CHOICES

- *Bacopa monnieri* Z8–12 H10–8
- *Chondropetalum tectorum* Z8–10 H10–8
- *Cyperus papyrus* 'Nanus' Z10–12 H12–6
- *Equisetum hyemale* Z5–10 H12–1
- *Iris brevicaulis* Z6–9 H9–5
- *Iris ensata* Z4–10 H9–1
- *Iris versicolor* Z3–10 H9–1
- *Iris virginica* Z4–9 H10–7
- *Juncus* 'Carman's Japan' Z7–10 H9–1
- *Scirpoides holoschoenus* Z6–10 H9–6

Acorus calamus 'Variegatus'
SWEET FLAG

☼ ☼ ◐ ● Z3–10 H12–2 ↕5ft (1.5m) ↔2ft (60cm)

A hardy philodendron relative with similar flowers used in arrangements. Its rhizomes and foliage are fragrant when bruised. Plants die to ground in winter.

Carex elata 'Aurea'
BOWLES' GOLDEN SEDGE

☼ ☼ ● pH Z3–10 H9–3
↕30in (70cm) ↔18in (45cm)

An evergreen clump, like a head of bright yellow hair, this is easy to grow in shallow water or wet ground and likes acid soil but can grow in any. Transplant and divide in spring or fall.

Thalia dealbata
POWDERY ALLIGATOR FLAG

Ⓝ ☼ ● Z9–10 H12–6
↕10ft (3m) ↔6ft (2m)

Arrow-shaped, gray-green leaves have straight-stemmed, spiky blue flowers. Hardy in unfrozen water, use it in a submerged container, in shallow water, or on the pond's edge. Groom often.

Colocasia esculenta 'Fontanesii'
BLACK STEM TARO

☼ ☼ ● Z10–12 H12–8
↕8ft (2.5m) ↔5ft (1.5m)

Arriving in Hawaii with Polynesians, this has edible starchy roots and papaya-scented, 1ft (30cm), yellow flowers in warmest climates. Dies to ground at 30°F (-1°C); lift in winter in cold parts of range.

Caltha palustris
MARSH MARIGOLD

Ⓝ ☼ ☼ ☼ ● Z3–8 H7–1
↕↔2ft (60cm)

Hardy from the northern US into Alaska, plant seeds or divisions in boggy soil, or a slightly submerged container. Used by ancient Americans as food, the greens are poisonous if not cooked several times.

HERBACEOUS PLANTS

Native perennials for desert gardens

Since the advent of air conditioning, more people have moved into hot interior and desert climates, where they find themselves forced to learn an entirely new way of gardening. These native plants can bring the desert atmosphere to your front door. Plant several species of penstemons from seeds in fall or as mature plants in spring. Provide sharp drainage.

Penstemon ambiguus
BUSH PENSTEMON
Ⓝ ☼ ☼ ◊ ◑ Z4–10 H9–1 ↕↔2ft (60cm)
Waves of bloom from early summer to early fall need a little shade in hottest zones and irrigation when rains are not adequate. For sandy soil in a high desert.

Penstemon pseudospectabilis
DESERT PENSTEMON
Ⓝ ☼ ☼ ◊ ◑ Z5–10 H9–5 ↕4ft (1.2m) ↔3ft (1m)
Native to desert washes, canyons, and slopes at moderate elevations, it can take some water to extend bloom if deadheaded. Clean up after spring bloom.

Oenothera caespitosa
WHITE EVENING PRIMROSE
Ⓝ ☼ ☼ ◊ ◑ Z4–10 H8–1 ↕↔8in (20cm)
Gray rounded foliage with a spring to fall bloom opening evenings, mostly in spring and early summer. Blooms more if irrigated twice a month in summer.

Penstemon palmeri
SCENTED PENSTEMON
Ⓝ ☼ ◊ ◑ Z7–10 H12–1 ↕6ft (2m) ↔3ft (1m)
Tall, fragrant spring flowers appear into summer after rain. This thrives in hot dry places but must have gravelly soil and sharp drainage; it dies in rich soil.

Zinnia grandiflora
MOUNTAIN ZINNIA
Ⓝ ☼ ◑ Z7–10 H12–1
↕↔1ft (30cm)
Tidy, low-mound blooms appear May through October after rains or irrigations. Shear off spent flowers. This works well in flowerbeds, spreads by rhizomes, and controls erosion on banks.

Zinnia acerosa
DESERT ZINNIA
Ⓝ ☼ ◑ Z7–10 H12–1 ↕10in (25cm) ↔2ft (60cm)
This has a profuse bloom spring and fall on thin hairy leaves, and a woody base and tap root. Needs excellent drainage: irrigate every two weeks in summer. Flowers turn papery tan.

MORE CHOICES

- *Argemone platyceras* Z8–11 H12–1
- *Bahia absinthifolia* Z9–11 H12–9
- *Hesperaloe parviflora* Z6–11 H12–6
- *Penstemon eatonii* Z4–10 H9–1
- *Thymophylla pentachaeta* Z8–10 H12–1
- *Verbena bipinnatifida* Z4–10 H7–1
- *Verbena goodingii* Z8–11 H12–8
- *Viguiera deltoidea* Z8–11 H12–10
- *Xylorhiza tortifolia* Z8–11 H12–2

Penstemon superbus
MEXICAN PENSTEMON

Ⓝ ☼ ◐ ◊ ◐ Z6–10 H9–6 ↕↔4ft (1.2m)

Handsome in desert gardens in well-drained soil, its
spring and early summer flowers bring hummingbirds.
It has gray foliage and will accept some summer water.

Melampodium leucanthum
BLACKFOOT DAISY

Ⓝ ☼ ◊ ◐ Z4–10 H9–1 ↕↔1ft (30cm)

A short-lived, long-blooming daisy on mounds, in rock
gardens, or near paths. Blooms all summer in desert if
irrigated, winter also in mild zones. Cut back in fall.

Sphaeralcea ambigua
APRICOT MALLOW

Ⓝ ☼ ◊ ◐ Z6–10 H12–8 ↕4ft (1.2m) ↔3ft (1m)

A rare color scheme, this is naturally well-groomed,
blooming in summer and fall with some irrigation.
Without water, it is summer deciduous in low deserts.

HERBACEOUS PLANTS

Perennials for use near swimming pools

The best plants for growing near swimming pools are clean, easy to care for, and attractive year round, especially in summer. Preferably, they should have leaves that stay on the plant until clipped off but no spines that might injure swimmers or flowers known to attract bees. Tropical plants work well in shade, but drought-resistant schemes are best in full sun.

Aspidistra elatior 'Varigeata'
VARIEGATED CAST IRON PLANT
☀ ☀ ◑ ● Z9–12 H12–1 ‡30in (75cm) ↔2ft (60cm)
Needs light sun or reflection to keep leaves variegated. Drought-resistant, reverts to green in rich soil. Spread earthworm castings to keep weevils from ruining foliage.

Dianella tasmanica
FLAX LILY
☀ ◑ ● Z9–12 H12–10 ‡4ft (1.2m) ↔3ft (1m)
Grasslike clumps of leaves, flower stems in spring and summer followed by two or more months of turquoise-blue berries, excellent cut; beware of staining carpets.

Epidendrum ibaguense
TERRESTRIAL ORCHID
☀ ◑ ● Z9–12 H12–6 ‡4ft (1.2m) ↔3ft (1m)
Many colors available. Plant in well-drained soil, east-facing or shaded south-facing raised bed. Arrange colors in bands like rainbow.

MORE CHOICES

- *Agapanthus* 'Snowy Owl' Z8–10 H10–8
- *Alstroemeria* Meyer Hybrids Z9–10 H12–7
- *Anigozanthos* Bush Gem Hybrids Z9–11 H12–10
- *Artemisia schmidtiana* 'Nana' Z5–10 H8–5
- *Canna* 'Tropical Rose' Z7–11 H12–1
- *Dierama pulcherrimum* Z8–10 H10–8
- *Gazania rigens* 'Sunglow' Z8–11 H12–1
- *Hedychium coccineum* Z8–10 H10–8
- *Hedychium gardnerianum* Z8–10 H12–9
- *Strelitzia reginae* Z9–12 H12–1
- *Zoysia tenuifolia* Z8–11 H12–8

Scaevola aemula 'Blue Wonder'
BLUE WONDER SCAEVOLA

☼ ◊◐ Z9–11 H12–1 ‡8in (20cm) ↔3ft (1m)

Clean, constant bloom. Use to fill a big pot next to pool. Spills flowers to ground but needs daily watering, monthly slow-release 14-14-14. Clip back tips.

Kniphofia uvaria
RED-HOT POKER

☼ ☼ ◊◐ Z5–9 H9–1 ‡4ft (1.2m) ↔2ft (60cm)

Plant in raised bed, on banks with excellent drainage, back from walks; foliage can be abrasive. Needs much water during growth and bloom. Flowers bring hummingbirds. Not successful near the coast.

Liriope spicata
CREEPING LILYTURF

☼ ☼ ◐ Z6–11 H12–1 ‡10in (25cm) ↔3ft (1m)

Hardy groundcover. Mow in early spring just before new growth begins. Then fertilize with lawn food. Control in raised bed; spreads slowly by rhizomes. Use with taller plants.

Hesperaloe parviflora
RED YUCCA

Ⓝ ☼ ◊◐ Z6–11 H12–6 ‡↔4ft (1.2m)

Grasslike clump sends up statuesque spikes of bloom several times a year. Summer monsoons in Southwest encourage successive flowering, bring hummingbirds.

Phormium tenax
NEW ZEALAND FLAX

☼ ☼ ◊◐◑ Z9–11 H12–6 ‡12ft (4m) ↔6ft (2m)

Hardy accent for dry, sunny bank or bed, back from paths. Many sizes and colors, attractive in light. Tall, statuesque flower spikes in summer.

Santolina chamaecyparissus
LAVENDER COTTON

☼ ◊◐ Z6–10 H9–4 ‡2ft (60cm) ↔3ft (1m)

For dry, sunny slopes, raised beds with good drainage. After flowers fade, shear into neat dome. Fragrant foliage. To renew: cut to 6 in (15cm) in earliest spring.

HERBACEOUS PLANTS

Pink drought-resistant perennials

Red, white, and blue is a patriotic color scheme, but try switching the red to pink, and adding yellow. This will leave you with the "spring colors": pink, white, blue, and yellow. You can even splash in a little lavender. You will never go wrong with this scheme: it is soft and pretty in sun or shade, in pots or the ground. Keep orange away, however, as it spoils the effect.

Liatris spicata
DENSE GAYFEATHER

Ⓝ ☼ ◐◑ Z4–9 H9–1 ↕4ft (1.2m) ↔18in (45cm)
Drought-resistant, like *L. punctata*, the best known variety, *L. spicata* 'Kobold', needs irrigation. Grow from bulbs or tuberous roots. All need a cold winter.

Chrysanthemum 'Clara Curtis'
CLARA CURTIS CHRYSANTHEMUM

☼ ☼ ◐◑ Z5–9 H9–1 ↕30in (75cm) ↔2ft (60cm)
For borders, with a late summer and fall bloom. Resistant to pests, diseases, and heat, this is also known as *Dendranthema* 'Clara Curtis'.

Oenothera speciosa
MEXICAN EVENING PRIMROSE

Ⓝ ☼ ☼ ◐◑ Z5–10 H8–1 ↕30in (75cm) ↔2ft (60cm)
Tough – taking heat, drought, and neglect – but invasive. Improved selections are deeper pink with slightly larger flowers and easier to control.

MORE CHOICES

- *Armeria* 'Bee's Ruby' Z5–10 H9–4
- *Gypsophila paniculata* 'Pink Fairy' Z4–9 H9–1
- *Pelargonium* 'Clorinda' Z9–11 H12–1
- *Phlox subulata* 'Marjorie' Z3–9 H8–1
- *Sedum spectabile* 'Brilliant' Z4–9 H9–1

Gaura lindheimeri 'Siskiyou Pink'
SISKIYOU PINK WHIRLING BUTTERFLIES

Ⓝ ☼ ◐ Z6–10 H9–6 ↕4ft (1.2m) ↔3ft (1m)
An improvement over the white variety, this is more compact, less invasive, and blends beautifully with *Achillea* 'Coronation Gold' and *Lavandula dentata*.

Red or purple drought-resistant perennials

Red is the symbol of life and strength, and purple is a cooled red. In China, red means luck and longevity, while red roses stand for love and fidelity. "Put a little red in every painting," an artist once advised. "It will tie everything together." The same is true in the garden. Red is an ingredient of sun colors, and will enliven spring shades if used in moderation.

Alcea rosea 'Nigra'
BLACK HOLLYHOCK
☼ ◐ ◊ ◊ Z3–10 H10–3 ↕6ft (2m) ↔3ft (1m)
An old-fashioned, Mediterranean cottage-garden plant. Black flowers fade to reddish purple in heat. Protect from snails. A tasteful choice against an adobe wall.

Dianthus chinensis 'Telstar Crimson'
CHINESE PINK
☼ ☼ ◊ ◊ Z9–11 H12–1 ↕14in (35cm) ↔8in (20cm)
A modern compact mound, smothered with spring bloom in mild zones, summer elsewhere. In mild-winter zones, plant seeds in flats in August, out in October.

MORE CHOICES

- *Aster novi-belgii* 'Crimson Brocade' Z4–9 H8–1
- *Bergenia* 'Abendglut' Z6–10 H9–6
- *Galvezia speciosa* 'Firecracker' Z8–11 H12–8
- *Papaver orientale* 'Allegro' Z4–9 H9–1
- *Tanacetum coccineum* 'Robinson's Red' Z5–10 H9–5

Salvia greggii 'Sierra Linda'
AUTUMN SAGE
Ⓝ ☼ ☼ ◊ ◊ ◊ Z7–10 H9–7 ↕↔4ft (1.2m)
A tidy shrubby mound, this blooms summer through fall, bringing hummingbirds. Cut off spent flowers and cut back in early spring before growth begins.

Penstemon eatonii
FIRECRACKER PENSTEMON
Ⓝ ☼ ☼ ◊ Z4–10 H9–1 ↕↔3ft (1m)
From higher elevations and deserts with heat-loving flower spikes above gray foliage, this needs drainage. It blooms spring into summer with a little water.

Yellow drought-resistant perennials

Yellow enhances alertness, decisiveness, and optimism. It is the color of sunshine, waking you up in the morning with light waves that stimulate the brain. A color scheme mixing yellows with shades of red and orange could be called the "sun colors," all the colors of sunshine. Add blue for sky and plenty of white for clouds – the result will be a bright and cheerful look.

HERBACEOUS PLANTS

Psilotrophe cooperi
PAPER DAISY
Ⓝ ☼ ◊◑ Z8–10 H12–10
↕1ft (30cm) ↔18in (45cm)
On a desert floor these are brightly lit morning or evening, as if light comes from within, and smothered in flowers after rains, March through October. Foliage is gray. Water occasionally.

Helianthus x *multiflorus* 'Flore Pleno'
DOUBLE-FLOWERED PERENNIAL SUNFLOWER
☼ ◑◑ Z5–10 H9–5 ↕5ft (1.5m) ↔3ft (1m)
Heat-resistant with six weeks of dahlia-like summer flowers on a rounded plant, this takes dryness in Oklahoma, Texas, and New Mexico, with summer rain; water if stressed.

Centaurea macrocephala
GIANT KNAPWEED
☼ ◑ Z3–10 H7–1 ↕4ft (1.2m) ↔2ft (60cm)
Combine this massive plant with blue salvias. It is easy to grow in back of bed. A long season of huge flower buds like artichokes does not repeat. Good cut flower.

Achillea 'Coronation Gold'
CORONATION GOLD YARROW
☼ ◊◑ Z3–10 H9–1 ↕3ft (1m) ↔2ft (60cm)
A vigorous hybrid and good cut flower, fresh or dry. Blooms stand upright without staking. Long-lasting in bright sun, mix with echinops, nepeta, and pink gaura.

MORE CHOICES

- *Baileya multiradiata* Z6–10 H9–6
- *Calylophus hartweggi* 'Sierra Sun Drop' Z3–10 H8–1
- *Cleome isomeris* H9–1
- *Coreopsis grandiflora* 'Early Sunrise' Z3–10 H9–1

Orange drought-resistant perennials

A garden without a splash of orange might be boring, but orange should be used with a careful hand. It sings with silver, gray, or lavender but clashes with pink. According to Chinese tradition, orange strengthens the immune system and wards off allergies. In India, orange stands for creativity and energy. It is said to encourage impulses of love and wisdom.

Kniphofia 'Bees' Sunset'
RED-HOT POKER
☼ ☀ ◊ ● Z6–9 H9–6 ↕3ft (1m) ↔4ft (1.2m)
Toothed grasslike leaves with a summer bloom, it needs water during growth and flowering, is well adapted to monsoon areas but must have drainage.

Alstroemeria aurea
PERUVIAN LILY
☼ ☀ ◊ ● ● Z7–10 H10–7 ↕4ft (1.2m) ↔1ft (30cm)
Extremely invasive with a massive June bloom, this is unforgettable in big drifts. In mild zones, it is largely replaced by non-invasive hybrids, blooming year round. 'Tricolor' has no seeds.

Lychnis chalcedonica
MALTESE CROSS
☼ ☀ ● Z4–9 H8–1
↕3ft (1m) ↔1ft (30cm)
With flaming orange-scarlet spring or summer bloom, this is a Russian, long-lived, upright plant. Cut to one foot after flowers fade for fall bloom. Full sun in mild zones.

Justicia spicigera
MEXICAN HONEYSUCKLE
☼ ☀ ◊ ● ● Z8–10 H12–10
↕5ft (1.5m) ↔4ft (1.2m)
This dependable, heat-resistant, shrublike evergreen is beloved by hummingbirds and has small flower clusters year round but mostly in spring and fall.

Leonotis leonurus
LION'S TAIL
☼ ● Z9–12 H12–6 ↕↔6ft (2m)
Heat-tolerant with a non-stop bloom. Cut faded stems and cut back old plants one-third at a time. If frost hits, cut off dead parts when growth resumes in spring.

MORE CHOICES

- *Anisacanthus quadrifidus* Z9–10 H10–9
- *Gaillardia* x *grandiflora* Z3–10 H8–1
- *Gazania rigens* 'Sunburst' Z8–11 H12–1
- *Heuchera* x *brizoides* Z4–10 H8–1
- *Sphaeralcea munroana* Z4–10 H12–8

Blue or lavender drought-resistant perennials

Blue gives the impression of space and distance and blends well with all other colors, toning down the hot shades. Scientific studies have even shown that blue triggers the release of melatonin, aiding relaxation and sound sleep. Violet is similarly cooling; it relieves tension. Meanwhile, lavender mixes well with soft spring shades and is an excellent foil for orange.

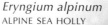

Convolvulus sabatius
GROUND MORNING GLORY
☼ ☀ ◑ Z7–10 H9–7
↕30in (75cm) ↔3ft (1m)
A Mediterranean plant, recently improved with bigger spring to fall flowers and more bloom. Plant with tough pink roses and white alyssum in a Mediterranean-style landscape.

Eryngium alpinum
ALPINE SEA HOLLY
☼ ☀ ◑ Z6–10 H9–6
↕30in (75cm) ↔18in (45cm)
Charming, drought-resistant, and self-sowing, this blooms in spring, summer, or fall. Its silvery blue foliage lights up in the morning and evening sun. Plant seeds in fall.

Centaurea montana
MOUNTAIN BLUET
☼ ◑ Z3–9 H9–1 ↕18in (45cm) ↔2ft (60cm)
Native to European mountains, which gives a hint as to where it will grow. Blooms late winter and early spring. Irrigate in dry zones. Vigorous and informal, this self-seeds under shrubs. Spread snail bait.

Campanula persicifolia
'Telham Beauty'
PEACH-LEAVED BLUEBELL
☼ ☀ ◑◑ Z3–10 H8–1
↕3ft (1m) ↔1ft (30cm)
Easy to grow from spring-planted seeds in most zones, it may bloom the first year in mild zones if planted in fall or late summer.

MORE CHOICES

- *Echinops ritro* 'Veitch's Blue'
  Z3–9 H12–1
- *Felicia amelloides* Z9–12 H12–1
- *Nierembergia hippomanica*
  Z7–11 H12–7
- *Perovskia atriplicifolia* 'Blue Spire'
  Z6–10 H9–6
- *Platycodon grandiflorus* Z4–9 H9–1

White or silver drought-resistant perennials

White massed next to bright or subtle hues acts like a frame around a picture, showing off good color combinations. Plant white flowers next to patios and you can see them at night. Keep in mind that white comes in many shades. Pure white flowers can make the creamy ones look dull, so separate the two groups with blue so the difference does not show.

Yucca filamentosa 'Color Guard'
VARIEGATED ADAM'S NEEDLE
Ⓝ ☼ ◊ Z6–10 H12–5 ↕30in (75cm) ↔5ft (1.5m)
A southeastern plant that provides much summer bloom with little water but needs good drainage. Do not plant near paths.
Y. wipplei needs no irrigation.

Cerastium tomentosum
SNOW IN SUMMER
☼ ☼ ◊◊ Z7–10 H7–1 ↕8in (20cm) ↔3ft (1m)
This may begin dying after several years. In November, pull all plants out, dig and amend the soil, and replant from flats. Apply granulated fertilizer in March.

Agapanthus praecox subsp. *orientalis* 'Albus'
WHITE LILY OF THE NILE
☼ ☼ ◊◊◊ Z9–12 H12–7
↕5ft (1.5m) ↔30in (75cm)
Summer bloom, any soil. Semishade in hottest zones. Drought tolerant. Store indoors during snowy winters.

Dictamnus albus 'Albiflorus'
GAS PLANT
☼ ☼ ◊◊ Z3–9 H8–1 ↕4ft (1.2m) ↔3ft (1m)
Wear gloves when planting this as the lemon-scented foliage may cause a rash. Do not divide – big clumps look best. Fragrance sparks at night if lit with a match.

MORE CHOICES

- *Asclepias linearis* Z3–9 H8–1
- *Convolvulus boissieri* Z7–10 H10–7
- *Leucanthemum vulgare* 'May Queen' Z3–10 H8–1
- *Lychnis coronaria* 'Alba' Z3–10 H8–1
- *Melampodium leucanthum* Z4–10 H9–1
- *Romneya* 'White Cloud' Z8–10 H9–2

HERBACEOUS PLANTS

Perennials for year-round bloom

In mild-winter climates, some perennials originating in tropical or subtropical climates may bloom year round – specifically, those whose bloom is not triggered by day-length. With these plants, the question arises: when is the right time to prune? The answer is that most could use a little pruning all through the year to keep them compact and encourage constant flowers.

Hemerocallis 'Happy Returns'
HAPPY RETURNS DAYLILY
☼ ☼ ● Z5–11 H12–1 ‡2ft (60cm) ↔3ft (1m)
Cut off spent stems and feed in spring. This may get daylily rust in some areas. Replace damaged plants with rust-resistant varieties. It remounts throughout spring, summer, and fall.

Nemesia caerulea 'Blue Bird'
BLUE BIRD NEMESIA
☼ ☼ ● Z9–10 H10–9 ‡2ft (60cm) ↔1ft (30cm)
Long-blooming in mild climates, the stems grow long and fall down, always with flowers on tips. Clip some back frequently to keep it more compact and feed.

Begonia 'Richmondensis'
RICHMONDENSIA BEGONIA
☼ ☼ ●● Z9–11 H12–1 ‡2ft (60cm) ↔4ft (1.2m)
Tropical from cool mountainsides, in mild zones, cut back old stems in fall or spring to new growth. An entire new plant, already blooming, arises from the ground, big tubs, or pots.

Gaura 'Perky Pink'
PINK WHIRLING BUTTERFLIES
Ⓝ ☼ ●● Z6–10 H9–2
‡30in (75cm) ↔2ft (60cm)
Long-blooming and compact with large flowers and dark foliage, this brings hummingbirds and butterflies. After lots of stems have bloomed, cut off handfuls.

Sutera cordata 'Snowflake'
SNOWFLAKE BACOPA
☼ ☼ ● Z9–12 H12–6 ‡8in (20cm) ↔4ft (1.2m)
Grow in a hanging basket with half shade only in the hottest climates. It dies without constant moisture and food. Lift up and cut dead growth from underneath.

Pennisetum setaceum 'Rubrum'
PURPLE FOUNTAIN GRASS
☼ ☼ ◊◗ z9–12 H12–8 ↕↔5ft (1.5m)
Beautiful when grown well, not when old growth mixes with new. Cut old plant to ground and apply lawn food. New growth begins from ground with first fall rain.

Streptocarpella saxorum 'Concord Blue'
CONCORD BLUE STREPTOCARPELLA
☼ ☼ ◊◗ z10–11 H12–1 ↕6in (15cm) ↔2ft (60cm)
Cascading from a basket or pot, this needs little pruning. Fertilize with 1tbsp (15ml) 14-14-14 slow-release pellets on top of soil monthly. Water daily.

Heliotropium arborescens
COMMON HELIOTROPE
☼ ☼ ◗ z9–12 H12–9 ↕4ft (1.2m) ↔2ft (60cm)
Beloved for its sweet fragrance, this grows big and shrubby. Plant in a flowerbed by a lawn in good drainage. Sprinklers can discolor foliage or flowers. Clip off all damaged parts.

Pentas lanceolata
STAR CLUSTER
☼ ☼ ◗ z9–11 H12–1 ↕↔3ft (1m)
Constant white, pink, or red blooms appear on outside of plant, which is much bigger in Hawaii. Cut this back lightly year round to keep neat and compact.

Pelargonium Multibloom Series
GARDEN GERANIUM
☼ ☼ ◊◗ z9–11 H12–1 ↕↔2ft (60cm)
Heat-resistant, self-cleaning for bedding. New varieties bloom in summer in many climates, winter in desert. Pinch, feed, and control budworms with Bt.

MORE CHOICES

- *Begonia* 'Bubbles' z9–11 H12–1
- *Heliotropium arborescens* 'Marine' z9–12 H12–1
- *Pelargonium peltatum* 'Pink Blizzard' z10–11 H12–1

HERBACEOUS PLANTS

Annuals for cut flowers

The best annual cut flowers are long-stemmed, long-lasting, quick to re-bloom, and easy to grow from seeds. Cut them in early morning, selecting those just opening. Then stand them in water and re-cut their stems underwater. To keep the vase water clear and the flowers fresh longer, mix one-half teaspoon of bleach into each quart of water before adding flowers.

Zinnia elegans 'Benary's Giant'
BENARY'S GIANT ZINNIA
☼ ● Z8–11 H12–1
↕4ft (1.2m) ↔2ft (60cm)
A variety developed for the cut-flower industry with strong cutting stems and no mildew. Plant seeds in warm weather as late as May. This is sometimes sold as 'Parks Picks'.

Psylliostachys suworowii
PINK POKERS
☼ ◐● Z6–10 H12–6 ↕18in (45cm) ↔1ft (30cm)
Sow seeds in early spring, thin according to package directions, and feed lightly. Tall thin spikes are covered with tiny everlasting flowers. Hang to dry or use fresh.

Mattholia incana 'Ten Weeks Trisomic'
GIANT STOCK
☼ ● Z6–10 H8–5 ↕↔4ft (1.2m)
Plant tall, cut-flower varieties in flats in early September. Keep moist and feed with fish emulsion. Nursery plants are not for cut flowers. Plant in well-drained soil in October.

Briza maxima
GREAT QUAKING GRASS
Ⓝ ☼ ◐● Z6–11 H12–1
↕2ft (60cm) ↔1ft (30cm)
Do not plant this invasive grass near wild lands. Sow in fall in mild zones, spring elsewhere, thin to 1ft (30cm). When grown, harvest all stems for dried and fresh arrangements.

Calendula officinalis 'Pacific Beauty'
POT MARIGOLD
☼ ◐ Z1–10 H6–1 ↕2ft (60cm) ↔18in (45cm)
Place each seed where you want it to grow. Do not bury seeds too deeply or they will not come up. Mix with wildflowers for early orange bloom.

MORE CHOICES

- *Celosia spicata* Flamingo Series Z10–11 H9–2
- *Lathyrus odoratus* 'Winter Elegance' Z9–10 H10–1
- *Matthiola* 'Mammoth Excelsior' Z8–9 H9–1
- *Scabiosa atropurpurea* Z10–11 H9–4

Perennials for cut flowers

Picking flowers is a type of pruning. As you cut these perennial blooms for the house and to share with friends, deadhead faded blooms at the same time to encourage re-blooming. In the case of cymbidiums, cutting does not increase bloom, but, given good year-round care, they will provide plenty of cut flowers and still have some left over for the winter display.

Cymbidium hybrids
CYMBIDIUM ORCHIDS

☼ ◐◑ Z9–11 H12–1 ↕4ft (1.2m) ↔3ft (1m)

This needs fertilizer and enough sun to turn its leaves yellow, plus a 20° range of temperatures in summer to bloom. Cut, this lasts six weeks in water.

Dahlia 'Bishop of Llandaff'
BISHOP OF LLANDAFF DAHLIA

☼ ☼ ◑ Z9–11 H12–5 ↕↔2ft (60cm)

A favorite variety, with dark bronze to purple foliage showing up well in beds. Dahlias need well-amended planting holes. Fill in as they grow and stake.

MORE CHOICES

- *Alstroemeria* 'Tricolor' Z9–10 H10–8
- *Aster pringlei* 'Monte Cassino' Z9–10 H8–1
- *Cymbidium* 'Santa Barbara White' Z9–11 H12–1
- *Leucanthemum* x *maximum* 'Snow Lady' Z5–10 H8–5
- *Trachelium caeruleum* Z9–11 H12–1

Limonium perezii
SEA LAVENDER

☼ ◐◑ Z10–11 H12–1 ↕↔3ft (1m)

Easy to grow in any soil in mild zones. Cut off faded flowers and feed occasionally to keep blooming. Shake old seeds heads over bare ground to sow more.

Gerbera jamesonii
TRANSVAAL DAISY

☼ ☼ ◐◑ Z8–11 H12–6 ↕18in (45cm) ↔8in (20cm)

Tricky in beds, its crown must never be covered, plants must dry between waterings, and mulch can rot them. Plant high in pots, water deeply, then dry out.

Perennials for English-style borders

An English-style, herbaceous border should have a good combination of colors and shapes, which change with the seasons in spring, summer, and fall. This can be a tough order in a hot dry climate, where temperatures soar for days in a row. It is better to bend the rules a bit and combine these perennials with heat-resistant flowering shrubs, roses, and climbers.

Aquilegia McKana Hybrids
MCKANA COLUMBINE
☼ ☼ ● Z3–10 H7–1
↕30in (75cm) ↔2ft (60cm)
An upright plant in many colors with spring bloom. Cut back after first bloom. This usually dies in summer; more arise from seeds, differing from parent. Transplant in fall.

Solidago 'Goldenmosa'
GOLDENROD
Ⓝ ☼ ☼ ● Z5–10 H9–5
↕30in (75cm) ↔18in (45cm)
Fall flowers erroneously thought to cause hay fever have a long bloom and stand up to heat. Mix with perovskia or blue asters.

Aurinia saxatilis
BASKET OF GOLD
☼ ☼ ● Z4–9 H8–1 ↕8in (20cm) ↔2ft (60cm)
Use in a rock garden, spilling over a low wall, or in front of dry border, with shade only in hottest zones. Not for coast. Drainage is essential. Cut back in fall.

Iris germanica
GERMAN IRIS
☼ ☼ ● ● Z4–10 H9–1 ↕↔4ft (1.2m)
A hardy and widely naturalized parent of many hybrids. This tough garden plant takes heat but needs afternoon shade in hottest zones. Divide in fall.

MORE CHOICES

- *Anthemis tinctoria* 'E. C. Buxton' Z4–10 H8–3
- *Callistephus chinensis* Ostrich Plume Series Z6–10 H9–1
- *Centaurea hypoleuca* 'John Coutts' Z5–9 H9–1
- *Delphinium* 'Pacific Hybrids' Z7–9 H6–1
- *Gypsophila paniculata* 'Bristol Fairy' Z4–10 H9–1
- *Linaria purpurea* 'Cannon J. Went' Z6–10 H8–5
- *Macleaya microcarpa* 'Kelway's Coral Plume' Z5–10 H9–1
- *Saponaria ocymoides* Z4–10 H8–1
- *Stachys byzantina* 'Silver Carpet' Z5–10 H8–1
- *Verbascum chaixii* 'Album' Z5–9 H9–5

Euphorbia polychroma
CUSHION SPURGE
☼ ☼ ◑ ◐ ◐ Z6–9 H9–5
↕18in (45cm) ↔2ft (60cm)
This rounded plant blooms midspring to midsummer. Short-lived but re-seeding, it is a good choice for rock gardens and needs well-drained soil and light shade in hottest zones.

Alchemilla mollis
LADY'S MANTLE
☼ ☼ ◐ Z4–9 H7–1 ↕2ft (60cm) ↔30in (75cm)
Chartreuse flowers and foliage are attractive next to gray walls, paths, and irises. As a groundcover, it brightens shade. Divide in February in mild zones. Not good for the coast.

Erysimum 'Bowles Mauve'
BOWLES MAUVE WALLFLOWER
☼ ☼ ◐ ◐ Z6–11 H8–5 ↕2ft (60cm) ↔6ft (2m)
A good filler with gray foliage that pops a flower on every tip year-round. Never cut back or it will die, though it will die anyway in three years.

Platycodon grandiflorus
BALLOON FLOWER
☼ ☼ ◐ Z4–10 H9–1
↕3ft (1m) ↔2ft (60cm)
Air-filled buds, like balloons, open to blue, pink, white, or purple flowers with purple veins and bloom from early to late summer. Deadhead to keep going. Deep fleshy roots.

Kniphofia 'Royal Standard'
ROYAL STANDARD RED-HOT POKER
☼ ◐ ◐ Z7–9 H9–4 ↕4ft (1.2m) ↔2ft (60cm)
This needs plenty of water during growth and bloom and is adapted to hot interior climates with summer rain and cold winters, not to dry summers and wet winters. Needs good drainage.

HERBACEOUS PLANTS

Annuals and perennials for herb gardens

When we speak of herb gardening, we are referring to plants used for medicine, flavoring, fragrance, or dyeing cloth. These fascinating plants have been treasured for thousands of years. Planting even a few of them will add history, mystique, and a healing atmosphere to your garden. Most grow well in dry climates. Only culinary herbs are used for food; a few should never be eaten.

Coriandrum sativum
CORIANDER, CILANTRO
☼ ☀ ◑ Z7–12 H10–1 ‡18in (45cm) ↔9in (22cm)
A winter annual that is an essential ingredient in Southwestern cooking. Plant from seeds or transplants above drip line in fall; comes back every year. Cut fresh leaves, or use dried seeds.

Tanacetum vulgare
COMMON TANSY
☼ ◑◑ Z4–10 H8–1 ‡36in (90cm) ↔18in (5cm)
Once used as medicine but not edible, with a strong odor. Clipping a piece on clothing is said to ward off insects. Rather invasive. Late summer bloom nice in herb gardens. Can be an ingredient of dried wreaths.

Stachys byzantina
LAMB'S EARS, WOOLLY BETONY
☼ ◑ Z5–10 H8–1 ‡18in (45cm) ↔24in (60cm)
Gray, softly felted leaves are the main attraction of this plant, beloved by children. Good drainage is essential. Nice in clumps on edge of decomposed-granite path, or sprouting in gravel terraces.

Dianthus 'Musgrave's Pink'
COTTAGE PINK
☼ ☀ ◑◑ Z5–10 H8–1
‡18in (45cm) ↔2ft (60cm)
Very fragrant spring flowers appear on this little perennial that is often treated as an annual. Plant in fall. Flowers are edible but only use the petals (base of flower is bitter).

HERBACEOUS PLANTS

Salvia elegans
PINEAPPLE SAGE

☼ ◆ Z8–11 H12–1 ‡6ft (2m) ↔3ft (1m)

Along with other salvias, this plant is often passed around by gardeners. Bright red flowers give tall color, spring to fall. Shear spent flowers three times each season. In spring, cut to new basal foliage (sprouting below). Pineapple-flavored leaves are good for garnish or iced tea.

Verbascum thapsus
DENSEFLOWER MULLEIN

☼ ◆ Z3–9 H9–1
‡4–6ft (1.2–2m) ↔18in (45cm)

Used since ancient times for dyeing cloth, plant this in fall for bloom the following year. Can rot if kept too wet. Once established, this comes back from seed.

Chamaemelum nobile
ROMAN CHAMOMILE

☼ ◑ ◆ Z5–10 H9–6
‡1ft (30cm) ↔3ftin (1m)

Plagued with sandy soil that dries out weekly, this charming filler reseeds freely and blooms nonstop in mild zones, even the desert. Cut back when blooms fade. Don't eat flowers or foliage – chamomile tea comes from another plant.

Mentha spicata
SPEARMINT

☼ ◑ ◆ Z5–10 H7–1
‡to 3ft (1m) ↔indefinite

A highly invasive, thirsty plant. Edible, light-blue flowers in summer. Pick leaves for flavoring drinks, desserts, or jellies. Grow in a container near a hose bib so watering is easy. Susceptible to whiteflies.

Artemisia dracunculus
TARRAGON

☼ ◆◆ Z6–10 H7–1
‡6ft (2m) ↔18in (45cm)

Although this is a perennial, it may not return another year but is worth fussing over in a pot. Leaves are great picked fresh to use in salad dressings, fish dishes, and sauces.

Anethum graveolens
DILL

☼ ◆ Z5–10 H12–1 ‡4ft (1.2m) ↔1ft (30cm)

Worth growing just for the swallowtail butterflies it brings, and a worthy candidate for vegetable gardens. Chop leaves to flavor sauce for salmon, cucumber salads, or tuna sandwiches. Use flowers in pickles or a garnish.

MORE CHOICES

- *Achillea millefolium* Z3–10 H9–1
- *Calendula officinalis* Z1–10 H6–1
- *Chenopodium ambrosioides* Z8–10 H8–1
- *Foeniculum vulgare* Z4–10 H9–1
- *Galium odoratum* Z5–10 H8–5
- *Petroselinum crispum* Z5–10 H9–1
- *Ruta graveolens* Z5–10 H9–5
- *Symphytum officinale* Z3–10 H9–1
- *Valeriana officinalis* Z4–10 H9–1

HERBACEOUS PLANTS

Annuals and perennials with edible flowers

Fifty years ago vegetable gardens were prosaic-looking places. Today vegetable gardens, particularly in the Southwest, are as ornamental as they are practical. For the most colorful appeal, do as the French and English do, and plant edible flowers among the crops. Picking flowers often for salads and garnishes keeps them blooming. Just be sure never to spray.

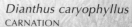

Dianthus caryophyllus
CARNATION
☼ ◑ Z7–10 H10–7
↕↔14in (35cm)
A flower beloved for its fragrance and the sweet clove flavor of its petals. Sometimes used as a garnish in fancy restaurants for sauces, tea, or sorbet. Before using petals, remove bitter white base.

Begonia 'Can Can'
CAN CAN TUBEROUS BEGONIA
☼ ◑ Z9–11 H12–1 ↕↔12in (30cm)
Tubers are dormant in winter, sprout in March, and flower in summer. For coastal zones, supply east-facing sun and afternoon shade. Let top half-inch of soil dry before watering. Petals have a citrus taste.

Bellis perennis
ENGLISH DAISY
☼ ☼ ◑ Z3–10 H8–1 ↕↔2–8in (5–20cm)
Many perennial or biennial varieties. Plant in early fall from seeds; flowers come the following year. Petals taste bitter and are more often used for garnish.

Chrysanthemum grandiflorum
FLORIST'S CHRYSANTHEMUM
☼ ◑ Z4–10 H9–1 ↕↔3ft (1m)
Pull petals from fall-blooming flowers you have grown (not store-bought, as they are sprayed). Cut off base of the petal, which is bitter, before using as a garnish surrounding a thick stew or on a salad.

Chrysanthemum coronarium
CROWN DAISY
☼ ◐◑◕ Z7–11 H12–1 ↕30in (75cm) ↔18in (45cm)
A perennial, naturalized in the Southwest. One type, called shungiku or chop suey greens, is edible. Use flowers as an ornamental garnish or remove petals and sprinkle on food. Cut off bitter base of petals.

Monarda didyma
BEE BALM, SWEET BERGAMOT

Ⓝ ☼ ◐ ◊ Z4–9 H10–1 ‡3ft (1m) ↔24in (60cm)

A perennial herb with a hot, sweet citrus flavor. Deadhead to keep blooming in summer and provide light shade in hottest zones. Brings hummingbirds.

Trifolium pratense
SCARLET CLOVER

☼ ◐ ◊ Z6–10 H9–6 ‡6in (15cm) ↔18in (45cm)

Sweet, chewable flowers can be chopped or used whole in salads, floated on cold soups, sautéed lightly and added to vegetables, or steeped for tea.

MORE CHOICES

- Allium schoenoprasum Z5–10 H9–1
- Allium tuberosum Z7–11 H8–1
- Calendula officinalis Z1–10 H6–1
- Chamaemelum nobile Z5–10 H9–6
- Helianthus annuus Z4–11 H12–1
- Hemerocallis 'Stella de Oro' Z3–9 H12–1
- Mentha spicata Z5–11 H7–1
- Salvia elegans Z8–11 H12–1
- Tagetes tenuifolia Z9–11 H12–1
- Tropaeolum majus Z8–11 H12–1
- Tulipa 'Fringed Elegance' Z5–10 H8–1
- Viola odorata Z6–10 H8–6
- Viola tricolor Z4–10 H12–1
- Viola x wittrockiana 'Jolly Joker' Z5–10 H9–1

Borago officinalis
BORAGE

☼ ◐ ◊ Z5–10 H12–1 ‡3ft (1m) ↔1ft (30cm)

Once grown, this comes back every winter in mild zones. Sweet flowers are nice on cheese, salad, soup, or ice cream. Young leaves have cucumber flavor.

Agastache foeniculum
ANISE HYSSOP

Ⓝ ☼ ◐ ◊ Z8–10 H9–5 ‡5ft (1.5m) ↔12in (30cm)

A perennial, easily grown from seeds but needs good drainage. Smells strongly of anise. Delicious, chewable flowers good in cookies, salads, pizza, and desserts.

HERBACEOUS PLANTS

Annuals and biennials for partial shade

When people move into a new house on a bare lot the first thing they do is plant trees, perhaps too many and in the wrong places. While the trees grow, the homeowners learn all about growing plants in sun. When the trees are full grown, gardeners have to relearn how to garden with shade. Small properties with big houses also suffer from too much shade.

Primula malacoides
FAIRY PRIMROSE
☼ ☀ ◑ Z8–11 H12–10 ‡12in (30cm) ↔5in (13cm)
For a winter bloom, set plants out in beds or in hanging baskets in October. Fill a sphagnum basket with potting soil, spread wires, and stick little roots through into the soil. Plant the top and feed.

Torenia fournieri 'Summer Wave'
WISHBONE FLOWER
☼ ☀ ◑ Z9–12 H6–1 ‡12in (30cm) ↔11in (28cm)
In cold-winter climates, this blooms in summer in shade and moist heat without mildew. It needs no deadheading. Mulch, pinch, and feed high potassium.

Begonia 'Organdy'
BEDDING BEGONIA
☼ ☀ ◑◑ Z5–10 H12–1 ‡↔8in (20cm)
This summer annual, actually a perennial, may last 2 years in mild zones. Mix pink ones with *Aeonium* 'Zwartkop' or use as an edging plant. No deadheading.

Browallia speciosa 'Vanja'
AMETHYST FLOWER
☀ ● Z9–11 H12–1 ↕2ft (60cm) ↔12in (30cm)
Blooms blue with a white eye, spring to fall. Pinch to control. The compact 'Powder Blue' needs no pinching and is free-flowering for a basket or bed.

Geranium maderense
MADIERA GERANIUM
☀ ◐ Z9–10 H9–8 ↕4ft (1.2cm) ↔5ft (1.5m)
For coastal zones, this biennial dies after its spring bloom, leaving progeny for sharing next year. Feed with winter rains and never cut leaves; they support plant.

MORE CHOICES

- *Digitalis purpurea* Z5–10 H9–1
- *Impatiens walleriana* Z9–12 H12–1
- *Lobelia erinus* Z7–11 H8–1
- *Nicotiana sylvestris* Z8–11 H12–1
- *Salvia coccinea* Z8–11 H12–1
- *Salvia splendens* Z1–11 H12–1
- *Salvia verticillata* Z6–10 H8–6
- *Schizanthus pinnatus* Z7–11 H8–1
- *Solenostemon scutellarioides* Z10–12 H12–1
- *Viola tricolor* Z4–10 H12–1

Gerbera jamesonii
TRANSVAAL DAISY
☀ ◐ ◊ Z8–11 H12–6
↕10in (25cm) ↔8in (20cm)
Plant in pots or the ground with crown high so it does not rot. Water deeply when pot is dry to one inch. Fertilize monthly with 14-14-14 and control snails. These make an excellent cut flower.

Nicotiana alata
FLOWERING TOBACCO
☀ ◐ ● Z7–11 H12–1
↕3ft (1m) ↔12in (30cm)
Grown more for its night fragrance than its beauty, this sticky and poisonous plant takes heat and dry air in hot climates if fed and watered. Plant near patios and outside windows to enjoy.

Myosotis alpestris
FORGET-ME-NOT
☀ ● Z4–10 H8–1 ↕↔12in (30cm)
A spreading plant with spring bloom in moist, partially shaded soil, this is persistent and may be carried from place to place by gardeners' shoes. It will not get going in sandy soil that dries out between waterings.

HERBACEOUS PLANTS

Annuals and biennials for cottage gardens

Like cottages themselves, cottage-garden plants have a nostalgic, almost fairy-tale appearance. This selection of annuals and biennials – plus one perennial – can be grown in any garden, but as a collection they would make the foundation for a delightful cottage-style garden. Most of these plants need regular watering and some of the taller ones should be staked.

Ammi majus
BISHOP'S FLOWER
☼ ◐ ◊　Z6–10 H9–1　‡36in (m)　↔12in (m)
Related to Queen Anne's lace, this carrot and parsley relative is difficult to start from seed. Plant in fall and pour boiling water on sprinkled seeds. Cover with potting soil, pat down, keep moist until germinated.

Nicotiana sylvestris
TOBACCO OF THE WOODS
☼ ◐ ◊　Z8–11 H12–1　‡5ft (1.5m)　↔2ft (60cm)
A summer-blooming annual. Plant from seeds in fall in well-amended adobe or clay that stays moist. Along the coast, freeze seeds overnight before planting.

Amaranthus caudatus
LOVE-LIES-BLEEDING
☼ ◐ ◊　Z8–11 H12–1　‡8ft (m)　↔3ft (m)
A summer annual to sow in late spring. Needs water but also likes heat. Produces edible grain (amaranth) and spinach-like leaves. Grown in vegetable gardens.

Dierama pulcherrimum
GRASSY BELLS
☼ ◊　Z8–10 H10–8　‡to 4ft (1.2m)
Grown from corms, this grasslike perennial has drooping flowers in late spring to summer. A second type, *D. pendulum*, has bell-shaped flowers.

MORE CHOICES

- *Campanula medium* Z6–10 H8–5
- *Campanula medium* var. *calycanthema* 'Ringing Bells' Z5–10 H8–5
- *Celosia argentea* var. *cristata* 'Coral Garden' Z1–12 H9–2
- *Cleome hassleriana* Z1–11 H12–1
- *Dianella tasmanica* Z8–10 H12–10
- *Dianthus barbatus* 'Summer Beauty' Z1–10 Hx–x
- *Eryngium alpinum* 'Amethyst' Z3–10 H9–6
- *Gaillardia pulchella* Z1–10 H12–1
- *Gypsophila paniculata* 'Bristol Fairy' Z4–9 H9–1
- *Lunaria annua* Z3–9 H9–1
- *Malva sylvestris* 'Magic Merlin' Z8–10 H10–8
- *Nigella damascena* Persian Jewels Series Z1–10 H10–1
- *Persicaria orientalis* Z6–9 H9–8
- *Rudbeckia hirta* Z5–10 H7–1
- *Salvia viridis* 'Claryssa' Z7–11 H12–10

Digitalis purpurea 'Excelsior'
EXCELSIOR COMMON FOXGLOVE
☀ ◐ ◗ z5–10 H10–1 ‡3–6ft (1–2m) ↔24in (60cm)
True biennials. Try sprouting seeds in June on a drip
line under sweet corn; transplant in early fall to final
site. Feed well for tall showy plants by spring.

Lavatera trimestris 'Silver Cup'
SILVER CUP ROSE MALLOW
☀ ◗ z8–11 H12–1 ‡5ft (1.5m) ↔3ft (1m)
An easy-to-grow annual in mild zones. Plant seeds
where you want them, thin as per package directions,
keep moist, and feed occasionally. This large plant is
covered with flowers in late spring, early summer.

Antirrhinum majus Sprite Series
SPRITE SNAPDRAGON
☀ ◗ z6–10 H9–1 ‡↔3ft (1m)
An old, rust-resistant variety, tall, easy to grow from
seeds planted in fall in mild zones or early spring where
winters are severe. Colors are available from catalogs.

Molucella laevis
BELLS OF IRELAND
☀ ◗ z7–10 H11–1
‡3ft (1m) ↔9in (23cm)
Easy to grow in fertile, moist, well-
drained soil with regular fertilizer. Not
for humid climates. Plant from seeds in
fall in mild zones. Grow as winter
annual in desert. Good cut flowers.

Nigella damascena Persian Jewels Series
LOVE-IN-A-MIST
☀ ◐ ◗ z6–10 H10–1
‡16in (40cm) ↔9in (22cm)
Plant in fall in mild zones,
earliest spring where colder.
Spring flowers followed
by unique seed capsules.
Does well in
rainy years and
sunny spots in
cool regions.

Alcea ficifolia Antwerp Mix
ANTWERP HOLLYHOCK
☀ ◐ ◗ z3–10 H10–8 ‡8ft (2.5m) ↔3ft (1m)
A beloved cottage-garden plant, easy to grow, and good in any garden.
Rust is a problem for most hollyhocks, but this form is relatively
resistant. Delightful single flowers with good colors.

HERBACEOUS PLANTS

Annuals for summer and fall bloom

Use warm-season annuals as quick fillers among perennials, or for summer bloom in pots and window boxes. Some are drought-tolerant, and easier to grow than many perennials, but all must be planted each year from seeds or transplants. Do not purchase and plant these flowers in fall even though many can still be found for sale. They will soon fade and die.

Portulaca grandiflora Sundance Hybrids
MOSS ROSE

☼   ◊ ◐   Z9–11 H12–1   ‡6in (15cm) ↔18in (45cm)
Plant in late spring for a summer bloom. 'Sundance' stays open longer during the day. It needs little care or fertilizer and no deadheading. Excellent in hot-interior zones, this self-sows but in a different form.

Tagetes erecta Lady Series
GIANT AFRICAN MARIGOLD

☼   ◊   Z5–10 H12–1   ‡↔18in (45cm)
Among the best annuals for hot-interior zones, this is tall and easy to grow from seeds planted in spring. Thin to 18in (45cm) apart, deadhead; no overhead watering.

Lobelia erinus
LOBELIA

☼ ☼   ◐   Z5–10 H8–1   ‡6in (15cm) ↔9in (23cm)
This blooms all winter in the desert, summer elsewhere. A great edging with sweet alyssum, sprinkle seeds into hanging baskets and window boxes of Balcon geranium.

MORE CHOICES

- *Amaranthus tricolor* 'Molten Fire' Z8–11 H12–5
- *Celosia argentea* Z6–12 H9–2
- *Celosia occidentalis* var. *pumila* Z6–12 H12–1
- *Cosmos sulphureus* Z5–12 H12–1
- *Gomphrena globosa* 'Buddy' Z6–12 H12–1
- *Lobularia maritima* Z5–10 H12–1
- *Sanvitalia procumbens* 'Mandarin Orange' Z6–10 H12–1
- *Tagetes erecta* 'Antigua Yellow' Z5–10 H12–1
- *Tagetes* Boy Series Z5–10 H12–1

HERBACEOUS PLANTS

Salvia splendens Sizzler Series
SCARLET SAGE

☼ ☼ ◐ z5–12 H12–1
↕↔3ft (1m)

An early-blooming annual that becomes a bit woody the second year. Grows large in Hawaii and gets giant whitefly.

Cleome hasslerana
CLEOME, SPIDER FLOWER

☼ ◊◐ z6–11 H12–1 ↕5ft (1.5m) ↔4ft (1.2m)

Plant from seeds when the weather warms up at the back of a flower bed or in a neglected part of the garden. These naturalizing, old-fashioned plants are long-blooming in hot interiors and make good cut flowers.

Cosmos bipinnatus 'Seashells'
COSMOS

Ⓝ ☼ ◐ z5–10 H12–1 ↕3ft (1m) ↔2ft (60cm)

An unusual variety of a native plant with a summer bloom, year-round in mild zones, that does not return from seeds unless you grow the common tall variety.

Petunia 'Magic Carpet'
MAGIC CARPET PETUNIA

☼ ◐ z6–10 H12–1 ↕8in (20cm) ↔12in (30cm)

This warm-season annual can be planted in fall for summer bloom in mild zones. It blooms all winter in the desert, and gets bud worms on the coast; use Bt.

Impatiens walleriana
BUSY LIZZIE

☼ ◐ z9–12 H12–1 ↕10in (25cm) ↔12in (30cm)

Place seeds on top of soil, do not cover, and keep damp; or start with plants. This never wilts facing east, but will west. Cut 1/3 of two large branches monthly.

Catharanthus roseus 'Parasol'
MADAGASCAR PERIWINKLE

☼ ☼ ◐ z6–10 H12–1 ↕↔12in (30cm)

One of the best summer annuals for hot zones, or in a hot spot in mild climates with good drainage, this never wilts in heat. Older varieties look coarse.

Cool-season annuals

In mild-winter climates cool-season annual flowers are planted in fall for winter and spring bloom. The trick is to plant them in October and feed them for bloom and growth. If you can get them into bloom before the winter solstice, they will bloom all winter into spring, otherwise in February. In cold climates these selections are planted in earliest spring.

Primula obconica
OBCONICA PRIMROSE
☀ ◐ Z9–10 H6–1
↕12in (30cm) ↔9in (23cm)
Offered for sale in spring, this is okay to use for filling in, but in mild climates they soon die. Start in fall so they will bloom all winter long.

Primula x polyantha
ENGLISH PRIMROSE
☀ ☀ ◐ Z6–10 H8–1 ↕12in (30cm) ↔9in (23cm)
Choose ones with taller stems (squat stems rot in heavy rains and are hard to deadhead). They grow well in pots or the ground and may last two years.

Papaver rhoeas 'Shirley Poppy'
SHIRLEY POPPIES
☀ ◐◐ Z5–10 H12–1 ↕3ft (1m) ↔12in (30cm)
Easy in well-drained soil, plant seeds in October or November for spring bloom. Sprinkle to sprout, fertilize lightly if foliage yellows, and deadhead.

MORE CHOICES

- *Antirrhinum majus* 'Sprite' Z5–10 H9–1
- *Bellis perennis* Z4–10 H8–1
- *Dianthus barbatus* Roundabout Series Z3–10 H9–1
- *Matthiola* Ten-week Group Z5–10 H9–1
- *Nemesia strumosa* 'Carnival Series' Z5–10 H10–1
- *Papaver somnifera* Z5–10 H9–2
- *Pericallis hybrida* Z10–11 H7–1
- *Primula malacoides* Z8–10 H10–8
- *Viola cornuta* Z6–10 H9–1

Brassica oleracea
FLOWERING CABBAGE, FLOWERING KALE

☼ ☼ ☼   ◊ ◊ ◊   Z8–10 H9–1   ↕↔18in (45cm)

Plant from seeds or from a small plant, which is easier. The first frost makes it even more colorful. In good soil, do not fertilize as it bolts. Protect with Bt from cabbage butterflies, though few appear in cool weather.

Viola tricolor
JOHNNY JUMP-UP

☼ ☼   ◊ ◊   Z3–10 H12–1
↕↔12in (30cm)

For bloom in spring to summer, sprinkle seeds around the edges of beds in fall, let them sift in naturally, or rake lightly on a bare ground. For winter bloom, plant in October.

Viola x wittrockiana 'Universal Plus'
PANSY

☼ ☼   ◊   Z6–10 H9–1
↕↔12in (30cm)

A superior, heat-resistant series with two-inch flowers that smother its foliage from fall to summer in mild zones. Fertilize to keep blooming. No deadheading in pots or ground.

Calendula officinalis
POT MARIGOLD

☼   ◊   Z5–11 H6–1
↕2ft (60cm)   ↔18in (45cm)

For double flowers, plant 'California Giant' in fall. Its seeds are big enough to grab so put them where you want them. Easy to grow, these bloom all winter.

Tropaeolum majus 'Empress of India'
NASTURTIUM

☼ ☼   ◊ ◊   Z5–11 H12–1
↕18in (45cm)   ↔12in (30cm)

A red compact variety with dark foliage, easy to grow from seeds. Others return as climbers, hiding flowers.

PART III

GARDENING TECHNIQUES

including Selecting Plants,
Planting, Pruning,
and Propagation

Once you've planned your SMARTGARDEN™
and have determined what you'd like
to grow, it's time to put on the gardening gloves.
Here are pointers on selecting healthy plants
and detecting potentially unhealthy ones;
planting them correctly; pruning trees, shrubs,
and vines; and propagating plants
by various methods.

SELECTING PLANTS

Choosing plants at the nursery or garden center does not need to be a long, complicated process: basically, look for plants that appear healthy and avoid extremes, such as too much top-growth compared to the root ball, or too little foliage on stems that barely support the leaves. Spend more time on choosing longer-lived and more expensive trees and shrubs than on herbaceous plants.

CHOOSING A TREE

Container-grown tree

Before buying one of these, remove it from its container to examine the roots. Do not buy a potbound tree (with a mass of congested roots) or one with thick roots protruding from the holes.

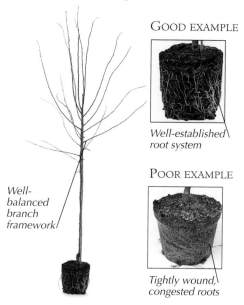

Well-balanced branch framework

GOOD EXAMPLE

Well-established root system

POOR EXAMPLE

Tightly wound, congested roots

Bare-root tree

These have virtually no soil around the roots. Examine the roots to check that they are not damaged or diseased and that there is no sign of dryness that may have been caused by exposure to air or sunlight.

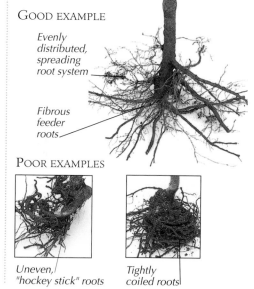

GOOD EXAMPLE

Evenly distributed, spreading root system

Fibrous feeder roots

POOR EXAMPLES

Uneven, "hockey stick" roots

Tightly coiled roots

Balled-and-burlapped tree

Buy and plant a balled-and-burlapped tree when it is dormant in fall or early spring, following the same basic examination criteria as for both container-grown and bare-root trees.

GOOD EXAMPLE

X CUPRESSOCYPARIS LEYLANDII

Firm root ball with the covering intact

SELECTING A CONTAINER-GROWN SHRUB

Look through the drainage holes (or carefully slide the shrub out of its container) to check for a well-developed root system. If present, the shrub is probably container-grown and is not containerized (meaning it was recently removed from the open ground and put into a container). The roots should have healthy, white tips. Reject plants with poorly developed root systems, with coiled roots or root balls, or with roots protruding from the container, since these rarely establish or grow well.

GOOD EXAMPLE

Vigorous, well-balanced top-growth

Healthy, white roots

PROSTANTHERA CUNEATA

POOR EXAMPLE

Twiggy, sparse stems showing little new growth

Potbound roots

Pruning congested roots

Tease out potbound roots, and cut back any that are very long and damaged.

SELECTING CLIMBERS

Climbing plants are usually sold container-grown, although a few may be sold bare-root. Choose a healthy-looking plant with a well-balanced framework of strong shoots, and reject any that show signs of pest infestation or disease. For potgrown plants, turn the pot over and check that the tips of the young roots are just showing. If so, the plant is well-rooted. Reject potbound plants – those that have tightly coiled roots or a mass of roots protruding through the drainage holes. Bare-root plants should have plenty of healthy, well-developed fibrous roots that are in proportion to the amount of top-growth.

GOOD EXAMPLE

Vigorous, sturdy stems

Healthy buds

LONICERA

POOR EXAMPLES

Spindly, weak growth with damaged buds

Roots coiled tightly around the root ball

SELECTING HEALTHY ROSES

Bare-root bush rose

Examine the plant carefully: if the stems appear dried out (the bark will be shriveled), or buds have started growing prematurely (producing blanched, thin shoots), do not buy it.

GOOD EXAMPLE

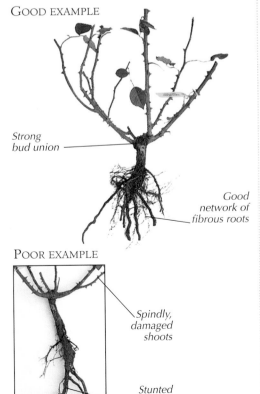

Strong bud union

Good network of fibrous roots

POOR EXAMPLE

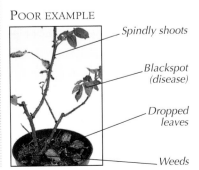

Spindly, damaged shoots

Stunted root sytem

Container-grown rose

Check that the plant has not been recently potted up: hold the plant by its main shoot and gently shake it. If it does not move around in the soil mix, it is well-established and a good buy.

GOOD EXAMPLE

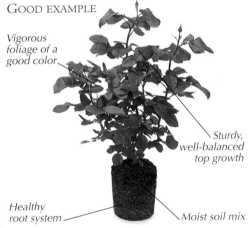

Vigorous foliage of a good color

Sturdy, well-balanced top growth

Healthy root system

Moist soil mix

POOR EXAMPLE

Spindly shoots

Blackspot (disease)

Dropped leaves

Weeds

Standard rose

Choose a standard rose with a balanced head of shoots, since it is likely to be viewed from all sides. A straight main stem is best, although a slightly crooked stem is acceptable.

GOOD EXAMPLE

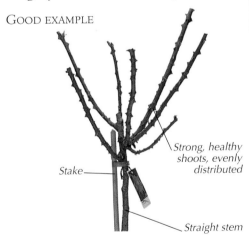

Strong, healthy shoots, evenly distributed

Stake

Straight stem

POOR EXAMPLE

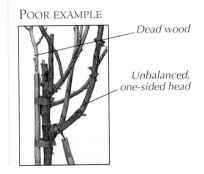

Dead wood

Unbalanced, one-sided head

CHOOSING HERBACEOUS PLANTS

Most herbaceous plants are sold container-grown, but bare-root plants are also sometimes available from fall to early spring, when they are dormant. If buying herbaceous plants at the beginning of the growing season, check that there are strong, emerging shoots. Plants that have a few fat, healthy-looking buds are better than those that have a large number of weaker ones.

GOOD EXAMPLE

IMPATIENS CULTIVAR

Bushy, sturdy growth

Healthy buds developing

Moist soil mix

GOOD EXAMPLE

Strong, healthy top growth

Moist soil mix

Established, vigorous roots

LUPINE

POOR EXAMPLES

Weak and weedy top-growth

Dry soil mix

Underdeveloped root system

Leggy, bare stems

Dead leaves

Moss and weeds growing on soil mix

Potbound roots

Yellowing, discolored leaves

SELECTING BULBS, CORMS, TUBERS, AND SIMILAR PLANTS

Most bulbs are sold in a dry state during their dormant period. Buy these as early as possible before they start into growth; most daffodils, for example, normally start producing roots in late summer, and most other spring-flowering bulbs will begin to grow by early fall. Fall-flowering crocuses and *Colchicum* species and hybrids especially benefit from early planting: specialized nurseries sell them in midsummer. All fall-flowering bulbs are best bought and planted by late summer. Summer-flowering bulbs (such as *Gladiolus*, *Dahlia*, and *Canna*) are available for purchase in spring.

Bulbs tend to deteriorate if kept dry too long; they will have a shorter growing period and take some time to recover and flower satisfactorily, so buy and plant them as soon as they are available. Do not buy or plant any bulbs that are mushy or slimy, or any that feel much lighter than a bulb of similar size of the same kind (they are probably dried up and dead).

GOOD EXAMPLES

DAFFODIL (SINGLE-NOSED)   DAFFODIL (TWIN-NOSED)

Fresh, plump tubers

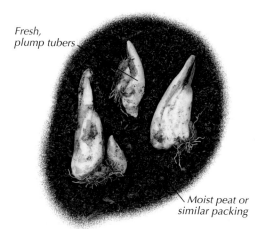

Moist peat or similar packing

ERYTHRONIUM OREGONUM

POOR EXAMPLES

Diseased tissue

Damaged outer scales

No tunic (covering)

Deterioration of bulb tissue

Small nose

Offset too small to flower

CORYDALIS SOLIDA

Distinct growing point on corm

SELECTING PLANTS FOR THE WATER GARDEN

When selecting aquatic plants at the nursery or garden center, look for clean, fresh-looking, and vigorous specimens growing in tanks that are free from algae and duckweed (*Wolffia*). Check that the undersides of the leaves are free from jellylike deposits of snail eggs and that there are no strands of blanketweed in the foliage. Mail-order plants should appear plump and green; if they look weak and limp, they are unlikely to grow well. If buying plants by mail order, use a specialized supplier.

Marginal plant

GOOD EXAMPLE

Strong flowering stem

Healthy leaves

CALTHA PALUSTRIS

Surface floater

GOOD EXAMPLE

Young, fresh growth

STRATIOTES ALOIDES

POOR EXAMPLE

Weak growth

Weed-infested soil mix

POOR EXAMPLE

Damaged growth

Old, rotting foliage

SELECTING CACTI AND OTHER SUCCULENTS

When buying cacti and other succulents, choose healthy, pest- and disease-free, unblemished plants that show strong new growth (unless you are buying the plants when they are dormant) or have flower buds forming. Do not buy damaged or even slightly shriveled specimens, or any with dull, dry, or limp segments. Also reject plants that have outgrown their pots.

GOOD EXAMPLE

Plump, fleshy leaves

Sturdy stem

CRASSULA OVATA

GOOD EXAMPLE

Healthy-looking body

New buds forming

REBUTIA SPECIES

POOR EXAMPLE

Damaged growth

POOR EXAMPLE

Shriveled and cut leaves

PLANTING

When selecting and planting trees, shrubs, and woody climbers, it is vital to take account of the general weather pattern of your area as well as your garden's individual microclimate, because these factors will determine whether a given plant is hardy and has a reasonable chance of surviving in your garden. Proper planting and aftercare will increase the likelihood of survival.

PLANTING A CONTAINER-GROWN TREE

First, thoroughly moisten the soil mix in the container – if it is very dry, stand the container in water for half an hour or until the soil mix is moist throughout (the bubbles will stop rising). Then remove the container, cutting it away if necessary, taking care not to damage the roots excessively. Gently tease out the roots with your fingers or a hand fork (or with pruners, if the roots are thickly congested) to encourage them to grow into the surrounding soil; this is essential with a potbound plant. If there are any broken or damaged roots, trim them back with pruners. It is important to check that the planting depth is correct. If a tree is planted too deeply, its roots may not receive enough oxygen and the tree may grow more slowly or even die; if planted too shallowly, the roots may dry out.

Mark out the area of the hole to be dug – about 3 or 4 times the diameter of the tree's root ball. Remove any grass or weeds, then dig out the hole to about 1½ times the depth of the root ball.

Scarify the sides and bottom of the hole with a fork. There is no need to improve the soil unless the quality is very poor, such as dense, heavy clay or very infertile sand.

Drive a stake into the hole, just off center and on the windward side. Lay the tree on its side and slide it out of the pot. Gently tease out the roots without breaking up the root ball.

Hold the tree next to the stake and spread out roots. Lay a stake across the hole to check the planting depth. Adjust by adding or removing soil. Plant tree at same depth it was in its container.

Backfill around the tree with more topsoil, working it down the root ball, and then gently firm the soil. Build up soil around the hole to form a watering ring.

Cut back damaged stems, long sideshoots, and weaker, lower branches (see inset). Apply a mulch 2–3in (5–7cm) deep around the area.

PLANTING A CONTAINER-GROWN SHRUB

Fall and spring are the optimum times for planting container-grown and containerized shrubs. Planting in fall allows the roots to establish while the ground is still warm, so the shrub should be growing vigorously before hot, dry weather the next summer. In some areas, planting can be carried out during mild weather in winter, but not when the ground is very cold or frozen. Roots will not begin growth in very cold soil, and there is a risk that they may freeze. A possible disadvantage to spring planting is that top-growth is likely to develop before the roots establish adequately and, if there is a long spell of hot, dry weather, watering may be required to help the plants survive.

Using a watering ring

To help retain water, create a shallow depression and a low wall of soil around the shrub. Cover the area with mulch, then allow the ring to settle on its own.

Placing one hand on top of the soil mix and around the shrub to support it, carefully ease the plant out of its container. Place the shrub in the prepared hole.

Lay a stake alongside to check that the soil level is the same as before. If necessary, adjust the planting depth by adding or removing topsoil beneath the shrub.

Backfill around the shrub with the removed soil, firming in stages to prevent air pockets from forming. Once the hole has been filled with soil, carefully firm around the shrub with your heel or hands.

Prune any diseased, damaged, or weak wood, and cut back any inward-growing or crossing stems to an outward-growing shoot or bud.

TRANSPLANTING A SHRUB

Careful selection and siting of a shrub should make transplanting unnecessary, although sometimes it may be desirable or unavoidable. In general, the younger the shrub, the more likely it is to reestablish after being moved. Most young shrubs may be lifted bare-root when dormant. Established shrubs that have large root systems should be lifted with a ball of soil around the roots before being moved. Spring (before bud break) and mid- to late fall are the best times to do this.

Using a spade, mark out a circle around the extent of the shrub's branches (here *Ilex aquifolium* 'Golden Milkboy'). Tie in (or prune off) any trailing stems, or wrap the shrub in burlap, to prevent the stems from being damaged. Dig a circular trench around the plant.

Use a fork to loosen the soil around the root ball. Continue to carefully fork away soil from around the shrub's root ball to reduce its size and weight.

Undercut the root ball with a spade, cutting through woody roots if necessary to separate them from the surrounding soil.

Pull some burlap up around the root ball and tie it securely. Remove the shrub from its hole, then transport it to its new location.

Remove or untie the burlap when replanting. Plant with the soil mark at the same level as before. Firm, water well, and mulch.

PLANTING A CLIMBER AGAINST A WALL

Before removing the plant from its pot, make sure that the soil mix is moist. Water the plant well, so that the root ball is thoroughly wet, and then allow it to drain for at least an hour. Remove the surface layer of soil mix to eliminate weeds, and then invert the pot, taking care to support the plant as it slides out. If the roots have begun to curl around inside the pot, gently tease them out. Any dead, damaged, or protruding roots should be cut back to the perimeter of the root ball. Position the plant so that the top of the root ball is just level with the surrounding soil. It is advisable to plant clematis more deeply, however. Climbers that have been grafted (as is the case with most wisterias) should be planted with the graft union 2½in (6cm) below soil level to encourage rooting of the cultivar.

Attach a support 12in (30cm) above the soil and 2in (5cm) from the wall. Dig a hole 18in (45cm) from the wall. Loosen the soil at the base and add compost.

Soak the climbers root ball well. Position it in the hole at a 45° angle, placing a stake across to check the planting level. Spread the roots away from the wall.

Fill in around the plant and firm and level the soil, ensuring that no air pockets remain between the roots and that the plant is fully supported.

Untie the stems from the central stake and select 4 or 5 strong shoots. Insert a stake for each shoot and attach it to the lowest wire. Tie in the shoots.

Using pruners, trim back any weak, damaged, or wayward shoots to the central stem. This establishes the initial framework for the climber.

Water the plant thoroughly (here *Jasminum mesnyi*). Cover the surrounding soil with a deep mulch to retain moisture and discourage weeds.

PLANTING A BARE-ROOT ROSE

Bare-root roses are best planted just before or at the beginning of their dormant period (in fall or early winter) to lessen the shock of transplanting. Early spring is better in areas that have bad winters. Plant roses as soon as possible after purchase. If there is any delay, perhaps because of unsuitable weather, it is best to heel them into a spare piece of ground, with the roots buried in a shallow trench. Alternatively, store the roses in a cool and frost-free place, and keep the roots moist. If the roots of a bare-root rose look dry before planting, soak the roots in a bucket of water for an hour or two until they are thoroughly moist.

Remove diseased, damaged , or crossing shoots and straggly stems; trim thick roots by one-third. Dig a hole and fork in compost mixed with bone meal or fertilizer.

Center the rose in the hole and spread out the roots evenly. Lay a stake across the hole to check that the bud union will be at the correct depth for the type of rose and your climate zone.

In 2 or 3 stages, water the hole and backfill with soil after the water has drained out. Do not walk on the backfilled soil to avoid compacting the soil and breaking the roots.

PLANTING A CLIMBING ROSE

Train climbers grown against a wall or fence along horizontal wires that are about 18in (45cm) apart and held in place by vine eyes or strong nails. If the brickwork or masonry is very hard, drill holes for the vine eyes with a ³⁄₁₆in (4.7mm) bit. Keep the wires 3in (7cm) away from the wall to allow air circulation and discourage diseases. The ground next to a wall is likely to be dry, since it is in a rain shadow and the masonry absorbs moisture from the soil. Plant about 18in (45cm) from the wall where the soil is less dry and water from eaves will not drip on the rose. Prepare the soil and planting hole, and trim the rose, as for bush roses. Fan out its roots. Train the shoots along stakes, but keep each stake far enough from the roots to avoid damaging them.

Place the rose in the planting hole, leaning it toward the wall at an angle of about 45° so that the shoots reach the lowest support wire. Place a stake across the hole to check the planting depth.

Use stakes to guide the shorter shoots toward the wires. Tie all the shoots to the stakes or wires with plastic straps (see insert).

PLANTING A STANDARD ROSE

A standard rose needs a stake, placed on the side of the prevailing wind, to support it. Paint the entire stake with a preservative that is not toxic to plants, then allow it to dry. Insert the stake very firmly near the center of the planting hole before positioning the rose to avoid damaging the roots and, as a result, encouraging suckers from below the graft union. Position the rose next to the stake, and check that it just reaches the base of the lowest branches; if necessary, adjust the height of the stake. Use a stake or rake handle to make sure that the bud union is at the correct level (above ground in warmer areas, below in colder).

Position the stake in the hole so that the rose stem will be in the center. Drive the stake into the ground and check that the top is just below the head of the rose.

Place a stake across the hole to check the planting depth. Use the old soil mark on the stem as a guide and plant at the correct depth. Fill in the hole, then water.

Use a tie just below the head of the rose, and another halfway up the stem, to attach the rose to the stake. Cut out weak or crossing shoots.

PLANTING A CONTAINER-GROWN PERENNIAL

Perennials grown in containers may be planted out at any time of year when the soil is workable, but the best seasons are spring and fall. Planting in fall helps the plants establish quickly before the onset of winter, because the soil is still warm enough to promote root growth, yet it is unlikely to dry out. In cold areas, however, spring planting is better for perennials that are not entirely hardy or that dislike wet conditions.

In a prepared bed, dig a hole 1½ times wider and deeper than the plant's root ball.

Gently scrape off the top 1¼in (3cm) of soil to remove weeds and weed seeds. Carefully tease out the roots around the sides and base of the root ball.

Check that the plant crown is at the correct depth when planted and fill in around the root ball. Firm gently around the plant, then water it in thoroughly.

PLANTING ANNUALS INTO OPEN GROUND

Before you plant out annuals, first prepare the bed, water the young plants thoroughly, and then allow them to drain for an hour or so. To remove a plant from its pot, invert it, supporting the stem with a finger on either side. Then tap the rim against a hard surface. If plants are in trays without divisions, hold the tray firmly with both hands, then tap one side sharply on the ground to loosen the medium.

Break the pack apart and carefully remove each seedling (here *Tagetes*) with its root ball intact.

Place each plant in a hole large enough to take its root ball, making sure the plant is slightly lower in the soil than it was in its container.

Gently firm the soil in the well around the plant so that there are no air pockets. Water the area.

PLANTING DEPTHS

ASTER

SISYRINCHIUM STRIATUM 'AUNT MAY'

GROUND-LEVEL PLANTING
The majority of perennials should be planted so that the crown of the plant is level with the surrounding soil.

RAISED PLANTING
Set plants that are prone to rot at the base, and variegated plants that tend to revert, with their crowns slightly above the ground.

While most perennials are best planted out at the same soil level as they were in their pots, a number grow better if planted higher or deeper, depending on their individual requirements. Some prefer a raised, well-drained site, while others thrive in deeper, moist conditions.

HOSTA

POLYGONATUM

SHALLOW PLANTING
Plant perennials that require a moist environment with their crowns about 1in (2.5cm) below ground level.

DEEP PLANTING
Plant perennials with tuberous root systems so that their crowns are about 4in (10cm) below the soil surface.

PLANTING LARGE BULBS IN GRASS

When planting bulbs that are to be naturalized in grass, first cut the grass as short as possible. Random rather than regimented planting achieves a more natural effect; scatter the bulbs gently by hand over the area and plant them where they have fallen, making sure that they are at least one bulb's width apart. Dig holes with a trowel or use a bulb planter, which cuts out plugs of sod and soil to a depth of about 4–6in (10–15cm); dig deeper if necessary for larger bulbs. Check that all the holes are at the correct depth and that the bulbs are the right way up before inserting them and replacing the sod, then give them a good watering.

Clean the bulbs (here daffodils), removing any loose outer coatings and old roots. Scatter the bulbs randomly over the planting area, then make sure that they are at least their own width apart.

Make an individual hole for each bulb, using a bulb planter to remove a circle of sod and a core of soil to a depth of about 4–6in (10–15cm).

Place a pinch of bone meal, mixed with a little of the soil from the core, into each hole and put in a bulb with the growing point uppermost.

Break up the underside of the core over the bulb so that it is completely covered with loose soil. Then replace the remains of the core on top of it.

Replace the lid of sod and firm it in gently, taking care not to damage the growing point of the bulb. Fill in any gaps in the grass with more soil.

PLANTING BULBS IN THE OPEN

Dry, loose bulbs should be planted as soon as possible after purchase, usually in late summer or early fall (plant summer-flowering bulbs in early to midspring); otherwise, keep them cool and dry until you can plant them. Bulbs are usually best planted several to a large hole dug out with a spade, but they may also be planted singly. Do not make the outline of the planting area or the spacing of the bulbs symmetrical: this looks unnatural, and if one or two bulbs fail, they will leave unsightly gaps.

Dig out a large hole in well-prepared ground. Plant the bulbs (here tulips), at least 3 times their own depth, and 2–3 widths apart.

For a natural effect, space the bulbs randomly. Once they are in position, gently draw the soil over them with your hand to avoid displacing or damaging them.

Planting bulbs

SINGLY
Plant each bulb in a separate hole at the appropriate depth. Draw back the prepared soil with a trowel, and firm it down gently afterward.

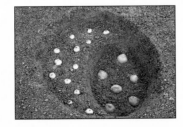

IN LAYERS
Two or more kinds of bulb may be planted in the same space. Plant each kind at its correct depth, carefully covering each layer before planting the next type of bulb.

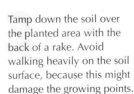

Tamp down the soil over the planted area with the back of a rake. Avoid walking heavily on the soil surface, because this might damage the growing points.

PLANTING DEEP-WATER AND MARGINAL PLANTS

Whether planting in beds or free-standing containers, settle the plants firmly in the soil, because they are very buoyant and may become dislodged. Always plant in moist soil, and soak containers well before immersing them in the pond. A top-dressing of grit, coarse sand, or pea gravel to a depth of 1in (2.5cm) prevents soil from floating out and clouding the water and discourages hungry or curious fish from disturbing the plants. When submerging the containers in deep water, thread string through the sides to form handles; this makes it much easier to position the basket, which can then be gradually lowered onto the bottom.

1 Choose a planting basket to accommodate the plant roots, and line it with burlap or closely woven polypropylene.

2 Fill the basket with heavy, moist soil to a depth of at least 2in (5cm). Center the plant (here *Aponogeton distachyos*).

3 Fill with more soil to within ½in (1cm) of the rim of the basket, firming the plant in well to give it good anchorage.

4 Top-dress the container with washed grit or pea gravel to a depth of 1in (2.5cm).

5 Trim away any surplus liner with scissors. Tie string handles to the rim of the basket on opposite sides.

6 Hold the basket by the string handles, then gently lower it onto blocks or the marginal shelf. Release the handles.

Surface floaters

With a new planting, include some surface-floating plants to discourage the growth of algae. When the ornamental plants become more established, some of the floaters should be removed. In a large pond, a line may be drawn across the pond from both ends to bring plants within reach. Duckweed in particular is very persistent, so choose less vigorous species.

Surface-floating plants have no anchorage because their roots obtain nutrients directly from the water. Their initial positioning is unimportant, since the groups are moved around on the surface by wind.

Surface-floating plants (here *Stratiotes aloides*) may be placed on the water's surface; in warm weather they multiply rapidly, giving valuable surface shade.

PLANTING IN A HANGING BASKET

A wide range of plants can be grown in a hanging basket, including annuals, tender perennials, succulents (as shown here) and even weak-stemmed shrubs, such as fuchsias. Make sure that the basket is completely clean. Wire baskets should be lined with a commercial liner or a layer of sphagnum moss. Do not line the basket with plastic, since this restricts drainage. If using a plastic basket that has an attached drainage tray, be sure to place a piece of screening over the drainage hole(s) to prevent the soil mix from washing out.

Line a wire hanging basket with a layer of moist sphagnum moss. The layer should be 1¼in (3cm) thick when compressed.

Fill the basket almost to the brim with a mix of 1 part sharp sand to 3 parts soil-based potting mix. Prepare a hole for the plant in the center of the basket.

Insert the plant (here a *Schlumbergera*), spreading out the roots. Fill in gently but firmly with soil mix so that there are no air pockets around the roots.

If planting succulents, as here, wait for 2–3 days after planting before watering the finished basket. Otherwise, water immediately and then allow the basket to drain before hanging it.

REPOTTING AN INDOOR PLANT

Indoor plants need repotting to accommodate their growth and to replenish the soil mix. A potbound plant has retarded growth, and water runs straight through the soil mix. Repot before this happens, so that the plant develops well. A few plants, such as amaryllis (*Hippeastrum*), enjoy confined roots, so repot them less often, and top-dress occasionally. The best time to repot is at the start of the growing season, although fast-growing plants may need repotting a few times in one season. The process may delay flowering, because the plant initially concentrates its energy on new root growth. Avoid repotting a dormant plant; it will not respond to the moisture and fertility, and it may rot.

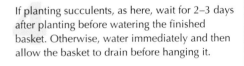

Before potting on a plant (here *Dracaena deremensis* 'Souvenir de Schriever'), make sure that its root ball is moist by watering it thoroughly about an hour beforehand. Select a pot that is one or two sizes larger than the old one. Make sure the pot is clean (whether washed, disinfected, or new) to avoid spreading diseases. The fresh potting mix should be of the same type as that in the old pot.

Remove the plant by inverting the pot and sharply tapping the rim on a hard surface to loosen the root ball. Support the plant as it slides out of the pot.

Gently tease out the root ball with a small fork or your fingers. Put some moist potting mix in the base of the new pot.

Insert the plant so that its soil mark is level with the rim base. Fill in with soil mix to within ½in (1.5cm) of the rim, firm, water, and place in position (right).

PRUNING

Pruning and training both aim to make sure that plants are as vigorous and healthy as possible, are at the least risk of infection from disease, and are free of structural weakness at maturity. They can also create striking features by enhancing ornamental qualities, such as bark, flowers, foliage, and fruit. However, pruning always causes some stress, so learn when and how to prune.

PRUNING AND TRAINING YOUNG TREES

Young trees benefit from formative pruning to make sure that they develop a strong, well-balanced framework of evenly spaced branches. This involves the removal of dead, damaged, and diseased wood, as well as any weak or crossing branches. Formative pruning may also be used to determine the tree's shape as it grows: for example, a young feathered tree may be pruned over several years to form a standard, or perhaps trained against a wall as an espalier.

Feathered Tree
Remove congested and crossing shoots, then cut out any laterals that are small, spindly, or badly positioned, to achieve a well-balanced framework of branches.

Feathered tree

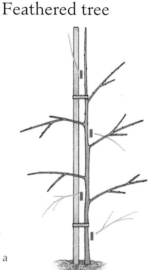

Central-leader standard

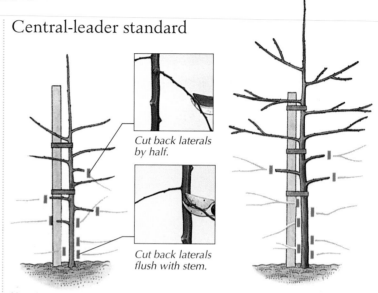

Cut back laterals by half.

Cut back laterals flush with stem.

Year 1
On the lowest third of the tree, cut back laterals to the main stem; on the middle third, cut back laterals by half. Remove any weak or competing leaders.

Years 2 and 3
Continue the process, removing the lowest laterals completely and cutting back by about half those laterals that are on the middle third of the tree.

Branched-head standard

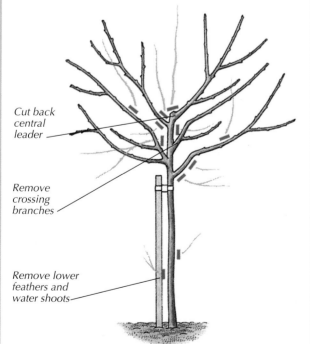

Cut back central leader

Remove crossing branches

Remove lower feathers and water shoots

Remove crossing laterals and any growths on the lower third of the tree. Cut back the leader to a healthy bud or shoot.

Weeping tree

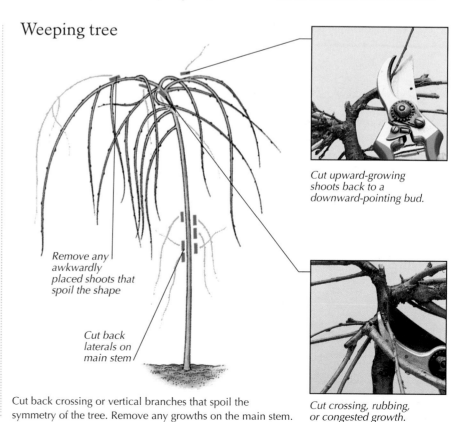

Remove any awkwardly placed shoots that spoil the shape

Cut back laterals on main stem

Cut back crossing or vertical branches that spoil the symmetry of the tree. Remove any growths on the main stem.

Cut upward-growing shoots back to a downward-pointing bud.

Cut crossing, rubbing, or congested growth.

FORMATIVE PRUNING AND TRAINING

The aim of formative pruning is to make sure that a shrub has a framework of well-spaced branches. The amount of formative pruning required depends very much on the type of shrub and on the quality of the plants available. (It is usually best to start with a quality plant from a good source.) Evergreen shrubs generally need little formative pruning. Excessive growth resulting in an unbalanced shape should be lightly pruned in midspring, after the shrub has been planted. Deciduous shrubs are much more likely to require formative pruning than evergreen shrubs. This should be carried out in the dormant season, between midfall and midspring, at or after planting.

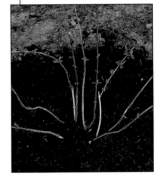

Coppicing a shrub for winter stem color

Coppicing stimulates the growth of colorful, vigorous stems. Cut back all stems to about 2–3in (5–8cm) from the base before growth begins in spring, and then fertilize and mulch well.

Prune back crossing or congested shoots to an outward-facing bud or cut right back to the base.

Prune out any very weak and spindly, or long and straggly, stems, cutting them right back to the base.

Also remove any very awkward stems that spoil the shape of the shrub, to leave an evenly balanced framework.

WHY, HOW, AND WHERE TO CUT

Pruning normally stimulates growth. The actively growing terminal shoot or dormant growth bud of a stem is often dominant, inhibiting by chemical means the growth of buds or shoots below it. Pruning to remove the ends of stems affects the control mechanism, resulting in more vigorous development of lower shoots or growth buds. Hard pruning promotes more vigorous growth than light pruning. This needs to be borne in mind when correcting the shape of an unbalanced shrub. Prune weak growth hard, but strong growth only lightly.

Opposite shoots
Prune stems with opposite buds to just above a strong pair of buds or shoots, using a clean, straight cut.

Alternate shoots
For plants with alternate buds, prune to just above a bud or shoot, using a clean, angled cut.

Making an angled cut
Angle the cut so that its lowest point is opposite the base of the bud and the top just clears the bud.

PRUNING ROSES

The purpose of pruning roses is to promote new, vigorous, disease-free shoots developing to replace the old, weakened ones, and so produce a reasonably attractive shape and the optimum display of blooms. Training a plant stimulates the production of flowering sideshoots and directs new growth. A pair of sharp, high-quality pruners is essential, and always wear thornproof gloves.

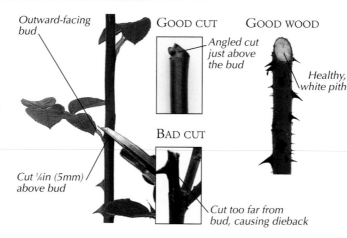

Outward-facing bud

Cut ¼in (5mm) above bud

GOOD CUT
Angled cut just above the bud

BAD CUT
Cut too far from bud, causing dieback

GOOD WOOD
Healthy, white pith

Pruning a newly planted bush rose

Prune a newly planted bush rose to about 3in (8cm) above ground level. Cut back to outward-facing buds, and remove any cold-damaged growth.

PRUNING HYBRID TEA AND GRANDIFLORA ROSES

Depending on the extent of winter kill and on the differences among cultivars, in colder areas the main shoots should be pruned back to between 8–10in (20–25cm). In milder areas, the shoots may be cut down less severely, to about 18–24in (45–60cm). For exhibition-quality blooms, cut the main shoots back hard to leave only two or three buds.

Cut out crossing, congested, and twiggy or spindly growth.

Remove dead wood and any that shows signs of damage or disease.

Prune main shoots to within about 8–10in (20–25cm) of ground level.

PRUNING FLORIBUNDA ROSES

When pruning Floribundas, cut out any unproductive wood as for Hybrid Teas. Reduce sideshoots by about one-third on smaller cultivars, and by two-thirds on taller-growing ones. Cut back the main shoots to 12–15in (30–38cm), but reduce the shoots of taller cultivars by about one-third. Do not prune them any harder, (unless growing for exhibition) because this will significantly reduce the number of blooms.

Remove crossing or congested wood and twiggy, spindly growth.

Prune out all dead, damaged or diseased wood to a healthy bud.

Prune main shoots to 12–15in (30–38cm) from ground level.

Reduce sideshoots by one- to two-thirds, cutting to a bud.

PRUNING STANDARD AND MINIATURE ROSES

Most standards are formed from Hybrid Teas or Floribundas budded onto a straight, unbranched stem. Prune as for their bush relatives, but cut back the main shoots so that they are all roughly equal in length. If the head is unbalanced, prune the shoots on the denser side less hard so that they do not produce as much new growth as those on the thinner side.

There are two methods: either give them the minimum of attention (remove dead growth, thin out tangles, and shorten overly long shoots) or treat them like small Hybrid Teas or Floribundas (remove all growth except the strongest shoots, and then cut them back by one-third or more).

Standard rose

After
All dead and damaged wood and any crossing stems have been removed to leave healthy shoots. The main shoots have been reduced to 8–10in (20–25cm), and the side-shoots by about one-third.

Before
In the spring, prune a standard rose to prevent the plant from becoming too top-heavy and to produce an evenly shaped, floriferous head.

Miniature rose

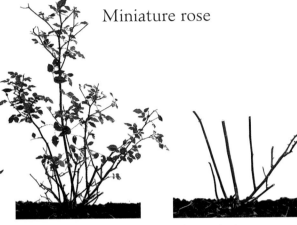

Before (Method Two)
Miniature roses often produce a mass of twiggy growth. The shape of this plant is unbalanced by overly vigorous shoots growing from the base.

After (Method Two)
Excessively twiggy and spindly growth, crossing shoots, and damaged wood have been removed, and vigorous shoots have been cut back by half.

DEALING WITH SUCKERS

Suckers usually look quite different from the rest of the plant, often with leaves of a different shape or color, and they often grow more strongly. Remove any suckers as soon as they appear. This prevents the rootstock from wasting energy on the sucker's growth. Damage to the roots, caused by severe cold or any accidental nicks from hoes, other implements, or a stake, may stimulate the production of suckers. Shoots on the stem of a standard rose are also suckers, since the stem is actually part of the understock. As with other grafted roses, any suckers will look different from the cultivar you want to grow.

REMOVING A SUCKER FROM A STANDARD ROSE
Pull away any suckers growing from the rose stem (see inset), taking care not to rip the bark.

With a trowel, carefully scrape away the soil to expose the top of the rootstock. Check that the suspect shoot arises from below the bud union.

Using gloves to protect your hands, pull the sucker down and away from the rootstock. Trim the wound, refill the hole, and gently firm the soil.

How a sucker grows

The sucker (right) grows directly from the rootstock. If cut back only at ground level it will regrow and divert further energy from the main part of the plant.

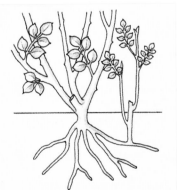

PEGGING DOWN ROSES

This technique is an effective (although time-consuming) way of increasing flower production on roses that tend to send up long, ungainly shoots with flowers only at the tips. In late summer or fall, bend the shoots over gently, taking great care not to snap them, then peg the shoots firmly into the ground. This has much the same result as horizontally training the shoots of climbing and rambler roses.

Select long, nonflowering shoots, and prune the soft tips. Gently bend each shoot over, then peg it to the soil with sturdy wire pins (see inset).

PRUNING GALLICA ROSES

Many of these old-fashioned roses produce a twiggy tangle of shoots that should be regularly thinned out to improve air circulation and bloom quality and to make the plant more attractive. After flowering, shorten the sideshoots only, and remove any dead or diseased wood. Gently clip Gallica roses used for hedging to maintain a neat shape. Follow their natural outline: do not attempt to shape them into a formal hedge, since this would remove many of the sideshoots on which flowers are produced in the following year.

Thin out twiggy growth regularly, and remove spent blooms by cutting back to the main shoot.

On mature plants, cut out up to one-quarter of old main shoots at the base.

Shorten side shoots, but not the main shoots, by about two-thirds. Cut out any dead, diseased, or weak wood.

PRUNING ALBA, CENTIFOLIA, DAMASK, AND MOSS ROSES

After flowering, reduce both main shoots and sideshoots. At the end of summer, cut back any overly long shoots that might whip about in the wind and cause wind-rock damage to the roots.

A general note on pruning the old-fashioned roses: some of these roses have a very individual growth habit and do not conform neatly to a specific pruning program. For these, it is best to observe the way the plant grows for the first few years, and then adapt a specific program (such as one of those given here) to how the rose reacts to the program. Some old-fashioned roses resent pruning and will respond by turning into very unattractive plants.

Cut back any overly long, whippy shoots by about one-third.

Prune sideshoots to about two-thirds of their length.

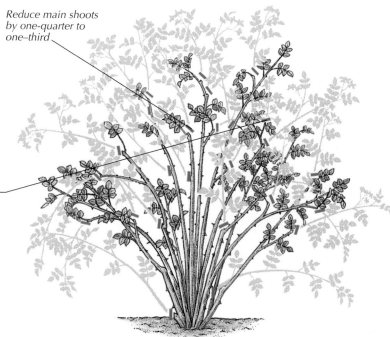

Reduce main shoots by one-quarter to one-third

PRUNING AND TRAINING CLIMBING ROSES

These roses require minor pruning but regular annual training. In their first year (and in their second unless they have made exceptional growth), do not prune climbers, except to remove any dead, diseased, or weak growth. Never hard prune climbing sports of bush roses (roses with the word "climbing" in their name; for example 'Climbing Peace') in the first two years, since they may revert to the bush form. Begin training as soon as the new shoots are long enough to reach the supports; train them sideways along horizontal supports to encourage flowering. Where this is not possible, choose a cultivar that is halfway between a tall shrub and a climbing rose. Many of these flower well from the plant base without special training.

Reduce the sideshoots by about two-thirds or about 6in (15cm), cutting above an outward-facing bud.

Tie all new shoots into horizontal wires 6–8in (15–20cm) apart. The shoots should not cross each other.

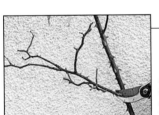

Remove any diseased, dead, or twiggy growth, cutting back to healthy wood or the main shoot.

PRUNING AND TRAINING MATURE RAMBLER ROSES

Ramblers produce much more growth from the base than most climbers and, if not carefully managed, grow into a vicious tangle of unmanageable shoots. Prune ramblers in summer, after they flower. In the first two years, restrict pruning to cutting back all the sideshoots by about 3in (7.5cm) to a vigorous shoot; also, remove dead or diseased wood. In later years, prune and train more heavily to maintain the framework: remove the oldest shoots to the ground, and train in new shoots that spring up from the base.

Cut sideshoots back to leave between 2 to 4 healthy buds or shoots.

Cut back any old, spent shoots to ground level, using loppers.

Tie all shoots to the wires as close to the horizontal as possible.

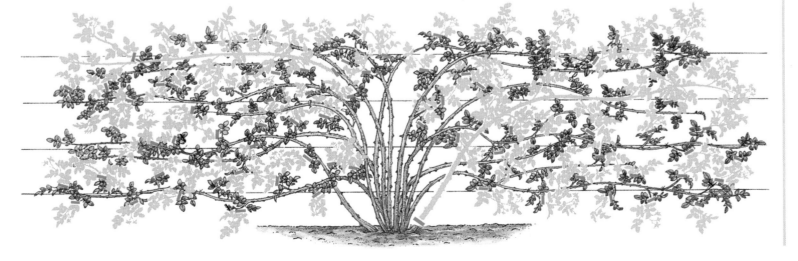

PROPAGATION

Producing new plants from existing ones is one of the most satisfying of all horticultural pursuits. From a simpler technique (sowing seeds) to the more elaborate (such as layering), growing your own allows you to raise a number of plants at minimum expense, such as for a hedge, and greatly increases your selections, especially if you grow annuals and vegetables from seed.

HARDWOOD CUTTINGS

Many deciduous trees and shrubs (as well as some evergreens) may be rooted from hardwood cuttings outdoors in fall and winter. If your winters are long and harsh or excessively wet, the cuttings usually die if left outside, but they can be rooted in deep boxes in a frost-free basement or root cellar instead. Select cuttings just after a hard frost. Choose strong, vigorous shoots of the current season's growth. For species that do not root easily, tie cuttings into small bundles, then plunge them into a sand bed.

Strip leaves and sideshoots from bottom half of cutting

For deciduous plants: trim off tips and cut stems into 8in (20cm) lengths. Make a horizontal cut just below a node, and a sloping cut to mark the top. Dip the base in hormone rooting compound. Insert them 2in (5cm) apart, 6in (5cm) deep, in soil-based rooting medium in pots, either in a cold place or outdoors.

For evergreens: cut shoots into sections 8–10in (20–25cm) long. Trim just above a leaf at the tip and below another at the base. Strip leaves from bottom half of cutting. Insert 5–8 cuttings in a 6in (15cm) pot. Place in a closed case with slight bottom heat, or in a clear plastic bag. Rooting occurs in 6–10 weeks.

SEMIRIPE CUTTINGS

Many conifers, as well as certain broadleaved evergreens such as hollies (*Ilex*) and *Magnolia grandiflora*, may be propagated readily from semiripe cuttings. After insertion, check the cuttings periodically, watering them only to keep them from drying out. Remove any fallen leaves as soon as they appear, since these may rot and spread disease to the cuttings. During cold spells, cold frames should be insulated with burlap or a similar covering.

The ideal semiripe cutting is taken from current season's growth that has begun to firm up; the base is quite firm, while the tip is soft and still actively growing. Such stems will offer some resistance when bent.

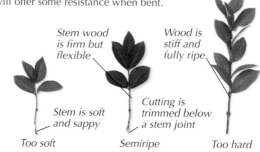

Stem wood is firm but flexible

Wood is stiff and fully ripe

Stem is soft and sappy

Cutting is trimmed below a stem joint

Too soft   Semiripe   Too hard

DISTINGUSHING SEMIRIPE WOOD

In mid- to late summer, select a healthy, semiripe shoot of the current season's growth (here, *Aucuba*), then sever the cutting just above a stem joint with clean, sharp pruners.

Remove sideshoots from the stem with a sharp knife. Trim the stem to 4–6in (10–15cm), cutting just below a stem joint. Remove the soft tip and the lowest pair of leaves.

To stimulate rooting, cut a shallow sliver of bark, ½–1in (1–2.5cm) long, from the base of the stem; do not expose the pith. This process is known as wounding.

Dip the base of the cutting in hormone rooting compound. Make sure that the entire wound receives the thinnest possible (but uniform) coating, then shake off the excess.

Place cuttings 2–3in (5–8cm) apart in standard rooting medium in a nursery bed outdoors (or in pots in a closed case). Label with name and date. Water and cover.

SOFTWOOD AND GREENWOOD CUTTINGS

This method of propagation is suitable for some tree species, although it is more commonly used for shrubs. Softwood cuttings are taken from the fast-growing tips of new shoots and usually root very easily. They wilt rapidly, however, so it is vital to prepare and insert them as quickly as possible after removing them from the parent plant.

SOFTWOOD CUTTINGS
Take softwood cuttings in spring and early summer from the new season's growth before it has begun to firm up. Choose vigorous nonflowering shoots with 2 or 3 pairs of leaves, cutting just below a stem joint.

GREENWOOD CUTTINGS
Take greenwood cuttings in late spring to midsummer, just as new stems begin to firm up. They are less prone to wilt and easier to handle than softwood and root as readily. Treat them exactly as for softwood cuttings

Remove the soft tip, because it is vulnerable to rot and scorch

Remove the soft tip just above a leaf joint, as well as the lowest pair of leaves. Cut large leaves in half to reduce moisture loss. Trim the base just below a leaf joint; the stem should be 1½–2in (4–5cm) long.

Fill a 5in (13cm) pot with rooting medium. Make 2 or 3 holes around the edge, then insert the cuttings so that the lowest leaves lie just above the surface and are not touching each other.

Vent of closed case will be opened gradually to harden off rooted cuttings

After watering thoroughly with a commercial fungicidal solution, label and place pots in a closed case heated, if possible, at the base to 59°F (15°C). Keep in a shaded place, out of direct sun.

Once cuttings have rooted, admit more air to harden them off. Knock out of the pot, tease apart, and pot up singly into 3½in (9cm) pots of soil mix. Pinch out growing tips to encourage bushy growth.

SIMPLE LAYERING

The long, trailing shoots of climbers may often be propagated by simple layering if they do not root naturally. A shoot is wounded and pegged down into the surrounding soil. This induces it to root at a node to provide a young plant that is later separated from the parent. Layers of many climbers that have been pegged down in spring will develop strong root systems by fall, at which time they can be separated from the parent plant. Layering also works for many shrubs and a few trees.

Dig a hole, about 3in (8cm) deep in prepared soil, with a shallowly sloping side next to the parent plant and a nearly vertical slope on the far side. Mix a little sand and organic matter into the bottom of the hole if soil is heavy.

Trim off sideshoots and leaves. At the point where the underside of the stem touches the soil, make a slanting cut through to the middle of the stem to make a "tongue" of bark, or remove a 1in (2.5cm) sliver of bark.

Dust the wound with some hormone rooting compound. Peg the stem down securely into the bottom of the hole using several U-shaped, galvanized wire pins, placing them on either side of the wound.

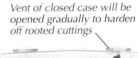

Bend the stem tip up against the vertical side of the hole and secure with a stake. Backfill, firm, and water in. Keep weed-free and moist. A layer should be well rooted within a year, and can be cut from the parent.

Plant the layer in a 5in (13cm) pot of standard soil mix, then water and label it. You could plant it into its permanent position in the garden if it has produced enough roots. Watch its watering needs carefully.

PROPAGATING PERENNIALS BY DIVISION

This method is suitable for propagating many perennials that have a spreading rootstock and produce plenty of shoots from the base. As well as being a way of increasing stocks, in many cases division rejuvenates the plants and keeps them vigorous, since old or unproductive parts are discarded. Most plants should be divided when they are dormant (or are about to go dormant, or are just emerging from dormancy) from late fall to early spring, but not in extremely cold, wet, or dry weather, because these conditions may make it difficult for the divided plants to reestablish successfully. Try to do this on an overcast, calm day.

Lift the plant to be divided, taking care to insert the fork far enough away from the plant so that the roots are not damaged. Shake off surplus soil.

Separate plants with a woody center by chopping through the crown with a spade. Use a trowel for smaller, less dense clumps.

Alternative method

Divide densely rooted herbaceous plants (here *Hemerocallis*) using 2 forks inserted back to back in the center. Larger, tougher clumps will require the help of an assistant.

Divide the plant into smaller pieces by hand, retaining only healthy, vigorous sections, each with several new shoots.

Cut back the old top-growth, then replant the divided sections to the same depth as before. Firm in and water thoroughly.

DIVIDING HOSTAS

Large hostas with tough rootstocks should be divided using a spade or back-to-back forks. Hostas that have looser, fleshy rootstocks may be separated by hand; this technique may be necessary to avoid damaging smaller-growing cultivars. For quick reestablishment of a clump, include several buds on an individual division, but if making many plants is your goal and you can wait longer for mature clumps, separate the clump into single or double buds, as long as each division has enough roots to sustain it. Trim any damaged parts with a knife, then replant as soon as possible. If there is a delay, store the plants under cover and keep moist.

Tough, fibrous roots
Divide the crown with a spade. Each section should include several developing buds.

Loose, fleshy roots
Divide small plants and those with a loose rootstock by pulling the clump apart by hand.

DIVIDING RHIZOMATOUS PLANTS

Divide plants with thick rhizomes, such as *Bergenia* and rhizomatous irises, by splitting the clump into pieces by hand, then cutting the rhizomes into sections, each with one or more growth points. Bamboos have tough rootstocks that either form dense clumps with short rhizomes or have long, spreading rhizomes. Divide dense clumps with a spade or two back-to-back forks; cut spreading rhizomes into sections (each of which should have three nodes or joints) with pruners. In all cases, trim excessively long roots before replanting.

Lift the plant to be divided (here an iris), inserting the fork well away from the rhizomes to avoid damaging them.

Shake the clump to remove any loose soil. Using your hands or a hand fork, split the clump into manageable pieces.

Discard any old rhizomes, then detach the new, young rhizomes from the clump and neatly trim off their ends.

Dust the cut areas with fungicide. Trim long roots by one-third. For irises, cut the leaves into a "fan" about 6in (15cm) tall to prevent wind-rock.

Plant the rhizomes at least 6in (15cm) apart. The rhizomes should be half buried, with their leaves and buds upright. Firm in well, then water.

PROPAGATING PERENNIALS BY ROOT CUTTINGS

This is a useful method of propagating perennials that have fairly thick, fleshy roots, such as *Papaver orientale*; it also works very well for horseradish (*Armoracia*). Take care to minimize damage to the parent plant when cutting its roots, and replant it immediately. Root cuttings are most successful when they are taken during the plant's dormant period, usually just before winter. Note: plants with thinner roots, such as *Anemone*, are done slightly differently. Lay the cuttings flat on the medium, then cover and treat as for thicker root cuttings.

Lift the plant (here *Acanthus*) when dormant and wash the roots. Cut roots of pencil thickness close to the crown.

Cut each into lengths of 2–4in (5–10cm). Make a straight cut at the upper end and an angled cut at the lower (inset).

Insert the cuttings into holes made in pots of moist rooting medium, then firm. The top end of each cutting should be flush with the surface.

Top-dress the pots of cuttings with coarse grit, label them, and place them in a cold frame until the cuttings root.

When the cuttings have developed young shoots, pot them up into individual pots filled with soil-based potting mix. Water and label the pots (see inset).

SOWING IN DRILLS

Seeds sown in drills produce seedlings growing in straight rows at regular intervals, so they are readily distinguished from weed seedlings, which are randomly distributed. Using either a trowel tip or the corner of a hoe, mark out shallow drills at a width depending on the ultimate size of the plants. Sow seeds thinly and evenly by sprinkling or placing them in each drill at the appropriate depth for the plants being sown, then carefully draw back the displaced soil. Label each row, then water gently but thoroughly with a fine spray. This technique is traditionally used for sowing vegetables, but it works equally well for annuals and biennials, especially in cutting gardens.

Using a line of string as a guide, make a furrow about 1in (2.5cm) deep with a hoe.

Alternative Step

If the seeds are pelleted, place them individually in the base of the drill.

Dribble the seeds from your hand to make sure they are scattered evenly.

Carefully rake the soil back over the drill without dislodging the seeds.

BROADCAST SOWING

Before sowing, mark the outline of the area for different plants with sand to keep track of the balance of colors, heights, and habits of each of the plants to be used, especially annuals. After sowing, label the area, then water the area gently but thoroughly with a fine spray. This method is particularly suitable for taprooted annuals, such as *Clarkia*, *Gypsophila*, and poppies (*Papaver*), which are best sown where they are to flower, since they do not transplant readily.

Prepare the soil by raking to produce a fine tilth. Scatter the seeds thinly over the prepared area from your hand or from the packet.

Rake over the area lightly at right angles to cover the seeds so that they are disturbed as little as possible. Water gently but thoroughly.

THINNING SEEDLINGS

To prevent overcrowding, seedlings usually need to be thinned. Do this when the soil is moist and the weather mild, taking care to retain the sturdier seedlings where possible and to achieve even spacing. To minimize disturbance to a seedling being retained, press the soil around it with your fingers as the surplus seedlings are extracted. Thinnings may be used to fill sparse areas caused by uneven sowing or irregular germination, or they may be planted elsewhere in the garden.

To thin small seedlings, nip them out at ground level so that the roots of the remaining seedlings are not disturbed.

Lift seedlings gently, keeping as much soil around them as possible. If moving them, place them in a clear plastic bag to retain moisture.

SOWING IN A TRAY

Many annuals, biennials, perennials, herbs, and vegetables are usually sown in containers so that they can germinate and develop under cover and then be planted out as young plants when conditions are favorable. Pots, seed pans (shallow pots), seed trays, and packs are all suitable containers, depending on the number of seeds to be sown and the space they require. Most seedlings will need to be pricked out before they are large enough to be planted out (see below). Peat pots are useful for seedlings that do not transplant well, since the whole pot may be planted out without disturbing the roots.

Fill the seed tray with a standard sowing medium, then level with a presser board to ½in (1cm) below the rim.

Sprinkle the seeds thinly over the surface of the medium to achieve an even distribution.

Cover the seeds with a layer of sieved, moist soil mix to about the same thickness as the seeds themselves. Water the seeds in lightly.

Place a piece of glass or clear plastic sheeting over the tray to maintain even humidity.

Shade the tray with netting if the tray is in direct sunlight. Remove both glass and netting as soon as germination starts.

PRICKING OUT OF A PACK

Seedlings raised in trays or pans need to be transplanted into larger containers before they become overcrowded, because they may quickly become weak and spindly if deprived of sufficient space or light, and damping off (a disease) may develop. This process is known as pricking out. It enables the seedlings to continue to develop properly until they are ready for planting out in the open garden. Fill the new containers with a soil-based mix, then firm gently to eliminate any air pockets. Small pots, no more than 3in (6cm) in diameter, or compartmentalized plastic packs are ideal for individual seedlings; larger pots, pans, or trays can be used for several plants.

Carefully separate the seedlings, handling them by their seed leaves, not their more delicate stems. Try to keep plenty of medium around the roots.

Transplant each seedling into a separate section of a pack. Firm the soil mix around each one with your fingers or a dibber, then water.

APPENDICES

GOVERNMENT RESOURCES: COOPERATIVE EXTENSION SERVICES

AZ
University of Arizona
Forbes 301, P.O. Box 210036
Tucson, AZ 85721-0036
(520) 621-7205
Fax: (520) 621-1314
http://cals.arizona.edu/extension

CA
Central Coast and South Regional Office
University of California #213
Highlander Hall, Bldg. 'C' Room 130
Riverside, CA 92521
(909) 787-3321
Fax: (909) 787-4675
http://ccsr.ucdavis.edu

Central Valley Regional Office
University of California
Kearney Agricultural Center
9240 South Riverbend Avenue
Parlier, CA 93648
(559) 646-6518
Fax: (559) 646-6513
http://cvr.ucdavis.edu

North Coast and Mountain Regional Office
DANR Building Hopkins Road
University of California Davis, CA 95616
(530) 754-8509
Fax: (530) 754-8540
http://ncmr.ucdavis.edu

HI
Hawaii Office of Cooperative Extension
3050 Maile Way, Gilmore 203
Honolulu, HI 96822
(808) 956-8139
Fax: (808) 956-9105
http://www2.ctahr.hawaii.edu

NV
University of Nevada
Mail Stop 404
Reno, NV 89557-0106
(775) 784-7070
Fax: (775) 784-7079
http://www.unce.unr.edu

NM
New Mexico State University
P.O. Box 30001
Las Cruces, NM 88003-8001
(505) 646-4115
http://www.cahe.nmsu.edu/ces

OK
Oklahoma State University
139 Agriculture Hall
Stillwater, Oklahoma 74078
(405) 744-5398
Fax: (405) 744-5339
http://www1.dasnr.okstate.edu/oces

TX
Texas A&M University
Room 225
Horticulture/Forestry Sciences Building
Mail Stop 2134
College Station, Texas 77843-2134
(979) 845-5341
http://agextension.tamu.edu

HORTICULTURAL ORGANIZATIONS AND GARDENING WEBSITES

The Internet is an ever-expanding wealth of information on all aspects of the horticultural world. These helpful sites offer links to others.

American Horticultural Society
http://www.ahs.org

American Rose Society
http://www.ars.org

Arizona Native Plant Society
http://aznps.org

California Native Plant Society
http://www.cnps.org

The Garden Web
http://www.gardenweb.com

Guide to the Art of Desert Gardening
http://www.hotgardens.net

Hort.net Gallery of Plants
http://www.hort.net/gallery

Las Pilitas Native Plants
http://www.laspilitas.com

Mediterranean Garden Society
http://www.mediterraneangardensociety.org

Native Seeds/SEARCH
http://www.nativeseeds.org

Native Hawaiian Plant Society
http://www.angelfire.com/hi4/nhps

Nevada Native Plant Society
http://heritage.nv.gov/nnps.htm

New Mexico Native Plant Society
http://npsnm.unm.edu

North American Native Plant Society
http://www.nanps.org/index.shtml

Oklahoma Native Plant Society
http://www.usao.edu/~onps

Texas Native Plant Society
http://www.npsot.org

SEED AND PLANT CATALOGS

Good sources for the toughest plants for your growing conditions, these offer plants and seeds not available at your local nursery.

Antique Rose Emporium
9300 Lueckemeyer Road
Brenham, TX 77833
(800) 441-0002
http://www.antiqueroseemporium.com

Botanical Interests, Inc.
660 Compton Street
Broomfield, CO 80020
(800) 486-2647
http://www.botanicalinterests.com

W. Atlee Burpee & Co.
300 Park Avenue
Warminster, PA 18974
(800) 333-5808
http://www.burpee.com

Bountiful Gardens
18001 Shafer Ranch Road
Willits, CA 95490
(707) 459-6410
http://www.bountifulgardens.org

Brent and Becky's Bulbs
7463 Heath Trail
Gloucester, VA 23061
http://www.brentandbeckysbulbs.com

Canyon Creek Nursery
3527 Dry Creek Road
Oroville, CA 95965
(530) 533-2166
http://www.canyoncreeknursery.com

The Cook's Garden
P.O. Box 1889
Southampton, PA 18966-0895
(800) 457-9703
http://www.cooksgarden.com

Digging Dog Nursery
P.O. Box 471
31101 Middle Ridge Road
Albion, CA 95410
(707) 937-1130
http://www.diggingdog.com

Heirloom Roses, Inc.
24062 NE Riverside Drive
St. Paul, Oregon 97137
(503) 538-1576
http://www.heirloomroses.com

High Country Gardens
2902 Rufina Street
Santa Fe, NM 87505
(800) 925-9387
http://www.highcountrygardens.com

Johnny's Selected Seeds
955 Benton Avenue
Winslow, ME 04901
http://www.johnnyseeds.com

McClure and Zimmerman
108 W. Winnebago Street
P.O. Box 368
Friesland, WI 53935-0368
(800) 883-6998
http://www.mzbulb.com

George W. Park Seed Co.
One Parkton Avenue
Greenwood, SC 29647-0001
(800) 213-0076
http://www.parkseed.com

Plants of the Southwest
Agua Fria Road
Route 6, Box 11A
Santa Fe, NM 87501
(505) 438-8888
http://www.plantsofthesouthwest.com

Seeds of Change
P.O. Box 15700
Sante Fe, NM 87506-5700
(888) 762-7333
http://www.seedsofchange.com

Seeds West Garden Seed
317 14th Street NW
Albuquerque, NM 87104
(505) 843-9713
http://www.seedswestgardenseed.com

Territorial Seed Co.
P.O. Box 158
Cottage Grove, OR 97424-0061
http://www.territorialseed.com

Thompson and Morgan
P.O. Box 1308
Jackson, NJ 08527
http://www.thompson-morgan.com

Willhite Seed, Inc.
P.O. Box 23
Poolville, TX 76487-0023
(800) 828-1840
http://www.willhiteseed.com

BOTANICAL GARDENS, ARBORETA, AND PARKS

Most have labeled collections of native and/or exotic plants. They can be an inspiration as well as an excellent source of information on what grows well in your region. Many offer seminars and demonstrations on various aspects of gardening. Additional sites worth a visit can be found on the American Association of Botanical Gardens and Arboreta website at http://www.aabga.org.

✲ All-America Selections Display Garden – see http://www.all-americaselections.org for more information.

Arizona
*Arboretum at Arizona State University
Facilities Management/Department Grounds
Tempe, AZ 85287-3305
(480) 965-8467
http://www.asu.edu/fm/arboretum.htm

Arboretum at Flagstaff
4001 South Woody Mountain Road
Flagstaff, AZ 86001-8776
(928) 774-1442
http://www.thearb.org

Arizona-Sonora Desert Museum
2021 N. Kinney Road
Tucson, AZ 85743-8918
(520) 883-1380
http://www.desertmuseum.org

Boyce Thompson Arboretum
37615 Highway 60
Superior, AZ 85273-5100
(520) 689-2811
http://ag.arizona.edu/BTA

Desert Botanical Garden
1201 N. Galvin Parkway
Phoenix, AZ 85008
(480) 941-1225
http://www.dbg.org

Tohono Chul Park
7366 North Paseo del Norte
Tucson, AZ 85704
(520) 742-6455
http://www.tohonochulpark.org

Tucson Botanical Gardens
2150 North Alvernon Way
Tucson, AZ 85712
(520) 326-9686
http://www.tucsonbotanical.org

University of Arizona Arboretum
P.O. Box 210036
Tucson, AZ 85721-0036
(520) 621-7074
http://arboretum.arizona.edu

California

*Arboretum of Los Angeles County
301 N. Baldwin Avenue
Arcadia, CA 91007
http://www.arboretum.org

Arboretum at the University of California,
Santa Cruz
1156 High Street
Santa Cruz, CA 95064
(831) 427-2998
http://www2.ucsc.edu/arboretum

Conservatory of Flowers
McLaren Lodge, Golden Gate Park
501 Stanyan Street
San Francisco, CA 94117
(415) 753-7271
http://www.conservatoryofflowers.org

Descanso Gardens
1418 Descanso Drive
La Canada Flintridge, CA 91011
(818) 952-4408
http://www.descanso.com

*Fullerton Arboretum
California State University
1900 Associated Road
Fullerton, CA 92831-3599
(714) 278-3579
http://www.arboretum.fullerton.edu

Ganna Walska Lotusland
695 Ashley Road
Santa Barbara, CA 93108
(805) 969-3767
http://www.lotusland.org

Guadalupe River Park & Gardens
50 W. San Fernando Street, #1100
San Jose, CA 95113
(408) 277-5998
http://www.grpg.org
Huntington Botanical Gardens
1151 Oxford Road

San Marino, CA 91108
(626) 405-3500
http://www.huntington.org

Mendocino Coast Botanical Gardens
18220 North Highway 1
Fort Bragg, CA 95437
(707) 964-4352
http://www.gardenbythesea.org

Pikake Botanical Gardens
15515 Villa Sierra Road
Valley Center, CA 92082-7651
(760) 749-4819
http://members.cox.net/pikakegardens

Quail Botanical Gardens Foundation
P.O. Box 230005
Encinitas, CA 92023-0005
(760) 436-3036
http://www.qbgardens.com

Quarryhill Botanical Garden
P.O. Box 232
Glen Ellen, CA 95442
(707) 996-3166
http://www.quarryhillbg.org

Rancho Santa Ana Botanic Garden
1500 North College Avenue
Claremont, CA 91711-3157
(909) 625-8767
http://www.rsabg.org

Ruth Bancroft Garden
P.O. Box 30845
Walnut Creek, CA 94598
(925) 944-9352
http://www.ruthbancroftgarden.org

San Luis Obispo Botanical Garden
P.O. Box 4957
San Luis Obispo, CA 93403
(805) 473-8988
http://www.slobg.org

Santa Barbara Botanic Garden
1212 Mission Canyon Road
Santa Barbara, CA 93105
(805) 682-4726
http://www.santabarbarabotanicgarden.org

Sherman Library and Gardens
2647 East Coast Highway
Corona del Mar, CA 92625
(949) 673-2261
http://www.slgardens.org
*Strybing Arboretum & Botanical Gardens
Ninth Avenue at Lincoln Way

San Francisco, CA 94122
(415) 753-7090
http://www.strybing.org

University of California, Davis Arboretum
One Shields Avenue
Davis, CA 95616
(530) 752-4880
http://arboretum.ucdavis.edu

University of California Botanical Garden
200 Centennial Drive #5045
Berkeley, CA 94720-5045
(510) 642-0849
http://www.mip.berkeley.edu/garden

Wrigley Memorial and Botanical Garden
P.O. 2739
Avalon, CA 90704
(310) 510-2288
http://www.catalina.com/memorial.html

Hawaii

Amy B. H. Greenwell Ethnobotanical Garden
82-6188 Mamalahoa Highway
Captain Cook, HI 96704
(808) 323-3318
http://www.bishopmuseum.org/greenwell

Foster Botanical Garden
50 North Vineyard Boulevard
Honolulu, HI 96817
(808) 522-7066

Hawaii Tropical Botanical Garden
P.O. Box 80
Papaikou, HI 96781
(808) 964-5233
http://www.hawaiigarden.com

Lyon Arboretum
3860 Manoa Rd.
Honolulu, HI 96822
(808) 988-0456
http://www.lyonarboretum.com

National Tropical Botanical Garden
3530 Papalina Road
Kalaheo, HI 96741
(808) 332-7324
http://ntbg.org
Waimea Arboretum and Botanical Garden
59-864 Kamehameha Highway
Halaiwa, HI 96712
(808) 638-8655

New Mexico
Rio Grande Botanic Garden
2601 Central Avenue, NW
Albuquerque, NM 87104
(505) 764-6210
http://www.cabq.gov/biopark/garden

Santa Fe Botanical Garden
P.O. Box 23343
Santa Fe, NM 87502-3343
(505) 428-1684
http://dir.gardenweb.com/directory/sfbg

Nevada
Desert Demonstration Gardens
3701 West Alta Drive
Las Vegas, NV 89153
(702) 258-3205
http://www.lvvwd.com/html/
spec_proj_gardens.html

Elko County Rose Garden
Sixth and Pine
Elko, NV 89801
http://www.elkorose.com/index.shtml

Frey Ranch Historical Complex and Gardens
1140 West Peckham Lane
Reno, NV 89509
(702) 825-3080

Reno Municipal Rose Garden
2055 Idlewild Drive
Reno, NV 89509
(702) 334-2270

Southern Nevada Zoological-Botanical Park
1775 North Rancho Drive
Las Vegas, NV 89106-1020
(702) 647-4685
http://www.lasvegaszoo.org

University of Nevada-Las Vegas
Arboretum and Xeric Garden
4505 Maryland Parkway, Box 451013
Las Vegas, NV 89154
(702) 895-3392
http://www.unlv.edu/facilities/landscape/
xeric.html
Wilbur D. May Arboretum
1502 Washington Street
Reno, NV 89503
(775) 785-4153
http://www.maycenter.com

Oklahoma
Jo Allyn Lowe Park
Price Road at Locust Road
Bartlesville, OK 74005
(918) 337-5267
http://home.okstate.edu/Okstate/dasnr/hort/
hortlahome.nsf/toc/joallyn

Lendonwood Botanical Gardens
1308 W. 13th Street
Grove, OK 74344
(918) 786-2938
http://www.lendonwood.org

Myriad Botanical Gardens and Crystal Bridge
301 West Reno
Oklahoma City, OK 73102
(405) 297-3995
http://www.myriadbotanicalgardens.com

North Oklahoma Botanical Garden
and Arboretum
1220 East Grand Avenue
Tonhawa, OK 74653
(580) 628-2220

Oklahoma Botanical Garden & Arboretum
Oklahoma State University
3425 West Virginia Street
Stillwater, OK 74078
(405) 744-5404
http://home.okstate.edu/Okstate/dasnr/hort/hort
lahome.nsf/toc/obgahead

Tulsa Garden Center
2435 South Peoria
Tulsa, OK 74114
(918) 746-5125
http://www.tulsagardencenter.com

Texas
Botanical Research Institute of Texas
509 Pecan Street
Fort Worth, TX 76102-1079
(817) 332-4441
http://www.brit.org

Carleen Bright Arboretum
9001 Bosque Boulevard
Woodway, TX 76712
(254) 399-9204

Corpus Christi Botanical Gardens
8545 South Staples Street
Corpus Christi, TX 78413
(361) 852-2100
http://www.ccbotanicalgardens.org

*Dallas Arboretum & Botanical Society
8617 Garland Road
Dallas, TX 75218
(214) 515-6500
http://www.dallasarboretum.org

East Texas Arboretum & Botanical Society
P.O. Box 2231
Athens, TX 75751
(903) 675-5630
http://dir.gardenweb.com/directory/etabs

Fort Worth Botanic Garden
3220 Botanic Garden Boulevard
Fort Worth, TX 76107
(817) 871-7686
http://www.fwbg.org

Houston Arboretum and Nature Center
4501 Woodway Drive
Houston, TX 77024
(713) 681-8433
http://www.houstonarboretum.org

Lady Bird Johnson Wildflower Center
4801 Lacross Avenue
Austin, TX 78739
(512) 292-4200
http://www.wildflower.org

Mercer Arboretum and Botanic Gardens
22306 Aldine Westfield Road
Humble, TX 77338-1071
(281) 443-8731
http://www.cp4.hctx.net/mercer

*Montgomery County Extension
Master Gardener Test Gardens
9020 FM 1484
Conroe, TX 77303

*San Antonio Botanical Garden
555 Funston Place
San Antonio, TX 78209
(210) 207-3255
http://www.sabot.org

Texas Discovery Gardens
P.O. Box 152537
Dallas, TX 75315
(214) 428-7476
http://www.texasdiscoverygardens.org

INDEX

Page numbers given in italics refer to catalog pages on which the plants are illustrated. In plant entries, topics that relate to the main entries appear first; subentries for species and cultivars always follow the general subentries.

A

Aaron's beard 174
Abelia
    'Edward Goucher' 217
    x grandiflora 199
    'Prostrate' 217
abelia, glossy 199
Abies nordmanniana 111
Abronia villosa 281
abutilon, Thompson's variegated 202
Abutilon
    megapotamicum 186, 225
    menziesii 54
    pictum var. thompsonii 202
acacia
    Bailey's 97, 115, 209
    Berlandier 54
    knife 213
    sweet 87
    twisted 94
    weeping 138
Acacia
    baileyana 97, 115, 209
    berlandieri 54
    constricta 135
    cultriformis 213
    farnesiana 87
    koa 54
    longifolia 159, 197
    pendula 138
    schaffneri 94
    willardiana 94
Acanthus 383
    mollis 260
Acca sellowiana 134
Acer
    campestre 123
    griseum 131
    japonicum 114
        'Acontifolium' 128
    macrophyllum 99, 113
        'Garnet' 128
    rubrum 99
    saccharinum 113
    tataricum subsp. ginnala 143
Achillea 14
    ageratifolia 267
    'Coronation Gold' 338
        Summer Shades 259
    'Moonshine' 265
    ptarmica 'The Pearl' 275
    tomentosa 308
Acorus calamus 'Variegatus' 331
Actinidia
    deliciosa 245
Adam's needle, variegated 341
Adenium obesum 212
Adiantum aleuticum 311
Aechmea
    fasciata 268
    Foster's Favorite Group 270
    gamosepala 268
Aegopodium podagraria 'Variegatum' 308

Aeonium
    arboreum 228
        'Zwartkop' 224
    haworthii 228
aeonium, black 224, 228
Aesculus
    californica 93, 132, 207
    x carnea 133
Agapanthus praecox subsp. orientalis
    'Albus' 341
Agastache
    aurantiaca 'Shades of Orange' 273
    foeniculum 351
agave
    cow horn 179
    foxtail 213
    Parry 303
    Queen Victoria 303
Agave
    americana 'Media Picta' 194
    attenuata 213
    bovicornuta 179
    parryi 303
    victoriae-reginae 303
Agonis flexuosa 141
Ajuga reptans 301
Akebia quinata 241
Albizia julibrissin 'Rosea' 108
Alcea
    filicifolia Antwerp Mix 355
    rosea 'Nigra' 337
Alchemilla mollis 347
alder. See Alnus
almond, all-in-one 147
Alnus cordata 99
aloe
    climbing 255
    dwarf 224, 299
    Thrask's 91
    tree 183, 191
Aloe 38
    arborescens 191
    aristata 224, 299
    ciliaris 255
    dichotoma 91
    thraskii 91
Alpinia zerumbet 268
Alstroemeria
    aurea 339
    'Parigo Charm' 277
Alyogyne huegelii 204
alyssum, sweet 279
Alyssum montanum 'Berggold' 272
amaranth, globe 279
Amaranthus
    caudatus 354
Amaryllis 373
    belladonna 263
amethyst flower 353
Ammi majus 286, 354
Ampelopsis brevipedunculata 237
Anacyclus pyrethrum var. depressus 300
Anchusa azurea 'Loddon Royalist' 297
Anemone 383
    blanda 319
    coronaria 'The Bride' 320
    fulgens 320
    x hybrida 296
anemone, Japanese 296
Anethum graveolens 349
angel's trumpet, Charles Grimaldi 178
Anigozanthos
    Bush Gem Hybrids 267
    'Bush Gold' 256
Anisodontea x hypomandarum
    'Tara's Wonder' 178
annuals
    for butterflies 279

    cool-season 288–289, 358–359
    for cottage gardens 354–355
    for cut flowers 344
    definition 34
    with edible flowers 350–351
    for herb gardens 348–349
    for partial shade 352–353
    planting techniques 370
    for summer and fall bloom 356–357
    wildflowers for desert gardens 280–281
Antigonon leptopus 230, 235
Antirrhinum majus Sprite Series 355
Apache plume 163
Aponogeton distachyos 372
Aporocactus flagelliformis 254
apple
    'Anna' 39, 124, 151
    large kangaroo 189
    low-chill golden 146
apricot
    Floragold 150
    Katy 151
    Moorpark 147
aprium, flavor delight 151
Aptenia cordifolia 307
aquatic plants 328–329
Aquilegia
    Dragonfly Hybrids 293
    formosa 312
    McKana Hybrids 275, 346
Arabis x arendsii 'Rosabella' 309
aralia, Japanese 173
Araucaria
    araucana 136
    heterophylla 110, 121
arborvitae 62, 135
Arbutus
    menziesii 133
    unedo 106
Archontophoenix cunninghamiana 156
Arctostaphylos
    densiflora 'Howard McMinn' 168
    'Emerald Carpet' 168
    pumila 208
    uva-ursi 'Point Reyes' 175
Arctotheca calendula 315
Ardisia crispa 172
Argyranthemum frutescens 222, 274
Armeria maritima 'Bloodstone' 300
Armoracia
Artemisia 42
    dranunculus 349
    ludoviciana 277
    'Powis Castle' 205
Asclepias tuberosa 278, 299
ash
    Arizona 113
    European weeping 139
    Mediterranean 95
Asparagus densiflorus 'Myersii' 261
aspen, weeping 113
asphodel, yellow 318
Asphodeline lutea 318
Aster 370
    x frikartii 'Wunder von Stäfa' 274
aster, Stokes' 274
Aucuba japonica 'Crotonifolia' 173
Aurinia saxatilis 346
azalea 38
    Alaska 178
    red wing 222
azara, boxleaf 172
Azara microphylla 172

B

Babania 37
    rubrocyanea 325
baboon flower 325
baby blue eyes 54, 288
baby's breath 275
Baccharis
    pilularis 'Pigeon Point' 168,
        sarothroides 166
bachelor's buttons 282, 288
bacopa, snowflake 342
Bahia absinthifolia 313
Baileya multiradiata 313
balloon flower 347
Ballota pseudodictamnus 259
balm, lemon 219
bamboo(s) 317, 383
    Buddha's belly 317
    giant timber 317
    golden goddess 215, 317
    Mexican weeping 317
    yellow groove 317
Bambusa
    multiplex
        'Alphonse Karr' 215
        'Golden Goddess' 317
    oldhammii 317
    tuldoides 317
banana, variegated ornamental 116
banana shrub 109
Banksia
    ericifolia 196
baobab, mini 213
barberry
    creeping 312
    Darwin's 198
    rose glow Japanese 210
    William Penn 197
    Wilson 194
basket of gold 346
    creeping 272
bat flower 295
Bauhinia
    x blakeana 108
    variegata 141
bay, sweet 96
bean
    castor 294
    Mescal 40, 90, 167
    scarlet runner 243
    screw 87, 92
    southwest coral 164
beardtongue 277
bear's breeches 260
Beaumontia grandiflora 230
bee balm 351
beech, weeping copper 138
begonia
    bedding 352
    cane 304
Begonia
    'Can Can' 350
    'Orange Rubra' 304
    'Organdy' 352
    'Richmondensis' 342
Belamcanda chinensis 276
bell flower, Chilean 243
bellflower, Italian 305
Bellis perennis 350
bells of Ireland 355
beneficial organisms 67–69
Berberis
    darwinii 198
    x gladwynensis 'William Penn' 197
    thunbergii var. atropurpurea 'Rose
        Glow' 210
    wilsoniae 194

bergamot, sweet *351*
Bergenia 383
   'Abendglut' *337*
Berlandiera lyrata 313
berry, lemonade *211*
betony, woolly *348*
Betula
   nigra 'Heritage' *100*
   papyrifera 131
   pendula 'Youngii' *138*
biennials
   for cottage gardens 354–355
   definition 34
   for partial shade 352–353
Billbergia rutans 260
birch
   Heritage River *100*
   silver *131*
   Young's weeping *138*
bird of paradise *179*
   giant *117, 137*
   Mexican *163*
birds *132, 134–135, 208–211, 243, 298–299*
bishop's flower *286, 354*
black-eyed Susan *294*
blanket flower
   double *283*
   perennial *283, 287*
bleeding heart, common *294*
Bletilla striata 326
bluebell
   peach-leaved *340*
   Texas *285*
bluebells, California desert *280*
bluebonnet, Texas *285, 288*
blue curls, woolly *214*
bluet, mountain *340*
borage *351*
Borago officinalis 351
Boronia megastigma 177
bottlebrush
   compact *198*
   lemon *135, 198*
   weeping *103*
Bougainvillea 24, 36, 38
   'Barbara Karst' *70, 230*
   x *buttiana* 'Golden Glow' *246*
   'Hawaii' *202*
   'La Jolla' *52, 240*
   'Orange King' *234*
Bouteloua
   curtipendula 313
   gracilis 14, 314
Bowiea-volubilis 254
box
   Brisbane *141*
   sweet *173*
   Victorian *134*
boxwood, Japanese *173*
Brachychiton 62
   acerifolius 102, 105
   discolor 132
Brahea
   aculeata 154
   armata 157
   edulis 152
brass buttons, New Zealand *309*
Brassica oleracea 359
Brazilian plume *188*
breath of heaven *215*
Breynia 44
Brighamia insignis 54
brittlebush *54, 167*
Briza maxima 344
brodiaea, white *325*
bromeliad, bottlebrush *268*
broom

butcher's *169*
   desert *166*
Browallia speciosa 'Vanja' *353*
Brugmansia 'Charles Grimaldi' *178*
Brunfelsia pauciflora 185, 223
buckeye
   California *93, 132, 207*
   Mexican *165*
Buddleia davidii 'Harlequin' *208*
bugleweed, carpet. See *Ajuga reptans*
bugloss, Italian *297*
Bulbine frutescens 264
bulbs
   hardy 318–319
   for naturalizing in mild-winter gardens 324–325
   planting and naturalization 371
   selection 364
   for summer and fall bloom 322–323
   for winter and spring bloom 320–321
bundle of strings *255*
bunny ears *212*
Bursera microphylla 86
busy Lizzie *357*
Butia capitata 152
butterflies *133, 206–207, 242, 278–279*
butterfly bush
   blue *184*
   harlequin *208*
butterfly weed *278, 299*
Buxus microphylla var. *japonica*
   'Green Beauty' *173*

C
cabbage, flowering *359*
cabbage lobelia, Olulu *54*
cabbage tree, mountain *116*
cactus(i)
   apple *226*
   beaver-tail *227*
   compass barrel *227*
   crab *224*
   golden barrel *227, 262*
   old man *226*
   orchid *254, 305*
   Peruvian old man *226*
   rattail *254*
   selection of *265*
   smaller, for garden accents *227*
   tall, for dramatic effects *10, 226*
   Thanksgiving *224*
   year round color with *35*
Caesalpinia mexicana 163
caladium, fancy-leaved *322*
Caladium bicolor 322
Calamagrostis x *acutiflora* 'Karl Foerster' *316*
Calendula officinalis 359
   'Pacific Beauty' *344*
Calibrachoa hybrids *305*
Calliandra 84
   californica 54, 160, 166
   eriophylla 160
   haematocephala 201
   tweedii 201, 217
calliopsis *286*
Callistemon
   citrinus 135
     'Compacta' *198*
   viminalis 97, 103
Calocedrus decurrens 111, 123
Calochortus superbus 318
Caltha palustris 331, 365
Calycanthus occidentalis 206
Camboba caroliniana 328
Camellia 38, 84
   'Dr. Clifford Parks' *223*
   japonica

'Elegans' *200*
   'Guilio Nuccio' *172*
   sasanqua 62
     'Mine-No-Yuki' *225*
     'Yuletide' *183, 220*
Campanula
   isophylla 'Alba' *305*
   persicifolia 'Telham Beauty' *340*
camphor tree *97, 141*
Campsis
   radicans 231
   x *tagliabuana* 'Madame Galen' *243*
candytuft
   evergreen *292, 301*
   snowflake *292*
Cantua buxifolia 182
cape weed *315*
cardinal flower *278*
Cardiospermum halicacabum 239
cardoon *269*
Carex
   comans 308
   elata 'Aurea' *331*
Carica papaya 'Sunset' *148*
Carissa macrocarpa 175
   'Fancy' *195*
carnation, cascading *290*
Carnegiea gigantea 54, 136
carob. See *Ceratonia siliqua*
Carpobrotus edulis 307
Carya illinoinensis 'Western Schley' *146*
Caryota urens 156
cashmere bouquet *176*
Cassia fistula 103, 104
Castanea 'Colossal' *147*
Castanospermum australe 99
Castilleja indivisa 285
cast iron plant *334*
catchfly *282, 286*
Catharanthus roseus 'Parasol' *357*
catmint *277*
cat's claw *240*
Cattleya aurantiaca 326
Ceanothus 54, 55
   'Blue Mound' *207*
   griseus var. *horizontalis 169*
   'Joyce Coulter' *169*
   maritimus 181
cedar
   blue atlas *107, 138*
   deodar *110*
   incense. See *Calocedrus decurrens*
   Japanese plume *111*
   of Lebanon *107*
   weeping atlas *138*
   western red *122*
Cedrus 62
   atlantica f. *glauca 107*
     'Pendula' *138*
   deodora 110
     'Pendula' *138*
   libani 107
Celtis laevigata var. *reticulata 95*
Centaurea
   cyanus 282, 288
   macrocephala 338
   montana 340
   pulcherrima 276
Centranthus ruber 34, 274
century plant *194*
Cephalocereus senilis 226
Cerastium tomentosum 309, 341
Ceratonia siliqua 96
Ceratostigma plumbaginoides 216
Parkinsonia florida 86, 90, 92, 95
Cercis
   canadensis 'Forest Pansy' *37*

occidentalis 93, 94
   siliquastrum 'Bodnant' *143*
Cereus uruguayanus 226
Ceropegia linearis subsp. *woodii 255*
Cestrum
   elegans 'Smithii' *187*
   nocturnum 177
Chamaecyparis nootkatensis 62
Chamaedorea elegans 153
Chamaemelum nobile 349
   'Treneague' *300, 314*
Chamaerops humilis 157
Chamelaucium unicinatum 196
chamisa *54, 165*
chamomile
   Roman. See *Chamaemelum nobile*
   Treneague lawn *300, 314*
cherry
   Catalina *175, 211*
   purple-leaved sand *203*
   sour *147*
chestnut
   colossal *147*
   Guiana *149*
   Moreton Bay *99*
   red horse *133*
   water *329*
Chilopsis linearis 90, 132
Chimonanthus praecox 176
chinaberry *89*
Chinese lantern *186, 225*
Chionanthus
   retusus 108
   virginicus 126
Chionodoxa luciliae 319
x *Chitalpa tashkentensis* 'Pink Dawn' *158*
chocolate flower *313*
Choisya ternata 176
cholla, teddy bear *54*
Chorisia speciosa 131, 132, 136
Chorizema ilicifolium 195
Christmas shrub, New Zealand *199*
Christmas tree, New Zealand *105*
Chrysanthemum
   'Clara Curtis' *296, 336*
   coronarium 350
   grandiflorum 350
Chrysothamnus nauseosus 54, 165
chuparosa *54, 160*
Cibotium glaucum 54
cigar plant *223*
cilantro *348*
cineraria *21*
Cinnamomum camphora 97, 141
cinquefoil *262*
Cistus 38
   'Doris Hibberson' *37, 180*
Citrus 29, 144–145
   aurantifolia 145
   limon 132
     'Bearss' *144*
     'Improved Meyer' *106*
   meyeri 125
   maxima 'Chandler' *144*
   'Oroblanco' *144*
   paradisi 'Rio Red' *144*
   reticulata 'Dancy' *125*
   sinensis
     'Lane Late' *145*
     'Moro' *144*
     'Valencia' *145*
   x *tangelo* 'Minneola' *145*
Clematis 368
   armandii 244
   'Polish Spirit' *236*
Cleome hasslerana 357
Clerodendrum
   bungei 176

myricoides var. ugandense 184
thomsoniae 234, 239
Clethra arborea 126
climate, Mediterranean and Southwest 38
climbers
    for butterflies 242
    for chain-link fences 246
    for cottage gardens 238–239
    for desert gardens 230
    drought-resistant 231
    with edible fruit 245
    with fragrant flowers 244
    for groundcover 240
    for groundcovers in shade 241
    for hummingbirds 243
    for Mediterranean-style gardens
        236–237
    roses 247–251
    selection of 363
    for subtropical gardens 232–233
    for tropical gardens 234–235
Clivia 52
    miniata 261
clover
    scarlet 351
    water 328
Clytostoma callistegioides 233
coastal gardens 25
Cobaea scandens 238
Codiaeum variegatum 'Pictum' 184
Coelogyne cristata 326
coffeeberry 93, 191
coffee tree, Kentucky 127
Colchicum 364
Coleonema pulchrum 'Golden Sunset' 215
coleus 44
Colocasia esculenta 'Fontanesii' 331
columbine 275, 293, 312, 346
    scarlet 312
Columnea x banksii 271
column plant 271
compost and composting 16, 30–31, 40,
        56–58
coneflower, purple 278, 284
Consolida ambigua 288
container gardening. See also hanging
        baskets
    shrubs for 222–223
    drip system for 15, 36
    succulents 224, 302–303
Convallaria majalis 290
Convolvulus
    cneorum 265
    sabatius 340
coppicing a shrub 375
Coprosma x kirkii 'Variegata' 175
coral bells. See Heuchera
coral plant 185
coral shrub 212
coral tree 84
coral-tree, cockspur 102
Cordia parvifolia 165
Cordyline
    australis 'Variegata' 116
    indivisa 116
Coreopsis
    grandiflora
        'Early Sunrise' 259
    lanceolata 282
    tinctoria 286
coriander 348
Coriandrum sativum 348
cornflower 282, 288
Cornus florida 'Cloud Nine' 172
Correa
    'Dusky Bells' 208
    pulchella 215
Corydalis solida 364

Corylus avellana 'Contorta' 39
Cosmos
    bipinnatus 'Seashells' 357
    sulphureus Ladybird Series 286
Cotinus 62
    coggygria 115
Cotoneaster
    atropurpureus 202
    dammeri 'Lowfast' 169
    lacteus 215
cotton, lavender 42, 219, 263, 335
    green 263
cottonwood
    black 159
    western 98
Cotyledon
    orbiculata var. oblonga 224, 229
cotyledon, fancy-leaved 224, 229
cover crops 31
coyote bush, dwarf 168
crabapple
    flowering 124
    white 133
crape myrtle 92, 115, 129
    Japanese 130
    Tuskegee 129
Crassula
    arborescens 224
    multicava 260, 306
    ovata 221
    perfoliata var. minor 229, 302, 303
creeper
    Australian bluebell 237
    blue star 301
    Carmel 169
    common trumpet 231
    Madame Galen trumpet 243
    Virginia 241
creeping Charlie 23, 311
crevillea, juniper-foliaged 196, 216
Crinum
    asiaticum 271
    x powellii 322
Crocosmia 'Lucifer' 324
Crocus vernus
    'Purpureus Grandiflorus' 321
crocus, Dutch 321
crop rotation 63
croton 184
crowfoot, water 328
crown of thorns 179, 212
Cryptomeria japonica 'Elegans' 111
Cuphea
    ignea 223
    x purpurea 295
x Cupressocyparis leylandii 122
    'Haggerston Grey' 120
Cupressus
    arizonica var. glabra 111
    macrocarpa 119
    sempervirens 117,
    torulosa 'Cashmeriana' 136
currant
    chapparal 170
    red flowering 168
Cyathea medullaris 104
Cycas revoluta 172
cyclamen
    florist's 321
    hardy 319
Cyclamen
    coum f. albissimum 319
    persicum 'Sierra White' 321
Cydonia oblonga 'Aromatnaya' 149
Cymbidium 21
    hookerianum 326
    hybrids 38, 345
    'Thurso' 268

Cynara cardunculus 269
Cyperus papyrus 330
cypress 29
    Arizona 111
    Haggerston Grey leyland 120
    Italian 117
    Kashmir 136
    leyland 120, 122
    Monterey 119
Cyrtomium falcatum 310

D
daffodil. See also Narcissus
    winter 323
Dahlia 364
    'Bishop of Llandaff' 345
    'Hayley Jane' 322
daisy
    annual African 289
    Blackfoot 333
    copper canyon 183
    crown 350
    English 350
    marguerite 222, 274
    Michaelmas 274
    Mount Atlas 300
    paper 338
    Santa Barbara 258
    Transvaal 345, 353
    whirligig freeway 265
Dalea
    frutescens 165
    pulchra 54, 162
dame's rocket 290
dandelion, desert 281
Daphne odora 'Leucanthe' 176
Dasylirion
    longissimum 166
    wheeleri 163
date, Chinese 148
dawn flower, blue 232, 246
daylily. See Hemerocallis
deer-resistant plants 214–215
Delonix regia 105
Delphinium elatum 292
desert spoon 163
Dianella tasmanica 334
Dianthus 22
    caryophyllus Hanging Mixed 290
    chinensis 'Telstar Crimson' 337
    'Musgrave's Pink' 348
Dicentra spectabilis 294
Dictamnus albus 'Albiflorus' 341
Dierama
    pulcherrimum 354
Dietes grandiflora 269
Digitalis
    purpurea 'Excelsior' 355
    'Tall Shirley' 34
dill 349
Dimorphotheca sinuata 289
Diospyros kaki 128
    'Hachiya' 125
disease 29, 36, 64, 142, 385
disease-resistant plants 38, 62, 142–143
Distictis buccinatoria 232
dittany, false 259
Dodecatheon meadia 282
Dodonaea viscosa 161
donkey tail 254, 305
dracaena 116, 373
    blue 116
Dracaena
    deremensis 'Souvenir de Schriever' 373
    draco 117
dragon tree 117
drainage
    runoff management 25, 43, 43–44

soil 18–19, 30, 37
Drosanthemum floribundum 306
drought-resistant plants
    adaptations of 36, 38, 42
    climbers 231
    climbing roses 248–249
    in the garden 26, 28, 37
    lawn and turf grass 14–15
    palms 154–155
    perennials 298–299, 336–341
    trees 94–97
duckweed 365, 372
Dudleya edulis 312
dudleya, Santa Catalina 312
Dymondia margaretae 309

E
Ebenopsis ebano 87
ebony, Texas 87
Eccremocarpus scaber 238
Echeveria elegans 303
Echinacea purpurea 284
    'Bright Star' 278
Echinocactus grusonii 227, 262
Echium fastuosum 70
elephant food 174, 229
elephant tree 86
elm. See Ulmus
empress tree 102
Encelia farinosa 54, 167
Epidendrum
    ibaguense 334
    x obrienianum 326
Epilobium angustifolium f. album 276
Epiphyllum
    crenatum 254
    hybrids 305
Eremurus robustus 277
Erigeron karvinskianus 258
Eriobotrya japonica 88
    'Champagne' 148
Erodium chrysanthum 272
Eryngium alpinum 340
Erysimum
    x allionii 283
    'Bowles Mauve' 347
Erythrina
    x bidwillii 212
    crista-galli 102
    flabelliformis 164
Erythronium oregonum 364
Escallonia
    x exoniensis 'Frades' 216
    'Langleyensis' 182
Eschscholzia
    californica 263, 288
    mexicana 280
espalier 124–125, 200–201
Espostoa lanata 226
eucalyptus 29
    flame 103
    lemon 52, 97
    lemon gum 52, 97
Eucalyptus
    cinerea 143
    citriodora 52, 97
    ficifolia 103
    globulus 121
    nicholii 159
    pauciflora 131
eugenia 100
Euonymus fortunei 'Golden Prince' 174
euphorbia
    Canary Island 91
    globe 303
    tree 91
Euphorbia 10, 36
    canariensis 91

candelabrum 91
    characias subsp. wulfenii 276
        'John Tomlinson' 212
    milii 212
        var. splendens 179
    obesa 303
    polychroma 347
Euryops pectinatus 182
    'Green Gold' 179
Eustoma grandiflorum 285
evapotranspiration map 44
everlasting, pink and white 268
Extension Services 38, 64, 77

F

Fagus sylvatica 'Purpurea Pendula' 138
fairy duster 54, 160, 166
Fallopia baldschuanica 231
Fallugia paradoxa 163
x Fatshedera lizei 241
Fatsia japonica 173
Felicia amelloides 'Santa Anita' 265
felt bush 229
fennel, common 267
fern(s) 23
    bird's nest 271
    black tree 104
    Boston 305
    five finger 311
    Hawaiian tree 54
    Japanese holly 310
    leatherleaf 311
    silver ribbon 270
    southern sword 261
    staghorn 305
Ferocactus cylindraceus 227
fertilizer 20
Festuca 14, 45
Ficus 62
    carica 'Brown Turkey' 114
    microcarpa 121
    rubiginosa 134
fig. See also Ficus
    edible. See Ficus carica
    Hottentot 307
    Indian laurel 121
    Port Jackson 134
    weeping 121
Filipendula rubra 'Venusta' 275
fir
    Douglas 112
    Nordmann 111
firebreaks 174–175, 262–263, 306–307
firethorn. See Pyracantha
fireweed, white 276
Firmiana simplex 117
flag
    crimson 323
    powdery alligator 331
    Spanish 243
    sweet 331
    yellow 330
flamboyant tree 105
flame bush, Brazilian 201, 217
flame of the woods 186
flame thrower 49–50
flame tree
    Australian 102, 105
    Chinese 108
    pink 132
flannel bush 54, 84, 181, 214
flax
    New Zealand 295, 335
    perennial 275, 287
    scarlet 288
Foeniculum vulgare 267
Foresteria neomexicana 90
forget-me-not 353

Fouquieria
    macdougalii 162
    splendens 54, 93, 164
foxglove 34, 355
    Chinese 259
Fragaria chiloensis 263
frangipani
    red 114
    white 222
Franklinia 62
    alatamaha 127
franklin tree 127
Fraxinus
    angustifolia 95
    excelsior 'Pendula' 139
    velutina 113
Fremontodendron 54
    'California Glory' 84, 214
    'Ken Taylor' 181
fringe tree
    Chinese 108
    white 126
Fritillaria camschatcensis 319
fruit 146–151, 245. See also espalier
fuchsia. See also Fuchsia
    Australian 208, 215
    California 54, 299
    tree 205
Fuchsia
    arborescens 205
    'Baby Chang' 62
    'Chance Encounter' 62
    'Dollar Princess' 62
    'Gartenmeister Bonstedt' 179
    'Golden West' 62
    'Lena' 225
    'Marinka' 225
    'Miniature Jewels' 62
    'Red Spider' 62
    'Swingtime' 223
fuki 329

G

Gaillardia
    aristata 283, 287
    pulchella 'Red Plume' 283
Galvezia speciosa 191
garden cleanup 59, 62
Gardenia jasminoides 'Veitchii' 217
gardening
    challenges and rewards 78
    environmentally responsible 40–51
    with a natural aesthetic 52–59
garden journal 70–73
garden plan
    adapting to existing conditions 26–31
    creation of the 10–15, 78
Garrya elliptica 199
gas plant 341
Gaura
    lindheimeri
        'Siskiyou Pink' 336
        'Whirling Butterflies' 258, 264
        'Perky Pink' 342
gayfeather, dense 322, 336
Gazania 37
Gelsemium sempervirens 244
Geraea canescens 281
geranium
    garden 343
    hardy. See Geranium
    ivy 304, 309
    Maderia 52, 353
    rica 269
    rose 218, 264
Geranium
    'Ann Folkard' 276
    maderense 52, 353

Gerbera jamesonii 345, 353
ginger, Kahili 188
Ginkgo 62
    biloba 'Autumn Gold' 129
Gladiolus communis 323
Gleditsia triacanthos 88
    'Elegantissima' 142
    'Ruby Lace' 159
globemallow 54, 256, 333
Gloriosa superba 'Rothschildiana' 238
glory bower 234
glory flower, Chilean 238
glory of the snow 319
goldenchain tree, Voss's 124
goldenrod 296, 346
golden shower tree 103, 104
Gomphrena globosa 279
gooseberry
    Chinese 245
    fuchsia flowering 214
gourd, trumpet 236
goutweed, variegated 308
grape
    California wild 54
    evergreen 241
    purpleleaf 236
    Thompson Seedless 245
grapefruit
    Oroblanco 144
    Rio red 144
grass(es) 256
    bamboos 317
    bent 14
    Bermuda 14
        'Santa Ana' 14
    black mondo 310
    blue gramma 14, 314
    buffalograss 14
    fescue 14, 45
    Foerster's feather reed 316
    heavy metal switch 316
    invasive 56
    Japanese silver 256, 316
    Kentucky bluegrass 14
    lawn. See lawn and turf
    maiden 256, 316
    mondo 310
    ornamental 316
    perennial rye 14
    purple fountain 316, 343
    quaking 344
    St. Augustine 14
    side oats grama 313
    zoysia 14
        'De Anza' 14
        'Victoria' 14
grass tree, Mexican 166
grassy bells 354
gray fingers 307
green carpet 301
Grevillea
    juniperina 196, 216
    'Noellii' 181
    robusta 62, 96
Grewia occidentalis 201
Griselinia
    littoralis 'Variegata' 220
groundcovers
    climbers 240–241
    herbaceous, for full sun 308–309
    for light foot traffic 314–315
    native perennial
        for dry shade 312
        for hot interiors 313
    perennial, for full shade 310–311
    succulent, for Zone 1 firebreaks
        306–307
    for Zone 2 firebreaks 262–263

growth habits 39
guajillo 66
guava
    pineapple 134
    strawberry 148
guinea plant, golden 200
gum
    American sweet 129
    blue 121
    ghost 131
    sour 129
Gunnera manicata 184
Gymnocladus dioicus 127
Gypsophila 384
    paniculata 'Bristol Fairy' 275,

H

hackberry, western 89, 95
hanging baskets 23, 34, 36, 225,
        304–305, 373
Hardiness Zones 22, 32, 35
harlequin flower 324
Harry Lauder's walking stick 39
hawthorn, Indian 45
hawthorn tree, Indian. See Rhaphiolepis
        indica
hearts on a string 255
Heat Zones 22, 32
Hebe 'Purple Queen' 181, 206
Hedera
    canariensis var. algeriensis 241
hedges 84, 123, 210
Hedychium
    coronarium 290
    gardnerianum 188
Helenium 'Wyndley' 287
Helianthus
    maximiliani 286
    x multiflorus 'Flore Pleno' 338
heliotrope
    common. See Heliotropium
        arborescens
    wild 280
Heliotropium arborescens 274, 343
hellebore, Corsican 260
Helleborus
    argutifolius 260
    niger 296
Hemerocallis 382
    'Betty Woods' 267
    'Black-eyed Stella' 62
    'Butterscotch Ruffles' 62
    'Cat's Cradle' 294
    'Frankly Scarlet' 62
    'Happy Returns' 342
    'Lavender Dew' 62
    'Little Joy' 62
    'Tootsie Rose' 62
herbaceous plants 256, 290–291
herb gardens 218–219, 348–349
herbicides and pesticides, chemical 50,
        65–66
Herniaria glabra 301
Hesperaloe parviflora 299, 335
Hesperis matronalis 290
Heteromeles arbutifolia 92, 175, 209
    subsp. macrocarpa 214
Heuchera
    'Firefly' 298
    micrantha 'Palace Purple' 292
    'Wendy' 312
Hibbertia scandens 240
hibiscus. See also Hibiscus
    blue 204
    Chinese 188, 198, 208
    coral 185, 188
    yellow 54
Hibiscus

brackenridgei 54
rosa-sinensis 188, 198
'Agnes Galt' 208
schizopetalus 185, 188
syriacus 'Minerva' 207
hidalgo 273
Hippeastrum 25, 373
holly 380
alpine sea 340
Burford's 197
California. See Heteromeles arbutifolia
English 367
Japanese 171
Oregon grape 180
variegated English 194
hollyhock
Antwerp 355
black 337
honey bush 213
honeysuckle 363
Australian 196
cape 209, 246
giant Burmese 243
Japanese 240, 242
late Dutch 241
Mexican 339
scarlet trumpet 236
hop bush 161
hops, golden 237
Hosta 370, 382
houseplants 373
Hoya carnosa 255
Humulus lupulus 'Aureus' 237
humus 31
hyacinth 21
Dutch 321
grape 319
white grape 321
Hyacinthus orientalis 'Ostra' 321
Hydrangea macrophylla 221, 223
Hypericum
androsaemum 171
calycinum 174
Hypoestes aristata 269
hyssop, anise 351

I

Iberis sempervirens 301
'Schneeflocke' 292
iceplant 307
orange 307
red apple 307
rosea 306
trailing 297, 307
ice plant, green apple 25
Ilex 380
aquifolium 'Gold Coast' 194
cornuta
'Burfordii' 197
crenata 'Helleri' 171
Impatiens 25, 35
walleriana 357
Indian paintbrush, Texas 285
indigo bush 54, 62
information resources 74, 76–77
integrated pest management (IPM) 60,
62–65, 67–69
invasive plants 56
Iochroma cyanea 186, 189
Ipomoea
indica 232, 246
lobata 243
tricolor 'Heavenly Blue' 238
iris. See also Iris
bearded 266
Del Norte County 324
German 346
Gladwin 260

Japanese water 330
Iris 383
'Beverly Sills' 293
'Dusky Challenger' 323
foetidissima 260
germanica 346
innominata 324
laevigata 330
pallida 266
pseudoacorus 330
ironwood, desert 90
irrigation 14, 15, 25, 36, 42–45
Iva hayesiana 174
ivy
Algerian 241
aralia 241
Ixora coccinea 186

J

Jacaranda mimosifolia 103, 104
Jacob's ladder 293
jade plant, silver 221
jade tree 224
Japanese lantern 185, 188
jasmine
angel wing 240
Arabian 177
Madagascar 244
night 177
pink 70
South African 237
star 244
Veitchii Cape 217
West Indian 84, 126
Jasminum
angulare 237
laurifolium 240
polyanthum 70
sambac 177
Jatropha
integerrima 221
podagrica 213
jessamine, Carolina yellow 244
johnny jump-up 359
jojoba 161
Joshua tree 137
Jubaea chilensis 155
Judas tree 143
Juglans
major 89
regia 'Pedro' 146
jujube 148
Juncus effusus 'Spiralis' 330
juniper. See Juniperus
Juniperus
chinensis 'Torulosa' 135
scopulorum
'Skyrocket' 112
'Tolleson's Blue Weeping' 139
squamata 'Blue Star' 203
Jupiter's beard 34, 274
Justicia
brandegeeana 'Yellow Queen' 187, 189
californica 54, 160
carnea 188
spicigera 339

K

Kalanchoe
beharensis 229
blossfeldiana 303
fedtschenkoi 302
pumila 229
tomentosa 302
kale, flowering 359
kangaroo paw 256, 267
Kerria japonica 'Golden Guinea' 200
Kigelia pinnata 105, 136

kitchen, outdoor 16
kiwi 245
knapweed 276
giant 338
Kniphofia
'Bees' Sunset' 339
'Royal Standard' 347
uvaria 335
knotweed 308
koa tree 54
Koelreuteria
bipinnata 108
paniculata 62, 140
Kokia drynarioides 54
koki'o tree 54
kopiko'ula tree 54
Kunzea baxteri 182

L

Laburnum x watereri 'Vossii' 124
lady's mantle 347
Lagenaria siceraria 236
Lagerstroemia
fauriei 'Fantasy' 130
indica 92
'Catawba' 115
'Tuskegee' 129
Lagunaria patersonii 120
lamb's ears. See Stachys
Lampranthus
aurantiacus 307
deltoides 307
spectabilis 297, 307
landscape
checklist of use 13
renewal 28, 28–29
Lantana
camara
'Feston Rose' 217
'Radiation' 208
montevidensis 191
Lapageria rosea 243
larkspur 288
candle 292
Lathyrus odoratus 'Cupani' 239
laurel
California 98
Carolina cherry 210
English 210
spotted Japanese 173
Texas mountain 40, 90, 167
variegated Portugal 123
Laurus nobilis 96
Lavandula
angustifolia 'Hidcote' 209, 218
dentata 204
Lavatera
assurgentiflora 55, 178
thuringiaca 'Barnsley' 199
trimestris 'Silver Cup' 355
lavender
English 209, 218
French 204
'Provence' 35
sea 265, 345
lawn and turf 13–14
alternatives 14, 14–15
irrigation 42–45
weed control 49
Layia platyglossa 284
lead ball tree, golden 90
leadwort, cape 240
lemon. See Citrus limon
lemonade berry 54, 211
Leonotis leonurus 298, 339
Leptinella squalida 309
Leptospermum
laevigatum 23

scoparium 115
'Nanum Tui' 222
'Ruby Glow' 182, 203
'Snow White' 198
Leucaena retusa 90
Leucojum
aestivum 'Gravetye Giant' 324
vernum 319
Leucophyllum
frutescens
'Compactum' 209
'Green Cloud' 163
var. compactum 161
laevigatum 166
Leucospermum cordifolium 196
Liatris spicata 322, 336
Ligustrum
lucidum 122
ovalifolium 206
lilac. See Syringa
California. See Ceanothus
Lilium
pardalinum 318
regale 290
lily
Aztec 323
blackberry 276
blood 270
cape 322
chocolate 319
flax 334
fortnight 269
foxtail 277
glory 238
green goddess cala 271
Guernsey 323
Kaffir 261
leopard 318
mariposa 318
Peruvian. See Alstroemeria
pink porcelain 268
regal 290
spider 271
white ginger 290
lily of the Nile, white 341
lily of the valley 290
lily-of-the-valley tree 126
lilyturf
big blue 261
creeping 310, 335
silver dragon 310
lime
Bearss 144
key 145
Limonium perezii 265, 345
Linaria moroccana 288
linden
African 220
silver 89
small-leaved 127
Linum
grandiflorum 'Rubrum' 288
lewisii 'Appar' 272
perenne 275, 287
lion's ears 298, 339
lion's tail 298, 339
lippia 14, 314
Liquidambar styraciflua 'Festival' 129
Liriodendron tulipifera 140
Liriope
muscari 261
spicata 335
'Silver Dragon' 310
Litchi chinensis 'Groff' 149
Livistona mariae 154
Lobelia
cardinalis 278
erinus 356

Lobularia maritima 'Snow Crystals' *279*
locust
    black *127*
    Elegantissima honey *142*
    honey *88, 142, 159*
    Idaho *159*
    New Mexico *94, 98*
    ruby lace honey *159*
Lonicera 363
    x *brownii* 'Dropmore Scarlet' *236*
    hildebrandiana 243
    japonica 'Halliana' *242*
    japonicum 'Halliana' *240*
    periclymenum 'Serotina' *241*
Lophostemon confertus 141
loquat. See *Eriobotrya japonica*
Loropetalum chinense 'Razzleberri' *203*
lotus *291*
Lotus berthelottii 304
love-in-a-mist *355*
love-lies-bleeding *354*
low-maintenance gardening 13, 14, 15, *15, 32*
Luma apiculata 109
lupine. See also *Lupinus*
    arroyo *299*
Lupinus 364
    arizonicus 280
    succulentus 299
    texensis 285
Lychnis
    chalcedonica 339

M
Macfadyena unguis-cati 240
Mackaya bella 189
Maclura pomifera 84, 142
madrone *133*
magic lantern *186, 225*
magnolia
    saucer *117*
    southern. See *Magnolia grandiflora*
    star *109*
    sweet bay *98*
    Veitch *102*
Magnolia
    grandiflora 127, 380
        'Little Gem' *125*
    x *soulangeana 117*
    stellata 109
    x *veitchii 102*
    virginiana 98
mahonia
    desert *211*
    longleaf *169*
Mahonia
    aquifolium 180
    fremontii 211
    nervosa 169
    repens 312
Malacothrix glabrata 281
mallow. See also *Lavatera*
    annual *289*
    apricot *54, 256, 333*
    Barnsley tree *199*
    silver cup rose *355*
    Tara's wonder cape *178*
    tree *55, 178*
Malosma laurina 54
maltese cross *339*
Malus
    'Adirondack' *124*
    'Anna' *39, 124, 151*
    'Dorset Golden' *146*
    'Snowdrift' *133*
Malva sylvestris 'Zebrina' *289*
Mandevilla sanderi 'Red Riding Hood' *223*
Mangifera indica 'Keitt' *149*

mango, Keitt *149*
manzanita. See *Arctostaphylos*
maple
    amur *143*
    bigleaf *99, 113*
    full moon *128*
    hedge *123*
    Japanese *114, 129*
    Oregon *99, 113*
    paperbark *131*
    red *99*
    sugar *113*
Maranta leuconeura var. *kerchoviana 311*
marguerite *222, 274*
    variegated blue *265*
marigold
    desert *313*
    giant African *356*
    marsh *331*
    pot. See *Calendula officinalis*
Markhamia hildebrandtii 120
marlberry *172*
marmalade bush *187, 223*
Marsilea quadrifolia 328
Master Gardeners 77
mat plant, purple *303*
Matthiola
    incana 'Ten Weeks Trisomic' *344*
    Trisomic Hybrids *291*
Maytenus boaria 138
Melaleuca linariifolia 131
Melampodium leucanthum 333
Melia azedarach 89
Melianthus major 213
Melissa officinalis 219
Mentha spicata 349
mesquite
    honey *87, 94*
    screwbean *87, 92*
Metasequoia 62
    glyptostroboides 142
Metrosideros
    excelsa 105
        'Spring Fire' *199*
    polymorpha 54
Mexican gem *303*
Mexican hat *284*
Mexican tree *162*
Michelia doltsopa 109
Mickey Mouse plant *184*
microclimates *24–25, 26*
milfoil, diamond *328*
million bells *305*
mimosa, red *108*
Mimulus aurantiacus Verity Hybrids *298*
mint, hummingbird *273*
Miscanthus sinensis 'Morning Light' *256, 316*
Molucella laevis 355
Monarda didyma 351
monkey flower *35*
    sticky *298*
monkey puzzle tree *136*
Monstera deliciosa 184, 187
montebretia *324*
morning glory. See also *Ipomoea*
    bush *265*
    ground *340*
Morus alba 101, 134, 141
moss, Scotch *300*
Mucuna bennettii 234
mulberry, white *101, 134, 141*
mulching *15, 40, 46, 46–48, 62*
mullein. See also *Verbascum*
    denseflower *349*
Musa acuminata 'Zebrina' *116*
Muscari
    armeniacum 319

    botryoides 'Album' *321*
Myoporum
    laetum 'Carsonii' *197*
    parvifolium 174
Myosotis alpestris 353
Myriophyllum aquaticum 328
myrtle
    common *171*
    lemon-leaf *109*
Myrtus communis 171

N
naked ladies *263*
Narcissus 364, 371
    'Cragford' *327*
    'February Gold' *327*
    'Fortune' *327*
    'Grand Soleil d'Or' *327*
    'Ice Follies' *327*
    'Tahiti' *320*
nasturtium. See *Tropaeolum*
native plants 52, 55
    for desert gardens 160–167, 332–333
    for dry shade 170
    groundcovers 312–313
    resistant to deer 214
    shrubs for birds 211
    shrubs for desert gardens 160–163
    trees for desert gardens 86–87
nature, working with 52–59
Nelumbo 'Mrs. Perry D. Slocum' *291*
Nemesia caerulea 'Blue Bird' *342*
Nemophila menziesii 54, 288
Nepeta x *faassenii 277*
Nephrolepis
    cordifolia 261
    exaltata 'Bostoniensis' *305*
Nerine sarniensis 323
Nerium oleander 38, 101
Nicotiana
    alata 353
    sylvestris 291, 354
Nigella damascena Persian Jewels Series *355*
nightshade, Costa Rican *231*
nogal *89*
Nolina
    bigelovii 54
    recurvata 137
Nototrichium sandwicense 54
nut, kulu'i 54
nutrients 19–20, 31
Nymphaea
    odorata 'Sulfurea Grandiflora' *329*
    'Panama Pacific' *329*
    tetragona 329
Nyssa sylvatica 129

O
oak
    Chinquapin *113*
    coastal scrub *170*
    cork *107, 130*
    Engelmann *54*
    holly *107, 119, 141*
    Holm *107, 119, 141*
    plateau live *88*
    silk *62, 96*
    valley *93*
Ochna serrulata 184
ocotillo. See *Fouquieria*
Oenothera
    caespitosa 332
    deltoides 280
    macrocarpa 287
    speciosa 336
    stubbei 313
ohe tree 54

ohi'a lehua tree 54
Olea europaea 97
oleander *38, 101*
    yellow *105*
olive *38*
    desert *90*
    sweet *177*
olive tree *97*
Olneya tesota 90
onion *38*
    climbing *254*
Ophiopogon
    japonicus 310
    planiscapus 'Nigrescens' *310*
Opuntia
    basilaris 227
    bigelovii 54
    microdasys 212
    robusta 226
    violacea 227
orange
    blood *144*
    Lane late navel *145*
    Osage *84, 142*
    sweet mock *177*
    Valencia *145*
    Wheeler's dwarf mock *216*
orange blossom, Mexican *176*
orchid(s)
    angel *326*
    Chinese ground *326*
    cymbidium. See *Cymbidium*
    reed *326*
    terrestrial *334*
orchid tree
    Hong Kong *108*
    purple *141*
oregano *219, 314*
    creeping *314*
organic matter 30–31. See also compost and composting
Origanum vulgare
    'Compactum' *314*
    'Roseum' *219*
Ornithogalum umbellatum 321
Osmanthus
    delavayi 171
    fragrans 177
Osteospermum 'Whirligig' *265*
Otatea acuminata var. *aztecorum 317*
Oxalis obtusa 297

P
Pachira aquatica 149
Pachycereus schotti 163
pagoda tree, Japanese *62, 88, 101*
palm(s)
    cabbage *157*
    California fan *86, 98, 152*
    Canary Island *152*
    Central Australian cabbage *154*
    Chilean wine *155*
    cliff date *154*
    for moist soil *156*
    date *152, 154*
    drought-resistant 154–155
    fan *38*. See also specific fan palms
    fancy natal *195*
    fishtail wine *56*
    foxtail *154*
    Guadalupe *152*
    Japanese sago *172*
    king *156*
    lady *153*
    Licury *155*
    loulu leo 54
    Mediterranean fan *157*
    Mexican blue *157*

Mexican fan *100, 155*
needle *157, 195*
parlor *153*
Pindo *152*
ponytail *137*
Puerto Rican hat *154*
pygmy date *114*
queen *156*
royal *153, 156*
sabal *194*
Sinaloa Hesper *154*
that survive frost *157*
that survive in desert heat *152–153*
traveler's *153*
for tropical gardens *153*
windmill *157*
palo blanco *94*
palo verde, blue *86, 90, 92,* 95
Pandanus tectorius 153
panda plant *302*
Pandorea
    jasminoides 233
Panicum virgatum 'Heavy Metal' *316*
pansy *297, 359*
Papaver
    orientalis 'Degas' *293*
    propagation techniques *383, 384*
    rhoeas 286
        'Shirley Poppy' *358*
papaya, sunset *148*
papyrus *330*
parasites and predators *68*
parrot's beak *304*
Parthenocissus quinquefolia 241
Passiflora
    x *alato-caerulea 232*
    'Amethyst' *242*
    caerulea 242
    edulis 'Frederick' *245*
    incarnata 'Incense' *244*
passion flower. See *Passiflora*
    Frederick *245*
Paulownia tomentosa 102
pea
    holly flame *195*
    sweet. See *Lathyrus odoratus*
peach
    Bonanza II *150*
    Florida prince *150*
pear
    evergreen *100*
    Japanese sand *124*
    prickly *226*
    Santa Rita prickly *227*
pecan *146*
Pelargonium
    'Amethyst' *264*
    graveolens 218, 264
    'Mrs. Henry Cobb' *67*
    Multibloom Series *343*
    peltatum 'Balcon' *304, 309*
    'Rica' *269*
Pennisetum setaceum 'Rubrum' *316, 343*
penstemon
    bush *332*
    desert *332*
    firecracker *337*
    Mexican *333*
    mountain *266*
    Rocky Mountain *283*
    scented *332*
Penstemon
    ambiguus 332
    barbatus 277
    centranthifolius 54
    eatonii 337
    heterophyllus 266
    palmeri 332

pseudospectabilis 332
    strictus 283
    superbus 333
Pentas lanceolata 89, 343
pepper, California *96, 123*
peppermint, Nichol's willow-leafed *159*
peregrina 221
perennials
    border
        English-style *346–347*
        fall and winter *296–297*
        spring *292–293*
        summer *294–295*
    for butterflies *278*
    for cottage gardens *274–275*
    for cut flowers *345*
    definition *34*
    drought-resistant
        blue or lavender *340*
        for hummingbirds *298–299*
        orange *339*
        pink *336*
        red or purple *337*
        white or silver *341*
        yellow *338*
    with edible flowers *350–351*
    for full sun *276–277*
    groundcovers *262–263, 310–313*
    grown as annuals *35*
    for hanging baskets *304–305*
    hardy *272–273*
    for hot dry shade *260–261*
    for herb gardens *348–349*
    for hot interior gardens *258–259*
    invasive *56*
    maintenance *56, 59*
    mild-zone
        fall and winter *268–269*
        spring *264–265*
        summer *266–267*
    native, for desert gardens *332–333*
    planting techniques *370*
    for shallow water *330–331*
    for tropical gardens *270–271*
    for use near swimming pools *334–335*
    for year-round bloom *342–343*
pergola *32*
periwinkle, Madagascar *357*
Perovskia atriplicifolia 'Blue Spire' *204*
persimmon
    Hachiya *125*
    Japanese *125, 128*
pesticides
    alternatives to chemical *67–69, 133*
    chemical *50, 65–66*
pest management *46, 47, 47, 48, 50, 50,*
        59, 60–69
pest-resistant plants *38, 62*
pests, common *64, 214–215*
Petasites japonicus 329
Petrea volubilis 234
Petunia 'Magic Carpet' *357*
pH, soil *19, 21, 30, 31*
Phacelia
    campanularia 280
    distans 280
    ramosissima 289
phacelia, fiddleneck *289*
Phaseolus 'Scarlet Runner' *243*
Philadelphus coronarius 177
philodendron
    Selloum *185*
    split-leaved *184*
Philodendron bipinnatifidum 185
Phlomis fruticosa 190
Phlox paniculata 'Eva Cullum' *295*
phlox, summer *295*
Phoenix

canariensis 152
    dactylifera 152
    roebelenii 114
    rupicola 154
Phormium 36
    'Apricot Queen' *258*
    tenax 335
        'Monrovia Red' *295*
Phyla nodiflora 14, 314
Phyllostachys aureosulcata 317
physically-challenged gardeners *13–14*
Picea abies 120
pickerel weed *328*
pincushion flower *278*
pine *29*
    Aleppo *119*
    bishop *119*
    bristlecone *112*
    Canary Island *110*
    fern *125, 140*
    Italian stone *106, 119*
    Japanese black *118*
    Japanese red *111*
    maritime *118*
    Mexican weeping *110*
    Norfolk Island *110, 121*
    piñon *111*
    screw *153*
    stone *106, 110, 119*
    Swiss stone *112*
    Torrey *54, 133*
    umbrella *106, 119*
    yew *122, 122*
pink. See also *Dianthus*
    bloodstone sea *300*
    Chinese *337*
    cottage *348*
Pinus
    aristata 112
    canariensis 110
    cembra 112
    densiflora 'Umbraculifera' *111*
    edulis 111
    halepensis 119
    muricata 119
    nigra 142
    patula 110
    pinaster 118
    pinea 106, 119
    thunbergii 118
    torreyana 133
pinwheel plant *228*
pistachio, Chinese *62, 129*
Pistacia chinensis 62, 129
Pittosporum
    crassifolium 190
    'Garnettii' *171*
    tobira 'Wheeler's Dwarf' *216*
    undulatum 134
planning your garden *10–15, 78*
plant collection issues *52, 55*
planting techniques *366–373*
plant selection *32–39, 52, 362–365*
plant stress *44, 59*
plant varieties and hybrids *38, 56, 62*
Platanus
    racemosa 54, 99, 130
    wrightii 87
Platycerium bifurcatum 305
Platycodon grandiflorus 347
Plectranthus verticillatus 23, 311
plum
    green gage European *147*
    natal. See *Carissa macrocarpa*
    prince's *273*
plumbago
    cape *240*
    dwarf *216*

Plumbago auriculata 240
plumcot, plum parfait *151*
Plumeria
    alba 84, 126
    auriculata var. *alba 222*
    rubra 114
pluot, flavor king *150*
Podocarpus 62
    gracilior 125, 140
    macrophyllus 122
Podranea ricasoliana 230
poker, red-hot *335, 339, 347*
pokers, pink *344*
Polemonium caeruleum 293
Polygala x *dalmaisiana 181*
Polygonum capitatum 308
pomegranate *107, 180, 200, 216*
Pontederia cordata 328
popcorn plant *188*
poplar, Lombardy *106*
poppy. See also *Papaver*
    California *35, 50, 263, 288*
    corn *286, 288, 358*
    Degas oriental *293*
    Matilija *38, 54, 264*
    Mexican *280*
Populus
    fremontii 98
    nigra
        'Italica' *106*
    tremula 'Pendula' *113*
    trichocarpa 159
Portulaca grandiflora Sundance Hybrids
        356
Portulacaria afra 174, 229
potato bush, blue *187*
Potentilla neumanniana 262
powder puff, pink *201*
Pratia pedunculata 301
prayer plant *311*
predators, common *68*
pride of London *260, 306*
pride of Madeira *70*
    blue *37*
primrose *25*
    birdcage *280*
    cape *270*
    English *358*
    fairy *34, 352, 358*
    Obconica *358*
    saltillo evening *313*
    white evening *332*
primrose tree *120*
Primula
    malacoides 352
    obconica 358
    x *polyantha 358*
princess flower *188*
Pritchardia hillebrandii 54
privet
    California *206*
    glossy *122*
propagation techniques *380–385*
propeller plant *229, 302*
Prosopis
    glandulosa 87
        var. *glandulosa 94*
    pubescens 87, 92
protea
    king *183*
    pincushion *196*
Protea cynaroides 183
pruning *29, 39, 59, 374–379*
Prunus
    armeniaca 'Moorpark' *147*
    'Bonanza II' *150*
    caroliniana 210
    x *cistena 203*

x *domestica* 'Green Gage' 147
dulcis 'All-In-One' 147
'English Morello' 147
'Flavor Delight' 151
'Flavor King' 150
glandulosa 'Katy' 151
ilicifolia subsp. *lyonii* 175, 211
laurocerasus 210
lusitanica 'Variegata' 123
persica 'Floridaprince' 150
'Plum Parfait' 151
sinensis 'Floragold' 150
Pseudotsuga menziesii 112
Psidium cattleianum 148
Psilotrophe cooperi 338
Psorothamnus spinosus 54, 95
Psychotria hawaiiensis 54
Psylliostachys suworowii 344
Pteris cretica 'Albolineata' 270
Pterocarya stenoptera 158
pumello
   Chandler pink 144
Punica granatum
   'Nana' 200, 216
   'Wonderful' 107, 180
pussywillow, pink 207
Pyracantha
   'Mohave' 210
   'Santa Cruz' 200
Pyrostegia venusta 70, 230, 246
Pyrus
   communis
      'Kieffer' 151
      'Moonglow' 146
   kawakamii 100
   pyrifolia 124

Q

queen of the prairie 275
queen's tears 260
queen's wreath 234
Quercus
   dumosa 170
   engelmannii 54
   fusiformis 88
   ilex 107, 119, 141
   lobata 93
   muehlenbergii 113
   suber 107, 130
Quillaja sasponaria 143
quince, Aromatnaya 149
quiver tree 91

R

rabbitbrush 54, 165
rain tree, golden 62, 140
raised beds 13, 14, 26, 28, 28, 43, 45
Ranunculus aquatilis 328
Raoulia australis 300
raspberry 245
Ratibida columnifera 284
Ravenala madagascariensis 153
redbud. See *Cercis*
red-hot poker 335, 339, 347
redwood, dawn 142
Rehmannia elata 259
resources for more information 74, 76–77
Rhamnus californica 191
Rhaphiolepis 45
   'Majestic Beauty' 109, 116
Rhapidophyllum hystrix 157, 195
Rhapis excelsa 153
Rhipsalis capilliformis 255
Rhodanthe chlorocephala subsp. *rosea* 268
Rhodochiton atrosanguineus 238
Rhododendron
   'Alaska' 178

'Phoenicia' 183
'Red Wing' 222
Rhoicissus capensis 241
rhubarb, giant 184
Rhus
   integrifolia 54, 211
   lancea 139
   ovata 211
   trilobata 160
   virens 167
ribbon bush 269
Ribes
   malvaceum 170
   sanguineum 168
   speciosum 214
Ricinus communis 'Carmencita Pink' 294
Robinia
   neomexicana 94
   pseudoacacia 'Frisia' 127, 159
rock cress, Rosabella 309
rock rose. See *Cistus*
Romneya
   coulteri 38, 54
   'White Cloud' 264
Rosa
   'Abraham Darby' 193
   'Alba Maxima' 62
   'Altissimo' 250
   'Amber Queen' 193
   'America' 251
   'Ballerina' 252
   banksiae 62, 249
      'Alba Plena' 231
      'Lutea' 192, 248
   'Belle Story' 253
   'Betty Boop' 252
   'Carefree Beauty' 252
   'Carefree' Series 62
   'Carefree Sunshine' 252
   'Climbing Cécile Brünner' 239, 249
   'Climbing Iceberg' 249
   'Climbing Mrs. Sam McGredy' 248
   'Climbing Queen Elizabeth' 249
   'Country Dancer' 252
   'De Rescht' 253
   'Dorothy Perkins' 239, 249
   'Dortmund' 247
   'Dream' Series 62
   'Dublin Bay' 62, 247
   'Duchesse de Brabant' 193
   'Evelyn' 192
   'Flower Carpet' 62
   'Fourth of July' 250
   'Frau Dagmar Hartopp' 190, 195
   gallica 'Versicolor' 205
   'Gene Boerner' 62
   'Gertrude Jekyll' 205
   'Golden Celebration' 247
   'Golden Showers' 193
   'Handel' 192
   'Iceberg' 16, 62, 178, 192
   'Joseph's Coat' 250
   'Lady Penzence' 195
   laevigata 248
   'Livin' Easy' 252
   'Margaret Merril' 62
   Mary Rose ('Ausmary') 192
   'Meg' 251
   'Mermaid' 236, 248
   'New Dawn' 247
   'Outta the Blue' 253
   'Pascali' 62
   planting techniques 368–369
   pruning techniques 376–379
   'Queen Elizabeth' 62
   'Ramona' 248
   'Royal Sunset' 251
   'Sally Holmes' 250

'Scabrosa' 249
'Souvenir de la Malmaison' 253
'Tamora' 253
'The Fairy' 253
'The Prince' 205
rose(s) See also *Rosa*
   Cherokee 248
   Christmas 296
   climbing
      drought-resistant 248–249
      for fences and arbors 247
      for hot interior zones 251
      for mild coastal zones 250
   desert 212
   for foggy coastal gardens 192–193
   growth requirements 36
   Lady Banks. See *Rosa banksiae*
   moss 356
   Raman's 190, 195
   rock. See *Cistus*
   rosa mundi 205
   shrub 252–253
   sweetheart 239, 249
   yellow Lady Banks 192, 248
rosemary. See also *Rosmarinus officinalis*
   coast 197, 202
   creeping 263
rose of Sharon 207
Rosmarinus officinalis 38, 191
   'Prostratus' 263
Roystonea regia 153, 156
Rubus 'Bababerry' 245
Rudbeckia fulgida var. *sullivantii*
   'Goldsturm' 294
rue
   meadow 292
   white Chinese meadow 294
Ruellia macrantha 186
Rumohra adiantiformis 311
Ruscus hypoglossum 169
rush
   corkscrew 330
   zebra 330
Russelia equisetiformis 185

S

Sabal
   causiarum 154
   minor 194
   palmetto 157
sacred flower of the Incas 182
sage
   autumn 299, 337
   blue spire Russian 204
   Chihuahuan 166
   dwarf silver leaf 273
   hummingbird 266
   indigo spires 275
   Jerusalem 190
   Kew red desert 160
   may night 273
   Mexican bush 183, 205
   pineapple 349
   prairie 266
   scarlet 357
   tropical 167, 285
   variegated 219
   white 277
Sagina subulata 300
saguaro 54, 136
St. John's bread. See *Ceratonia siliqua*
St. John's wort 171
   creeping 174
Salix
   babylonica var. *pekinensis* 'Tortuosa' 137
   caprea 'Kilmarnock' 207
   gooddingi 86

x *sepulcralis* var. *chrysocoma* 138
Salvia
   azurea 'Nekan' 266
   coccinea
      'Lady in Red' 285
      Pink Form 167
   daghestanica 273
   elegans 349
   greggii 299
      'Sierra Linda' 337
   'Indigo Spires' 275
   leucantha 183, 205
   microphylla 'Kew Red' 160
   officinalis 'Tricolor' 219
   spathacea 266
   splendens Sizzler Series 357
   x *sylvestris* 'Mainacht' 273
sandalwood, mountain 54
Santalum paniculatum 54
Santolina 42
   chamaecyparissus 335
   pinnata 219
   rosmarinifolia 263
Sapindus oahuensis 54
Saponaria ocymoides 293
Sarcococca confusa 173
Satureja
   hortensis 219
   montana 219
sausage tree 105, 136
savory
   summer 219
   winter 219
Scabiosa columbaria 'Butterfly Blue' 278
Scadoxus multiflorus subsp. *katherinae* 270
Scaevola aemula 'Blue Wonder' 335
scarlet bugler 54
Schaffner's wattle 94
Schefflera
   actinophylla 116
   arboricola 221
Schinus molle 96, 123
Schizostylis coccinea 'Sunrise' 323
Schlumbergera truncata 224
Schoenoplectus lacustris subsp.
   tabernaemontani 'Zebrinus' 330
Scilla peruviana 320
sedge. See also *Carex*
   Bowles' golden 331
   New Zealand hair 308
Sedum 36
   acre 306
   morganianum 254, 305
   spathulifolium 'Purpureum' 303
   spectabile 'Brilliant' 303
   spurium 'Bronze Carpet' 306
seed sowing techniques 384–385
Senecio
   confusus 235, 242
   madraliscae 303
   mandraliscae 307
   rowleyanus 255
senita 163
senna
   shrubby 164
   spiny 165
Senna
   alata 188
   armata 165
   wislizeni 164
sequoia, giant 112
Sequoiadendron giganteum 112
shade and light 23, 29, 36, 37, 352
shaving brush tree 149
shooting stars 282
shrimp bush, yellow 187, 189
shrubs

for hummingbirds 208–209
for butterflies 206–207
with colorful foliage 203
for containers 222–223
for cottage gardens 204–205
coppicing 375
for desert gardens 160–163
    evergreen 166–167
for desert-style gardens 164–165
for dry shade 168–171
for espalier 200–201
for fall and winter bloom 182–183
with fantastic shapes 212–213
with flowers for tropical effects
    188–189
with fragrant flowers 176–177
for use near swimming pools 220–221
for hanging baskets 225
for herb gardens 218–219
for informal screens 197–199
invasive 56
for moist soil
    in deep shade 173
    in partial shade 172
native
    for birds 211
    for desert gardens 160–163
for the oceanfront 190–191
planting and transplanting 367
to plant under windows 216–217
roses 252–253
for sandy soil 196
selection 362
for spring or summer bloom 180–181
for subtropical gardens 186–187
that create thorny barriers 194–195
for tropical gardens 184–185
with variegated foliage 202
for year-round bloom 178–179
for Zone 3 firebreaks 174–175
Silene armeria 282
silk tassel, coast 199
silk tree 108
    floss 131, 132, 136
silver carpet 309
silver dollar tree 143
Simmondsia chinensis 161
site assessment 16–25, 37
skunkbush 160
smog-resistant trees 140–141
smoke tree. See *Cotinus coggygria;*
    Psorothamnus spinosus
snapdragon
    baby 288
    island bush 191
    sprite 355
sneezeweed 287
snowbell, fragrant 127
snowbush 44
snowflake
    Gravetye giant 324
    spring 319
snow in summer. See *Cerastium*
    tomentosum; Melaleuca linariifolia
soapbark tree 143
soapberry, O'ahu 54
soapwort, rock 293
soil
    adapting to existing conditions 30,
        37–38
    assessment 16, 18–19
    improvement 16, 18, 26, 30–31
    surface, and temperature 25
    test report for 18
    urban 21
Solandra maxima 233
Solanum
    jasminoides 232

laciniatum 189
ratonnettii 'Royal Robe' 187
wendlandii 231
Solenostemon 44
Solidago
    'Goldenmosa' 346
    sphacelata 'Golden Fleece' 296
Sollya heterophylla var. *parviflora* 237
solomon's-seal 370
Sophora
    japonica 62, 101
    'Regent' 88
    secundiflora 40, 90, 167
sotol 163
Sparaxis tricolor 324
Sparmannia africana 220
Spathodea campanulata 104
spearmint 349
Sphaeralcea ambigua 54, 256, 333
spice bush 206
spider flower 357
spiderwort 285
Sprekelia formosissima 323
spruce, Norway 120
spurge. See also *Euphorbia*
    cushion 347
squill
    Peruvian 320
    Siberian 269
Stachys 42
    albotomentosa 'Hot Spot Coral' 273
Stanleya pinnata 273
star cluster 189, 343
star flower, lavender 201
star of Bethlehem 321
Stephanotis floribunda 244
stepping stones, plants between 300–301,
    314–315
Sternbergia lutea 323
stewardship in your garden 40–51, 52, 57
Stigmaphyllon ciliatum 235
stock 291, 344
Stokesia laevis 274
stonecrop. See also *Sedum*
    brilliant 303
    gold moss 306
stork's bill, yellow 272
Stratiotes aloides 372
strawberry 46
    beach 263
strawberry tree 106
Strelitzia
    nicolai 117, 137
    reginae 179
Streptocarpella saxorum 'Concord Blue'
    343
Streptocarpus 'Constant Nymph' 270
Streptosolen jamesonii 187, 223
string of beads 255
Strongylodon macrobotrys 235
structures 24–25
Styrax obassia 127
succulents 35, 36
    climbing and trailing 254–255
    for dry landscaping or containers
        302–303
    groundcovers for Zone 1 firebreaks
        306–307
    selection 365
    shrubby
        for containers 224–225
        for rocky landscapes 228–229
    treelike, for dry gardens 91
sugar bush 211
sumac. See also *Rhus*
    African 139
    evergreen 167†
sundrops, Ozark 287

sunflower 34
    desert 281
    double-flowered perennial 338
    maximillian 286
    torch Mexican 279, 287
Sutera cordata 'Snowflake' 342
sweet pea. See *Lathyrus odoratus*
sweet pea shrub 181
swimming pools 37, 116–117, 334–335
Syagrus
    coronata 155
    romanzoffiana 156
sycamore
    Arizona 87
    California 54, 99, 130
Syzygium paniculatum 100

T

Tabebuia impetiginosa 84, 104
Tagetes 370
    erecta Lady Series 356
    lemmonii 183
Tanacetum vulgare 348
tangelo, Minneola 145
tangerine, Dancy 125
tansy, common 348
taro, black stem 331
tea tree, New Zealand. See *Leptospermum*
    scoparium
Tecoma capensis 209, 246
temperature range and climate 21, 22–23,
    35, 36, 38, 59
terragon 349
Tetraplasandra hawaiiensis 54
Texas ranger. See *Leucophyllum frutescens*
Thalia dealbata 331
Thalictrum
    aquilegifolium 292
    delavayi 'Album' 294
Thevetia peruviana 105
thistle 50
thorn, white 135, 177
Thuja
    occidentalis 'Reingold' 135
    plicata 'Green Giant' 122
Thunbergia
    alata 24, 233
    gregorii 246
thyme
    common 219
    creeping 262
    woolly 315
Thymus
    pseudo-lanuginosus 315
    serpyllum 262
    vulgaris 219
Tibouchina urvilleana 188
tickseed
    early sunrise 259, 338
    golden 286
tidytips 284
tiger flower 322
Tigridia pavonia 322
Tilia
    cordata 127
    tomentosa 89
time as an element in garden plan 13,
    28–29, 39
Tithonia rotundifolia 'Torch' 279, 287
toadflax 288
tobacco, flowering 353
tobacco of the woods 291, 354
tomato
    Better Boy VFN 36
    sea 190, 195
topography 25
Torenia fournieri 'Summer Wave' 352
toyon. See *Heteromeles arbutifolia*

Trachelospermum jasminoides 244
Trachycarpus fortunei 157
Tradescantia andersoniana 285
transplanting techniques 59, 367, 384,
    385
Trapa natans 329
trees
    for adobe soil 100–101
    for birds 134–135
    for butterflies 133
    citrus. See *Citrus*
    with colorful fall foliage 128–129
    conifers
        for interior zones 111
        for mild-winter zones 110
        for mountain zones 112
    deciduous
        interior fruit and nut 146–147
        for mountain zones 113
    for desert gardens 86–90, 152
    drought-tolerant
        evergreen 96–97
        deciduous 94–95
    espalier 39, 124–125, 374
    evergreen
        for mountain zones 112
        for screens 122
    with fantastic shapes 136–137
    fast-growing broadleaf 158–159
    flowering
        with fragrant flowers 126–127
        large subtropical 102–103
        medium, for mild zones 108
        small, for front yards 115
        small, for mild zones 109
    forms 39
    fruit and nut
        interior 146–147
        low-chill 150–151
        tropical or exotic 148–149
    for hummingbirds 132
    for informal hedges 123
    invasive 56
    for Mediterranean-style gardens
        106–107
    for the oceanfront 118–119
    with ornamental bark 130–131
    for patios 114
    planting technique 366
    resistant to oak-root fungus 142–143
    resistant to smog 140–141
    selection 362
    for windbreaks 120–121
    that survive without irrigation 92–93
    thinning, limbing up, and pruning of
        28–29, 39, 59, 374–375
    for wet soil 98–99
    for tropical gardens 104–105
    for use near swimming pools 116–117
    with a weeping habit 138–139
    when to call the arborist 29
Trichostema lanatum 214
Trifolium pratense 351
tristania 141
Triteleia hyacinthina 325
Tropaeolum majus 'Empress of India' 359
trumpet tree
    gold 120
    pink 84, 104
Tulipa 21
    bakeri 'Lilac Wonder' 325
tulip tree 140
    African 104
tupelo 129

U

Ulmus 'Morton' 159
Umbellularia californica 98
umbrella plant, variegated 221
umbrella tree, Queensland 116
Ungnadia speciosa 165
Urginea maritima 269
urn plant 268

V

valerian, red 34, 274
Vanda 'Miss Joaquim' 270
vase plant, hieroglyphic 271
vegetables 49, 59, 63
Verbascum 36
    'Banana Custard' 256
    thapsus 349
verbena
    butterfly 258, 274
    sand 281
    white Peruvian 314
Verbena
    bonariensis 258, 274
    peruviana 'Alba' 314
viburnum
    Korean spice 206
    leatherleaf 173
    Pere David 220
    sweet 176
Viburnum
    awabuki 176
    carlesii 206
    davidii 220
    rhytidophyllum 173
Vinca minor 'Variegata' 262
vine(s). See also climbers
    amethyst passion 242
    balloon 239
    black-eyed Susan 24, 233
    blood red trumpet 232
    blue crown passion 242
    bower 233
    chocolate 241
    coral 230, 235
    cup and saucer 238
    cup of gold 233
    Easter lily 230
    flame 70, 230, 246
    Guinea gold 240
    incense passion 244
    invasive 56
    jade 235
    Mexican flame 70, 230, 235, 242, 246
    orange clock 246
    orchid 235

passion. See Passiflora
    porcelain 237
    potato 232
    purple bell 238
    red jade 234
    red trumpet 230
    silver lace 231
    violet trumpet 233
Viola
    tricolor 359
    x wittrockiana
        'Jolly Joker' 297
        'Universal Plus' 359
violet bells 186, 189
vitex, beach 54
Vitis vinifera
    'Purpurea' 236
    'Thompson Seedless' 245
Vriesea hieroglyphica 271

W

wallflower, Siberian 283
walnut
    Arizona 89
    Pedro English 146
Washingtonia
    filifera 86, 152
    robusta 100, 155
water
    conservation techniques 42–45
    effects on microclimate 25
    evapotranspiration map 44
    quality issues 43
    stress 44
water garden 24, 256, 328–331, 365, 372
waterlily
    American white 329
    Panama Pacific 329
    pygmy 329
water shield, Carolina 328
Watsonia 36
    'Stanford Scarlet' 325
wattle
    Cootamundra 97, 115, 209
    Sydney golden 159, 197
wax flower, Geralton 196
wax plant 255
weed barriers 48
weeds and weeding 15, 48–50, 57, 59
Westringia fruticosa 197
    'Morning Light' 202
whirling butterflies. See Gaura
wildflowers 10, 16, 40, 55
    annual
        cool-season 288–289

for desert gardens 280–281
    for mountain zones 282–283
    for summer and fall 286–287
    for Texas 284–285
wildlife 40, 42, 50–51, 51
willow
    corkscrew 137
    desert 90, 132
    golden weeping 138
    peppermint 141
    San Joachin 86
wind 24, 25, 37, 59, 120–121
windflower
    Grecian 319
    scarlet 320
wine cup, lacquered 270
wingnut, Chinese 158
wintercreeper 174
wintersweet 176
wishbone flower 352
wisteria
    Chinese 32, 232
    Japanese 114, 231
    silky 242
Wisteria 368
    brachybotrys 242
    floribunda
        'Alba' 114
        'Macrobotrys' 231
    sinensis 32, 232
Wodyetia bifurcata 154
Wolffia 365, 372
woody plants 35, 84
wormwood. See Artemisia
wort
    creeping St. John's 174
    rupture 301

X

Xylosma congestum 201

Y

yarrow. See also Achillea
    woolly 308
yesterday, today, and tomorrow 185
yucca. See also Yucca
    red 299, 335
Yucca 36, 38
    brevifolia 137
    filamentosa 'Color Guard' 341
    rigida 162

Z

Zantedeschia aethiopica 'Green Goddess' 271
Zauschneria californica 54, 299
    subsp. latifolium 170
Zelkova serrata 'Japanese Selko' 101
zinnia
    desert 332
    mountain 332
Zinnia
    acerosa 332
    elegans
        'Benary's Giant' 344
        'Peter Pan Gold' 279
    grandiflora 332
Ziziphus jujuba 'Li' 148

ACKNOWLEDGMENTS

DK Publishing Inc. and the American Horticultural Society (AHS) would like to express special thanks to Dr. H. Marc Cathey for his vision of a SMARTGARDEN™ and for promoting these important principles to the American gardener; to Katy Moss Warner for her keen eye and superb leadership; to Arabella Dane for the use of her Showtime database; to Mary Ann Patterson for believing in and coordinating this project from its conception; to Mark Miller, Jessie Keith, and Elaine Lee for hours of research; to David Ellis for his editor's savvy. Rita Pelczar, author of the core text for the SmartGarden™ Regional Guides, has written for several American gardening magazines and has contributed to several books. As an associate editor for The American Gardener, she wrote a four-year series of articles highlighting principles of the SmartGarden™ plan.

Patricia R. Welsh is the author of Southern California Gardening: A Month-by-Month Guide and other books. She's a well-known speaker throughout Southern California and winner of many awards. The author thanks Nan Sterman for her consultation and contributions to the plant category lists. She thanks the many people who allowed her to photograph their gardens, and the following people for help with lists: Linda Chisari, Laurie Nies, Becky Dembitsky, Evelyn Weidner, Mary Weidner, Vincent Lazaneo, Carol L. Dalu, and Katherine Jean Jones. Pat says: "I give my deepest thanks to Denise Holcombe, without whose unfailing support and help I could never have completed this book. Denise donated more than one day a week for over a year and helped me through every stage of the work. She also wrote the appendix."

PHOTO CREDITS

Abbreviations Key
T = Top B= Bottom C=Center L= Left R = Right

American Camellia Society: 225 TR

American Gardener Magazine: Mary Yee 18L, 19TR

Ball Horticultural Company: 77R

Trevor Cole: 94 TL, 100 TL, 108 TR, 127 BR, 131 BR, 146 TC, 188 BL, 192 TL, 239 TR, 248 BL, 249 TC, 258 TC, 262 BL, 278 BL, 283 TL, 284 BC, 284 BR, 293 BR, 315 TC, 340 BL

Corbis: W. Perry Conway 51TR; Dave G. Houser 54BL, 76BR; Joe McDonald 51TL, 51BL; Douglas Peebles 54 TR; Peter Reynolds 51TR

Dave Wilson Nursery: 146 BL, 147 TL, 147 TR, 147 BL, 147 CR, 147 BR, 150 TL, 150 TR, 150 BL, 150 BR, 151 TL, 151 TR, 151 C, 151 BR, 151 BL, 154 BL

Emerald Coast Growers: 264BL

FLPA: S. Maslowski 61

Gardenphotos.com: Judy White 87 BL, 88 TL, 105 BL, 125 TR, 130 L, 136 BC, 178 TR, 187 BL, 189 TL, 194 TL, 219 TR, 231 BL, 232 BR, 239 CL, 239 CR, 244 TL, 244 TR, 277 TC, 279 BR, 299 TC, 301 BC, 306 TR, 309 TR, 312 BR, 341 TR; Graham Rice: 305 BR

Garden & Wildlife Matters Photo Library: 60BL, 65TR, 68BR, 93 BL, 94BL 98 R, 111 TC, 131 BL, 205 C, 214 TR, 214 BC, 236 BC, 239 BL, 249 TR, 276TR, 282 TR, 334 R; M. Collins 60BR; John Feltwell 92 B, 99TL, 156 BL; Colin Milkins 51BL; Steffie Shields 231 TC; Debi Wager 47BL

Garden Picture Library: Philippe Bonduel 266 BC; Christi Carter 170BR, 211 TL; Brian Carter 211BR; Densey Clyne 156TL, 236BL; Christopher Fairweather 200B; Vaughan Fleming 152BL; John Glover 127 TR; Jacqui Hurst 293BL; Jane Legate 29TR; Marie O'Hara 70BL; Howard Rice 278TL; JS Sira 179BL, 191BC, 286CR, 293TL, 302BR; Friedrich Strauss 217TC; Mel Watson 152TC; Didier Willery 282B

Courtesy of Heirloom Roses: 205 CR, 250 BL, 250 TR, 250 BR, 251 TL, 251 BL, 252 TL, 252 TC, 252 TR, 252 CR, 252 BL, 252 BR, 253 TL, 253 TR, 253 BC, 253 BR

High Country Gardens:
www.highcountrygardens.com: 272 TR, 272 BR, 273 TR, 273 BL, 273 BC, 273 BR

Horticopia: Edward F. Gilman 148 TR, 148 BL, 149 TR, 149 BR, 154 TL, 154 TR, 154 C, 154 BR, 155 BR

Huntington Library, Art Collections and Botanical Gardens: 76 BL

Charlie Jones: 175TR, 211BL

Monrovia: 5 TL, 5 BL, 90 TR, 100 BR, 106 TL, 107 TL, 108 TL, 108 BL, 111 TR, 116 BC, 116 BR, 119 BC, 122 BR, 124 TR, 125 TL, 125 BL, 129 TL, 129 BC, 132 BL, 132 BR, 138 C, 138 BL, 139 BL, 140 BR, 141 TR, 143 TL, 157 TR, 158 TR, 161 TR, 168 TL, 173 C, 174 TC, 176 TL, 176 TR, 176 BL, 177 CR, 177 BC, 178 BR, 179 TR, 181 TL, 182 TL, 183 TR, 185 TL, 187 TL, 195 BR, 199 BL, 201 TR, 201 BL, 202 TR, 207 TL, 207 TR, 209 TR, 210 BL, 215 TL, 215 TR, 215 BR, 216 BL, 216 BR, 217 TL, 217 CL, 217 BR, 220 CR, 220 BR, 221 BR, 222 BR, 230 TC, 230 TR, 231 TL, 232 TL, 234 TL, 236 TL, 240 TL, 240 TR, 243 TC, 244 BL, 246 TL, 258 BL, 262 TR, 273 TL, 292 BR, 295 TR, 298 BR, 299 BL, 300 TL, 306 BL, 310 TL, 312 TL, 316 TL, 317 TL, 317 TR, 317 BL, 317 BC, 317 BR, 335 BC, 336 BL, 342 TL

Mountain States Wholesale Nursery: George Hull 86 TL, 86 TR, 86 BL, 86 BR, 87 TL, 87 TR, 87 BR, 88 B, 89 TR, 89 BL, 90 TL, 90 TC, 90 BC, 90 BR, 92 TR, 93 TL, 93 BR, 94 TC, 94 TR, 94 BR, 95 TL, 95 TR, 135 TR, 138 TL, 139 TL, 160 TC, 160 TR, 160 BL, 162 TC, 162 TR, 162 B, 163 TL, 163 BR, 163 BL, 164 TL, 164 BL, 164 R, 165 TL, 165 TC, 165 TR, 165 BL, 166 TR, 166 CL, 166 CR, 166 BL, 167 TL, 167 TR, 170 TL, 269 BL,332 TL, 332 TC, 332 TR, 332 BL, 332 BC, 332 BR, 333 TL, 333 BL, 337 TR, 337 BR, 338 TL

Steven Nikkila: 88TR, 159BC

Plant Delights Nursery: Tony Avent 266 R, 275 TR, 290 BC, 310 BC

Courtesy of Proven Winners:
www.provenwinners.com: 292 TC, 342 BC, 342 BR

Scott Millard Photography: 144 TL, 144 TR, 144 BL, 144 BC, 144 BR, 145 TL, 145 TR, 145 BL, 145 BR, 148 TL, 166 TL, 168 TR, 168 BR, 169 TL, 169 C, 169 BR, 245 TR, 245 BL, 280 TL, 280 BL, 281 TC, 308 TL, 313 TL, 313 BL

USDA-NRCS Plants Database: Gary A. Monroe 280 TR, 280 BC, 281 TL, 281 B; J.S.Peterson 170 TR, 170 CL

Patricia R. Welsh: 7 TC, 7 CR, 7 BR, 10 BL, 11, 14 TL, 14 BL, 14 BR, 15 T, 16 BL, 17, 19 TL, 19 BR, 21 TR, 21 BL, 21 BR, 23 L, 23 TR, 23 BR, 24 B, 25 TL, 25 TR, 25 BR, 26 TR, 26 BL, 27, 28 T, 28 C, 28 B, 30 BL,32 BL, 32 BR, 33, 34 BL, 34 BR, 35 TL, 35 TR, 35 BL, 35 BC, 35 BR, 36 TR, 36 BL, 36 BR, 37 TL, 37 TR, 37 BL, 37 BR, 38 BR, 40 TR, 42 TL,42 BR, 43 BR, 44 BR, 45 TR, 45 BL, 46 T, 47 TR, 48 BR, 49 R, 50 TL, 50 BR, 52 BL, 53, 55 TC, 55 CR, 55 BL, 59 BR, 62 TL, 67 TR, 69 B, 71 TL,

71 TR, 71 BL, 71 BR, 72 TL, 72 TR, 73 TR, 73 B, 75, 79, 90 BL, 91 TR, 92 TL, 92 TC, 96 BR, 97 TL, 97 TR, 97 BL, 97 BC, 100 BL, 109 BL, 114 TR, 115 TL, 115 TR, 115 BR, 116 TL, 116 BL, 117 TR, 117 BR, 119 TR, 120 TL, 120 BR, 121 TL, 121 TR, 121 BC, 121 BR, 124 BL, 130 TR, 133 TL, 134 CR, 134 BR, 135 TL, 135 BL, 152 BR, 153 BL, 155 L, 156 BR, 159 TC, 165 BR, 167 B, 168 BL, 175 TL, 178 TL, 179 TL, 180 TR, 182 BL, 183 TL, 184 TR, 191 BR, 197 TL, 200 TR, 201 CL, 202 BR, 203 BC, 203 R, 211 TR, 221 TR, 222 TL, 222 BL, 223 TR, 225 TL, 226 BR, 232 TR, 237 BL, 246 BL, 246 C, 247 TL, 250 TL, 251 R, 256 TR, 256 BL, 257, 259 TL, 263 TR, 264 BC, 265 TR, 266 TL, 267 TR, 269 TR, 276 TC, 284 L, 297 BR, 304 TL, 305 TL, 305 CL, 307 BC, 309 TC, 309 C, 309 L, 316 TR, 316 BL, 324 BR, 340 BR, 342 TR, 342 BL, 343 BR, 344 TC, 344 BR, 345 TL, 345 BL, 347 BL, 353 BL, 356 TR, 358 TR, 359 TL, 359 BL

The Publisher would also like to thank the following DK Photographers who have contributed to this book:

Peter Anderson, Sue Atkinson, Blooms of Bressingham, Michael Booher, Booker Seeds, Clive Boursnell, Deni Brown, Jonathan Buckley, Andrew Butler, Cambridge Botanic Garden, Beth Chatto, Eric Crichton, Geoff Dann, Andrew de Lory, Christine M. Douglas, Alistair Duncan, Andreas Einsiedel, John Fielding, Neil Fletcher, Roger Foley, John Glover, Derek Hall, David W. Hardon, Jerry Harpur, Stephan Hayward, Dr. Alan Hemsley, C. Andrew Henley, Ian Howes, Jacqui Hurst, Anne Hyde, International Coffee Organization, Dave King, Jane Miller, RHS Garden Wisley, Howard Rice, Tim Ridley, Barbara Rothenberger, Royal Botanical Garden, Edinburgh, Bob Rundle, Les Saucier, Savill Garden, Windsor, Mike Severns, Steven Still, Joseph Strach, Richard Surman, R. Tidman, Juliette Wade, Colin Walton, Matthew Ward, Alex Watson, Steven Wooster, Francesca York